Scott, Foresman

WORLD ATLAS

2nd Edition

Scott, Foresman and Company

Editorial Offices: Glenview, Illinois
Regional Sales Offices: Sunnyvale, California • Tucker, Georgia •
Glenview, Illinois • Oakland, New Jersey • Dallas, Texas

Maps and index by
Bill Willett, Cartographic Editor, George Philip
and Son Ltd., London

David Gaylard, Joan Russell,
and Raymond Smith, George Philip
and Son Ltd., London

Maps prepared by
George Philip Cartographic Services Ltd.,
London under the direction of Alan Poynter,
Director of Cartography, George Philip and Son
Ltd., London

Acknowledgments for the photographs, maps,
and index are included in the acknowledgments
section on page 159. The acknowledgments
section is an extension of the copyright page.

Introductory text prepared by
Dr. Douglas C. Wilms. Dr. Wilms is a professor
of geography and planning at East Carolina
University in Greenville, North Carolina. He is
the author of many books, including *Earth and
Man: A Systematic Geography* (1981), *North
Carolina: A Geographic Review* (1980), and
*North Carolina: A Teacher's Guide to Map
Skills and Study Activities* (1978). Dr. Wilms has
published articles and reviews in dozens of
journals and has taught geography at the high
school level. He is actively involved in the
movement to improve geographic education in
the United States and has conducted many
workshops on the teaching of geography and
map and globe skills.

ISBN: 0-673-43339-0

23456789—WEB—91908988

Contents

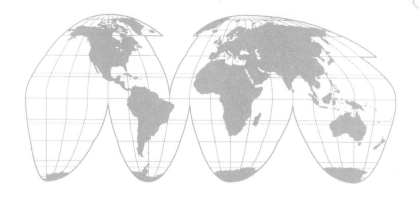

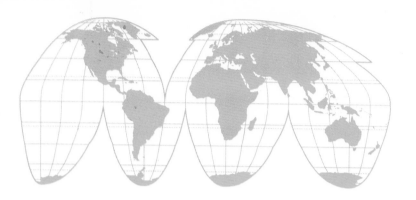

How to Use This Atlas

Atlas was the imaginary giant of Greek mythology who carried the world on his shoulders. His name is used today to refer to a book of reference maps. An atlas is an important reference tool for finding the location of a town or country or natural features, such as islands, lakes, and deserts.

The *Scott, Foresman World Atlas* is divided into four parts. The first part is introductory. It includes tips on how to use the atlas plus a glossary of geographical terms. Note the latitude and longitude diagram (page 7), the key to symbols (page 8), and the landforms diagram (page 9). They will help you understand the maps in the atlas.

The second part of the atlas gives data about the world as a whole. It includes diagrams and maps of the solar system, seasons, and time zones, as well as volcanoes, glaciers, and other natural forces that make the earth's landscapes so varied. Also in this part of the atlas are world thematic maps that focus on special subjects—or themes—such as climate regions, minerals, and major crops.

For example, look at the map of climate regions on pages 26–27. Suppose you want to know where Africa's deserts are located. Using the color-coded map key, you can see that a huge desert stretches across northern Africa and a smaller desert runs along the coast of southwestern Africa. Use the map scale to estimate the size of these deserts. You will find that the desert in northern Africa—the Sahara—is more than 3,500 miles from east to west and 1,500 miles from north to south. This is larger than the entire United States.

Many of the thematic maps in this atlas use dots to represent a certain quantity. See, for example, the world population distribution map on pages 32–33. Here each dot is used to represent 1 million persons. You can see at a glance which parts of the world are most densely populated (northwest Europe, south Asia, and east

Asia). The world food resources maps on pages 34–36 also use dots. For example, the map on page 34 uses a blue dot to represent 2 million tons of potatoes, and you can quickly see that most potatoes are grown in Europe.

The third and largest part of this atlas contains detailed physical and political maps of the world's continents, regions, and countries. These are the maps you will most often use to find states, towns, mountains, rivers, and other features. The easiest way to locate a place is to use the index on pages 141–159. The index pages are tinted blue to make them easy to find. The index lists thousands of place names in alphabetical order. The page on which a place name can be found is listed in bold (dark) type before the name. The numbers following the place name show its latitude and longitude.

Let's assume that you want to find Melbourne, Australia. What steps should you take? First, turn to the index and look up Melbourne. The number in bold type, 121, is the atlas page that you should turn to. Use the geographical coordinates provided (latitude 37°50'S and longitude 145°0'E), to help you find Melbourne on page 121. If you want to see where Australia is in relation to other countries, refer to the world political map on pages 46–47.

Note that smaller towns generally appear only on large scale maps, such as the United States regional maps (pages 52–61). In densely populated areas, many smaller towns are omitted in order to make the map easier to read.

Some atlas pages have small maps called inset maps. For example, the map of Italy and the Balkan States on pages 88–89 has two inset maps. Inset maps have several uses. The inset map of southeast Europe makes it easier to see the international boundaries in this part of the world. The inset map of Malta shows you details of a tiny island country south of Italy. On page 102 the inset map of southern India shows a part of India that extends southward beyond the

main map area. If southern India were shown in its proper place, then the map of South Asia would have to be much smaller. Always refer to a world map or map of the region to see where the places shown in the inset maps are actually located.

The fourth part of this atlas includes handy reference tables as well as the index described on page 5. Here you can find national and city population figures, flags, lists of products, and other information about the world's countries and major dependencies. There are also facts and figures about U.S. regions and states. Note that the index also gives you guidelines for pronouncing many foreign place names.

The Basic Skills of Map Reading

Scale. Scale refers to the relationship between a map and the part of the earth it represents. Scale is the proportional relationship between map distance and actual ground distance. It may be shown in one of three ways. First, it may be shown as a ratio, such as 1:40,000,000. Such a ratio appears on the South America map on page 70. The ratio means that one inch on the map equals 40,000,000 inches on the ground.

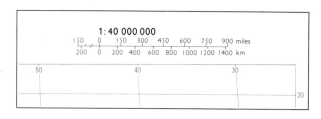

Second, a map's scale may also be stated in words, such as "One inch equals 631 miles." This statement means that one inch on the map equals 631 miles on the earth's surface. To arrive at this figure, divide 40,000,000 inches by 63,360 inches (the number of inches in a mile). The answer is 631 miles. Third, scale may be shown with a bar scale. Using the bar scale on the United States map on pages 52–53, estimate

the distance between Chicago, Illinois, and Cleveland, Ohio. You will see that the distance is about 300 miles.

On most maps in this atlas, scale is shown both as a ratio and by means of a bar scale. These guides will help you estimate distances between places on the map.

The scale on atlas maps varies from map to map. One inch might equal 100 miles on one map and 500 miles on another. For example, compare the scale of the British Isles (1:4,000,000) on page 80 to that of South America (1:40,000,000) on page 70. The map of the British Isles has the larger scale: one inch on the map represents 63 miles on the ground. The scale of the South American map is smaller: one inch equals 631 miles. Always keep in mind that a larger scale map shows a smaller area in greater detail.

Some typical scales would be:
1 inch : 10 feet (plan of a classroom)
1 inch : 200 feet (a builder's plan)
1 inch : 10 miles (a highway map)

Latitude and Longitude. Mapmakers use a grid system to identify locations on earth. The system, as shown in the latitude and longitude diagram on page 7, makes use of imaginary lines called parallels and meridians. The parallels run east and west around the earth. They measure latitude—the distance measured in degrees (°) north and south of the Equator. The distance between each degree of latitude is about 70 miles. The Equator is 0° latitude and divides the earth into two hemispheres (half spheres): the Northern Hemisphere and the Southern Hemisphere. All degrees of latitude are either north of the Equator or south of it. The North Pole is 90°N, and the South Pole is 90°S.

Look at the line representing 30°N latitude on the diagram. You can see that the city of New Orleans is located on this parallel. Because it is north of the Equator, New Orleans has a north latitude position. Pôrto Alegre, located at 30°S latitude, is in the southern latitudes. Now turn to the United States map on pages 52–53 and

locate New Orleans. Find 30°N latitude along the margin of either page and move your finger across the parallel until you come to New Orleans. Use the same method to locate the Brazilian city of Pôrto Alegre on page 74.

Meridians are the lines that run north and south from pole to pole. They are not parallel; rather, they meet at the poles. The Prime Meridian, which is shown on the diagram below, passes through Greenwich, England. It is located at 0° longitude. The Prime Meridian divides the earth into Eastern and Western hemispheres. Every location to the east, up to 180°, is east longitude. Every place to the west, up to 180°, is west longitude. As you can see from the atlas map on pages 122–123, the 180° longitude line passes through the country of Fiji in the South Pacific.

Turn again to the United States map on pages 52–53. You will see that longitude 90°W intersects New Orleans. Now turn to the South American map on page 74 and estimate the longitude of Pôrto Alegre. It is about 51°W. Thus, the latitude and longitude of this city is approximately 30°S and 51°W.

Degrees of latitude and longitude are further divided into small units called minutes. There are 60 minutes in each degree, and they are marked by the symbol ('). New Orleans is actually located at 30°0'N and 90°5'W. Pôrto Alegre is actually located at 30°7'S and 50°55'W.

Map Symbols. The map key on page 8 shows various symbols used throughout the atlas. Symbols can stand for many different things. Dots, circles, squares, and larger symbols are used for towns. These will vary with the size of the town. Larger communities tend to have larger symbols and larger and bolder printed names.

Bold red-orange lines on top of broken dark lines show international boundaries—the border

Latitude and Longitude Diagram

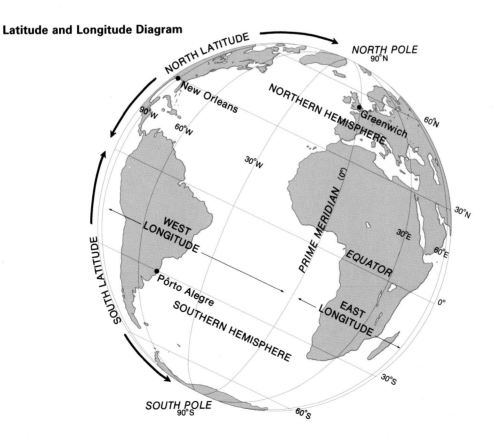

lines that separate one country from another. Lighter red lines are used for internal boundaries, such as U.S. states and Canadian provinces. Thin red lines show roads, while thin black lines show railways.

Blue represents water, and blue lines indicate rivers. Swamps, marshes, and ice fields each have their own unique symbols. Notice, for example, the many swamp symbols found in the low-lying areas of southern Florida and eastern North Carolina. (See pages 56–57.)

Color is also used to show varying elevations of land areas and depth of water bodies. As land increases in elevation, the colors change from green to yellow, to orange, brown, and purple.

Turn to the map of Mexico on pages 64–65 and look at the color key in the margin. Note how the darker colors are used to show plateaus and mountainous areas, while green shows low-lying areas, such as the coastal plain that borders the Gulf of Mexico.

Take a moment to review the basic skills of map reading: scale, latitude and longitude, and symbols. With a little practice you will master each of these useful skills.

Key to Symbols

SETTLEMENTS

Settlement symbols in order of size

LONDON　　Osaka　　Venice　　Andropov　　Toledo　　Cromer　　Interlaken

Settlement symbols and type styles vary according to the scale of each map and indicate the importance of towns on the map rather than specific population figures.

ADMINISTRATION

—————　International Boundaries

--- --- ---　International Boundaries
(Undemarcated or undefined)

International boundaries show the 'de facto' situation where there are rival claims to territory.

·········　Internal Boundaries

—···—　U.S. State Boundaries

TRANSPORTATION

～～　Principal Roads

————　Principal Railways

··········　Principal Canals

- - - -　Tracks and Seasonal Roads

- - - - -　Railways under construction

—·—·—　Principal Oil Pipelines

⊣---⊢　Road Tunnels

⊣---⊢　Railway Tunnels

✿　Principal Airports

⊃⊂　Passes

PHYSICAL FEATURES

～～　Perennial Streams

　Swamps and Marshes

▲ 8848　Elevations in meters

- - - -　Seasonal Streams

　Permanent Ice and Glaciers

▼ 8050　Sea Depths in meters

　Seasonal Lakes and Salt Flats

∪　Wells in Desert

1134　Height of Lakes

ELEVATION

ft	m
12,000	4000
9000	3000
6000	2000
4500	1500
3000	1000
1200	400
600	200
Sea Level 0	0
200	600
2000	6000
m	ft

Glossary of Geographical Terms

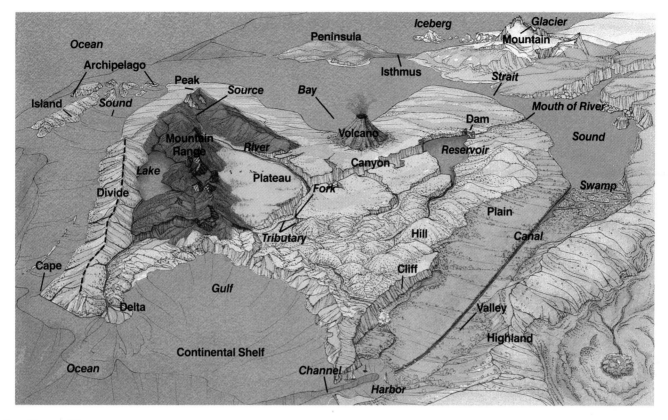

Landforms Diagram

agriculture science, art, or occupation of cultivating the soil to produce crops, and also of raising livestock.

altitude height above the earth's surface. The altitude of a place is usually expressed in feet or meters above or below sea level.

archipelago (är′kə pel′ə gō) a group of many islands. *See diagram.* The Aleutian Islands form an archipelago.

atmosphere the mass of gases that surrounds the earth and is held to it by the force of gravity.

atoll (at′ol) a circular-shaped coral island or group of islands enclosing or partly enclosing a body of water called a lagoon.

barrier a wall built by people to break the impact of waves, often near the entrance to a harbor.

basin 1 all the land drained by a river and the streams that flow into it. 2 land enclosed by higher land.

bauxite (bôk′sīt) a claylike mineral from which aluminum is obtained.

bay part of an ocean or a lake extending into the land, having a wide opening. A bay is usually smaller than a gulf and larger than a cove. *See diagram.*

butte (byüt) a steep, flat-topped hill that stands alone on a plain; found in the dry regions of the western United States. A large butte is called a mesa.

canal a waterway dug across land for transportation, irrigation, or water supply. *See diagram.* The Panama Canal connects the Atlantic and Pacific oceans.

canyon a long, narrow valley with high, steep sides, often with a river flowing through it. *See diagram.* The Grand Canyon in North America is one mile deep, and it contains the Colorado River.

cape a point of land which projects out into a body of water. *See diagram.* Cape Horn is at the southern tip of South America.

channel 1 the bed of a river or a stream. 2 a small body of water that joins two larger bodies of water, like the English Channel. *See diagram.*

cliff a steep slope of rock or soil. *See diagram.*

climate 1 the kind of weather a place has. Climate includes conditions of heat and cold, moisture and dryness, clearness and cloudiness, wind and calm. 2 region with certain conditions of heat and cold, rainfall, wind, sunlight, etc.

consumer goods products made to satisfy human wants directly, such as clothing and food.

continent any one of the seven largest masses of land on the earth. The continents, in order of size, are Asia, Africa, North America, South America, Antarctica, Europe, and Australia. Sometimes Asia and Europe are considered to be a single continent called Eurasia.

Pronunciation Key

a hat	i it	oi oil		a in about
ā age	ī ice	ou out		e in taken
ä far	o hot	u cup	ə =	i in pencil
e let	ō open	ů put		o in lemon
ē equal	ô order	ü rule		u in circus
ėr term				

continental drift according to the theory of plate tectonics, the movement of continents on huge plates that slide across the surface of the earth's mantle.

continental shelf a plateau beneath the ocean from which the continents rise. *See diagram.*

copra (kō'prə) the dried meat of coconuts pressed for coconut oil—used for cooking, soap, shampoo, and margarine.

coral a limestone formation built on underwater rocks by colonies of polyps, small marine animals. Coral may form islands or reefs, sometimes developing on the tops of volcanoes to build atolls.

cordillera (kor'də lyer'ə) a system of mountain ranges, usually set in parallel ridges.

cove 1 a small, sheltered bay; inlet on the shore; mouth of a creek. **2** a sheltered place among hills or woods.

crater a bowl-shaped depression in the earth or around the opening of a volcano. The Great Meteor Crater near Flagstaff, Arizona, probably resulted from the impact of a large meteorite. Crater Lake in Oregon occupies the crater of an extinct volcano.

dam a wall built across a stream or river to hold back water. *See diagram.*

delta a more or less triangular deposit of sand and soil that collects at the mouth of some rivers. *See diagram.* The Nile River has a large delta.

desert a region with sparse vegetation due to little or no rainfall. A desert may be hot or cold. Local words for desert are often used as place names, like Sahara and Gobi.

divide a ridge of land between two regions drained by different rivers. *See diagram.* The Continental Divide in western North America separates streams flowing toward the Pacific Ocean from those flowing toward the Atlantic Ocean.

downstream the direction toward which a river flows.

Equator imaginary circle around the middle of the earth, halfway between the Poles.

erosion the wearing away of the surface of the earth by all processes, including weathering.

estuary (es'chü er'ē) a broad river mouth into which the tide flows.

export article sent to another country for sale.

fiord or **fjord** a long, narrow inlet of the sea bordered by steep cliffs. Formed by glaciers, fiords can be found along the coasts of Norway, Alaska, and New Zealand.

fork the place where a stream or tributary joins a river. *See diagram.*

glacier a large mass of ice formed over many years from snow on high ground wherever winter snowfall exceeds summer melting. It moves very slowly down a mountain, through a valley, or over a wide stretch of land. *See diagram.*

gulf an arm of an ocean or sea extending into the land. It is usually larger than a bay. *See diagram.*

harbor a sheltered area of water where ships can anchor safely. *See diagram.*

highland an area of mountains, hills, or plateaus. *See diagram.*

hill a raised part of the earth's surface with sloping sides—smaller than a mountain. *See diagram.*

iceberg a large mass of ice floating in the ocean. *See diagram.*

import an article for sale brought in from another country.

island a body of land smaller than a continent and completely surrounded by water. *See diagram.* Greenland is the world's largest island. New Guinea is the second largest.

isthmus (is'məs) a narrow strip of land with water on both sides, connecting two larger bodies of land. *See diagram.* The Isthmus of Panama connects North America and South America.

jute (jüt) a strong fiber obtained from two tropical plants related to the linden, used for making rope and coarse fabrics.

lake a large body of water completely surrounded by land. *See diagram.*

lowland a region that is lower and flatter than surrounding land. Broad regions of flat lowlands are called plains.

meridians imaginary lines running from Pole to Pole around the earth. They indicate degrees of longitude. The meridian at 0° longitude is called the Prime Meridian.

mesa (mā'sə) a large butte; a steep, flat-topped hill that stands alone on a plain.

metal any of a class of elements which usually have a shiny surface, conduct heat and electricity, and can be hammered into thin sheets.

mineral any natural substance obtained by mining or quarrying; a mineral may be a metal, such as gold, a liquid, such as petroleum, or a combination of various minerals, such as bauxite.

monsoon a seasonal wind of the Indian Ocean and southern Asia, blowing from the southwest from April to October and from the northeast during the rest of the year.

mountain a raised part of the earth's surface with a pointed or rounded top—higher than a hill. *See diagram.*

mountain range a row of connected mountains. *See diagram.*

mouth (of a river) the part of a river where its waters flow into another body of water. *See diagram.*

oasis (ō ā'sis) a fertile place in the desert where there is water and vegetation.

ocean 1 the great body of salt water that covers almost three-quarters of the earth's surface. *See diagram.* **2** any of its four main divisions: the Pacific, Atlantic, Indian, and Arctic oceans.

parallels imaginary circles running parallel to the Equator around the earth. They indicate degrees of latitude. The parallels at the Poles, 90°N and 90°S, are points not circles.

peak the pointed top of a mountain or hill. *See diagram.*

peninsula (pə nin′sə lə) a piece of land jutting out from the mainland and almost surrounded by water. *See diagram.* Florida and Italy are peninsulas.

plain a broad and flat or gently rolling area. *See diagram.*

plateau (pla tō′) a plain at a height considerably above sea level. *See diagram.* The Plateau of Tibet is the highest in the world.

polder a tract of lowland reclaimed from the sea or other body of water and protected by dikes. The Netherlands has extensive polder areas along the North Sea.

population density number of people living per unit of the earth's surface.

prairie (prer′ē) a large area of flat or rolling land covered with grass and very few trees.

precipitation moisture in the form of rain, dew, snow, and so on.

Prime Meridian imaginary line from which longitude east and west is measured; it runs through Greenwich, England, and its longitude is 0°.

rainforest a dense forest in a region where rain is heavy throughout the year. Rainforests are usually in tropical areas, though some may also be found in marine west coast climate areas like the Pacific Northwest coast of North America.

range a row of mountains.

reef a narrow ridge of rocks, sand, or coral lying at or near the surface of the water. The Great Barrier Reef off the northeast coast of Australia is over 1,200 miles long.

relief the differences in elevation between high and low spots in a particular area.

reservoir a place where water is collected and stored. *See diagram.*

resources the actual and potential wealth of a country; supplies that will meet a need, such as farmland or minerals.

rift valley a long, narrow depression with steep walls caused by the shifting of the earth's crust. The Great Rift Valley extends from Israel and Jordan all the way to Mozambique. The Dead Sea, Red Sea, and Lake Nyasa are part of this valley.

river a natural stream of water that flows into a lake or an ocean. *See diagram.* Small rivers are called brooks, creeks, rills, or runs.

river valley depression cut by the action of flowing water in a river.

savanna (sə van′ə) tall grassland with scattered trees between equatorial rainforests and steppes. The length of grass depends on the total rainfall.

savanna climate a tropical climate in which rain falls during the high sun season; also known as the "tropical wet-and-dry climate."

sea any large body of salt water. The word may refer to the oceans as a whole, to a part of an ocean, or to a smaller body of salt water like the Caspian Sea.

sound **1** a narrow body of water separating a large island from the mainland. **2** an inlet of the ocean.

source (of a river) the place where a river or stream begins. *See diagram.*

staple crops the most important or principal farm products grown in a place.

steppe like the savanna, a treeless grassland, but drier and with short grass. Gradually, as the area of dryness increases, it merges into the desert.

strait a narrow waterway connecting two larger bodies of water. *See diagram.* The Strait of Gibraltar connects the Mediterranean Sea with the Atlantic Ocean.

subsistence farming small-scale farming in which the final products are consumed by the grower's family.

swamp a piece of low-lying land in which water collects. *See diagram.*

taiga (tī′gə) the needleleaf forest that lies south of the tundra in North America, Scandinavia, and the Soviet Union.

topography the shape and elevation of an area's terrain.

tributary stream that flows into a larger stream or body of water; part of a river system. *See diagram.*

tropical rainforest a dense forest of trees, vines, ferns, and flowers near the Equator that receives abundant rainfall the year round.

tundra (tun′drə) area of land between timberline and polar regions on which only mosses, lichens, and a few shrubs grow. The ground just beneath the thin topsoil may remain frozen the year round, as permafrost. Tundra exists in high latitudes and high altitudes.

uplands a hilly region; contrasted with highlands, a mountainous region.

upstream the direction from which a river flows.

urbanization the growth of cities.

valley low land between hills or mountains. *See diagram.*

volcano an opening in the earth's crust through which steam, ashes, and molten rock are forced out. *See diagram.* A volcano may be active (capable of erupting at any time), dormant (not currently active), or extinct (no longer active and unlikely to be so again). The state of Hawaii is located on the tops of the world's highest volcanoes, which lie mainly beneath the sea.

weathering process which wears away the earth's surface by changes of temperature, by wind, rain, frost, and so on.

Pronunciation Key

a	hat	i	it	oi	oil			
ā	age	ī	ice	ou	out		a	in about
ä	far	o	hot	u	cup	ə =	e	in taken
e	let	ō	open	u̇	put		i	in pencil
ē	equal	ô	order	ü	rule		o	in lemon
ėr	term						u	in circus

THE SOLAR SYSTEM

The Solar System is a tiny part of one of the countless galaxies that make up the Universe. It consists of the Sun at the center with nine planets and various moons, comets, dust particles and gases revolving around it. All the planets revolve around the Sun in the same direction, anti-clockwise when viewed from the Northern Heavens, and almost in the same plane.

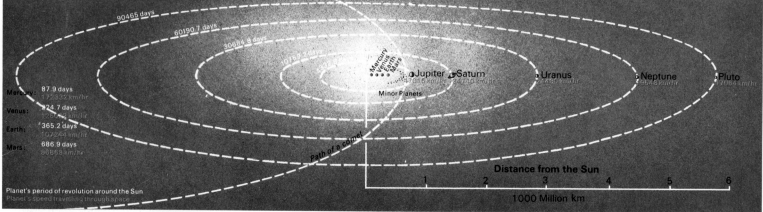

90465 days

60190.7 days

30684.8 days

Mercury
Venus
Earth

Jupiter   Saturn   Uranus   Neptune   Pluto

Minor Planets

Mercury: 87.9 days
          172332 km/hr
Venus: 224.7 days
          126000 km/hr
Earth: 365.2 days
          107244 km/hr
Mars: 686.9 days
          86868 km/hr

Path of a comet

Planet's period of revolution around the Sun
Planet's speed travelling through space

Distance from the Sun

1   2   3   4   5   6

1000 Million km

THE PLANETS IN RELATION TO THEIR SIZE

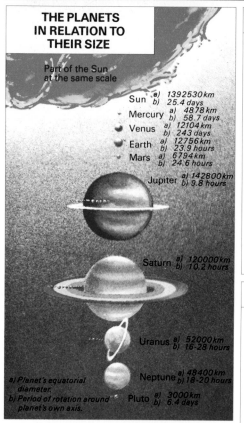

Part of the Sun at the same scale

Sun	a)	1392530km
	b)	25.4 days
Mercury	a)	4878km
	b)	58.7 days
Venus	a)	12104km
	b)	243 days
Earth	a)	12756km
	b)	23.9 hours
Mars	a)	6794km
	b)	24.6 hours
Jupiter	a)	142800km
	b)	9.8 hours
Saturn	a)	120000km
	b)	10.2 hours
Uranus	a)	52000km
	b)	16-28 hours
Neptune	a)	48400km
	b)	18-20 hours
Pluto	a)	3000km
	b)	6.4 days

a) Planet's equatorial diameter
b) Period of rotation around planet's own axis.

ECLIPSES

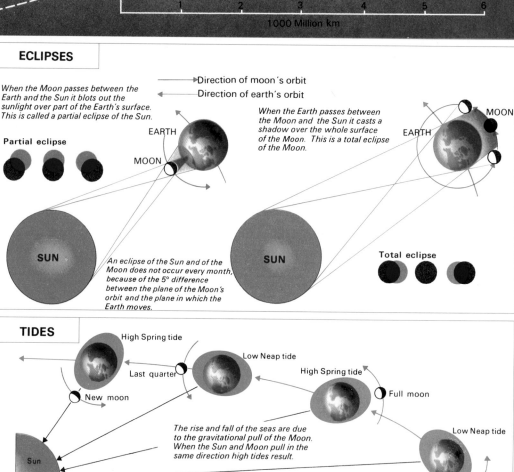

When the Moon passes between the Earth and the Sun it blots out the sunlight over part of the Earth's surface. This is called a partial eclipse of the Sun.

→ Direction of moon's orbit
← Direction of earth's orbit

When the Earth passes between the Moon and the Sun it casts a shadow over the whole surface of the Moon. This is a total eclipse of the Moon.

Partial eclipse

EARTH

MOON

SUN

MOON

EARTH

SUN

Total eclipse

An eclipse of the Sun and of the Moon does not occur every month, because of the 5° difference between the plane of the Moon's orbit and the plane in which the Earth moves.

TIDES

High Spring tide

Low Neap tide

Last quarter

High Spring tide

Full moon

New moon

Low Neap tide

The rise and fall of the seas are due to the gravitational pull of the Moon. When the Sun and Moon pull in the same direction high tides result.

Sun

First quarter

THE PHASES OF THE MOON

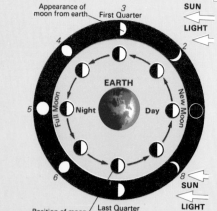

The Moon, like the planets, has no light of its own and shines only by reflecting sunlight.

Appearance of moon from earth

First Quarter   3

SUN

LIGHT

4   2

EARTH

Full Moon   Night   Day   New Moon

5

6   8

Last Quarter

Position of moon   7

SUN

LIGHT

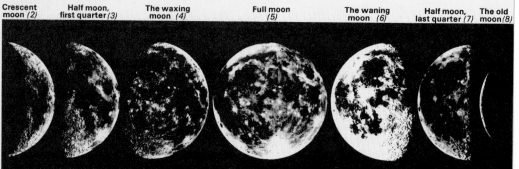

The Moon rotates on its own axis in just over 27 days, which is the same as its period of revolution around the Earth, so that it always presents the same face (hemisphere) to us. Because the Earth has moved on its own orbital plane around the Sun, while the Moon is revolving around it, the time from one full Moon to the next is 29½ days.

| Crescent moon (2) | Half moon, first quarter (3) | The waxing moon (4) | Full moon (5) | The waning moon (6) | Half moon, last quarter (7) | The old moon (8) |

THE SEASONS

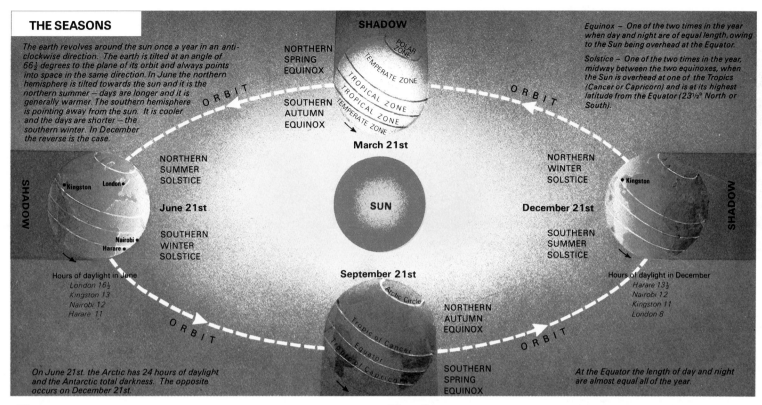

The earth revolves around the sun once a year in an anti-clockwise direction. The earth is tilted at an angle of 66½ degrees to the plane of its orbit and always points into space in the same direction. In June the northern hemisphere is tilted towards the sun and it is the northern summer – days are longer and it is generally warmer. The southern hemisphere is pointing away from the sun. It is cooler and the days are shorter – the southern winter. In December the reverse is the case.

Equinox – One of the two times in the year when day and night are of equal length, owing to the Sun being overhead at the Equator.

Solstice – One of the two times in the year, midway between the two equinoxes, when the Sun is overhead at one of the Tropics (Cancer or Capricorn) and is at its highest latitude from the Equator (23½° North or South).

NORTHERN SPRING EQUINOX
SOUTHERN AUTUMN EQUINOX

March 21st

SUN

NORTHERN SUMMER SOLSTICE
June 21st
SOUTHERN WINTER SOLSTICE

NORTHERN WINTER SOLSTICE
December 21st
SOUTHERN SUMMER SOLSTICE

September 21st

NORTHERN AUTUMN EQUINOX
SOUTHERN SPRING EQUINOX

Hours of daylight in June
London 16½
Kingston 13
Nairobi 12
Harare 11

Hours of daylight in December
Harare 13½
Nairobi 12
Kingston 11
London 8

On June 21st. the Arctic has 24 hours of daylight and the Antarctic total darkness. The opposite occurs on December 21st.

At the Equator the length of day and night are almost equal all of the year.

Time

1. The Year – the time taken by the Earth to revolve around the Sun, or 365¼ days.

2. The Month – the approximate time taken by the Moon to revolve around the Earth. The twelve months of the year in fact vary from 28 (29 in a Leap Year) to 31 days.

3. The Week – an artificial period of 7 days, not based on astronomical time.

4. The Day – the time taken by the Earth to complete one revolution on its Axis.

5. The Hour – 24 hours make one day. Usually the day is divided into hours A.M. (ante meridiem or before noon) and P.M. (post meridiem or after noon), although most timetables now use the 24-hour system, from midnight to midnight, for example, 1 p.m. = 13.00 hours.

Time Zones

Each day has a period of daylight when the sun is above the horizon, and a period of night when it is below. This is because the Earth rotates from west to east, so that part of its surface is in shadow at any one time. Time thus alters longitudinally, noon being reckoned as the point when the sun crosses a meridian. Places having the same longitude will have approximately the same time, and the world is therefore divided into 24 time zones, each centered on a meridian at a 15° interval. The base zone, centered on the Greenwich Meridian, is known as Greenwich Mean Time, GMT. The twelve zones to the west of this are behind GMT; the twelve to the east are ahead. Thus when it is noon at Greenwich it is 7 a.m. in New York and 2 p.m. in Moscow. A line roughly following the 180° meridian divides the eastern and western zones; this is the International Date Line. Time Zone boundaries do not always follow the appropriate meridians, as in many cases, these cut across country boundaries and obviously it is more convenient for a country to have a standard time throughout its area. A few countries with very great areas have several time zones, for example, the U.S.A. and U.S.S.R.

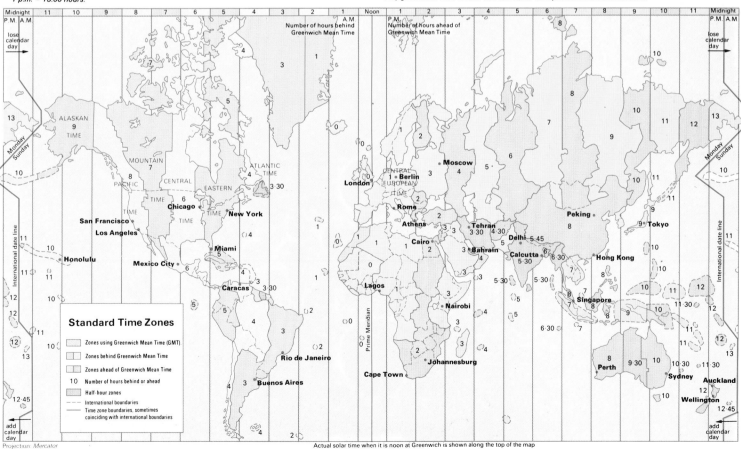

Standard Time Zones

- Zones using Greenwich Mean Time (GMT).
- Zones behind Greenwich Mean Time
- Zones ahead of Greenwich Mean Time
- **10** Number of hours behind or ahead
- Half-hour zones
- --- International boundaries
- — Time zone boundaries, sometimes coinciding with international boundaries

Number of hours behind Greenwich Mean Time

Number of hours ahead of Greenwich Mean Time

Actual solar time when it is noon at Greenwich is shown along the top of the map

Projection: *Mercator*

Projection: Hammer Equal Area

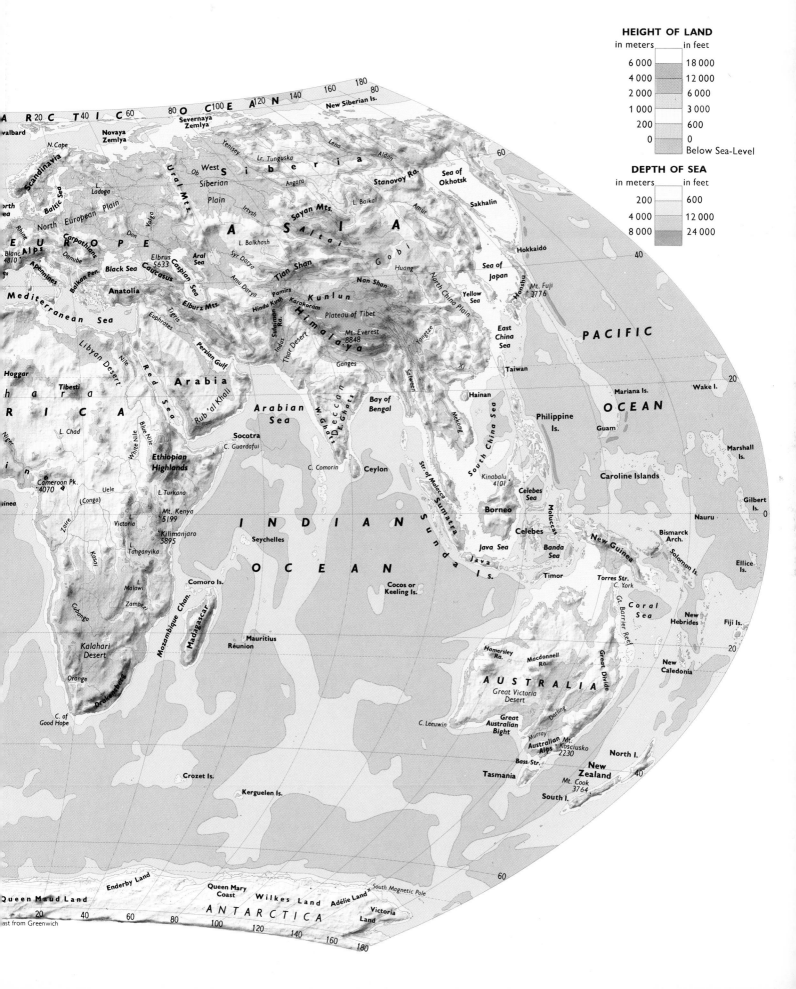

HEIGHT OF LAND

in meters		in feet
6 000		18 000
4 000		12 000
2 000		6 000
1 000		3 000
200		600
0		0
		Below Sea-Level

DEPTH OF SEA

in meters		in feet
200		600
4 000		12 000
8 000		24 000

ARCTIC OCEAN

Svalbard
N. Cape
North Sea
Baltic Sea
L. Ladoga
Scandinavia
EUROPE
Rhine
Alps
Mt. Blanc 4810
Apennines
Carpathians
Danube
Don
Volga
Black Sea
Caucasus
Elbrus 5633
Caspian Sea
Aral Sea
Balkan Pen.
Anatolia
Mediterranean Sea
Libyan Desert
Nile
Red Sea
Euphrates
Tigris
Persian Gulf
Elburz Mts.
Hindu Kush
Pamirs
Karakoram
Sulaiman Ra.
Indus
Thar Desert

Novaya Zemlya
Severnaya Zemlya
Yenisey
Ob
West Siberian Plain
Ural Mts.
Siberia
Irtysh
L. Balkhash
Syr Darya
Amu Darya
Tian Shan
ASIA
Altai
Sayan Mts.
Angara
Lr. Tunguska
Lena
Aldan
Stanovoy Ra.
Amur
L. Baikal
Gobi
Kunlun
Nan Shan
Huang
Plateau of Tibet
Himalaya
Mt. Everest 8848
Ganges

New Siberian Is.
Sea of Okhotsk
Sakhalin
Hokkaido
Sea of Japan
Honshu
Mt. Fuji 3776
North China Plain
Yellow Sea
East China Sea
Yangtze
Xi
Taiwan
Hainan

PACIFIC OCEAN
Mariana Is.
Wake I.
Guam
Caroline Islands
Marshall Is.
Gilbert Is.
Nauru
Ellice Is.

Hoggar
Tibesti
L. Chad
Sahara
Niger
Guinea
Cameroon Pk. 4070
Uele
(Congo)
Zaire
Kasai
L. Victoria
Arabia
Rub' al Khali
Socotra
C. Guardafui
Ethiopian Highlands
White Nile
Blue Nile
L. Turkana
Mt. Kenya 5199
Kilimanjaro 5895
L. Tanganyika
Arabian Sea
W. Ghats
Deccan
E. Ghats
C. Comorin
Ceylon
Bay of Bengal
Salween
Mekong
Str. of Malacca
Sumatra
Sunda Is.
Java
Java Sea
South China Sea
Kinabalu 4101
Borneo
Celebes Sea
Celebes
Moluccas
Banda Sea
Timor
Philippine Is.
New Guinea
Bismarck Arch.
Solomon Is.

INDIAN OCEAN
Seychelles
Comoro Is.
Madagascar
Mozambique Chan.
Mauritius
Réunion
Cocos or Keeling Is.
Torres Str.
C. York
Coral Sea
New Hebrides
New Caledonia
Fiji Is.

L. Malawi
Zambezi
Cubango
Orange
Kalahari Desert
Drakensberg
C. of Good Hope

Crozet Is.
Kerguelen Is.

Hamersley Ra.
Macdonnell Ra.
Great Divide
AUSTRALIA
Great Victoria Desert
C. Leeuwin
Great Australian Bight
Murray
Darling
Australian Alps
Mt. Kosciusko 2230
Bass Str.
Tasmania
North I.
New Zealand
Mt. Cook 3764
South I.

Queen Maud Land
Enderby Land
Queen Mary Coast
Wilkes Land
Adélie Land
South Magnetic Pole
Victoria Land
ANTARCTICA
East from Greenwich

The origin of the earth is still open to much conjecture although the most widely accepted theory is that it was formed from a solar cloud consisting mainly of hydrogen. Under gravitation the cloud condensed and shrank to form our planets orbiting around the sun. Gravitation forced the lighter elements to the surface of the earth where they cooled to form a crust while the inner material remained hot and molten. Earth's first rocks formed over 3·5 billion years ago but since then the surface has been constantly altered.

Until comparatively recently the view that the primary units of the earth had remained essentially fixed throughout geological time was regarded as common sense, although the concept of moving continents has been traced back to references in the Bible of a break up of the land after Noah's floods. The continental drift theory was first developed by Antonio Snider in 1858 but probably the most important single advocate was Alfred Wegener who, in 1915, published evidence from geology, climatology and biology. His conclusions are very similar to those reached by current research although he was wrong about the speed of break-up.

The measurement of fossil magnetism found in rocks has probably proved the most influential evidence. While originally these drift theories were openly mocked, now they are considered standard doctrine.

The jigsaw
As knowledge of the shape and structure of the earth's surface grew, several of the early geographers noticed the great similarity in shape of the coasts bordering the Atlantic. It was this remarkable similarity which led to the first detailed geological and structural comparisons. Even more accurate fits can be made by placing the edges of the continental shelves in juxtaposition.

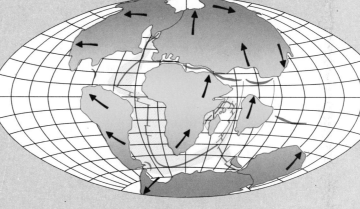

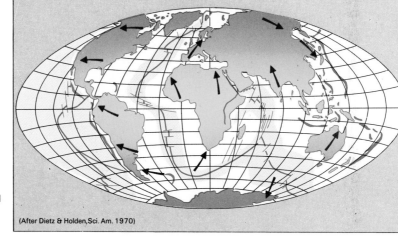

(After Dietz & Holden, Sci. Am. 1970)

180 million years ago.
The original Pangaea land mass had split into two major continental groups. The southern group, Gondwana-land, had itself started to break up, India and Antarctica-Australia becoming isolated. A rift had begun to appear between South America and Africa and, in the East, Africa was closing up the Tethys Sea.

135 million years ago.
Both Gondwanaland and Laurasia continued to drift northwards but the widening of the splits in the North Atlantic and Indian Oceans persisted. The South Atlantic rift continued to lengthen and a further perpendicular rift appeared which will eventually separate Greenland from North America. India continues heading northward towards Asia.

65 million years ago.
South America, completely separated from Africa, moved quickly north and westwards. Madagascar broke free from Africa but, as yet, there is no sign of the Red Sea Rift which will split Africa from the Arabian Peninsula. The Mediterranean Sea is recognizable. In the south, Australia is still connected to Antarctica.

Today.
India has moved northwards and is colliding with Asia, crumpling up the sediments to form the folded mountain range of the Himalayas. South America has rotated and moved west to connect with North America. Australia has separated from Antarctica.

	Trench
	Rift
	New Ocean Floor
	Zones of slippage

The earth's surface is slowly but continually being rearranged. Some changes such as erosion and deposition are extremely slow but they upset the balance which causes other more abrupt changes often originating deep within the earth's interior. The constant movements vary in intensity, often with stresses building up to a climax such as a particularly violent volcanic eruption or earthquake.

The crust (below and right)
The outer layer or crust of the earth consists of a comparatively low density, brittle material varying from 3 mi. to 30 mi. deep beneath the continents. This consists predominately of silica and aluminum; hence it is called 'sial'. Extending under the ocean floors and below the sial is a basaltic layer known as 'sima', consisting mainly of silica and magnesium.

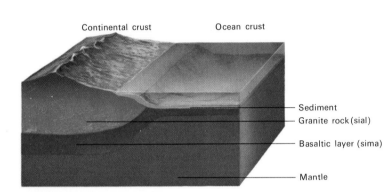

Crust
Mantle
Outer core
Inner core

Continental crust   Ocean crust

Sediment
Granite rock (sial)
Basaltic layer (sima)
Mantle

Volcanoes (right, below and far right)
Volcanoes occur when hot liquefied rock beneath the crust reaches the surface as lava. An accumulation of ash and cinders around a vent forms a cone. Successive layers of thin lava flows form an acid lava volcano while thick lava flows form a basic lava volcano. A caldera forms when a particularly violent eruption blows off the top of an already existing cone.

The mantle (above)
Immediately below the crust, at the mohorovicic discontinuity line, there is a distinct change in density and chemical properties. This is the mantle - made up of iron and magnesium silicates - with temperatures reaching 1 600 °C. The rigid upper mantle extends down to a depth of about 600 mi. below which is the more viscous lower mantle which is about 1 200 mi. thick.

The core (above)
The outer core, approximately 1 300 mi. thick, consists of molten iron and nickel at 2 000 °C to 5 000 °C possibly separated from the less dense mantle by an oxidised shell. About 3 000 mi. below the surface is the liquid transition zone, below which is the solid inner core, a sphere of 1 700 mi. diameter where rock is three times as dense as in the crust.

Shield volcano   **Cinder cone**   **Hornit cone**   **Caldera**

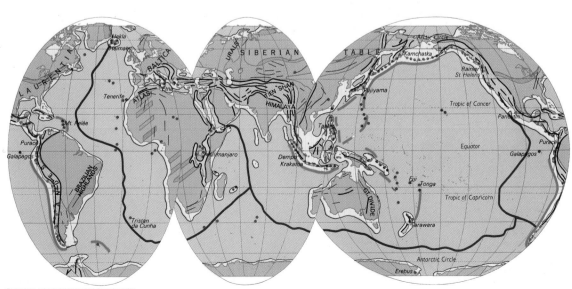

Volcanoes and structure

- • Volcanoes
- ▬ Sea floor spreading center
- ▬ Ocean trench
- ▬ Continental shelf

Structure
After L. Kober and others

Pre-Cambrian
Caledonian folding
Hercynian folding
Tertiary folding
Great Rift Valley
// /// Main trend lines

Projection: Interrupted Mollweide's Homolographic

The making of landscape

The major forces which shape our land would seem to act very slowly in comparison with the average life span of human beings but in geological terms the erosion of rock is in fact very fast. Land goes through a cycle of transformation. It is broken up by earthquakes and other earth movements, temperature changes, water, wind and ice. Rock debris is then transported by water, wind and glaciers and deposited on lowlands and on the sea floor. Here it builds up and by the pressure of its own weight is converted into new rock strata. These in turn can be uplifted either gently as plains or plateaus or more irregularly to form mountains. In either case the new higher land is eroded and the cycle begins again.

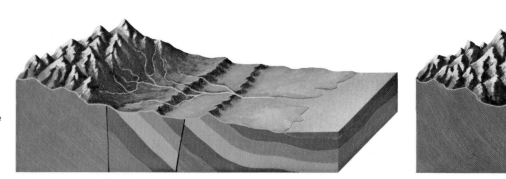
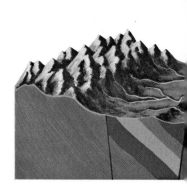

Rivers

Rivers shape the land by three basic processes: erosion, transportation and deposition. A youthful river flows fast eroding downwards quickly to form a narrow valley (1). As it matures it deposits some debris and erodes laterally to widen the valley (2). In its last stage it meanders across a wide flat flood plain depositing fine particles of alluvium (3).

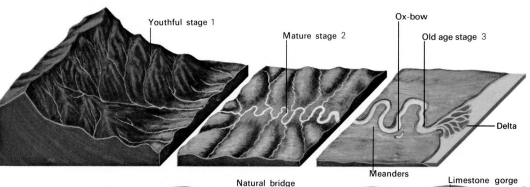

Youthful stage 1

Mature stage 2

Ox-bow

Old age stage 3

Delta

Meanders

Underground water

Water enters porous and permeable rocks from the surface moving downward until it reaches a layer of impermeable rock. Joints in underground rock, such as limestone, are eroded to form underground caves and caverns. When the roof of a cave collapses a gorge is formed. Surface entrances to joints are often widened to form vertical openings called swallow holes.

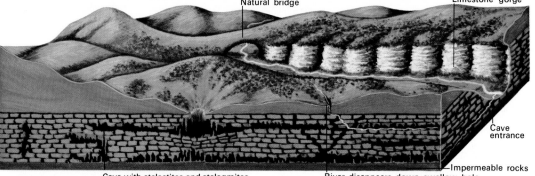

Natural bridge

Limestone gorge

Cave entrance

Cave with stalactites and stalagmites

River disappears down swallow hole

Impermeable rocks

Wind

Wind action is particularly powerful in arid and semi-arid regions where rock waste produced by weathering is used as an abrasive tool by the wind. The rate of erosion varies with the characteristics of the rock which can cause weird shapes and effects (right). Desert sand can also be accumulated by the wind to form barchan dunes (far right) which slowly travel forward, horns first.

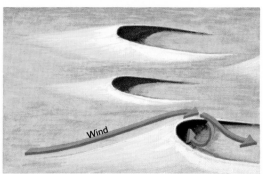

Wind

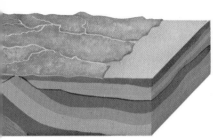

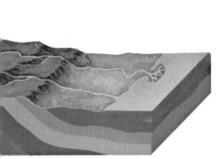

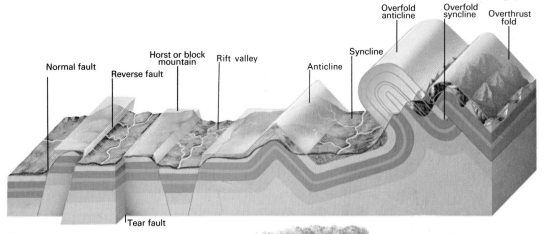

Normal fault · Reverse fault · Horst or block mountain · Rift valley · Anticline · Syncline · Overfold anticline · Overfold syncline · Overthrust fold · Tear fault

Folding and faulting

A vertical displacement in the earth's crust is called a fault or reverse fault; lateral displacement is a tear fault. An uplifted block is called a horst, the reverse of which is a rift valley. Compressed horizontal layers of sedimentary rock fold to form mountains. Those layers which bend up form an anticline, those bending down form a syncline : continued pressure forms an overfold.

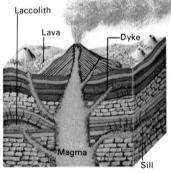

Laccolith · Lava · Dyke · Magma · Sill

Volcanic activity

When pressure on rocks below the earth's crust is released the normally semi-solid hot rock becomes liquid magma. The magma forces its way into cracks of the crust and may either reach the surface where it forms volcanoes or it may collect in the crust as sills, dykes, or laccoliths. When magma reaches the surface it cools to form lava.

Waves

Coasts are continually changing, some retreat under wave erosion while others advance with wave deposition. These actions combined form steep cliffs and wave cut platforms. Eroded debris is in turn deposited as a terrace. As the water becomes shallower the erosive power of the waves decreases and gradually the cliff disappears. Wave action can also create other features (far right).

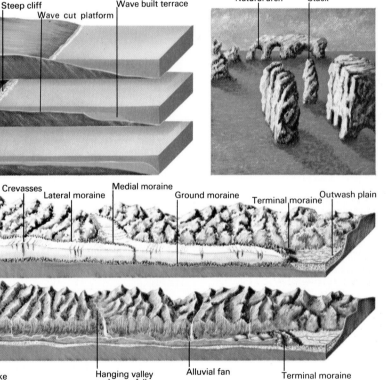

Steep cliff · Wave cut platform · Wave built terrace

Natural arch · Stack

Ice

These diagrams (right) show how a glaciated valley may have formed. The glacier deepens, straightens and widens the river valley whose interlocking spurs become truncated or cut off. Intervalley divides are frost shattered to form sharp arêtes and pyramidal peaks. Hanging valleys mark the entry of tributary rivers and eroded rocks form medial moraine. Terminal moraine is deposited as the glacier retreats.

Pyramidal peak · Arête · Crevasses · Lateral moraine · Medial moraine · Ground moraine · Terminal moraine · Outwash plain

Cirque with lake · Hanging valley and waterfall · Alluvial fan · Terminal moraine

Subsidence and uplift

As the land surface is eroded it may eventually become a level plain - a peneplain, broken only by low hills, remnants of previous mountains. In turn this peneplain may be uplifted to form a plateau with steep edges. At the coast the uplifted wave platform becomes a coastal plain and in the rejuvenated rivers downward erosion once more predominates.

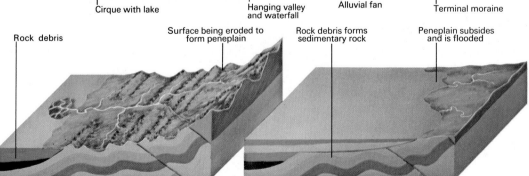

Rock debris · Surface being eroded to form peneplain · Rock debris forms sedimentary rock · Peneplain subsides and is flooded

Its surface

Highest point on the earth's surface: Mt. Everest, Tibet - Nepal boundary   29 029 ft
Lowest point on the earth's surface: The Dead Sea, Israel - Jordan   below sea level 1 296 ft
Greatest ocean depth : Challenger Deep, Mariana Trench   36 161 ft
Average height of land   2 756 ft
Average depth of seas and oceans   12 493 ft

The Figure of Earth

An imaginary sea-level surface is considered and called a geoid. By measuring at different places the angles from plumb lines to a fixed star there have been many determinations of the shape of parts of the geoid which is found to be an oblate spheriod with its axis along the axis of rotation of the earth. Observations from satellites have now given a new method of more accurate determinations of the figure of the earth and its local irregularities.

Land and Sea Hemispheres.

About 85% of the total land area is contained in the hemisphere centred on a point between Paris and Brussels.

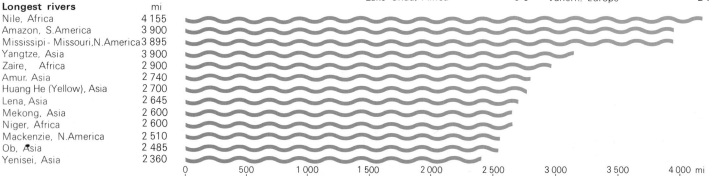

Dimensions

Superficial area	197 000 000 mi^2
Land surface	57 000 000 mi^2
Land surface as % of total area	29·2 %
Water surface	139 000 000 mi^2
Water surface as % of total area	70·8 %
Equatorial circumference	24 888 mi.
Meridional circumference	24 845 mi.
Equatorial diameter	7 922 mi.
Polar diameter	7 895·2 mi.
Equatorial radius	3 960·9 mi.
Polar radius	3 947·6 mi.
Volume of the Earth	672 686 x 10^6 mi^3
Mass of the Earth	5·9 x 10^{21} tonnes

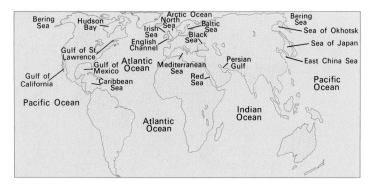

Oceans and Seas
Area in 1000 mi^2

Pacific Ocean	63 985	North Sea	222
Atlantic Ocean	31 529	Black Sea	173
Indian Ocean	28 356	Red Sea	170
Arctic Ocean	5 541	Baltic Sea	163
Mediterranean Sea	1 145	Persian Gulf	92
Bering Sea	878	St. Lawrence, Gulf of	91
Caribbean Sea	750	English Channel & Irish Sea	69
Mexico, Gulf of	700	California, Gulf of	62
Okhotsk, Sea of	590		
East China Sea	482		
Hudson Bay	475		
Japan, Sea of	405		

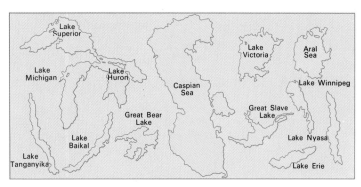

Lakes and Inland Seas
Areas in 1000 mi^2

Caspian Sea (Salt), Asia	163·8	Lake Ontario, N.America	7·5
Lake Superior, N.America	31·8	Lake Ladoga, Europe	7·1
Lake Victoria, Africa	26·8	Lake Balkhash, Asia	6·7
Aral Sea (Salt), Asia	24·6	Lake Maracaibo, S.America	6·3
Lake Huron, N.America	23·0	Lake Onega, Europe	3·8
Lake Michigan, N.America	22·4	Lake Eyre (Salt), Australia	3·7
Lake Tanganyika, Africa	12·7	Lake Turkana (Salt), Africa	3·5
Lake Baikal, Asia	12·2	Lake Titicaca, S.America	3·2
Great Bear Lake, N.America	12·0	Lake Nicaragua, C.America	3·1
Great Slave Lake, N.America	11·2	Lake Athabasca, N.America	3·0
Lake Nyasa, Africa	11·0	Reindeer Lake, N.America	2·4
Lake Erie, N.America	9·9	Issyk-Kul, Asia	2·4
Lake Winnipeg, N.America	9·4	Lake Torrens (Salt), Australia	2·3
Lake Chad, Africa	8·0	Koko Nor (Salt), Asia	2·3
		Lake Urmia, Asia	2·3
		Vänern, Europe	2·2

Longest rivers

	mi
Nile, Africa	4 155
Amazon, S.America	3 900
Mississipi - Missouri, N.America	3 895
Yangtze, Asia	3 900
Zaire, Africa	2 900
Amur, Asia	2 740
Huang He (Yellow), Asia	2 700
Lena, Asia	2 645
Mekong, Asia	2 600
Niger, Africa	2 600
Mackenzie, N.America	2 510
Ob, Asia	2 485
Yenisei, Asia	2 360

0   500   1 000   1 500   2 000   2 500   3 000   3 500   4 000 mi

The Highest Mountains and the Greatest Depths.

Mount Everest defied the world's greatest mountaineers for 32 years and claimed the lives of many people. Not until 1920 was permission granted by the Dalai Lama to attempt the mountain, and the first successful ascent came in 1953. Since then the summit has been reached several times. The world's highest peaks have now been climbed but there are many as yet unexplored peaks in the Himalayas, some of which may be over 25 000 ft.

The greatest trenches are the Mariana Trench (36 161 ft), the Tonga Trench (35 505 ft), the Mindanao Trench (34 439 ft), and the Puerto Rico Deep (30 184 ft). The trenches represent less than 2% of the total area of the seabed but are of great interest as lines of structural weakness in the Earth's crust and as areas of frequent earthquakes.

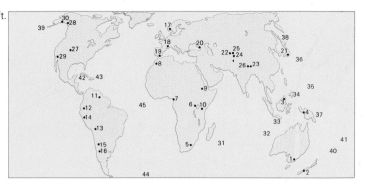

High mountains

Mountain heights in feet

1 Kosciusko 7 316 · 2 Mt. Cook (N.Z.) 12 349 · 3 Kinabalu 13 455 · 4 Jaya (Irian) 16 400 · 5 Mt. aux Sources 10 822 · 6 Ruwenzori 16 795 · 7 Cameroon peak 13 350 · 8 Dj. Toubkal 13 661 · 9 Ras Dashen 15 158 · 10 Kilimanjaro 19 340 · 11 Roraima 9 219 · 12 Chimborazo 20 561 · 13 Illimani 21 151 · 14 Huascaran 22 205 · 15 Ojos del Salado 22 572 · 16 Aconcagua 22 831 · 17 Galdhøpiggen 8 097 · 18 Mont Blanc 15 781 · 19 Mulhacen 11 420 · 20 Elbrus 18 481 · 21 Fujiyama 12 388 · 22 Communism Peak 24 590 · 23 Kanchenjunga 28 208 · 24 K2 28 250 · 25 Muztagh 24 388 · 26 Everest 29 029 · 27 Mt. Elbert 14 431 · 28 Mt. Logan 19 850 · 29 Mt. Whitney 14 495 · 30 Mt. McKinley 20 320

Oceania · Africa · South America · Europe and Asia · North America

Bathyscaphe

Ocean depths in feet

Sea level

31 Mauritius basin 20 100 · 32 W. Australian basin 21 200 · 33 Java trench 25 340 · 34 Mindanao trench 34 439 · 35 Mariana trench 36 161 · 36 Japan trench 34 620 · 37 Bougainville deep 30 000 · 38 Kuril trench 34 040 · 39 Aleutian trench 25 660 · 40 Kermadec trench 32 960 · 41 Tonga trench 35 505 · 42 Cayman trough 25 190 · 43 Puerto Rico trough 30 184 · 44 S. Sandwich trench 27 100 · 45 Romanche deep 25 320

Indian Ocean · Pacific Ocean · Atlantic Ocean

Waterfall

Notable Waterfalls heights in feet

Angel, Venezuela	3 215
Tugela, S. Africa	2 798
Mongefossen, Norway	2 539
Yosemite, California	2 421
Mardalsfossen, Norway	2 149
Cuquenan, Venezuela	2 001
Sutherland, N.Z.	1 899
Reichenbach, Switzerland	1 798
Wollomombi, Australia	1 699
Ribbon, California	1 611
Gavarnie, France	1 384
Tyssefallene, Norway	1 358
Krimml, Austria	1 214
King George VI, Guyana	1 200
Silver Strand, California	1 168
Geissbach, Switzerland	1 148
Staubbach, Switzerland	981
Trümmelbach, Switzerland	951
Chirombo, Zambia	879
Livingstone, Zaire	849
King Edward VIII, Guyana	840
Gersoppa, India	830
Vettifossen, Norway	820
Kalambo, Zambia	787
Kaieteur, Guyana	741
Maletsunyane, Lesotho	630
Terui, Italy	590
Kabarega, Uganda	400
Victoria, Zimbabwe-Zambia	351
Cauvery, India	318
Boyoma, Zaire	200
Niagara, N.America	167
Schaffhausen, Switzerland	98

Dam

Notable Dams heights in feet

Africa

Cabora Bassa, Zambezi R.	551
Akosombo Main Dam Volta R.	462
Kariba, Zambezi R.	420
Aswan High Dam, Nile R.	360

Asia

Nurek, Vakhsh R., U.S.S.R.	1 040
Bhakra, Sutlej R., India	741
Kurobegawa, Kurobe R., Japan	610
Charvak, Chirchik R., U.S.S.R.	551
Okutadami, Tadami R., Japan	515
Bratsk, Angara R., U.S.S.R.	410

Oceania

Warragamba, N.S.W., Australia	449
Eucumbene, N.S.W., Australia	380

Europe

Grande Dixence, Switz.	931
Vajont, Vajont, R., Italy	856
Mauvoisin, Drance R., Switz.	777
Contra, Verzasca R., Switz.	754
Luzzone, Brenno R., Switz.	682
Tignes, Isère R., France	590
Amir Kabir, Karadj R., U.S.S.R.	590
Vidraru, Arges R., Rom.	541
Kremasta, Acheloos R., Greece	541

North America

Mica, Columbia R., Can.	794
Oroville, Feather R.,	771
Hoover, Colorado R.,	725
Glen Canyon, Colorado R.,	708
Daniel Johnson, Can.	702
New Bullards Bar, N. Yuba R.	636
Mossyrock, Cowlitz R.,	603
Shasta, Sacramento R.,	600
W.A.C. Bennett, Canada.	600
Don Pedro, Tuolumne R.,	584
Grand Coulee, Columbia R.,	551

Central and South America

Guri, Caroni R., Venezuela.	347

Earth's thin coating (right)

The atmosphere is a blanket of protective gases around the earth providing insulation against otherwise extreme alternations in temperature. The gravitational pull increases the density nearer the earth's surface so that 5/6ths of the atmospheric mass is in the first 15 kms. It is a very thin layer in comparison with the earth's diameter of 12 680 kms., like the cellulose coating on a globe.

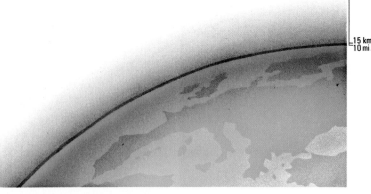

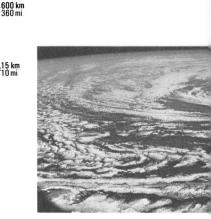

Exosphere (1)

The exosphere merges with the interplanetary medium and although there is no definite boundary with the ionosphere it starts at a height of about 600 kms. The rarified air mainly consists of a small amount of atomic oxygen up to 600 kms. and equal proportions of hydrogen and helium with hydrogen predominating above 2 400 kms.

Ionosphere (2)

Air particles of the ionosphere are electrically charged by the sun's radiation and congregate in four main layers, D, E, F1 and F2, which can reflect radio waves. Aurorae, caused by charged particles deflected by the earth's magnetic field towards the poles, occur between 65 and 965 kms. above the earth. It is mainly in the lower ionosphere that meteors from outer space burn up as they meet increased air resistance.

Stratosphere (3)

A thin layer of ozone contained within the stratosphere absorbs ultra-violet light and in the process gives off heat. The temperature ranges from about -55°C at the tropopause to about -60°C in the upper part, known as the mesosphere, with a rise to about 2°C just above the ozone layer. This portion of the atmosphere is separated from the lower layer by the tropopause.

Troposphere (4)

The earth's weather conditions are limited to this layer which is relatively thin, extending upwards to about 8 kms. at the poles and 15 kms. at the equator. It contains about 85% of the total atmospheric mass and almost all the water vapour. Air temperature falls steadily with increased height at about 1°C for every 100 meters above sea level.

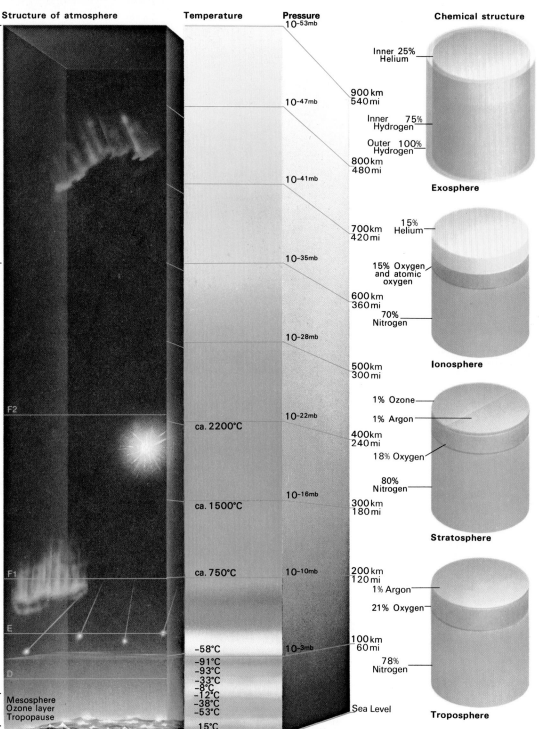

Structure of atmosphere

F2

F1

E

D

Mesosphere
Ozone layer
Tropopause

Temperature

ca. 2200°C

ca. 1500°C

ca. 750°C

-58°C
-91°C
-93°C
-33°C
-8°C
-12°C
-38°C
-53°C

15°C

Pressure

10^{-53}mb

10^{-47}mb

10^{-41}mb

10^{-35}mb

10^{-28}mb

10^{-22}mb

10^{-16}mb

10^{-10}mb

10^{-3}mb

10^{3}mb

600 km
360 mi

15 km
10 mi

900 km
540 mi

800 km
480 mi

700 km
420 mi

600 km
360 mi

500 km
300 mi

400 km
240 mi

300 km
180 mi

200 km
120 mi

100 km
60 mi

Sea Level

Chemical structure

Inner 25% Helium

Inner 75% Hydrogen

Outer 100% Hydrogen

Exosphere

15% Helium

15% Oxygen and atomic oxygen

70% Nitrogen

Ionosphere

1% Ozone

1% Argon

18% Oxygen

80% Nitrogen

Stratosphere

1% Argon

21% Oxygen

78% Nitrogen

Troposphere

Pacific Ocean
Cloud patterns over the Pacific show the paths of prevailing winds.

Circulation of the air

Circulation of the air
Owing to high temperatures in equatorial regions the air near the ground is heated, expands and rises producing a low pressure belt. It cools, causing rain, spreads out then sinks again about latitudes 30° north and south forming high pressure belts.

High and low pressure belts are areas of comparative calm but between them, blowing from high to low pressure, are the prevailing winds. These are deflected to the right in the northern hemisphere and to the left in the southern hemisphere (Coriolis effect). The circulations appear in three distinct belts with a seasonal movement north and south following the overhead sun.

Cloud types

Clouds form when damp air is cooled, usually by rising. This may happen in three ways: when a wind rises to cross hills or mountains; when a mass of air rises over, or is pushed up by another mass of denser air; when local heating of the ground causes convection currents.

Cirrus (1) are detached clouds composed of microscopic ice crystals which gleam white in the sun resembling hair or feathers. They are found at heights of 6 000 to 12 000 meters.

Cirrostratus (2) are a whitish veil of cloud made up of ice crystals through which the sun can be seen often producing a halo of bright light.

Cirrocumulus (3) is another high altitude cloud formed by turbulence between layers moving in different directions.

Altostratus (4) is a grey or bluish striated, fibrous or uniform sheet of cloud producing light drizzle.

Altocumulus (5) is a thicker and fluffier version of cirro cumulus, it is a white and grey patchy sheet of cloud.

Nimbostratus (6) is a dark grey layer of cloud obscuring the sun and causing almost continuous rain or snow.

Cumulus (7) are detached heaped up, dense low clouds. The sunlit parts are brilliant white while the base is relatively dark and flat.

Stratus (8) forms dull overcast skies associated with depressions and occurs at low altitudes up to 1500 meters.

Cumulonimbus (9) are heavy and dense clouds associated with storms and rain. They have flat bases and a fluffy outline extending up to great altitudes.

10 000 m
30 000 ft

High clouds
1

8 000 m
25 000 ft

2

6 000 m
18 000 ft

3

Middle clouds

4 000 m
12 000 ft

4

5

2 000 m
6 000 ft

6

Low clouds

7

8

Sea Level

1 Cirrus

2 Cirrostratus

3 Cirrocumulus

4 Altostratus

5 Altocumulus

6 Nimbostratus

7 Cumulus

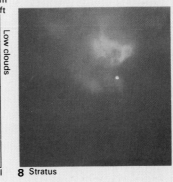

8 Stratus

9 Cumulonimbus

THE WORLD : Temperature and Ocean Currents

1:190 000 000

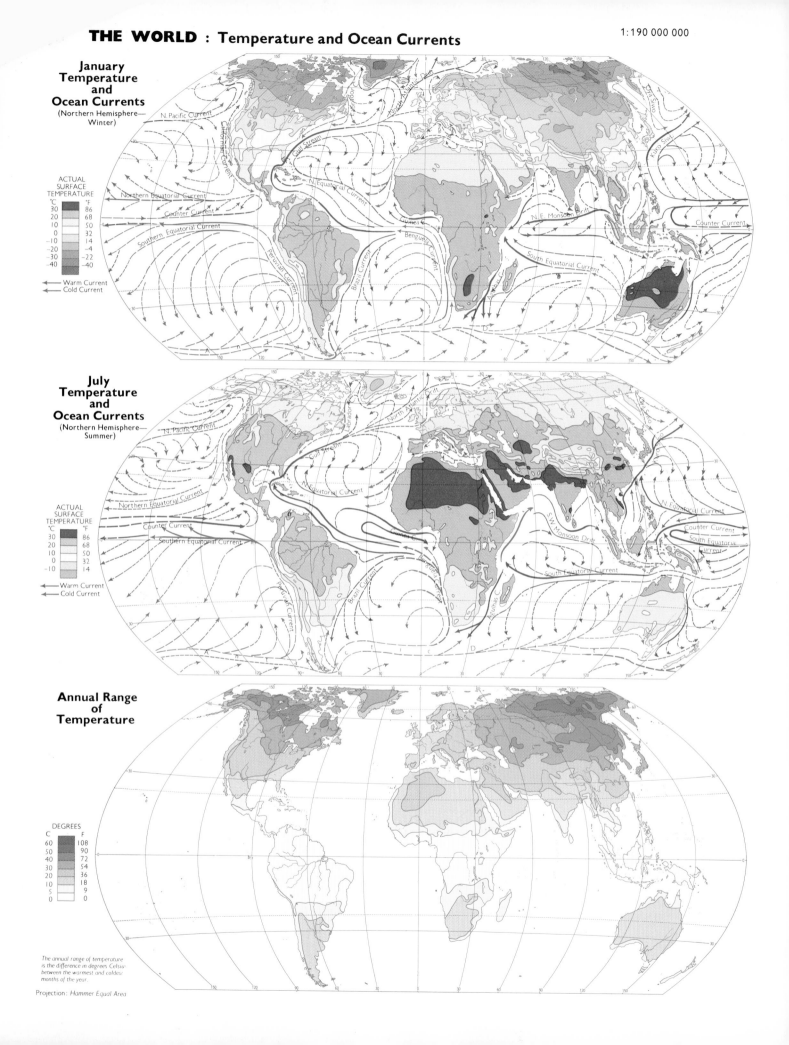

January Temperature and Ocean Currents
(Northern Hemisphere—Winter)

ACTUAL SURFACE TEMPERATURE

°C	°F
30	86
20	68
10	50
0	32
-10	14
-20	-4
-30	-22
-40	-40

⟵ Warm Current
⟵ Cold Current

July Temperature and Ocean Currents
(Northern Hemisphere—Summer)

ACTUAL SURFACE TEMPERATURE

°C	°F
30	86
20	68
10	50
0	32
-10	14

⟵ Warm Current
⟵ Cold Current

Annual Range of Temperature

DEGREES

C	F
60	108
50	90
40	72
30	54
20	36
10	18
5	9
0	0

The annual range of temperature is the difference in degrees Celsius between the warmest and coldest months of the year.

Projection: Hammer Equal Area

1:190 000 000

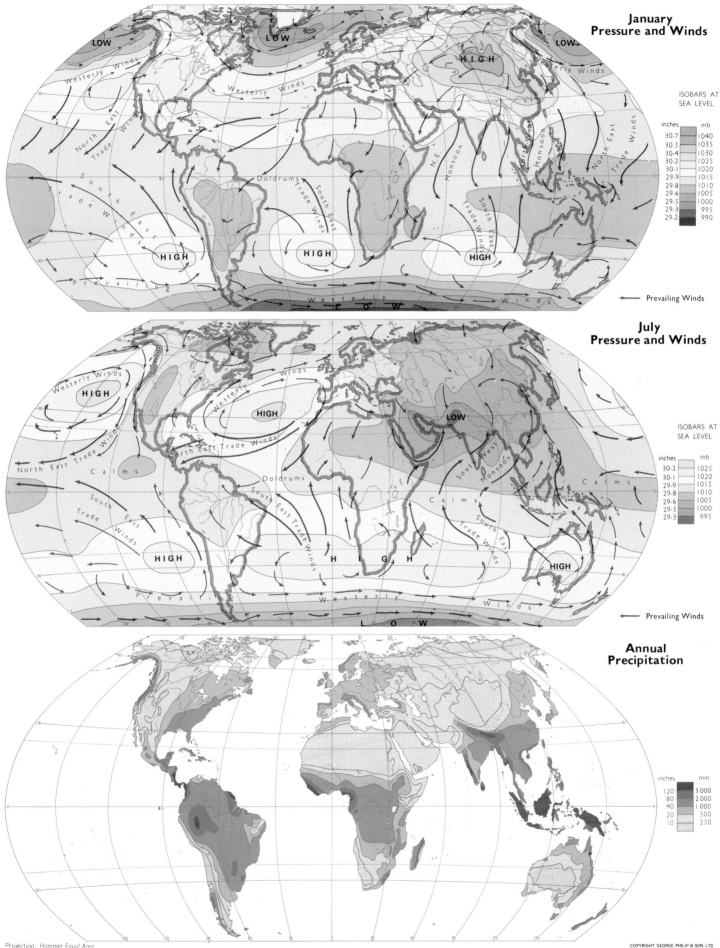

January Pressure and Winds

ISOBARS AT SEA LEVEL

inches	mb
30·7	1040
30·5	1035
30·4	1030
30·2	1025
30·1	1020
29·9	1015
29·8	1010
29·6	1005
29·5	1000
29·3	995
29·2	990

⟵ Prevailing Winds

July Pressure and Winds

ISOBARS AT SEA LEVEL

inches	mb
30·2	1025
30·1	1020
29·9	1015
29·8	1010
29·6	1005
29·5	1000
29·3	995

⟵ Prevailing Winds

Annual Precipitation

inches	mm
120	3 000
80	2 000
40	1 000
20	500
10	250

Projection: *Hammer Equal Area*

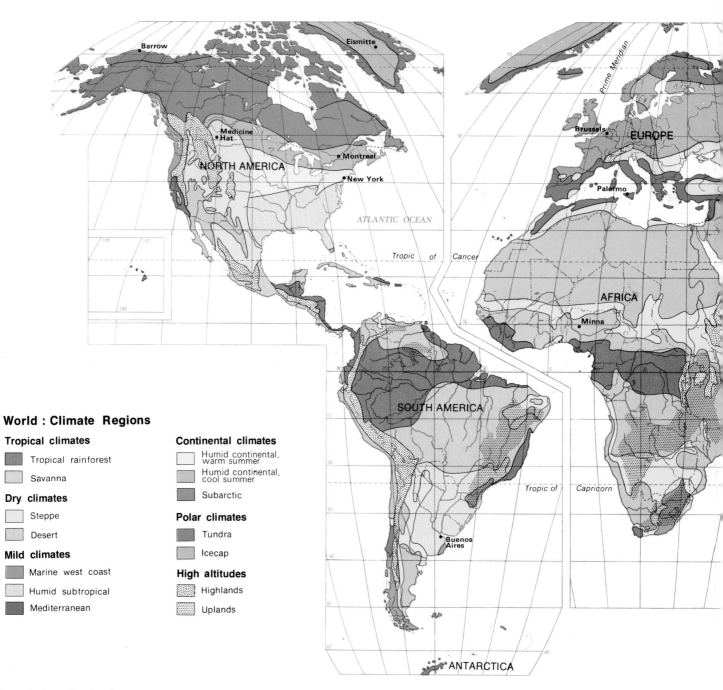

World : Climate Regions

Tropical climates

- Tropical rainforest
- Savanna

Dry climates

- Steppe
- Desert

Mild climates

- Marine west coast
- Humid subtropical
- Mediterranean

Continental climates

- Humid continental, warm summer
- Humid continental, cool summer
- Subarctic

Polar climates

- Tundra
- Icecap

High altitudes

- Highlands
- Uplands

Each graph shows the climatic conditions experienced in a location for each month of the year.

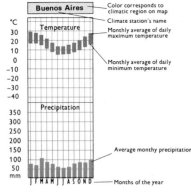

Color corresponds to climatic region on map
Climate station's name
Monthly average of daily maximum temperature
Monthly average of daily minimum temperature
Average monthly precipitation
Months of the year

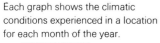

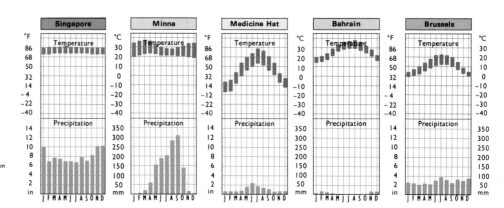

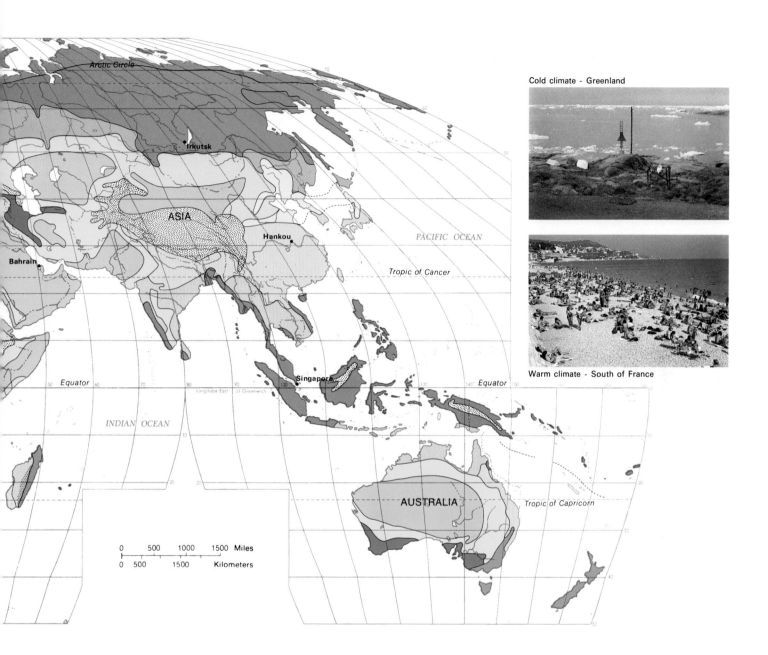

Cold climate - Greenland

Warm climate - South of France

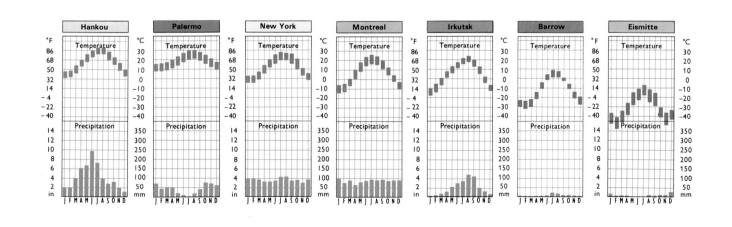

| Hankou | Palermo | New York | Montreal | Irkutsk | Barrow | Eismitte |

World: Natural Vegetation Regions

- Broadleaf forest—rainforest
- Broadleaf forest—deciduous
- Broadleaf forest—other
- Needleleaf forest
- Mixed forest (broadleaf and needleleaf)
- Grassland
- Desert—little or no vegetation
- Desert—scrub with grassy patches
- Tundra
- Ice-covered land
- High mountains (climate varies with elevation)

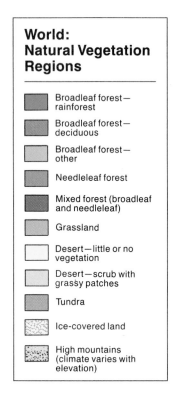

Broadleaf forest (tropical rainforest) - Peru

Broadleaf forest (deciduous forest) - U.S.A.

Broadleaf forest (Mediterranean scrub) - Australia

Needleleaf forest - Sweden

Mixed forest (broadleaf and needleleaf) - Canada

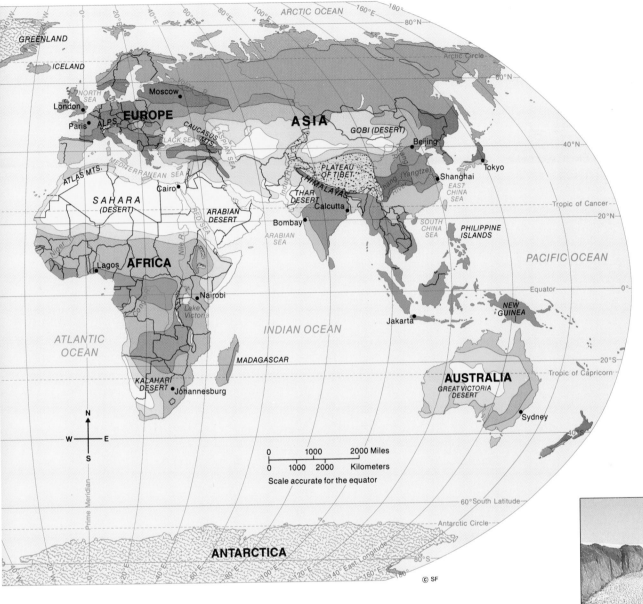

GREENLAND
ICELAND
ARCTIC OCEAN
80°N
Arctic Circle
60°N
London
NORTH SEA
Moscow
EUROPE
ASIA
Paris
ALPS
CAUCASUS MTS.
BLACK SEA
CASPIAN SEA
GOBI (DESERT)
40°N
Beijing
Tokyo
ATLAS MTS.
MEDITERRANEAN SEA
PLATEAU OF TIBET
Shanghai
EAST CHINA SEA
Cairo
HIMALAYAS
SAHARA (DESERT)
THAR DESERT
RED SEA
ARABIAN DESERT
Calcutta
Tropic of Cancer
20°N
Niger R.
Nile R.
Bombay
ARABIAN SEA
SOUTH CHINA SEA
PHILIPPINE ISLANDS
PACIFIC OCEAN
AFRICA
Lagos
Congo R.
Nairobi
Lake Victoria
Equator
0°
NEW GUINEA
Jakarta
ATLANTIC OCEAN
INDIAN OCEAN
MADAGASCAR
20°S
AUSTRALIA
Tropic of Capricorn
KALAHARI DESERT
Johannesburg
GREAT VICTORIA DESERT
Sydney
N
W E
S
0   1000   2000 Miles
0   1000   2000   Kilometers
Scale accurate for the equator
60°South Latitude
Antarctic Circle
Prime Meridian
ANTARCTICA
© SF

Ice-covered land - Greenland

Savanna grassland - Kenya

Desert (little or no vegetation) - Australia

Desert (scrub with grassy patches) - U.S.A.

Tundra - Greenland

World: Land Use

- Hunting, fishing, and gathering
- Subsistence farming
- Ranching
- ◆ Mining
- Urban land use
- Nomadic herding
- Commercial farming
- Lumbering
- Commercial fishing
- Little or no economic activity

Fishing - Malawi

Subsistence farming - Kenya

Ranching - Uruguay

Mining - Jamaica

Urban land use - Turkey

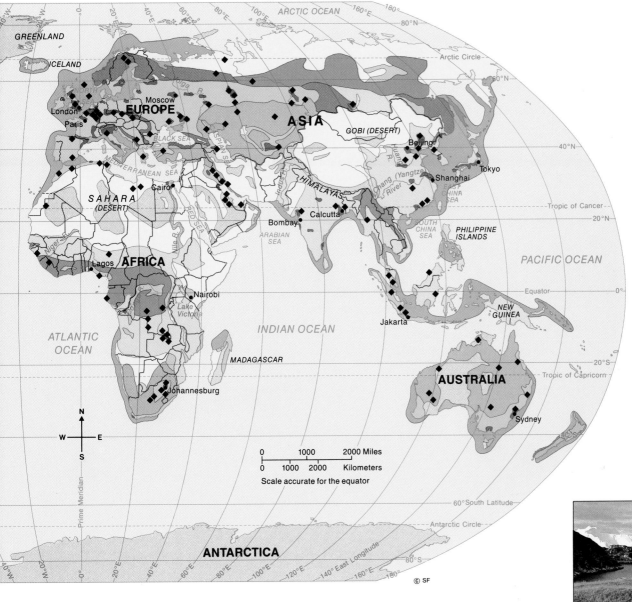

GREENLAND
ICELAND
EUROPE
London
Paris
Moscow
ASIA
GOBI (DESERT)
Beijing
Tokyo
Shanghai
HIMALAYAS
Chang (Yangtze) River
Huang River
EAST CHINA SEA
SAHARA (DESERT)
Cairo
NILE R.
RED SEA
CASPIAN SEA
BLACK SEA
MEDITERRANEAN SEA
Calcutta
Bombay
ARABIAN SEA
SOUTH CHINA SEA
PHILIPPINE ISLANDS
PACIFIC OCEAN
AFRICA
Lagos
Niger
Nairobi
Lake Victoria
ATLANTIC OCEAN
INDIAN OCEAN
MADAGASCAR
Jakarta
NEW GUINEA
Johannesburg
AUSTRALIA
Sydney
ANTARCTICA
ARCTIC OCEAN
Arctic Circle
Tropic of Cancer
Equator
Tropic of Capricorn
Antarctic Circle
60° South Latitude
Prime Meridian
East Longitude

N W E S

0   1000   2000 Miles
0   1000   2000 Kilometers
Scale accurate for the equator

© SF

Little or no economic activity - Greenland

Nomadic herding - Sudan

Commercial farming - Canada

Lumbering - Indonesia

Commercial fishing - North Sea

Population distribution
(right and lower right)
People have always been unevenly distributed in the world. For centuries Europe contained nearly 20% of the world's population, but after the 16th - 19th century explorations and migrations this proportion declined rapidly. In 1750 the Americas had 2% of the world's total. In 2000 AD they are expected to contain 16%.

The most densely populated regions are in India, China, and Europe where the average density is between 60 and 120 per square mile. There are also many other pockets of extremely high density. In contrast Australia has 0·9 people per square mile. On the map on the lower right, the countries have been redrawn to make their areas proportional to their populations.

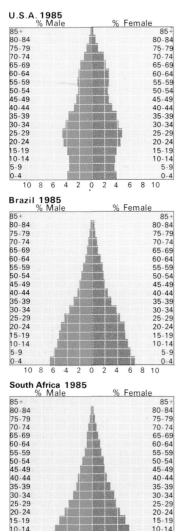

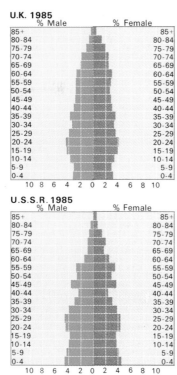

U.S.A. 1985

U.K. 1985

Brazil 1985

U.S.S.R. 1985

South Africa 1985

India 1985

Age distribution
The U.S.A. shows many demographic features characteristic of developed countries. Birth and death rates have declined with a moderate population growth — there are nearly as many old as young. In contrast, India and several other countries have few old and many young because of the high death rates and even higher birth rates. It is this excess that is responsible for the world's population explosion.

World population increase
Until comparatively recently there was little increase in the population of the world. About 6000 B.C. it is thought that there were about 200 million people. In the following 7000 years there was a slow increase of about 100 million more. In the 1800s there were about 1 billion people. Now there are over 5 billion, and by the year 2000 there may be more than 6 billion.

1650   1700   1750   1800

World population distribution

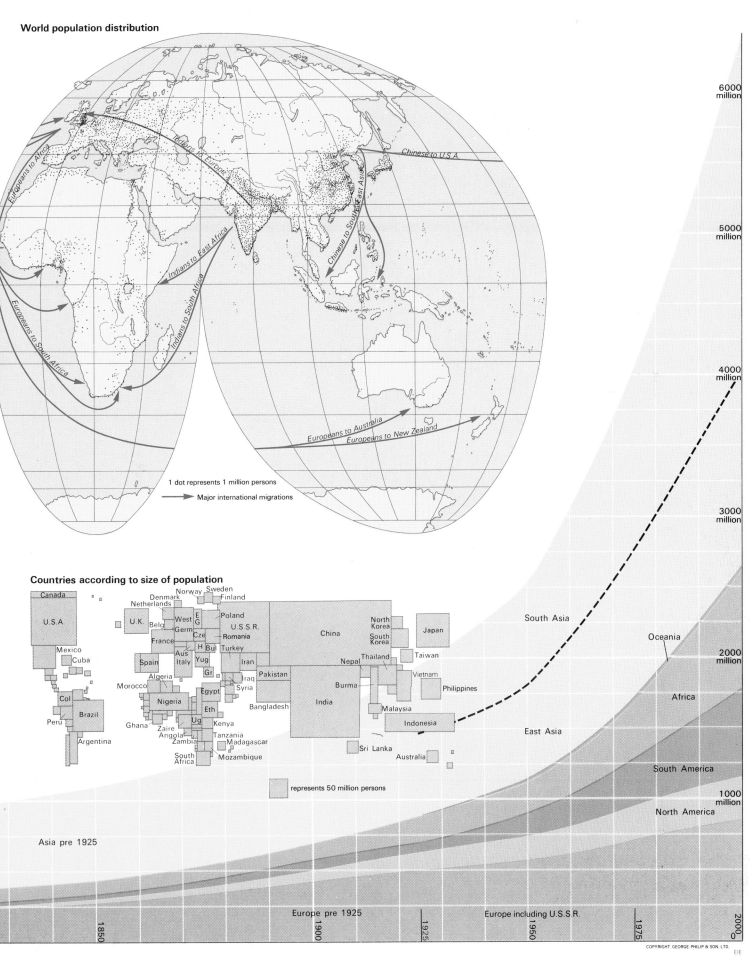

1 dot represents 1 million persons

→ Major international migrations

Europeans to Africa
Indians to Europe
Chinese to U.S.A.
Indians to East Africa
Chinese to South-East Asia
Europeans to South Africa
Indians to South Africa
Europeans to Australia
Europeans to New Zealand

Countries according to size of population

Canada
U.S.A.
Mexico
Cuba
Col
Peru
Brazil
Argentina

Norway Sweden
Denmark Finland
Netherlands
U.K. West E Poland
Belg Germ G
France Cze U.S.S.R.
Spain Aus H Bul Romania China North Korea Japan
Italy Yug Turkey South Korea
Algeria Gr Iran Taiwan
Morocco Egypt Iraq Pakistan Nepal Thailand Vietnam
Nigeria Syria Burma Philippines
Ghana Eth Bangladesh India Malaysia
Zaire Ug Kenya Indonesia
Angola Tanzania Sri Lanka Australia
Zambia Madagascar
South Mozambique
Africa

☐ represents 50 million persons

South Asia
Oceania
Africa
East Asia
South America
North America

Asia pre 1925
Europe pre 1925
Europe including U.S.S.R.

6000 million
5000 million
4000 million
3000 million
2000 million
1000 million

1850
1900
1925
1950
1975
2000
0

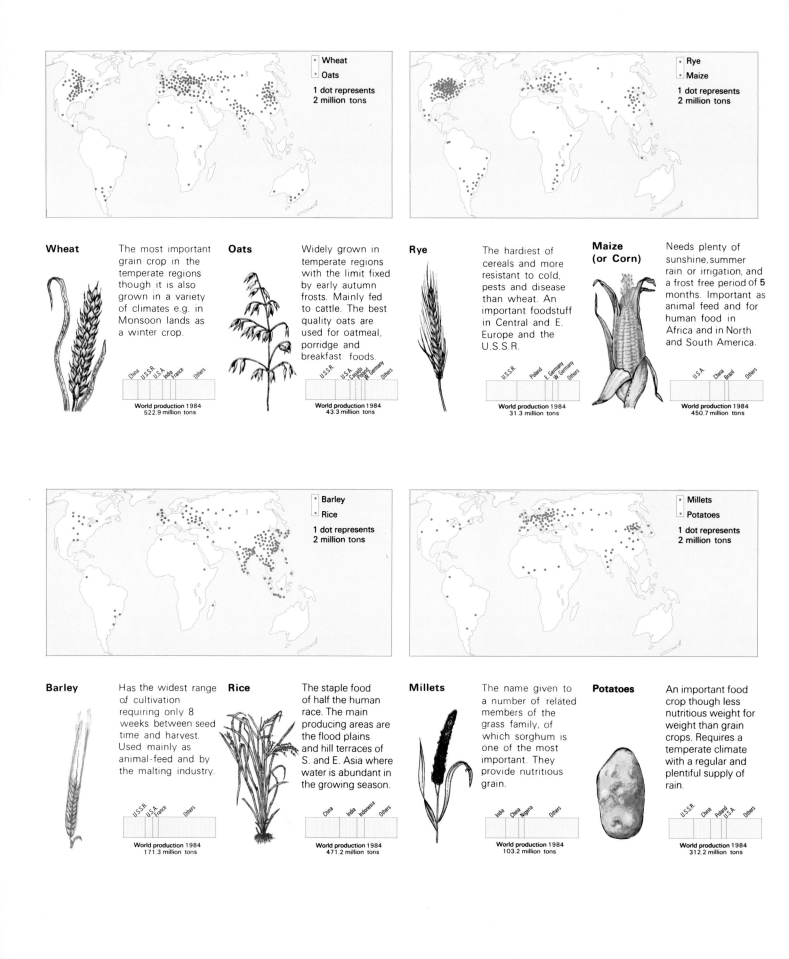

Wheat
The most important grain crop in the temperate regions though it is also grown in a variety of climates e.g. in Monsoon lands as a winter crop.

China U.S.S.R. U.S.A. India France Others

World production 1984
522.9 million tons

Oats
Widely grown in temperate regions with the limit fixed by early autumn frosts. Mainly fed to cattle. The best quality oats are used for oatmeal, porridge and breakfast foods.

U.S.S.R. U.S.A. Canada Poland W.Germany Others

World production 1984
43.3 million tons

Rye
The hardiest of cereals and more resistant to cold, pests and disease than wheat. An important foodstuff in Central and E. Europe and the U.S.S.R.

U.S.S.R. Poland E.Germany W.Germany Others

World production 1984
31.3 million tons

Maize (or Corn)
Needs plenty of sunshine, summer rain or irrigation, and a frost free period of 5 months. Important as animal feed and for human food in Africa and in North and South America.

U.S.A. China Brazil Others

World production 1984
450.7 million tons

Barley
Has the widest range of cultivation requiring only 8 weeks between seed time and harvest. Used mainly as animal-feed and by the malting industry.

U.S.S.R. U.S.A. France Others

World production 1984
171.3 million tons

Rice
The staple food of half the human race. The main producing areas are the flood plains and hill terraces of S. and E. Asia where water is abundant in the growing season.

China India Indonesia Others

World production 1984
471.2 million tons

Millets
The name given to a number of related members of the grass family, of which sorghum is one of the most important. They provide nutritious grain.

India China Nigeria Others

World production 1984
103.2 million tons

Potatoes
An important food crop though less nutritious weight for weight than grain crops. Requires a temperate climate with a regular and plentiful supply of rain.

U.S.S.R. China Poland U.S.A. Others

World production 1984
312.2 million tons

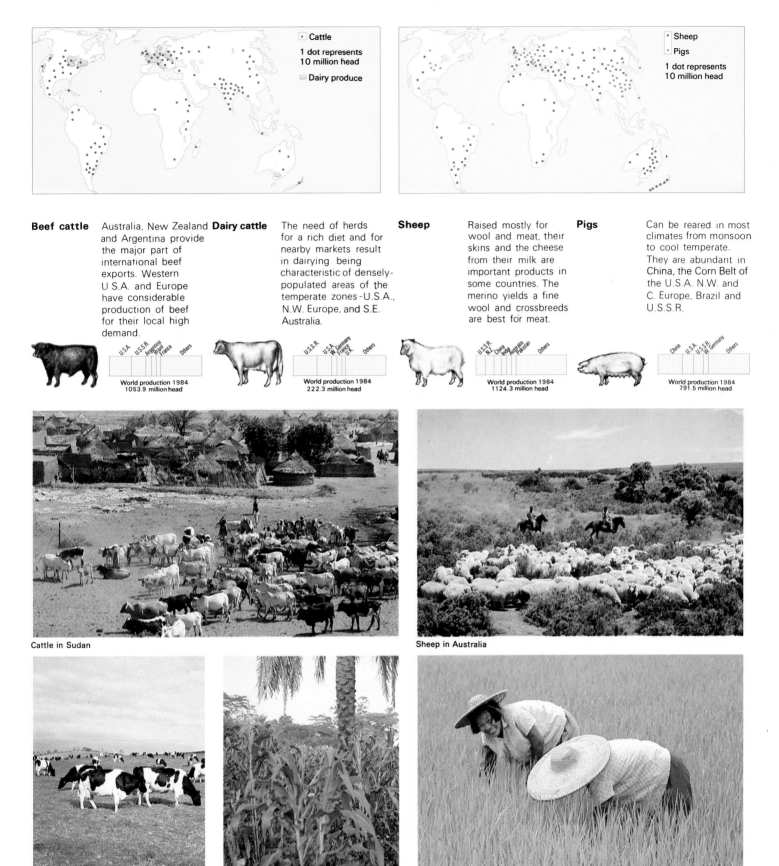

Beef cattle Australia, New Zealand and Argentina provide the major part of international beef exports. Western U.S.A. and Europe have considerable production of beef for their local high demand.

World production 1984
1053.9 million head

Dairy cattle The need of herds for a rich diet and for nearby markets result in dairying being characteristic of densely-populated areas of the temperate zones - U.S.A., N.W. Europe, and S.E. Australia.

World production 1984
222.3 million head

Sheep Raised mostly for wool and meat, their skins and the cheese from their milk are important products in some countries. The merino yields a fine wool and crossbreeds are best for meat.

World production 1984
1124.3 million head

Pigs Can be reared in most climates from monsoon to cool temperate. They are abundant in China, the Corn Belt of the U.S.A. N.W. and C. Europe, Brazil and U.S.S.R.

World production 1984
791.5 million head

Cattle in Sudan

Sheep in Australia

Dairy Cattle in England

Corn in Nigeria

Rice in China

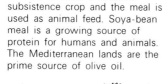

Peanuts
Soya beans
Sunflower seed
1 dot represents
1 million tons

Tea
Cacao
Coffee
1 dot represents
100 000 tons

Vegetable oilseeds and oils

Despite the increasing use of synthetic chemical products and animal and marine fats, vegetable oils extracted from these crops grow in quantity, value and importance. Food is the major use- in margarine and cooking fats.

Peanuts are also a valuable subsistence crop and the meal is used as animal feed. Soya-bean meal is a growing source of protein for humans and animals. The Mediterranean lands are the prime source of olive oil.

Tea and cacao

Tea requires plentiful rainfall and well-drained, sloping ground, whereas cacao prefers a moist heavy soil. Both are grown mainly for export.

Coffee

Prefers a hot climate, wet and dry seasons and an elevated location. It is very susceptible to frost, drought and market fluctuations.

Peanut

Soya bean

Sunflower

Cacao

Tea

World production 1984
5.2 million tons

Brazil | Colombia | Indonesia | Mexico | Others

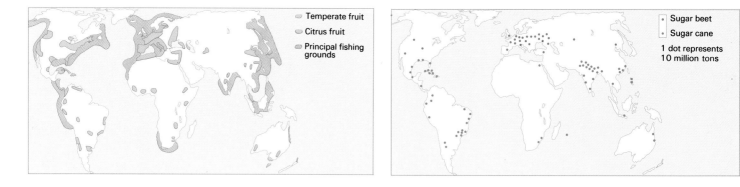

Temperate fruit
Citrus fruit
Principal fishing grounds

Sugar beet
Sugar cane
1 dot represents
10 million tons

Fruit

With the improvements in canning, drying and freezing, and in transport and marketing, the international trade and consumption of deciduous and soft fruits, citrus fruits and tropical fruits has greatly increased. Recent developments in the use of the peel will give added value to some of the fruit crops.

Fish

Commercial fishing requires large shoals of fish of one species within reach of markets. Freshwater fishing is also important. A rich source of protein, fish will become an increasingly valuable food source.

Sugar beet

Requires a deep, rich soil and a temperate climate. Europe produces over 90 % of the world's beets mainly for domestic consumption.

Sugar cane

Also requires deep and rich soil but a tropical climate. It produces a much higher yield per hectare than beet and is grown primarily for export.

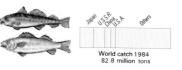

Japan | U.S.S.R. | China | U.S.A. | Others

World catch 1984
82.8 million tons

World production 1984
293.5 million tons

U.S.S.R. | France | U.S.A. | W. Germany | Poland | Others

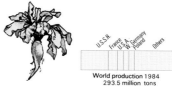

Brazil | India | Cuba | China | Others

World production 1984
935.8 million tons

Energy is the name given to the ways we drive our machines or keep ourselves warm. Wood and dried animal dung, coal and peat, oil, natural gas and nuclear power are sources of energy. Because they are used up they are called 'expendable energy sources'. The following sources of energy go on for ever: power from the sun, the wind, rivers, tides, waves and hot water and steam from deep in the Earth. To make energy in large quantities from these sources requires large, complicated and expensive machines, and so it is often cheaper to use the expendable sources. As these expendable energy sources run out these means of creating energy will be used. Electricity is the most useful form of energy that we know and it is carried from the power station to our homes and industries through cables.

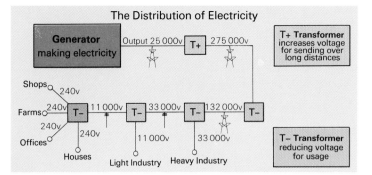

The Distribution of Electricity

Coal

Coal comes from the forests and swamps of millions of years ago. These forests were buried and crushed by later layers of rocks and the wood converted to coal. Coal can be mined by deep or open cast mines. Peat is a very young form of coal and is cut on the surface. The softer brown coals, or 'lignites', are younger than the harder 'bituminous coals'. Coal is principally used in power stations to make electricity. It is also converted into coke for the manufacture of iron and used in the chemical industry.

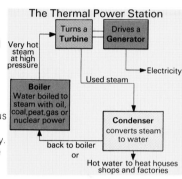

The Thermal Power Station

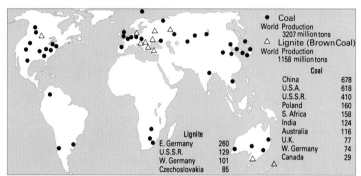

Coal	
World Production	
3207 million tons	
Lignite (Brown Coal)	
World Production	
1158 million tons	
Coal	
China	678
U.S.A.	618
U.S.S.R.	410
Poland	160
S. Africa	158
India	124
Australia	116
U.K.	77
W. Germany	74
Canada	29
Lignite	
E. Germany	260
U.S.S.R.	129
W. Germany	101
Czechoslovakia	85

Oil and natural gas

These are also geological deposits or 'fossil fuels' which are found by drilling deep into the earth's crust. Crude oil is refined near the drilling area, or is carried by pipeline or tanker to refineries where it is converted into the different types of petroleum products. It also provides the raw material for the plastic and chemical industries. Natural gas is often found in association with crude oil and can be moved by pipeline or be turned into liquid form by lowering its temperature to −160°C.

Boiling temperatures °C	Product	Use
−10–0	Propane and Butane	Household cooking
25–80	Gasoline (Petrol)	Vehicles
80–150	Naphtha	To make chemicals
150–250	Kerosene (Paraffin)	Household heating Aeroplanes
250–350	Gas oil	Diesel engines
350	Residual oil	Large engines Bitumen for roads

The gas from the crude oil condenses and separates into its parts at the various temperatures up the tower. It gets cooler upwards

Crude oil heated into a gas +350°C

At the heart of the oil refinery is the **Fractioning Tower**

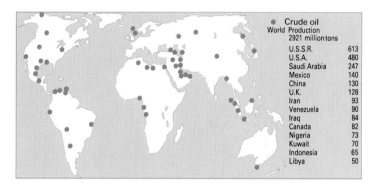

Crude oil	
World Production	
2921 million tons	
U.S.S.R.	613
U.S.A.	480
Saudi Arabia	247
Mexico	140
China	130
U.K.	128
Iran	93
Venezuela	90
Iraq	84
Canada	82
Nigeria	73
Kuwait	70
Indonesia	65
Libya	50

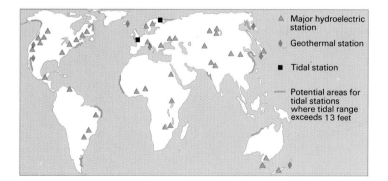

▲	Major hydroelectric station
●	Geothermal station
■	Tidal station
—	Potential areas for tidal stations where tidal range exceeds 13 feet

Hydroelectricity

Coal, oil and nuclear power heat water to make steam which drives turbines that in turn generate electricity. This is called thermal electricity. If a river is dammed a higher level of water is created and water can be shot down pipes to drive turbines and make electricity. This is called hydroelectricity. At one or two places in the world the incoming tide flows into an estuary and at low tide the trapped water escapes back to the sea through turbines to generate electricity.

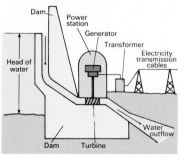

A Hydroelectric Power Station

Nuclear Power

Everything is made up of atoms. If the atom is broken energy is released. Uranium is a substance whose atoms can be easily split. In a nuclear power station this energy heats water to make steam and the electricity is generated as in a coal powered station. The nuclear reaction is very powerful and the machinery has to be massively controlled to prevent accidents. More and more countries are generating electricity by nuclear reaction and some sea vessels are also nuclear powered.

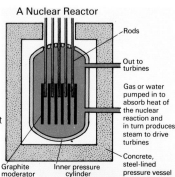

A Nuclear Reactor

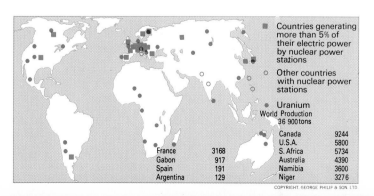

■	Countries generating more than 5% of their electric power by nuclear power stations
●	Other countries with nuclear power stations
□	Uranium

World Production 36 900 tons

France	3168	Canada	9244
Gabon	917	U.S.A.	5800
Spain	191	S. Africa	5734
Argentina	129	Australia	4390
		Namibia	3600
		Niger	3276

Iron

Iron was used by early humans and still forms the backbone of the modern world. Iron ore is mined in open cast sites and is usually carried overseas in large ore carriers. It is refined in a blast furnace. The blast furnace principle is used in refining other metals – lead and copper, for example.

Steel is iron which is refined further and other metals are added to give special properties to the steel to form alloy steels.

Types of Iron Ore

Type	Mined in
Hematite (or Red hematite)	Sweden, Belgium, Canada, Australia, U.S.A.
Limonite (or Brown hematite)	France, Germany, Spain, Australia
Magnetite	Sweden, Norway, U.S.S.R.
Siderite	U.K.

A Blast Furnace

Gases extracted (used again)

Iron ore, limestone, and coke added to furnace via double bell hopper.

FURNACE

Hot air blown into furnace

Slag drawn off

Molten iron drawn off for pig-casting or to steel plant.

Iron ore — World Production 531 million tons

U.S.S.R.	148
Brazil	99
China	61
Australia	51
U.S.A.	33
India	26
Canada	24
S. Africa	15
Sweden	11
Liberia	10
Venezuela	8

The Iron and Steel Processes

Iron ore — Coke — Limestone

IRON MAKING — Blast furnace

Pig iron → Uses of pig iron

Alloys — Steel scrap

STEEL MAKING

Basic oxygen furnace | Open hearth furnace | Electric arc furnace | Bessemer converter

Ingots for further working | Cast into strip | Rolling mill to produce bars, plates, pipes and sheets

Strip mill

Pig iron — World Production 493 million tons

The molten iron is tapped off and allowed to solidify into ingots or pigs and in this state is called pig iron, which is then removed to other places for further working. Molten iron can also be taken to the steel furnaces situated nearby.

Pig Iron (million tons)

U.S.S.R.	111	Italy	12
Japan	80	Poland	10
U.S.A.	47	Canada	10
China	40	U.K.	10
W. Germany	30	Czechoslovakia	10
Brazil	17	Romania	10
France	15		

To make one ton of steel

Iron ore 18 cwt.
Coal (coke) 16 cwt.
10 cwt. Steel scrap
8 cwt. Limestone
TON OF STEEL
Air 1·5 tons
Electricity 150 kWh
Water 2472 ft³

Steel production — World Production 707 million tons

U.S.S.R.	154
Japan	106
U.S.A.	84
China	43
W. Germany	39
Italy	24
France	19
Brazil	18
Poland	17
U.K.	15
Czechoslovakia	15
Canada	15
Spain	13
Belgium	11

Types of Alloy Steels and Their Uses

Alloying elements	Properties given to steel	Uses
Nickel	—hardness —rust resistance —non magnetic and resists passage of electricity	stainless steel
Chromium	—hardness —resistant to wear and corrosion	stainless steel armour plating cutlery
Manganese	—gives good hot-working properties —toughness —combats brittleness	pipelines rifle barrels cars farm implements
Molybdenum	—improves workability of steel —resists corrosion	high speed steels
Tungsten	—very hard and still hard at high temperatures	cutting tools
Vanadium	—high strength —helps get rid of impurities in steel	high speed steels and tools girders
Cobalt	—highly magnetic —hard —rust resistant	permanent magnets turbines artificial human joints
Silicon	—gives elasticity	bridges car springs reinforcing rods
Boron	—strength —toughness —hardness	used as a cheaper substitute for nickel and chromium

The car – a major user of steel

Charging a basic-oxygen furnace

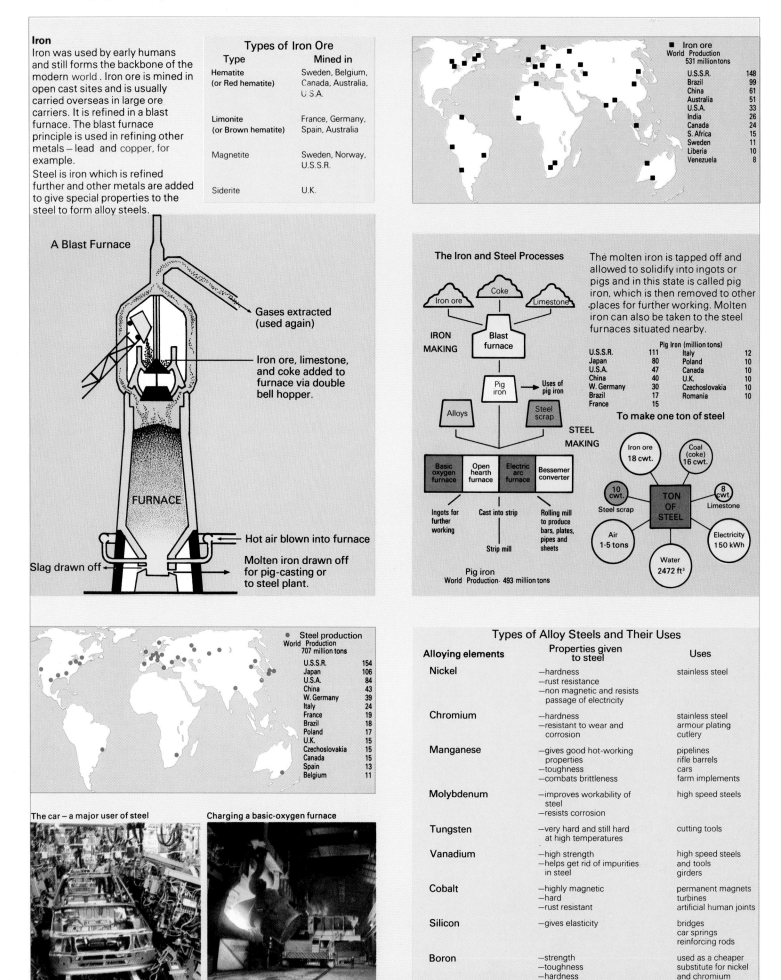

Nickel

Nickel ore comes from open-cast and deep mines. Refining is by crushing, flotation then melting, or by electrolysis. Nickel adds hardness when added to iron and steel, is resistant to corrosion from sea-water and acids (used in pipework), and forms the anti-corrosion layer beneath chromium plating. It gives great strength; is used in gear wheels and drive-shafts, in armour plating and in crushing plant for gold and copper ores. Nickel/chromium alloy provides resistance wires in electricity (e.g. sparking plugs). Nickel/copper alloy (30/70) is used in silver coins (e.g. Kwacha).

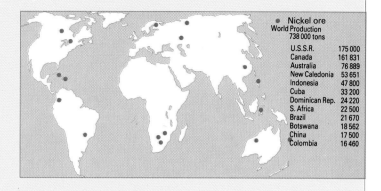

Nickel ore World Production 738 000 tons	
U.S.S.R.	175 000
Canada	161 831
Australia	76 889
New Caledonia	53 651
Indonesia	47 800
Cuba	33 200
Dominican Rep.	24 220
S. Africa	22 500
Brazil	21 670
Botswana	18 562
China	17 500
Colombia	16 460

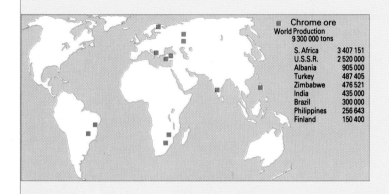

Chrome ore World Production 9 300 000 tons	
S. Africa	3 407 151
U.S.S.R.	2 520 000
Albania	905 000
Turkey	487 405
Zimbabwe	476 521
India	435 000
Brazil	300 000
Philippines	256 643
Finland	150 400

Chromium

Chrome ore is found in association with iron, manganese and aluminum. The metal is produced in a furnace or by "electrolysis". It is electroplated on to a nickel base to give chrome plating. As an alloying element to steel it gives increased strength and resistance to corrosion. As a metal it is used in "stainless steel" Chromium has a very high melting point and is used to line vessels for melting other metals. It is used for making chemicals (e.g. dyes and saccharin), as a coloring in paints (yellow and green), for fixing colors in textiles and in tanning.

Titanium

This metal is found widely on earth and in the sea. It is very difficult and expensive to extract the pure metal from the ore. Titanium is light, strong and resistant to corrosion and is used in the manufacture of chemical plants and aircraft parts, particularly in engines, and in the frame and skin of the faster-than-sound (supersonic) aircraft. Used as a pigment in paints.

Manganese

Manganese and iron ores are mixed in the blast furnace to produce "Ferro-manganese". This is added to steel to give corrosion resistance and hardness (e.g. Army helmets). Also provides coloring in glass Manganese is essential to plant growth and is added to soil as fertilizer, especially for citrus crops. Used in the manufacture of dry cell electric batteries.

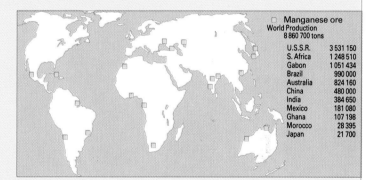

Manganese ore World Production 8 860 700 tons	
U.S.S.R.	3 531 150
S. Africa	1 248 510
Gabon	1 051 434
Brazil	990 000
Australia	824 160
China	480 000
India	384 650
Mexico	181 080
Ghana	107 198
Morocco	28 395
Japan	21 700

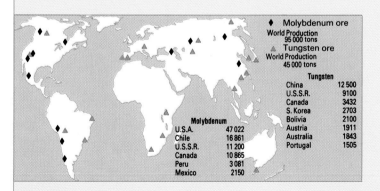

Molybdenum ore World Production 95 000 tons

Tungsten ore World Production 45 000 tons

Tungsten	
China	12 500
U.S.S.R.	9100
Canada	3432
S. Korea	2703
Bolivia	2100
Austria	1911
Australia	1843
Portugal	1505

Molybdenum	
U.S.A.	47 022
Chile	16 861
U.S.S.R.	11 200
Canada	10 865
Peru	3 081
Mexico	2150

Molybdenum

This metal has a very high melting point (2600°C) and can remain strong and hard where high temperatures develop. It resists corrosion and is light in weight. Used in manufacture of nuclear reactors, wireless valves, switchgear, rocket parts, pigments and dyes. It is added to grease and oils to help them to operate at high temperatures. Used as a plant nutrient.

Tungsten (Wolfram)

Very hard metal. Highest melting point of any metal (3400°C) and retains its strength at these high temperatures. When alloyed in steel it allows a cutting edge or a drill's sharpness to be retained at high speeds. Used as a filament in electric light bulbs and to protect the outside of space vehicles on re-entry into the earth's atmosphere.

Vanadium

Principal use is as an alloy steel to give strength, hardness and wear. Used in concrete reinforcing rods, girders, car parts and the chemical industry.

Cobalt

The ore is found in association with many other minerals – iron, nickel and copper. It is present in plants and animals, in meteorites, in the sun and in small nodules on the floor of the ocean, from where it may be mined in the future. It is highly magnetic and so is used in permanent magnets. Very hard and resistant to rust. Used in razor blades, turbine blades, knee and hip joints and a number of other medical uses, and as a blue dye in glass, pottery and paints.

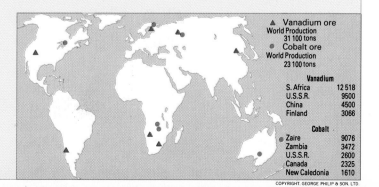

Vanadium ore World Production 31 100 tons

Cobalt ore World Production 23 100 tons

Vanadium	
S. Africa	12 518
U.S.S.R.	9500
China	4500
Finland	3066

Cobalt	
Zaire	9076
Zambia	3472
U.S.S.R.	2600
Canada	2325
New Caledonia	1610

Aluminum

Aluminum is the most plentiful metal in the earth's crust. It occurs as an ore (aluminum oxide) or Bauxite. It is found in abundance in tropical sites where heavy rainfall has washed the ore into deep and rich pockets. It is crudely refined near the mining site to make alumina. Alumina is refined into pure metal where there are abundant sources of cheap electricity, hydroelectricity for example.

Aluminum is light, corrosion resistant, non-magnetic, reflects light and is an excellent conductor of heat and electricity. It can be easily worked and cast. Alloyed with copper, magnesium, silicon, zinc, nickel and iron it makes castings with special properties. It is used in aircraft and car manufacture, food and drink packaging (foil and cans), cladding of buildings, electric cables, synthetic rubies and sapphires (jewels in watches), paint pigments, cosmetics and medicines.

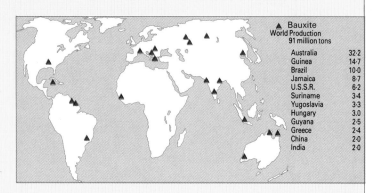

▲ Bauxite
World Production
91 million tons

Australia	32·2
Guinea	14·7
Brazil	10·0
Jamaica	8·7
U.S.S.R.	6·2
Suriname	3·4
Yugoslavia	3·3
Hungary	3·0
Guyana	2·5
Greece	2·4
China	2·0
India	2·0

To make 1 ton of aluminum

5 tons bauxite
USING:
1 ton oil
3 cwt. caustic soda

2 tons alumina
USING:
15 000 kWh
9 cwt. carbon anodes
1 cwt. cryolite

1 ton aluminum

Aluminum
World Production
16 million tons

U.S.A.	4·10
U.S.S.R.	2·30
Canada	1·22
W. Germany	0·78
Norway	0·76
Australia	0·76
Brazil	0·45
China	0·43
Venezuela	0·39
Spain	0·38
France	0·34
U.K.	0·29
India	0·27

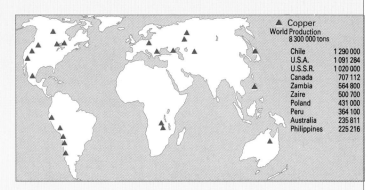

▲ Copper
World Production
8 300 000 tons

Chile	1 290 000
U.S.A.	1 091 284
U.S.S.R.	1 020 000
Canada	707 112
Zambia	564 800
Zaire	500 700
Poland	431 000
Peru	364 100
Australia	235 811
Philippines	225 216

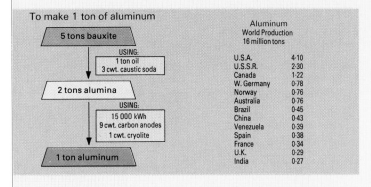

■ Tin ore
World Production
194 000 tons

Malaysia	41 307
Indonesia	23 225
Thailand	21 960
Brazil	19 957
Bolivia	19 911
U.S.S.R.	17 000
China	16 000
Australia	9300
U.K.	5216

Copper

Copper ore is mined in open-cast and deep mines. It is often found with nickel, zinc and lead. The ore is "dressed" by the flotation method or by roasting to get rid of impurities. Further refining is made by smelting. After silver, copper has the highest conductivity of heat and electricity. Much of the world's copper is used in the electrical industry. Alloyed with zinc it makes Brass and with tin, Bronze. Silver coins are made from a copper-nickel alloy and copper coins are made from an alloy of copper, zinc and tin.

Refined copper
World Production
9 600 000 tons

U.S.A.	1 509 400
U.S.S.R.	1 380 000
Japan	935 156
Chile	879 200
Zambia	523 300
Canada	504 262
Belgium	427 707
W. Germany	378 916
Poland	372 300
China	320 000

Tin

Tin is obtained by washing out river deposits or from open pit mines. Tin has a very low melting point and is refined in a blast furnace or by electric smelting. Its widest use is for making tin plate for the canning industry. A very thin coating of tin is put on to thin rolls of steel. Tin is alloyed with lead to make solder; with antimony, copper and lead to make bearings for the wheels of heavy vehicles; with antimony and copper to make *Pewter* and with copper to make *Bronze* .

Tin dredging in Malaysia

Lead

The ore of lead – galena – is found in association with the ores of zinc, copper and silver. Because of its low melting point (327°C) it is easy to refine. Much new metal is obtained from scrap. Used in electric storage batteries, acid containers (because of its resistance to chemical attack), radiation shields in x-ray departments, nuclear plants, pipes and cable covering, ammunition, printing metal, paint pigments, solders, additives to petrol and bearing metals.

Zinc

The ore is mined open-cast or underground and is often refined in the country of production, electrolytically or by smelting. The metal is highly resistant to corrosion and melts easily for use in casting. It is used to coat iron and steel goods and sheets; this is called "galvanizing". Zinc is widely used in casting, particularly toys. Alloyed with copper it is known as *Brass*. It is used in the manufacture of rubber, paints, medicines and printing plates.

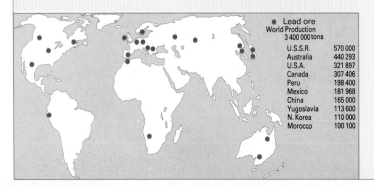

● Lead ore
World Production
3 400 000 tons

U.S.S.R.	570 000
Australia	440 293
U.S.A.	321 897
Canada	307 406
Peru	198 400
Mexico	181 968
China	165 000
Yugoslavia	113 600
N. Korea	110 000
Morocco	100 100

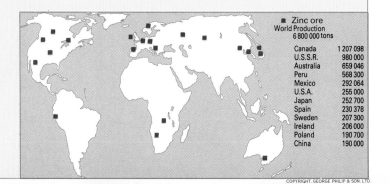

■ Zinc ore
World Production
6 800 000 tons

Canada	1 207 098
U.S.S.R.	980 000
Australia	659 046
Peru	568 300
Mexico	292 064
U.S.A.	255 000
Japan	252 700
Spain	230 378
Sweden	207 300
Ireland	206 000
Poland	190 700
China	190 000

Gold

The most prized and historic of metals. Three-quarters of all the world's gold is held in bank vaults. The ore is mined from deep mines or from river sands. It is a very expensive metal to produce, ten tons of rock producing only three ounces of metal. The pure metal is very soft and alloys (copper, silver, nickel and zinc) are added. Pure gold is said to be 24 Carats (12 Carat gold is half gold, half alloy). Its uses are in jewelry, coinage, electrical and electronic industries and in dentistry.

Pouring gold bars

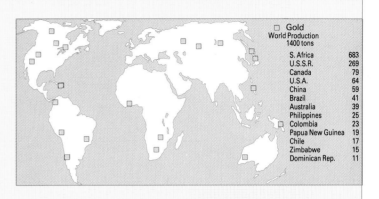

Gold World Production 1400 tons	
S. Africa	683
U.S.S.R.	269
Canada	79
U.S.A.	64
China	59
Brazil	41
Australia	39
Philippines	25
Colombia	23
Papua New Guinea	19
Chile	17
Zimbabwe	15
Dominican Rep.	11

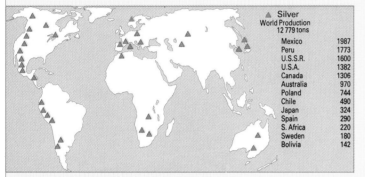

Silver World Production 12 779 tons	
Mexico	1987
Peru	1773
U.S.S.R.	1600
U.S.A.	1382
Canada	1306
Australia	970
Poland	744
Chile	490
Japan	324
Spain	290
S. Africa	220
Sweden	180
Bolivia	142

Silver

Silver is usually found in association with the ores of lead, copper and zinc and the pure metal is extracted along with these metals. It is an excellent conductor of electricity and is widely used for making electrical contacts. It is used in coinage, jewelry, light reflectors and for dental fillings. Silver bromide forms the coating of photographic films.

Inside a silver mine

Platinum

It is found in river sands and also as an ore in association with copper, nickel, gold, iron and sulfur. Highly resistant to the attack from other chemicals. It has a high melting point (1770°C), is heavy, soft and workable. Used in containers for melting and processing other metals, glass manufacture, sensitive thermo-meters, electrical contacts, dentist's fillings, jewelry and chemical processes.

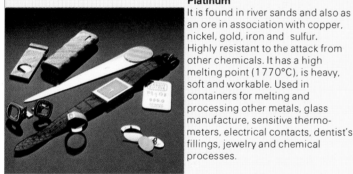
Platinum jewelry and articles

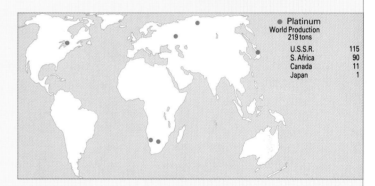

Platinum World Production 219 tons	
U.S.S.R.	115
S. Africa	90
Canada	11
Japan	1

Diamond necklace

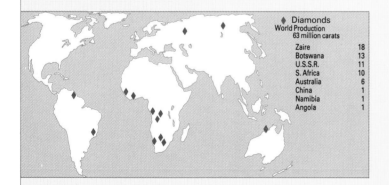

Diamonds World Production 63 million carats	
Zaire	18
Botswana	13
U.S.S.R.	11
S. Africa	10
Australia	6
China	1
Namibia	1
Angola	1

Diamonds

The hardest naturally occuring substance known. They are mined from deep mines as in South Africa or from river sands as in Zaire. They are divided into gemstones and industrial diamonds. The gemstones are taken to centers such as Antwerp and Amsterdam where they are cut and polished into perfect shapes. The industrial diamonds are used mainly to tip cutting and grinding tools. Small diamonds are used in styluses for record players. Diamonds are weighed in Carats (100 Carats = 0·7 ounces)

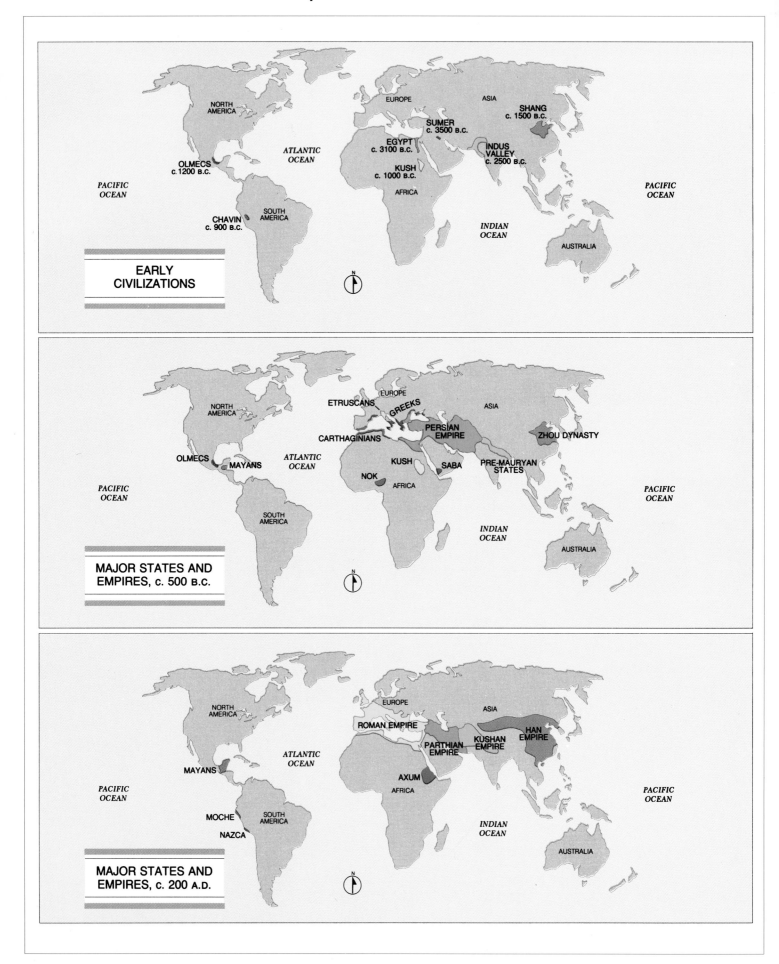

EARLY
CIVILIZATIONS

NORTH
AMERICA

ATLANTIC
OCEAN

PACIFIC
OCEAN

OLMECS
c.1200 B.C.

CHAVIN
c. 900 B.C.

SOUTH
AMERICA

EUROPE

ASIA

SHANG
c. 1500 B.C.

SUMER
c. 3500 B.C.

EGYPT
c. 3100 B.C.

INDUS
VALLEY
c. 2500 B.C.

KUSH
c. 1000 B.C.

AFRICA

PACIFIC
OCEAN

INDIAN
OCEAN

AUSTRALIA

MAJOR STATES AND
EMPIRES, c. 500 B.C.

NORTH
AMERICA

ATLANTIC
OCEAN

PACIFIC
OCEAN

OLMECS

MAYANS

SOUTH
AMERICA

ETRUSCANS

GREEKS

EUROPE

ASIA

CARTHAGINIANS

PERSIAN
EMPIRE

ZHOU DYNASTY

KUSH

SABA

NOK

AFRICA

PRE-MAURYAN
STATES

PACIFIC
OCEAN

INDIAN
OCEAN

AUSTRALIA

MAJOR STATES AND
EMPIRES, c. 200 A.D.

NORTH
AMERICA

ATLANTIC
OCEAN

PACIFIC
OCEAN

MAYANS

MOCHE

NAZCA

SOUTH
AMERICA

ROMAN EMPIRE

EUROPE

ASIA

PARTHIAN
EMPIRE

KUSHAN
EMPIRE

HAN
EMPIRE

AXUM

AFRICA

PACIFIC
OCEAN

INDIAN
OCEAN

AUSTRALIA

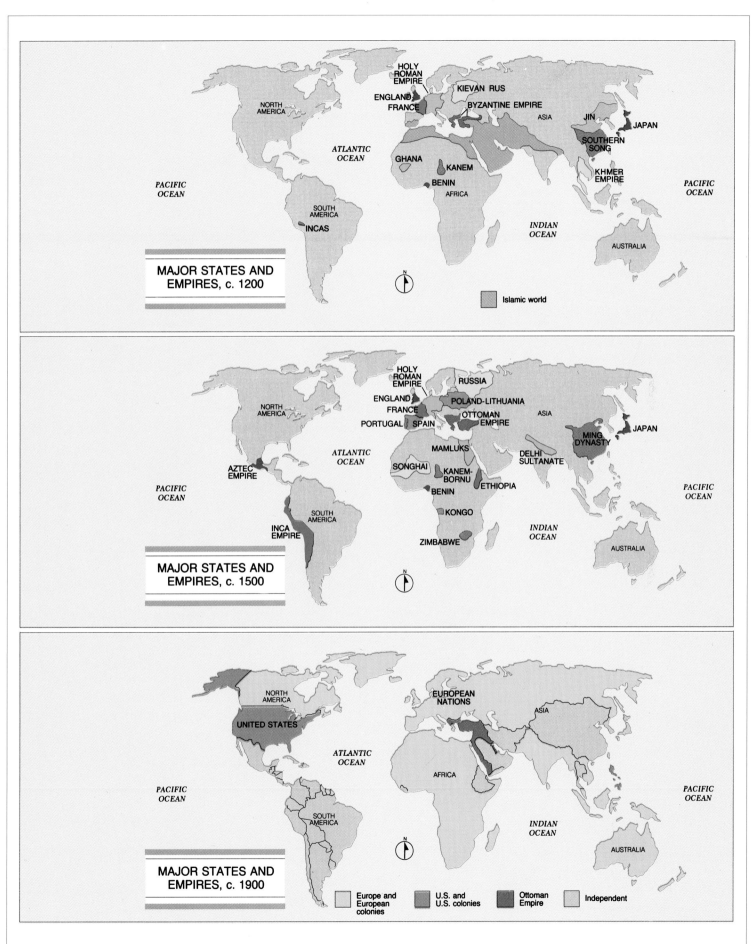

MAJOR STATES AND EMPIRES, c. 1200

NORTH AMERICA

HOLY ROMAN EMPIRE

KIEVAN RUS

ENGLAND
FRANCE

BYZANTINE EMPIRE

JIN

JAPAN

ASIA

SOUTHERN SONG

KHMER EMPIRE

ATLANTIC OCEAN

GHANA

KANEM

BENIN

AFRICA

PACIFIC OCEAN

SOUTH AMERICA

INCAS

INDIAN OCEAN

PACIFIC OCEAN

AUSTRALIA

N

Islamic world

MAJOR STATES AND EMPIRES, c. 1500

NORTH AMERICA

HOLY ROMAN EMPIRE

RUSSIA

ENGLAND
FRANCE

POLAND-LITHUANIA

PORTUGAL   SPAIN

OTTOMAN EMPIRE

ASIA

MING DYNASTY

JAPAN

AZTEC EMPIRE

ATLANTIC OCEAN

MAMLUKS

DELHI SULTANATE

SONGHAI

KANEM-BORNU

BENIN

ETHIOPIA

PACIFIC OCEAN

SOUTH AMERICA

INCA EMPIRE

KONGO

ZIMBABWE

INDIAN OCEAN

PACIFIC OCEAN

AUSTRALIA

N

MAJOR STATES AND EMPIRES, c. 1900

NORTH AMERICA

EUROPEAN NATIONS

ASIA

UNITED STATES

ATLANTIC OCEAN

AFRICA

PACIFIC OCEAN

SOUTH AMERICA

INDIAN OCEAN

PACIFIC OCEAN

AUSTRALIA

N

Europe and European colonies

U.S. and U.S. colonies

Ottoman Empire

Independent

Language is human speech, either spoken or written. It makes it possible for people to talk to other people and to write their thoughts and ideas.

Spoken Language

Wherever there are people, there is language. About 3,000 languages exist. This number does not include dialects, which are local forms of a language.

Many languages are spoken only by a few hundred or a few thousand persons. More than 150 languages have a million or more speakers each. Fourteen languages each have over 60 million speakers. These are Chinese, English, Hindustani, Russian, Spanish, Arabic, Portuguese, Bengali, German, Japanese, Indonesian, French, Korean, and Vietnamese.

Language Families

The world's languages are divided into families. Each family is made up of groups of similar languages. They are thought to have developed from common parent languages.

Assyrian (carved)

Ancient Hebrew (painted)

Egyptian hieroglyphic (painted)

Some modern non-latin type faces

Greek
ΑΒΓΔΕΖΗΘΙΚΛΜΝΞΟΠΡΣΤΥΦΧΨΩς

Cyrillic
АБВГДЕЖЗИЙІКЛМНОПРСТУФХЦЧШ

Arabic
فى عام ١٨٩٧ وصل إلى إنجلترا أ نموذج

Bengali
১৮৯৭ খ্রীস্টাব্দে আধুনিক মডেলের একটি

Telugu
నిన్న న్యూయింంట్ఈ వచ్చిన యుతిథ యేమియు

Japanese
国土の位置と地形

Chinese
父獨子出有之限地位司，
司在提印芬刷奥業司上有

For example, the first nine language groups on the map are part of the Indo-European language family. About half the people in the world speak languages in this family. English and German are Germanic languages. French, Italian, Spanish and Portuguese are Romance languages. Russian is a Slavic language. Bengali and Hindustani are Indo-Aryan languages. Speakers of all these languages once lived in an area extending from northern India to western Europe. Now, they live in other parts of the world.

The Sino-Tibetan family is the next largest. This family includes Chinese, which has about half a dozen dialects.

Written Language

Languages have different systems of writing. In fact, not all languages have a written form. Some writing systems are based on words and symbols, such as Japanese and Chinese. Others are based on alphabets, such as Greek. The chart shows some different systems in use now and in the past.

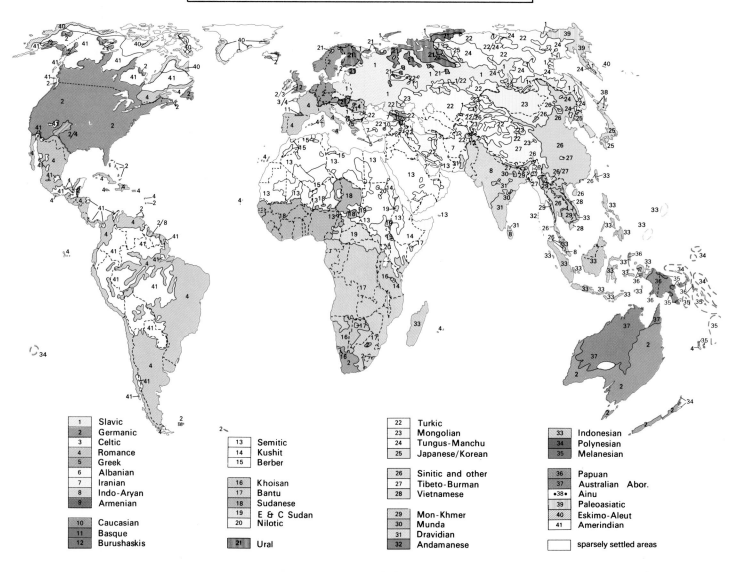

1	Slavic		
2	Germanic		
3	Celtic		
4	Romance		
5	Greek		
6	Albanian		
7	Iranian		
8	Indo-Aryan		
9	Armenian		
10	Caucasian		
11	Basque		
12	Burushaskis		
13	Semitic	22	Turkic
14	Kushit	23	Mongolian
15	Berber	24	Tungus-Manchu
16	Khoisan	25	Japanese/Korean
17	Bantu	26	Sinitic and other
18	Sudanese	27	Tibeto-Burman
19	E & C Sudan	28	Vietnamese
20	Nilotic	29	Mon-Khmer
21	Ural	30	Munda
		31	Dravidian
		32	Andamanese
33	Indonesian	36	Papuan
34	Polynesian	37	Australian Abor.
35	Melanesian	38	Ainu
		39	Paleoasiatic
		40	Eskimo-Aleut
		41	Amerindian
			sparsely settled areas

Many religions are practiced in the world today. Each of them has a system of beliefs based on traditions and teachings.
Christianity is the most widespread religion. In western Europe and N. and S. America, most Christians are either Roman Catholics or Protestants. In other parts of the world, many Christians belong to the Orthodox and other Eastern churches.
Judaism dates back to the 1200s B.C. Jews have always considered Israel their religious home. Today, most Jews live in Israel or in cities around the world.
Islam was founded by Muhammad (A.D. 570-632). Most Muslims (followers of Islam) live in northern Africa, the Middle East, and Indonesia. There are two branches of Islam – the Sunni and Shia.
Hinduism is the traditional religion of India, and most of the world's Hindus live there.
Buddhism is an offshoot of Hinduism and was founded by Gautama Buddha (563–483 B.C.). Although Buddhism began in India, it spread eastward to Tibet, China, Japan, Korea, and south-eastern Asia.

Confucianism was founded by Confucius (551–479 B.C.). It is an important religion in China.
Shintoism is a religion founded in Japan, and its beginnings have been traced back 2,500 years.
Tribal religions exist among the native peoples of Africa, Asia, Australia, North and South America, and the Pacific Islands. Most of these religions center on the practical needs of the people.

Christian monastery

Jewish holy place

Hindu temple

Muslim mosque

Buddhist temple

- ▲ Roman Catholicism
- Orthodox and other Eastern Churches
- • Protestantism
- Sunni Islam
- Shia Islam
- Buddhism
- Hinduism
- Confucianism
- Judaism
- Shintoism
- Tribal religions
- Uninhabited

Polar Routes

Pacific
Routes

Pacific
Routes

Principal Air Routes
Distances in km

Anchorage

Queen Elizabeth Is.

Victoria I.

Baffin I.

GREENLAND

ICELAND

Churchill

Hudson
Bay

NORTH

Newfoundland

**UNITED
KINGDOM**
Glasgow
IRELAND
Lond

Edmonton

Vancouver
Calgary
C A N A D A

Winnipeg

Seattle

AMERICA

Quebec
Montreal

FRAN

San Francisco

Denver
St. Louis

Chicago
Detroit
Toronto
Boston
New York
Washington

PORTUGAL
Lisbon
Madr
SPA

Azores

Los Angeles

UNITED   STATES

Dallas

Casablanca
Canary Is.
MOROCCO
W. SAHARA
AL

Hawaiian
Islands
(U.S.)

Tropic of Cancer

Houston
MEXICO

New Orleans

A T L A N T I C

Gulf of
Mexico
Miami
BAHAMAS

MAURITANIA

A   F

Mexico

Havana CUBA
West Indies

JAMAICA HAITI
DOMINICAN REP.
Puerto
Rico (U.S.)

BELIZE
GUATEMALA HONDURAS
EL SALVADOR
NICARAGUA
COSTA
RICA PANAMA

Caribbean
Sea

Palmyra Is.
(U.S.)

Tabuaeran

Kiritimati

Equator

P A C I F I C

Caracas

VENEZUELA
Bogota
COLOMBIA

GUYANA
SURINAME
FR.
GUIANA

O C E A N

SENEGAL
GAMBIA
GUINEA-BISSAU

C. VERDE IS.

BURKI
FA

GUINEA
SIERRA
LEONE
IVORY
COAST
LIBERIA

Quito
ECUADOR

Belém

Manaus

Galapagos Is.
(Ecuador)

SOUTH
B R A Z I L
AMERICA
Brasília

Phoenix Is.

Tokelau Is.
(N.Z.)

O C E A N

PERU
Lima

Recife

Ascension
(Br.)

Samoan Is.

TONGA

Society Is.
(Fr.)

Tuamotu
Archipelago
(Fr.)

La Paz
BOLIVIA

Salvador

St. Helena
(Br.)

Tropic of Capricorn

Tubuai Is.
(Fr.)

Easter I.

PARAGUAY
Asunción

Rio de Janeiro
São Paulo

Kermadec Is.
(N.Z.)

Santiago

ARGENTINA

URUGUAY
Montevideo
Buenos
Aires

Tristan da
Cunha
(Br.)

Chatham Is.
(N.Z.)

CHILE

Falkland Is.

S. Georgia

Tierra del Fuego

FALKLAND IS.   DEPENDENCIES (Br.)

ROSS DEPENDENCY

A N T A R C T I C A
BRITISH ANTARCTIC TERRITORY

NORWE

West from Greenwich

Projection: Hammer Equal Area

Pacific
Routes

Pacific
Routes

ARCTIC OCEAN

Svalbard

Novaya
Zemlya

NORWAY
SWEDEN FINLAND
Oslo
Stockholm
Copenhagen
Helsinki
DEN.
BRUSSELS
POLAND Warsaw
Berlin
GERMANY
Vienna
Paris
ITALY YUGOSLAVIA
Rome
ROMANIA
BULGARIA
Tunis
GREECE
Athens
Algiers
Istanbul
TUNISIA
Tripoli
TURKEY
ALGERIA

Arkhangelsk

Leningrad

Moscow

UNION   OF   SOVIET   SOCIALIST   REPUBLICS

Sverdlovsk

Novosibirsk

Irkutsk

Ulaanbaatar

MONGOLIA

Vladivostok
Sapporo

N.
KOREA
Beijing
Dalian
S.
Pusan
JAPAN
Tokyo
Osaka

Bering
Sea

Baku
Tashkent
Tehran
SYRIA
Baghdad
IRAQ
ISRAEL
JORDAN
IRAN
AFGHANISTAN
Kabul
Islamabad
Lahore
PAKISTAN
Karachi
Delhi
Ahmadabad
INDIA
Mecca
Bombay
OMAN
SOUTH
YEMEN
YEMEN
SUDAN
EGYPT
LIBYA
SAUDI
ARABIA
BAHRAIN
QATAR
U.A.E.
KUWAIT
Red Sea
Cairo
Alexandria

CHINA
Chongqing
Shanghai

TAIWAN
Hong Kong

A   S   I   A

NEPAL
BANGLA-
DESH
Dhaka
Calcutta
BURMA
Rangoon
Madras
Bengal
Bay of
THAILAND
Bangkok
Phnom
Penh
CAM-
BODIA
Ho Chi Minh
City
Hanoi
Hue
VIETNAM
LAOS

PACIFIC

OCEAN

Tropic of Cancer

Wake I.
(U.S.)

Northern
Marianas
(U.S.)
Guam
(U.S.)

MARSHALL IS.

NIGER
CHAD
Khartoum
NIGERIA
Niamey
Kano
N'Djamena
Lagos
CAMEROON
Douala
EQUATORIAL
GUINEA
GABON
CABINDA
Kinshasa
ZAIRE
Luanda
ANGOLA
CENTRAL
AFRICAN
REPUBLIC
Addis Ababa
ETHIOPIA
SOMALI
REP.
DJIB.
Mogadishu
UGANDA
KENYA
Nairobi
RWANDA
BURUNDI
Mombasa
TANZANIA
Dar-es-Salaam
ZAMBIA
Harare
ZIMBABWE
NAMIBIA
BOTSWANA
MALAWI
MOZAMBIQUE
Johannesburg
SOUTH
AFRICA
LES.
SWAZ.
Durban
Cape Town

Arabian
Sea

Colombo
SRI LANKA

MALDIVES

SEYCHELLES

INDIAN

OCEAN

Crozet Is.
(Fr.)

Kerguelen Is.
(Fr.)

Antananarivo
MADAGASCAR
MAURITIUS

Manila
PHILIPPINES

Palau
(U.S.)

FEDERATED STATES
OF MICRONESIA

Equator

KIRIBATI

Kuala
Lumpur
Singapore
Padang
Sumatra
Borneo
BRUNEI
MALAYSIA
Jakarta
Surabaya
INDONESIA
Darwin
New
Guinea
PAPUA
NEW GUINEA
Port Moresby
SOLOMON IS.
TUVALU

VANUATU

FIJI

Coral
Sea

New
Caledonia
(Fr.)

Alice Springs
AUSTRALIA
Tropic of Capricorn
Perth
Adelaide
Sydney
Canberra
Melbourne
Brisbane
Tasmania
Hobart
NEW
ZEALAND
Auckland
Christchurch
Dunedin

DEPENDENCY   AUSTRALIAN   DEPENDENCY   ADELIE LAND
East from Greenwich

Copyright, George Philip & Son, Ltd.

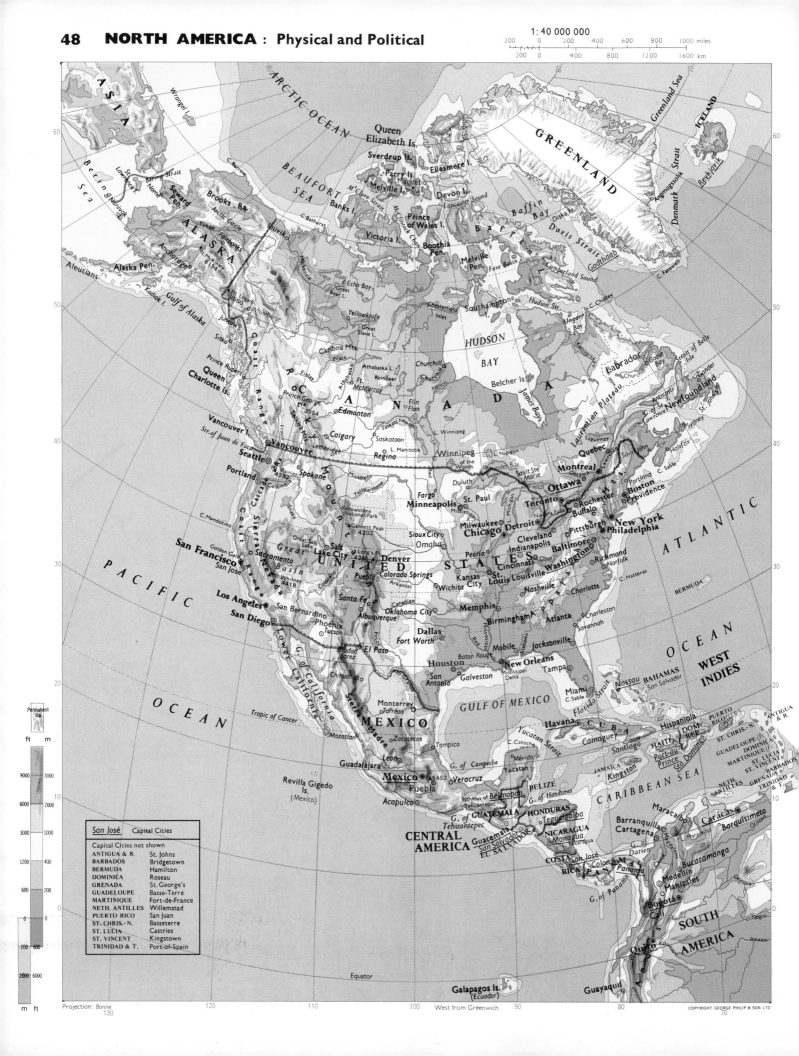

Climate Regions

Tropical climates
- Tropical rainforest
- Savanna

Mild climates
- Marine west coast
- Humid subtropical
- Mediterranean

Dry climates
- Steppe
- Desert

Continental climates
- Humid continental, warm summer
- Humid continental, cool summer
- Subarctic

Polar climates
- Tundra
- Icecap

High altitudes
- Highlands

(after Trewartha 1957)

Natural Vegetation

- Broadleaf forest – rainforest
- Broadleaf forest – deciduous
- Broadleaf forest – other
- Needleleaf forest
- Mixed forest
- Grassland
- Desert – scrub with grassy patches
- Tundra
- Ice-covered land
- High mountains (climate varies with elevation)

Land Use

- Hunting, fishing, and gathering
- Subsistence farming
- Ranching
- Urban land use
- Nomadic herding
- Commercial farming
- Lumbering
- Commercial fishing
- Little or no economic activity

Mining
- Petroleum
- Coal
- Iron Ore
- Other Mining

Population

- 100,000 people

North America's Ten Largest Cities

1. New York	17 807 000
2. Mexico	14 750 000
3. Los Angeles	12 373 000
4. Chicago	8 035 000
5. Philadelphia	5 755 000
6. San Francisco	5 685 000
7. Detroit	4 577 000
8. Boston	4 027 000
9. Houston	3 566 000
10. Washington	3 429 000

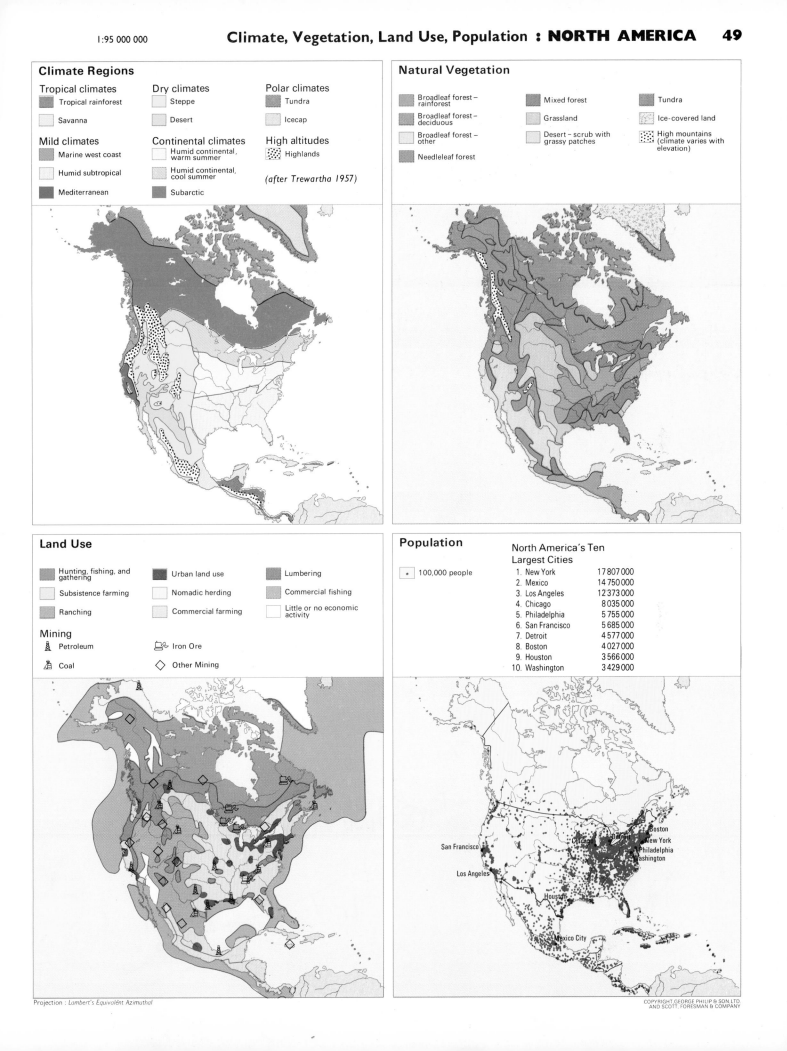

Projection : *Lambert's Equivalent Azimuthal*

ALASKA (U.S.)
1:30 000 000
100 0   100 200   300 miles
100 0   200   400 km

Projection: Bonne

West from Greenwich

1:15 000 000

100 50 0 100 200 300 400 miles

100 0 100 200 300 400 500 600 km

Main map labels

Devon Island
Lancaster Sound
Brodeur Peninsula
Baffin Bay
GREENLAND
Svartenhuk Peninsula
Disko I.
Sondre Stromfjord
Davis Strait
2134 Bylot I.
C. Hewett
Pond Inlet
Home B.
Fury & Hecla Str.
2591 Cumberland Peninsula
C. Dyer
C. Mercy
Cumberland Sd.
Melville Peninsula
Committee B.
Prince Charles I.
Foxe Basin
Nettilling L.
Frobisher Bay
Amadjuak L.
Foxe Penin.
C. Dorchester
Foxe Channel
Wager B.
Southampton I.
Frobisher Bay
Resolution I.
Roes Welcome Sd.
Coats I.
Mansel I.
Ivujivik
Maricourt (Wakeham Bay)
Koartac
Akpatok I.
C. Chidley
Hudson Strait
Bellin (Payne Bay)
Ungava Bay
Payne L.
Port Nouveau-Quebec (George R.)
Ungava Peninsula
Leaf R.
George R.
Nain
Hudson Bay
Ottawa Isls
257
Kuujjuaq
Koksoak
L. Minto
Leaf L.
N E W
Hopedale
C. Harrison
King George Is.
Clearwater L.
Lac Bienville
Schefferville
Petitsikapau L.
Kaniapiskau L.
Indian Harbour
Rigolet
L. Melville
Cartwright
Belcher Is.
Poste de la Baleine (Great Whale River)
LABRADOR
Michikamau L.
Happy Valley Goose Bay
Battle Harb.
C. Henrietta Maria
Ft. George
Kaniapiskau R.
Churchill
Str. of Belle Isle
D
Big Trout L.
James Bay
Akimiski I.
Eastmain
1128
Gagnon
Q U E B E C
Mingan
Natashquan
Corner Brook 814
Grand Falls
Bonavista
Winisk
Attawapiskat
Fort Rupert (Rupert House)
Rupert R.
Mistassini L.
Manicouagan L.
Sept Iles
Port Cartier
Anticosti
NEWFOUNDLAND
St. John's
Severn
Albany
Moosonee
o Chibougamau
Baie Comeau
R. St. Lawrence
Gaspé
Gulf of St. Lawrence
Corner Brook
Channel-Port aux Basques
C. Race
St. Joseph
Missinaibi
Gouin Reservoir
St. John
Saguenay
Matane
Gaspé Pen.
Cabot Str.
Carbonear
Hearst
Geraldton
L. Abitibi
Rimouski
Campbellton
Rivière du Loup
Bathurst
PR. EDWARD I.
Cape Breton I.
Glace Bay
Nipigon
Oba
Timmins
Rouyn
Vol d'Or
Edmundston
Chatham
Summerside
Charlottetown
Sydney
Thunder Bay
Lake Superior
Kirkland Lake
La Tuque
NEW BRUNSWICK
Moncton
Northumberland Str.
New Glasgow
Lake Superior
Marquette
Sault Ste. Marie
Sudbury
North Bay
Cabonga Reservoir
Shawinigan
Trois Rivieres
1190
QUÉBEC
Fredericton
Saint John
Amherst
NOVA SCOTIA
Truro
Dartmouth
Halifax
Sault Ste. Marie
Georgian Bay
St. Catharines
MONTREAL
St. Hyacinthe
Sherbrooke
MAINE
Kentville
B. of Fundy
Bridgewater
Sable I. (Nova Scotia)
Escanaba
Wausau
Green Bay
Appleton
Traverse City
TORONTO
Hamilton
Ottawa
Hull
L. Champlain
Bangor
Yarmouth
C. Sable
6309
MILWAUKEE
Madison
Saginaw
L. Ontario
Oshawa
Peterboro
Kingston
Burlington
917
Lewiston
Portland
NEW HAMPSHIRE
Manchester
WISCONSIN
Grand Rapids
Kitchener
London
Niagara Falls
Rochester
Syracuse
Albany
Springfield
Concord
MASS.
BOSTON
C. Cod
Rockford
Windsor
Lake Erie
BUFFALO
NEW YORK
Binghamton
CONN.
Providence
CHICAGO
Gary
DETROIT
Toledo
Erie
CLEVELAND
Akron
PENNSYLVANIA
Scranton
New Haven
R.I.
ILLINOIS
INDIANA
OHIO
Allentown
Newark
NEW JERSEY
NEW YORK

West from Greenwich

Inset map

NEWFOUNDLAND

1:7 000 000

25 0 25 50 100 miles

25 0 25 50 100 150 km

NEWFOUNDLAND
QUÉBEC
L'Anse au Loup
Fortau
Bradore Bay
St.-Augustin-Saguenay
Battle Harbour
Str. of Belle Isle
Belle I.
St. Anthony
Hare B.
Groais I.
Bell I.
Roddickton
Englee
Horse Is.
C. St. John
Long Range Mts.
White B.
Notre Dame B.
Fogo
Fogo I.
C. Freels
GROS MORNE NAT. PARK
Springdale
Lewisporte
Wesleyville
Bonavista B.
Trout River
Deer Lake
Howley
Botwood
Windsor
Gander
Bonavista
Catalina
Bay of Islands
Buchans
Red Indian
Badger
Grand Falls
Bishop's Falls
Trinity B.
Corner Brook 814
Grand L.
Stephenville
Victoria Res.
Grey Res.
Clarenville
Conception B.
Port au Port B.
St. George's B.
Salmon Res.
381
Carbonear
St. John's
Mt. Pearl
C. St. George
Long Range Mts.
White Bear Res.
Spaniard's B.
Argentia
Avalon Peninsula
Cabot Str.
C. Ray
Channel-Port aux Basques
Miquelon
Grand Bank
St. Lawrence
Placentia B.
St. Mary's B.
C. St. Mary's
C. Pine
C. Race
Langlade
St. Pierre
SAINT-PIERRE & MIQUELON (Fr.)

HAWAII
1:10 000 000

Projection: Albers' Equal Area with two standard parallels.   West from Greenwich

National Capital ★
State Capital ■ • • • •

1:12 000 000

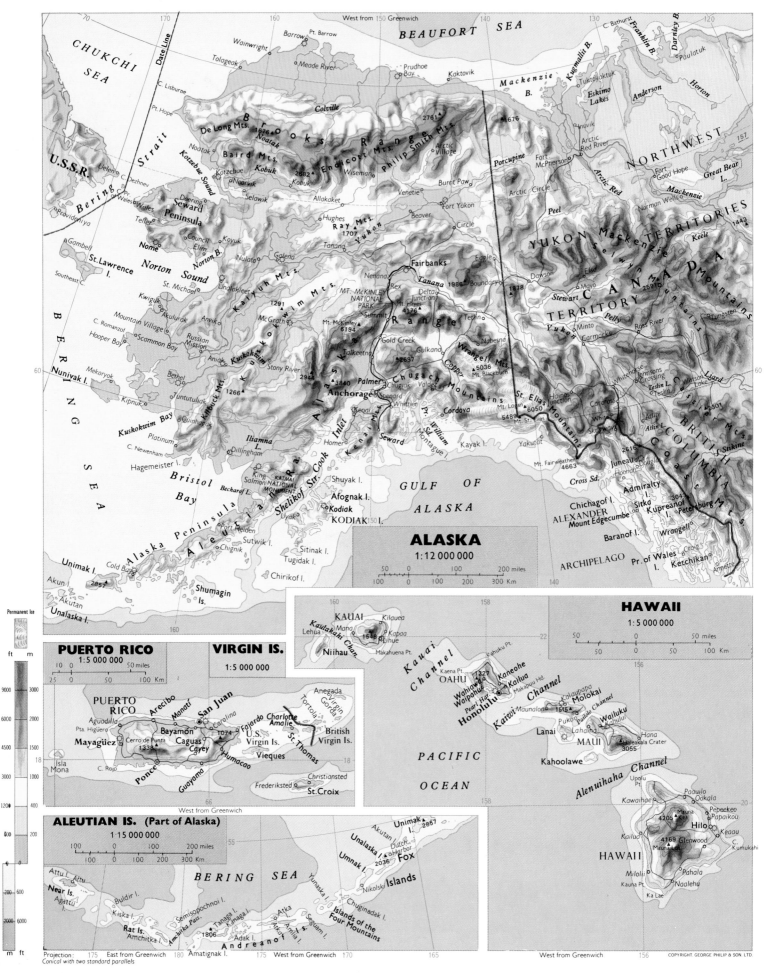

ALASKA
1:12 000 000

HAWAII
1:5 000 000

PUERTO RICO
1:5 000 000

VIRGIN IS.
1:5 000 000

ALEUTIAN IS. (Part of Alaska)
1:15 000 000

Permanent Ice

Projection:
Conical with two standard parallels

COPYRIGHT. GEORGE PHILIP & SON. LTD.

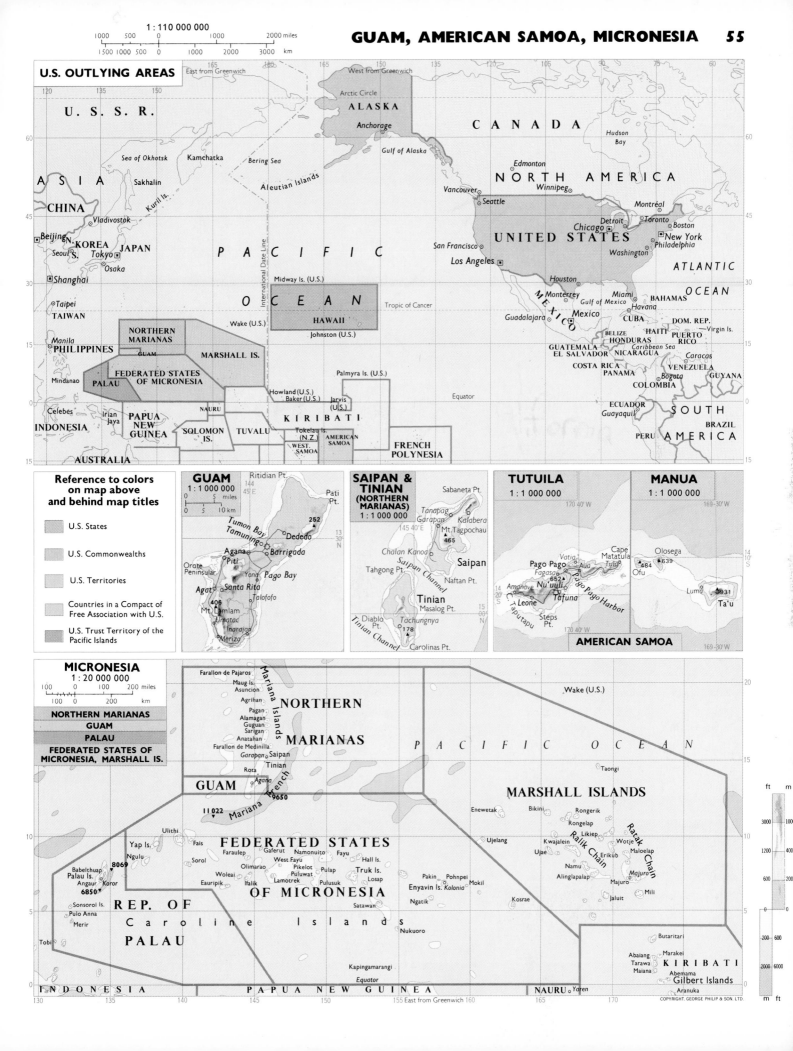

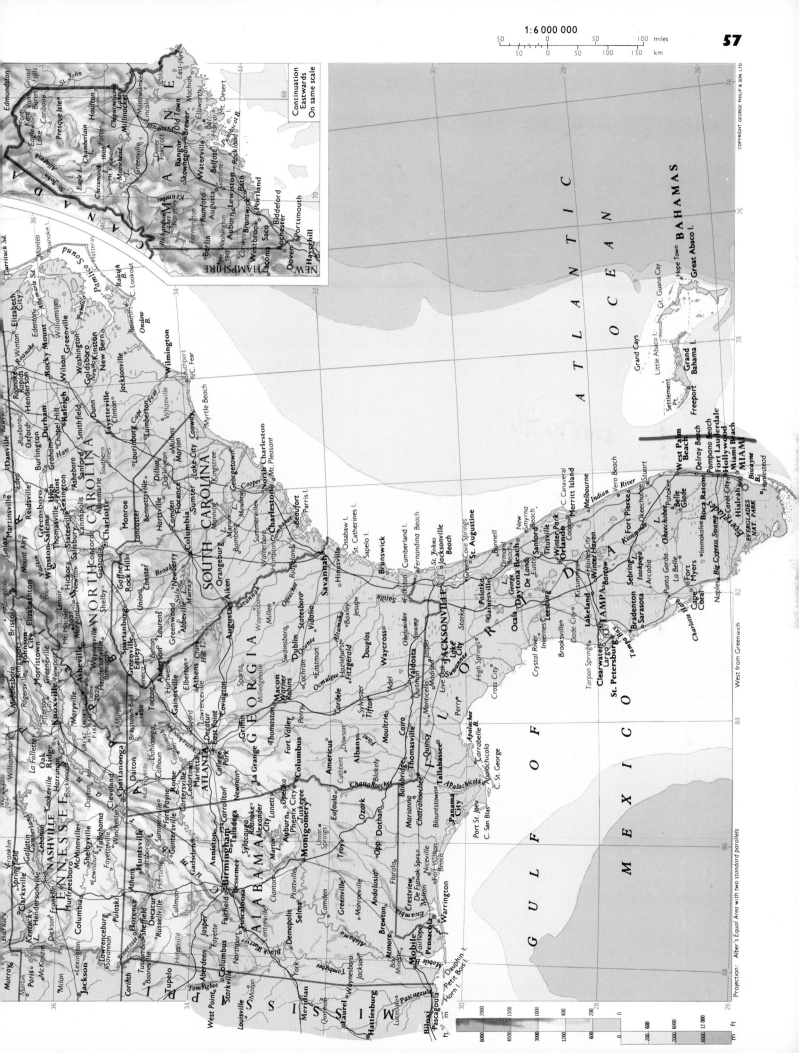

1 : 6 000 000

50   0   50   100   miles
50   0   50   100   150   km

Continuation
Eastwards
On same scale

COPYRIGHT GEORGE PHILIP & SON LTD.

Maine inset

Edmundston
Grand Falls
Fort Kent
Van Buren
Eagle L.
Caribou
Presque Isle
St. John
Chamberlain
Chesuncook
L.
Lincoln
Old Town
Millinocket
Mattawamkeag
Machias
Dover-Foxcroft
Moosehead L.
Greenville
East Port
Mt. Katahdin
1605
M A I N E
Bangor
Brewer
Skowhegan
Waterville
Belfast
Rockland
Mt. Desert
Ellsworth
Bath
Kennebec
Farmington
Rumford
Augusta
Gardiner
Brunswick
Lewiston
Auburn
Berlin
Mt. Washington
1917
Conway
Portland
Biddeford
Saco
Westbrook
Portsmouth
Dover
Rochester
Laconia
N E W
H A M P S H I R E
Hayerhill

C A N A D A

Main map

Murray
Paris
Martin
Milan
Jackson
Corinth
West Point
Columbus
Starkville
Louisville
Aberdeen
Tupelo
Holly Spgs.
M I S S I S S I P P I
Meridian
Laurel
Hattiesburg
Lucedale
Bay St. Louis
Pascagoula
Biloxi

Franklin
Springfield
Clarksville
Gallatin
NASHVILLE
Murfreesboro
Columbia
Lawrenceburg
Savannah
Tullahoma
Lewisburg
Shelbyville
McMinnville
Fayetteville
Pulaski
Lebanon
Cumberland
Cookeville
Crossville
T E N N E S S E E
Dickson
Lexington

Middlesboro
Williamsburg
La Follette
Jefferson
Jellico
Rogersville
Kingsport
Johnson City
Bristol
Abingdon
K E N T U C K Y

Oak Ridge
Clinton
Morristown
Newport
Greeneville
Maryville
KNOXVILLE
Mt. Mitchell 2037
Murphy

G R E A T
S M O K Y
MTS. NAT.
PARK
Mt. Guyot
2024

Martinsville
Danville
Reidsville
Eden
Mount Airy
Galax
Elkin
Yadkin
North Wilkesboro
Boone
Lenoir
Morganton
Marion
Hickory
Statesville
V I R G I N I A
Roxboro
Oxford
Henderson
Durham
Chapel Hill
Graham
Burlington
Greensboro
High Point
Winston-Salem
Thomasville
Lexington
Salisbury
Kannapolis
N O R T H   C A R O L I N A
Asheville
Waynesville
Brevard
Hendersonville
Shelby
Gastonia
Charlotte
Concord
Spartanburg
Gaffney
Rock Hill
Monroe
Albemarle

Roanoke R.
Emporia
Weldon
Roanoke Rapids
Henderson
Louisburg
Raleigh
Wilson
Rocky Mount
Goldsboro
Smithfield
Dunn
Sanford
Fayetteville
Clinton
Kinston
New Bern
Jacksonville
Washington
Greenville
Williamston
Winton
Elizabeth City
Edenton
Albemarle Sd.
Plymouth
Currituck Sd.
Manteo
Roanoke I.
Pamlico Sd.
C. Hatteras
Beaufort
Onslow B.
C. Lookout

Laurinburg
Lumberton
Whiteville
Southport
C. Fear
Wilmington
Myrtle Beach
Conway
Marion
Dillon
Florence
Hartsville
Bennettsville
Cheraw
Darlington
Lake City
Sumter
Camden
Kingstree
Georgetown

S O U T H   C A R O L I N A
Columbia
Orangeburg
Lancaster
Chester
Union
Newberry
Saluda
Greenwood
Abbeville
Anderson
Greenville
Easley
Clemson
Seneca
Pickens
Walhalla
Laurens
Clinton
Batesburg
Aiken
Augusta
Summerville
North Charleston
Charleston
Mt. Pleasant
Moncks Corner
Walterboro
Beaufort
Parris I.
St. Helena

G E O R G I A
ATLANTA
Decatur
East Point
College Park
Marietta
Griffin
Newnan
La Grange
West Point
Carrollton
Villa Rica
Cedartown
Rome
Cartersville
Dalton
Calhoun
Dahlonega
Gainesville
Lawrenceville
Buford
Athens
Elberton
Hartwell
Toccoa
Washington
Thomson
Covington
Madison
Milledgeville
Eatonton
Macon
Warner Robins
Forsyth
Perry
Cochran
Dublin
Swainsboro
Statesboro
Millen
Waynesboro
Sandersville
Wrightsville

Thomaston
Fort Valley
Columbus
Phenix City
Americus
Cordele
Cuthbert
Dawson
Albany
Sylvester
Tifton
Fitzgerald
Hazlehurst
Eastman
Ocmulgee
Douglas
Adel
Valdosta
Waycross
Jesup
Vidalia
Baxley
Hinesville
Savannah
Brunswick
St. Catherines I.
Sapelo I.
Ossabaw I.
Blackbeard I.
Cumberland I.
Fernandina Beach
Jacksonville Beach
St. Johns
St. Augustine

A L A B A M A
Birmingham
Bessemer
Fairfield
Tuscaloosa
Northport
Jasper
Fayette
Gadsden
Anniston
Talladega
Sylacauga
Alexander City
Tuskegee
Auburn
Opelika
Lanett
MONTGOMERY
Prattville
Wetumpka
Union Springs
Troy
Ozark
Dothan
Enterprise
Opp
Andalusia
Greenville
Camden
Monroeville
Brewton
Atmore
Selma
Demopolis
Marengo
Clanton
Roanoke

Cairo
Bainbridge
Thomasville
Quitman
Madison
Monticello
Perry
Live Oak
Lake City
Jasper
Tallahassee
Quincy
Marianna
Chattahoochee
Blountstown
Panama City
Port St. Joe
Apalachicola
C. San Blas
C. St. George
Apalachee B.
Carrabelle
Crestview
De Funiak Spgs.
Milton
Niceville
Fort Walton Beach
Pensacola
Warrington

Mobile
Fairhope
Dauphin I.
Petit Bois I.
Horn I.
Mobile B.

Starke
Gainesville
High Springs
Cross City
Suwannee
Crystal River
Inverness
Brooksville
Tarpon Springs
Clearwater
Largo
St. Petersburg
TAMPA
Bradenton
Sarasota
Punta Gorda
Fort Myers
Cape Coral
Naples
Ocala
Leesburg
Eustis
Sanford
Orlando
Winter Park
Kissimmee
Winter Haven
Lakeland
Haines City
Bartow
Sebring
Arcadia
La Belle
Immokalee
Big Cypress Swamp
EVERGLADES
NAT. PARK

F L O R I D A
De Land
Daytona Beach
Ormond Beach
New Smyrna Beach
Titusville
Cocoa
Cape Canaveral
C. Canaveral
Merritt Island
Melbourne
Vero Beach
Fort Pierce
Stuart
Okeechobee
L. Okeechobee
Pahokee
Belle Glade
West Palm Beach
Delray Beach
Boca Raton
Pompano Beach
Fort Lauderdale
Hollywood
MIAMI
Miami Beach
Hialeah
Carol City
Homestead
Biscayne B.
Indian River
Bunnell
Palatka
Green Cove Springs
Folkston
Okefenokee
Swamp

Kissimmee L.
Istokpoga L.
George L.
Dade City
Plant City
Winter Garden

A T L A N T I C   O C E A N

G U L F   O F   M E X I C O

B A H A M A S
Great Abaco I.
Little Abaco I.
Gt. Guana Cay
Hope Town
Grand Cays
Grand Bahama
Freeport
Settlement Pt.

West from Greenwich

Projection: Alber's Equal Area with two standard parallels

ft   m
6000   2000
4500   1500
3000   1000
1200
600
0   0
200
600
2000
6000
12 000
ft   m

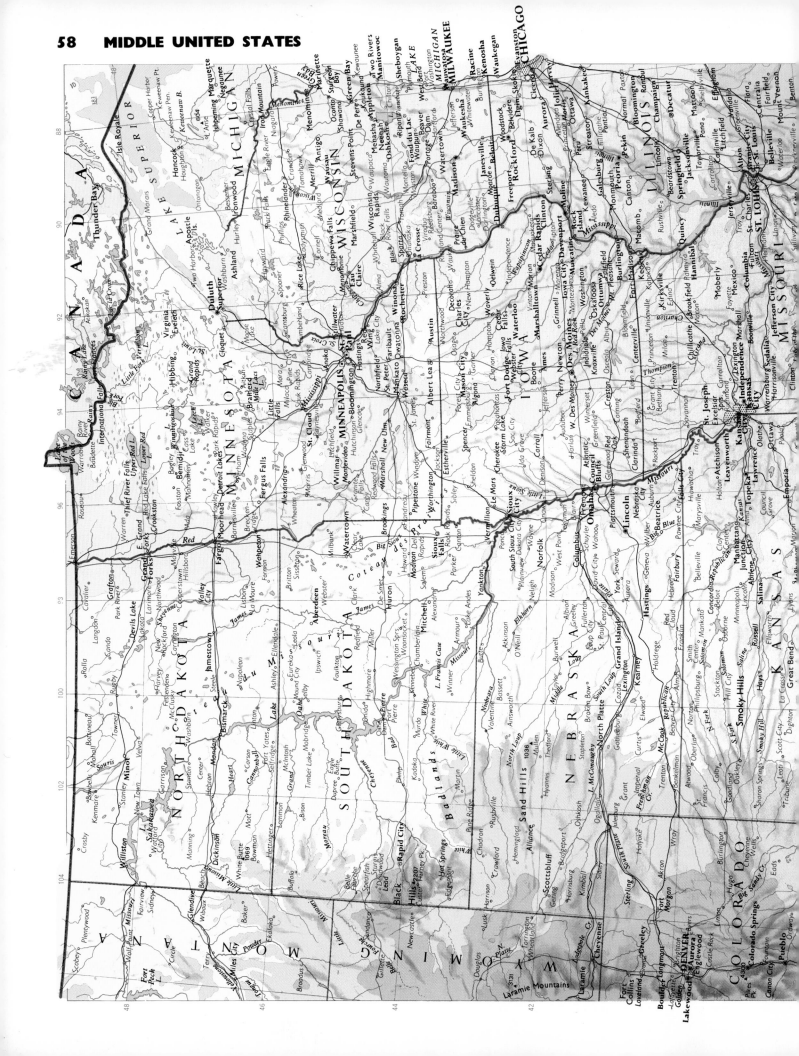

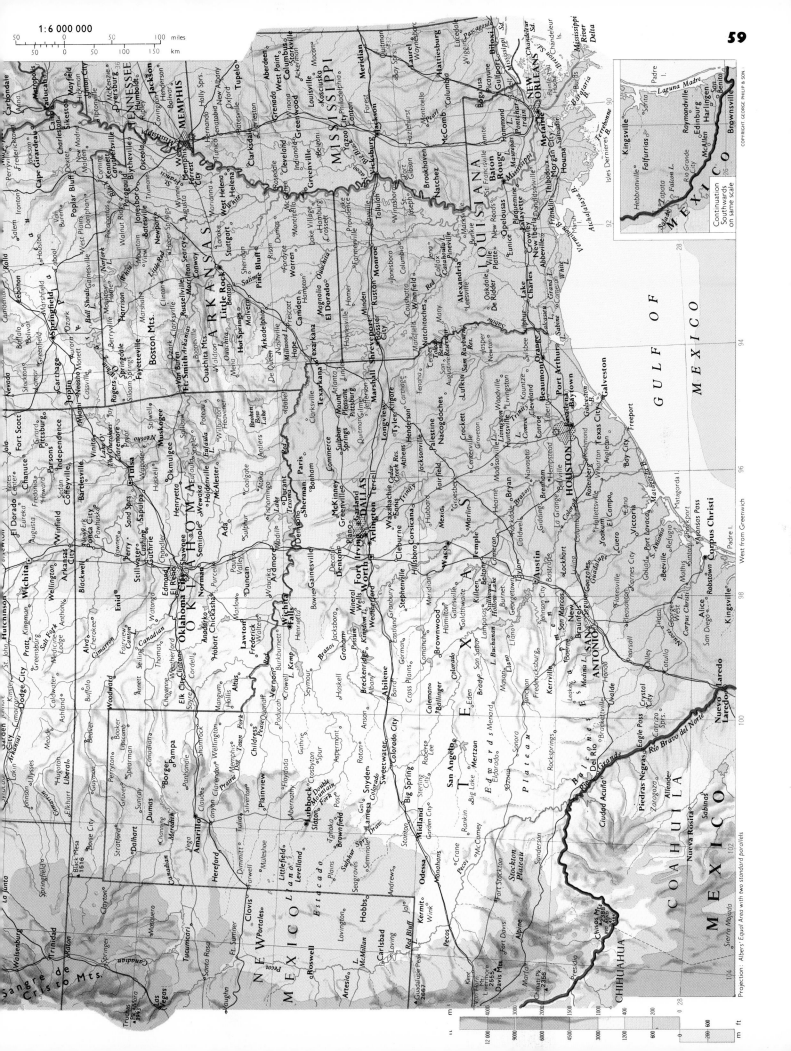

1 : 6 000 000

50   0   50   100 miles
50   0   50   100   150 km

Laguna Madre

Kingsville
Falfurrias
Raymondville
Harlingen
Hebbronville
Edinburg
McAllen
Brownsville
Rio Grande
Zapata
Falcon L.
Salado
S. Benito

Continuation
Southwards
on same scale

M E X I C O

Isles Dernieres

TENNESSEE

MEMPHIS

MISSISSIPPI

ARKANSAS

Little Rock

LOUISIANA

NEW ORLEANS

Baton Rouge

G U L F   O F   M E X I C O

O K L A H O M A

Oklahoma City

Tulsa

DALLAS

Fort Worth

T E X A S

HOUSTON

San Antonio

Austin

Corpus Christi

Laredo
Nuevo Laredo

N E W   M E X I C O

C O A H U I L A

C H I H U A H U A

M E X I C O

Sangre de Cristo Mts.

Llano Estacado

Edwards Plateau

Stockton Plateau

Rio Grande

West from Greenwich

Projection: Albers' Equal Area with two standard parallels

ft
m

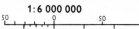

1:6 000 000

COPYRIGHT: GEORGE PHILIP & SON, LTD

PACIFIC OCEAN

Projection: Albers' Equal Area with two standard parallels

West from Greenwich

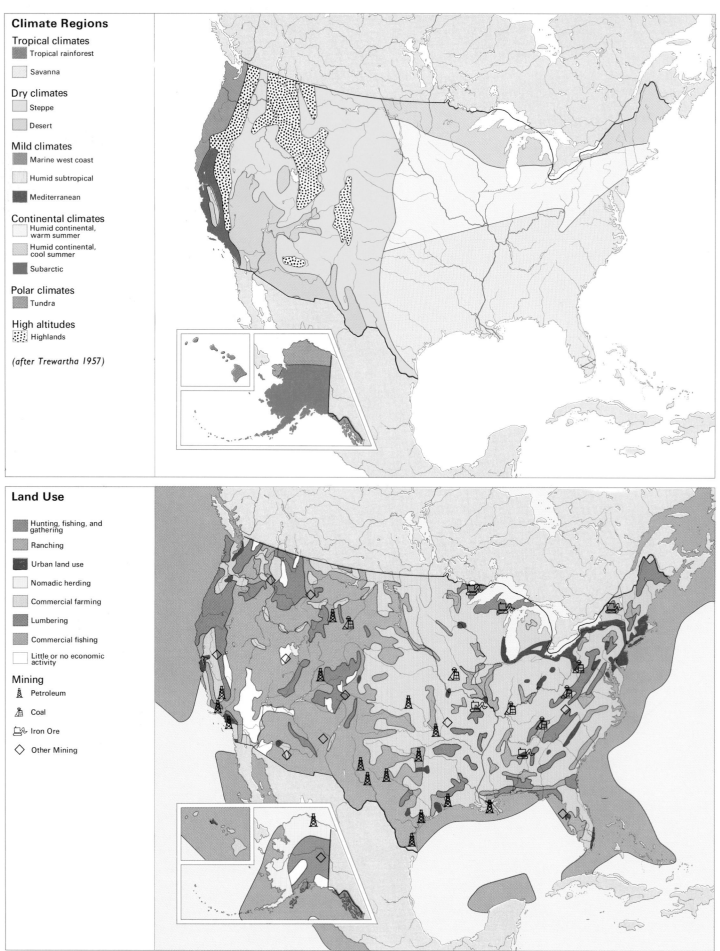

Climate Regions

Tropical climates
Tropical rainforest

Savanna

Dry climates
Steppe

Desert

Mild climates
Marine west coast

Humid subtropical

Mediterranean

Continental climates
Humid continental, warm summer

Humid continental, cool summer

Subarctic

Polar climates
Tundra

High altitudes
Highlands

(after Trewartha 1957)

Land Use

Hunting, fishing, and gathering

Ranching

Urban land use

Nomadic herding

Commercial farming

Lumbering

Commercial fishing

Little or no economic activity

Mining
Petroleum

Coal

Iron Ore

Other Mining

Projection : *Albers Equal Area with two standard parallels*

Natural Vegetation

- Broadleaf forest – rainforest
- Broadleaf forest – deciduous
- Broadleaf forest – other
- Needleleaf forest
- Mixed forest
- Grassland
- Desert – scrub with grassy patches
- Tundra
- High mountains

—6— Length of growing season (in months)

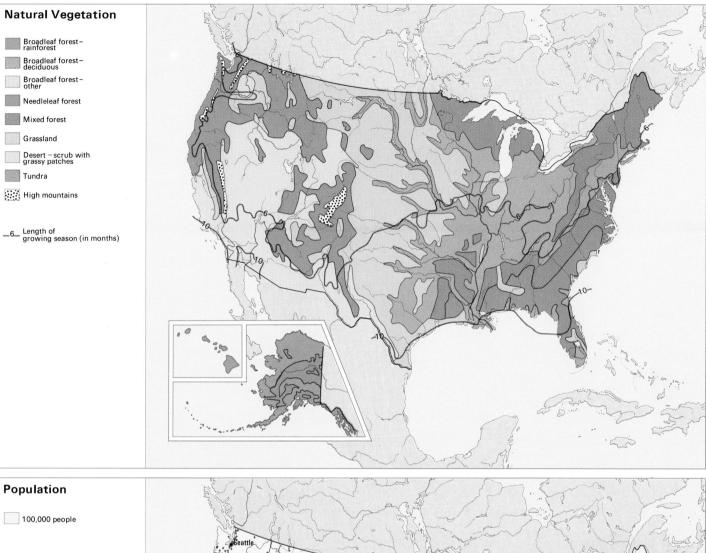

Population

100,000 people

United States' Twenty Largest Cities

1.	New York	17 807 000
2.	Los Angeles	12 373 000
3.	Chicago	8 035 000
4.	Philadelphia	5 755 000
5.	San Francisco	5 685 000
6.	Detroit	4 577 000
7.	Boston	4 027 000
8.	Houston	3 566 000
9.	Washington	3 429 000
10.	Dallas	3 348 000
11.	Miami	2 799 000
12.	Cleveland	2 788 000
13.	St. Louis	2 398 000
14.	Atlanta	2 380 000
15.	Pittsburgh	2 372 000
16.	Baltimore	2 245 000
17.	Minneapolis – St. Paul	2 231 000
18.	Seattle	2 208 000
19.	San Diego	2 064 000
20.	Tampa	1 811 000

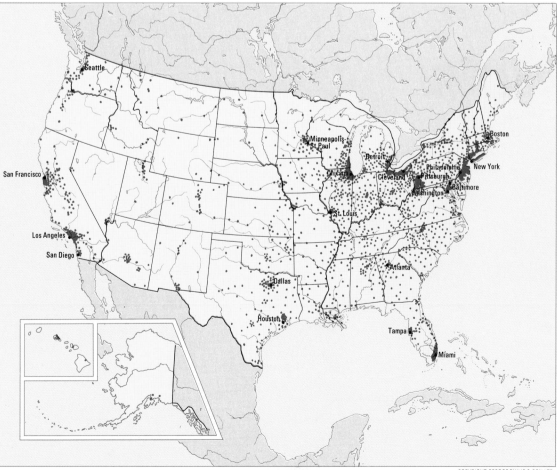

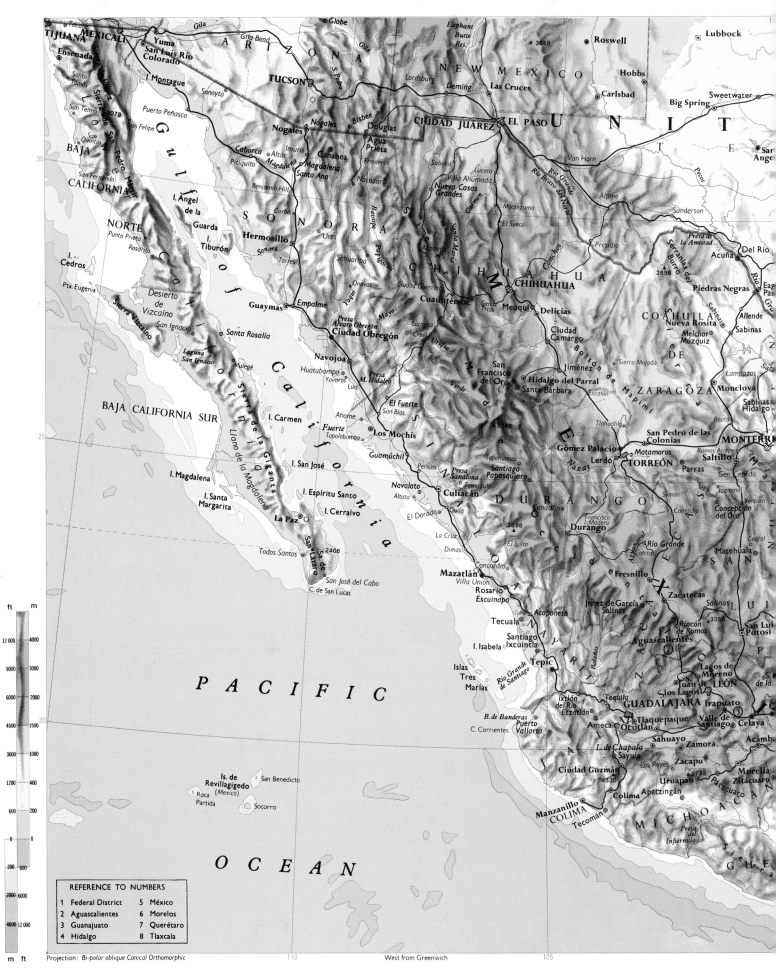

ft   m

12 000   4000

9000   3000

6000   2000

4500   1500

3000   1000

1200   400

600   200

0   0

200   600

2000   6000

4000   12 000

m ft

REFERENCE TO NUMBERS

1 Federal District   5 México
2 Aguascalientes   6 Morelos
3 Guanajuato   7 Querétaro
4 Hidalgo   8 Tlaxcala

Projection: *Bi-polar oblique Conical Orthomorphic*   110   West from Greenwich   105

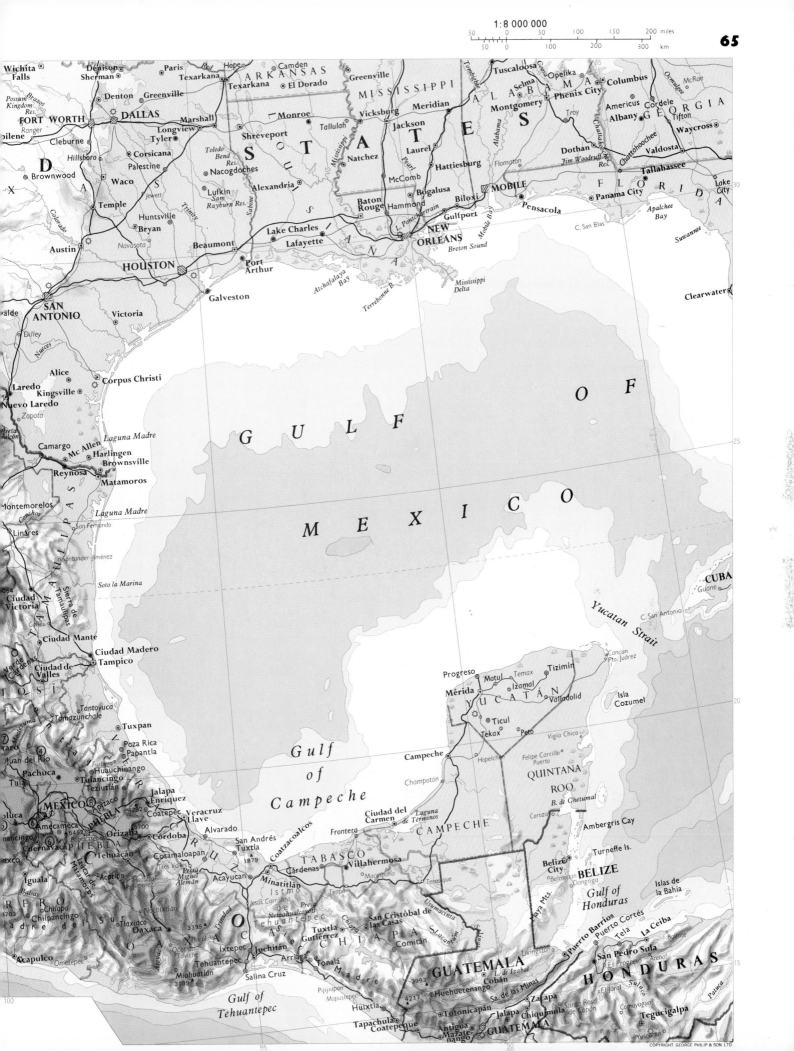

1:8 000 000

50   0   50   100   150   200 miles
50   0   100   200   300 km

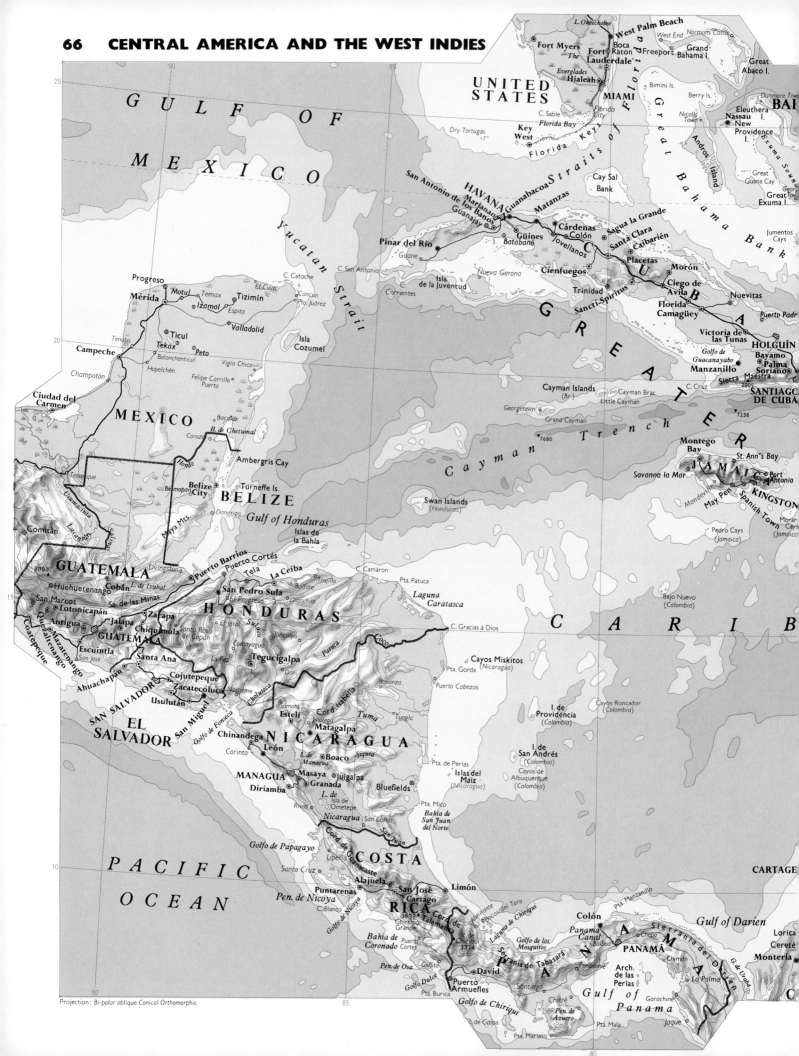

GULF OF MEXICO

UNITED STATES

Fort Myers
Fort Lauderdale
Boca Raton
West Palm Beach
West End
Normans Castle
Freeport
Grand Bahama I.
Great Abaco I.
L. Okeechobee
Everglades
Hialeah
MIAMI
The Everglades
C. Sable
Florida City
Florida Bay
Key West
Dry Tortugas
Bimini Is.
Berry Is.
Nicolls Town
Eleuthera I.
Nassau
New Providence
Great Guana Cay
Great Exuma I.
Jumentos Cays
Dunmore Tov
BAI

Straits of Florida

HAVANA
San Antonio de los Baños
Guanabacoa
Marianao
Guanajay
Matanzas
Pinar del Río
Guane
Güines
Batabanó
Cárdenas
Colón
Jovellanos
Sagua la Grande
Santa Clara
Caibarién
Placetas
Morón
Cienfuegos
Isla de la Juventud
Nueva Gerona
Trinidad
Sancti-Spíritus
Ciego de Avila
Florida
Camagüey
Nuevitas
Puerto Padr
Victoria de las Tunas
HOLGUÍN
Golfo de Guacanayabo
Bayamo
Palma Soriano
Manzanillo
Sierra Maestra
SANTIAGO DE CUBA
2005
7238

C U B A

G R E A T E R

Cay Sal Bank
Corrientes
C. San Antonio
C. Catoche

Yucatan Strait

Progreso
Motul
Temax
Tizimín
Mérida
Izamal
Espita
Cancún
Pto. Juárez
El Cuyo
Ticul
Tekax
Peto
Valladolid
Isla Cozumel
Campeche
Tenabo
Bolonchenticul
Hopelchén
Champotón
Felipe Carrillo Puerto
Vigía Chico

MEXICO

Ciudad del Carmen
Bacalar
B. de Chetumal
Corozal
Hondo
Ambergris Cay
Tenosique
Usumacinta
Belmopan
Belize City
Turneffe Is.
Dangriga
BELIZE
Maya Mts.
Comitán
Lacantún
Salinas
Livingston
G. de Izabal
Puerto Barrios
Puerto Cortés
Tela
La Ceiba
Trujillo
C. Camarón
Pta. Patuca

Gulf of Honduras

Swan Islands (Honduras)

Islas de la Bahía

Cayman Islands (Br.)
Georgetown
Grand Cayman
Cayman Brac
Little Cayman
C. Cruz
7680

Cayman Trench

Montego Bay
St. Ann's Bay
Savanna la Mar
JAMAICA
Port Antonio
Mandeville
May Pen
Spanish Town
KINGSTON
Morar
Pedro Cays (Jamaica)

8993
Huehuetenango
Cobán
Sa. de las Minas
San Marcos
Totonicapán
Zacapa
El Progreso
San Pedro Sula
Olanchito
Aguán
Yoro
HONDURAS
Laguna Caratasca
Antigua
Jalapa
Chiquimula
Santa Rosa de Copán
GUATEMALA
Quezaltenango
Mazatenango
Coatepeque
San José
Escuintla
Santa Ana
Cojutepeque
Zacatecoluca
Usulután
Ahuachapán
San Miguel
SAN SALVADOR
EL SALVADOR
Golfo de Fonseca
Corinto
Comayagua
La Paz
Nacaome
Choluteca
El Jicaral
Sulaco
Juticalpa
Tegucigalpa
Danlí
Patuca
Coco
C. Gracias á Dios
Cayos Miskitos (Nicaragua)
Pta. Gorda
Bonanza
Puerto Cabezas

C A R I B

Somoto
Estelí
Jinotega
Matagalpa
Cord. Isabelia
Tuma
Tunla
Chinandega
León
NICARAGUA
L. de Managua
Boaco
Siquia
Pta. de Perlas
I. de Providencia (Colombia)
Cayos Roncador (Colombia)
MANAGUA
Masaya
Granada
Juigalpa
Diriamba
L. de Nicaragua
Bluefields
Islas del Maiz (Nicaragua)
I. de San Andrés (Colombia)
Cayos de Albuquerque (Colombia)
Rivas
L. de Isla de Ometepe
San Carlos
Pta. Mico
Bahía de San Juan del Norte
Nicaragua
San Juan

PACIFIC OCEAN

Golfo de Papagayo
Cord. de Guanacaste
Santa Cruz
Liberia
COSTA
Puntarenas
Pen. de Nicoya
Alajuela
San José
Cartago
Limón
RICA
C. Blanco
Golfo de Nicoya
Cord. de Talamanca
3837
Cerro Chirripó
Grande
Bahía de Coronado
Puerto Cortés
Pen. de Osa
Golfito
Golfo Dulce
Puerto Armuelles
Pta. Burica
Golfo de Chiriqui
David
Santiago
Chitré
Pen. de Azuero
Pta. Mariato
de Coiba
Almirante
Bocas del Toro
Laguna de Chiriquí
Golfo de los Mosquitos
Serranía de Tabasará
Penonomé
Arch. de las Perlas
Chimán
Balboa
Panamá Canal
Colón
Pta. Manzanillo
PANAMÁ
Serranía del Darién
Gulf of Darien
G. de Urabá
Lorica
Cereté
Montería
La Palma
Garachiné
Jaqué
Sierra de Santa Fe
CARTAGE

C A R I B

Bajo Nuevo (Colombia)

CARTAGE

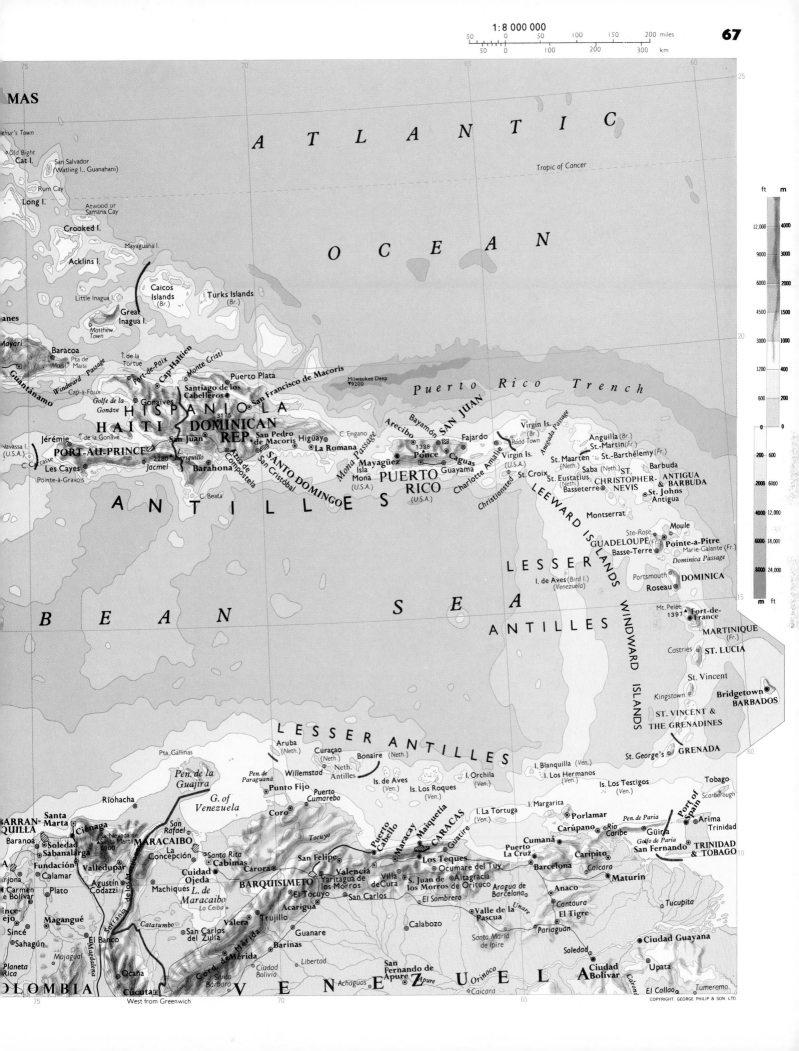

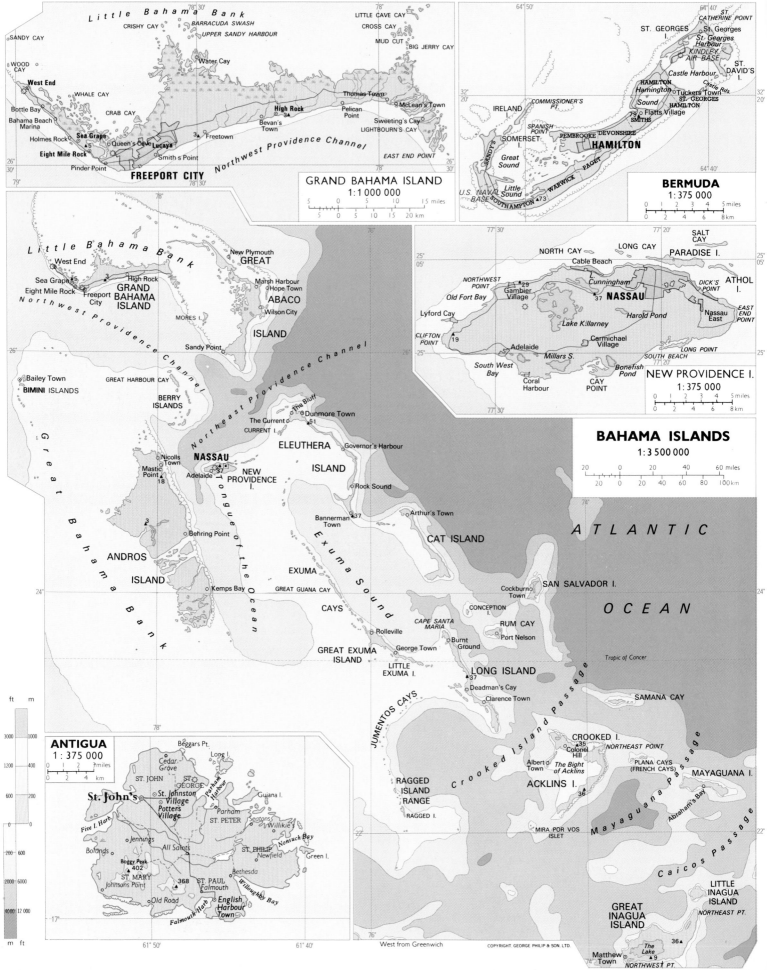

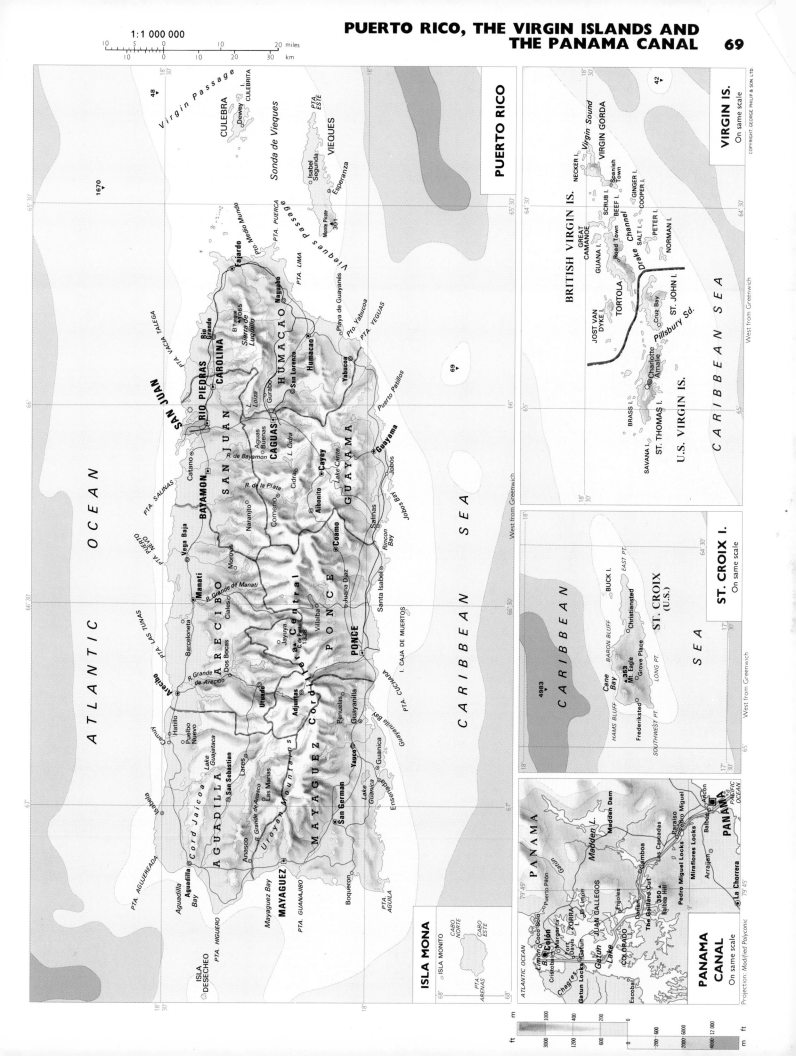

1:1 000 000

PUERTO RICO

ATLANTIC OCEAN

CARIBBEAN SEA

Virgin Passage

CULEBRA
Dewey
I. CULEBRITA

Sonda de Vieques
Isabel Segunda
Esperanza
VIEQUES
Monte Pirate 301
PTA. ESTE

SAN JUAN
RIO PIEDRAS
CAROLINA
BAYAMON
Catano
Vega Baja
Manati
Barceloneta
Arecibo
Hatillo
Pueblo Nuevo
AGUADILLA
Aguadilla Bay
Isabela
ARECIBO
Utuado
Adjuntas
Lares
Las Marias
San Sebastian
Lake Guajataca
Lake Guayo
MAYAGUEZ
Mayaguez Bay
San German
Yauco
Boqueron
Guanica
Lake Guanica
Ensenada

Sierra de Luquillo
El Yunque 1065
Rio Grande
HUMACAO
San Lorenzo
Humacao
Yabucoa
CAGUAS
Cayey
Aibonito
Coamo
GUAYAMA
Guayama
Salinas
Santa Isabel
Juana Diaz
PONCE
Villalba
Ciales
Cord. Central
Naranjito
Comerio
Cidra
Aguas Buenas
Gurabo

ISLA MONA
CABO NORTE
ISLA MONITO
CABO ESTE
PTA. ARENAS

ISLA DESECHEO

VIRGIN IS.
On same scale

BRITISH VIRGIN IS.
NECKER
VIRGIN GORDA
Spanish Town
SCRUB I.
GUANA I.
GINGER I.
BEEF I.
COOPER I.
SALT I.
PETER I.
NORMAN I.
TORTOLA
Road Town
Drake Channel
JOST VAN DYKE
GREAT CAMANOE
Virgin Sound
ST. JOHN I.
Cruz Bay
Pillsbury Sd.
Charlotte Amalie
ST. THOMAS I.
BRASS I.
SAVANA I.
U.S. VIRGIN IS.

CARIBBEAN SEA

West from Greenwich

COPYRIGHT GEORGE PHILIP & SON LTD.

ST. CROIX I.
On same scale

CARIBBEAN SEA

BUCK I.
EAST PT.
BARON BLUFF
Christiansted
Cane Bay
Mt. Eagle 353
Grove Place
ST. CROIX (U.S.)
Frederiksted
HAMS BLUFF
LONG PT.
SOUTHWEST PT.
4983

West from Greenwich

PANAMA CANAL
On same scale

PANAMA
ATLANTIC OCEAN
Limon Bay
Colon
Cristobal
Coco Solo
Fort Davis
Gatun Locks
Gatun
Margarita
Escobal
ZORRA
Puerto Pilon
Madden L.
Madden Dam
Chagres
Gatun Lake
COLORADO
JUAN GALLEGOS
Frijoles
Fort San Lorenzo
El Limon
Gamboa
The Gaillard Cut
Las Cascadas
Pedro Miguel Locks
Paraiso
Pedro Miguel
Miraflores Locks
Balboa Hill 350
Arraijan
Balboa
Ancon
PANAMA
PACIFIC OCEAN
La Chorrera

Projection: Modified Polyconic

ft m
3000 1000
1200 400
600 200
0 0
ft m
600 200
6000 2000
12 000 4000

1:40 000 000

150   0   150   300   450   600   750   900 miles
200   0   200   400   600   800 1000 1200 1400 km

NORTH

ATLANTIC

OCEAN

Cape
Verde
Islands

G. of
Campeche
Yucatan Str.
Cuba
Hispaniola
G. of Honduras
Kingston
Port-au-Prince
Santo Domingo
S. Juan
Puerto Rico
Leeward Is.
CARIBBEAN   SEA
Windward Is.
Guatemala
Tegucigalpa
San Salvador
Managua
CENTRAL
AMERICA
San José
San José
Panamá
G. of
Panamá
Barranquilla
G. of Darien
Maracaibo
Curaçao (Neth.)
Caracas
Barquisimeto
Orinoco
Trinidad
VENEZUELA
GUYANA
Georgetown
SURINAME
Paramaribo
FR. GUIANA
Cayenne
Medellín
Manizales
Bogotá
Roraima
2810
Sierra Pacaraima
Kaieteur Falls
Cali
COLOMBIA
ECUADOR
Quito
Chimborazo
6267
Cotopaxi
5897
Guayaquil
C. Pariña
Iquitos
Marañón
Putumayo
Japurá
Negro
Amazon
Manaus
Marajó I.
Pará
Belém
Equator
Equator
São Luis
Fernando Noronha
Chiclayo
Trujillo
Ucayali
Purus
Madeira
Roosevelt
Tapajós
Santarem
Xingu
Tocantins
Araguaia
Parnaiba
Fortaleza
Natal
C. de São Roque
João Pessoa
Recife
C. Branco
PERU
Callão
Lima
Cuzco
Titicaca
6850
Arequipa
La Paz
Cachabamba
Oruro
Sucre
BOLIVIA
Selvas
São Francisco
Maceió
Salvador
B R A Z I L
Plateau of Mato Grosso
Cuiabá
Goiâna
Brasília
Brazilian Highlands
Belo Horizonte
Arica
Iquique
Antofagasta
Tropic of Capricorn
Pilcomayo
PARAGUAY
Asunción
Ribeirão Prêto
Campinas
São Paulo
Santos
Niteroi
Rio de Janeiro
C. Frio
SOUTH
Ojos del Salado
6863
Tucumán
Paraná
Iguaçu Falls
Curitiba
Gran Chaco
Juan Fernández (Chile)
Aconcagua
6980
Córdoba
Mendoza
Rosario
Viña del Mar
Valparaiso
Santiago
ARGENTINA
Santa Fé
URUGUAY
Montevideo
Buenos Aires
La Plata
Rio de la Plata
Pôrto Alegre
Lagoa dos Patos
ATLANTIC
Toltas
Concepción
Temuco
Colorado
Negro
Bahia Blanca
Pta. Mogotes
Valdivia
Puerto Montt
Chiloé
G. of San Matias
Chubut
PACIFIC
Chonos Arch.
G. of San Jorge
Patagonia
OCEAN
OCEAN
Falkland Is. (Br.)
Stanley
Punta Arenas
C. Froward
Magellan's Str.
Tierra del Fuego
Staten I.
C. Horn
South Georgia (Br.)
Drake Passage
South Shetland Is.
Elephant I.
South Orkney Is. (Br.)
South Sandwich Is. (Br.)
Palmer Arch.
Joinville I.
Antarctic Peninsula

Permanent Ice

ft	m
12 000	4000
6000	2000
3000	1000
1200	400
600	200
0	0
200	600
2000	6000

m   ft

Georgetown   Capital Cities

Climate Regions

Tropical climates
- Tropical rainforest
- Savanna

Dry climates
- Steppe
- Desert

Mild climates
- Marine west coast
- Humid subtropical
- Mediterranean

High altitudes
- Highlands
- Uplands

(after Trewartha 1957)

Natural Vegetation
- Broadleaf forest – rainforest
- Broadleaf forest – deciduous
- Broadleaf forest – other
- Mixed forest
- Grassland
- Desert – little or no vegetation
- Desert – scrub with grassy patches
- High mountains

Land Use
- Hunting, fishing, and gathering
- Subsistence farming
- Ranching
- Urban land use
- Commercial farming
- Lumbering
- Commercial fishing
- Little or no economic activity

Mining
- Petroleum
- Coal
- Iron Ore
- Other Mining

Population

100,000 people

South America's Ten Largest Cities
1. Buenos Aires   9 927 000
2. São Paulo   8 493 000
3. Lima   5 258 000
4. Rio de Janeiro 5 091 000
5. Bogotá   4 486 000
6. Santiago   4 132 000
7. Caracas   2 944 000
8. Medellin   1 812 000
9. Belo Horizonte 1 781 000
10. Salvador   1 502 000

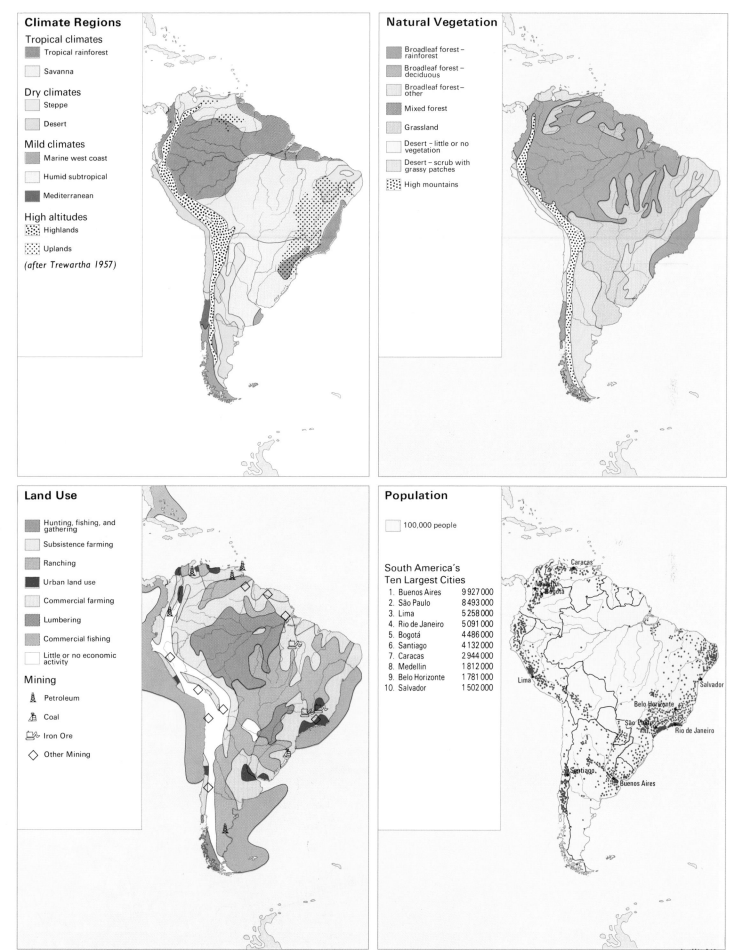

Projection : *Lambert's Equivalent Azimuthal*

NORTH SEA

IRISH SEA

North Channel

NORTHERN IRELAND

SCOTLAND

ENGLAND

Southern Uplands

Cheviot Hills

Pennines

CUMBRIA

NORTHUMBERLAND

DURHAM

NORTH YORKSHIRE

CLEVELAND

TYNE & WEAR

HUMBERSIDE

N. York Moors

LINCOLN

NOTTS

DERBY

SOUTH YORKSHIRE

W. YORKSHIRE

GREATER MANCHESTER

LANCASHIRE

MERSEYSIDE

CHESHIRE

CLWYD

GWYNEDD

Anglesey

ISLE OF MAN

Belfast
Bangor
Newtownards
Larne

Stirling
Falkirk
Airdrie
Coatbridge
Motherwell
Wishaw
Hamilton
Glasgow
Clydebank
Paisley
Greenock
Dumbarton
Edinburgh
Leith
Dunfermline
Kirkcaldy
Ochil Hills

Kilmarnock
Ayr
Troon
Dumfries
Merrick 843

Carlisle
Penrith
Skiddaw 931
Helvellyn 950
Cumbrian Mts.
Sca Fell 978
Kendal
Windermere
Ullswater

Berwick-upon-Tweed
The Cheviot 816
Hexham
Newcastle
Gateshead
Morpeth
Blyth
Tynemouth
South Shields
Sunderland
Hartlepool
Stockton
Middlesbrough
Darlington

Whitby
Scarborough
Bridlington
Flamborough Hd.
Beverley
Hull
Grimsby
Scunthorpe
Doncaster
York
Harrogate
Leeds
Bradford
Halifax
Huddersfield
Wakefield
Barnsley
Rotherham
Sheffield
Chesterfield
Mansfield
Worksop
Newark
Lincoln
Nottingham
Loughborough
Grantham
Derby
Burton-on-Trent
Stoke-on-Trent
Newcastle-under-Lyme
Crewe
Macclesfield
Stockport
Manchester
Salford
Oldham
Bolton
Bury
Blackburn
Preston
Blackpool
Fleetwood
Morecambe
Lancaster
Barrow-in-Furness
Whitehaven
Workington

Southport
Formby Pt.
Liverpool
Birkenhead
Wallasey
St. Helens
Wigan
Warrington
Runcorn
Wrexham
Snowdon 1085
Caernarfon
Bangor
Holyhead
Colwyn Bay
Rhyl

NORFOLK
The Wash
LINCOLN

1:2 000 000

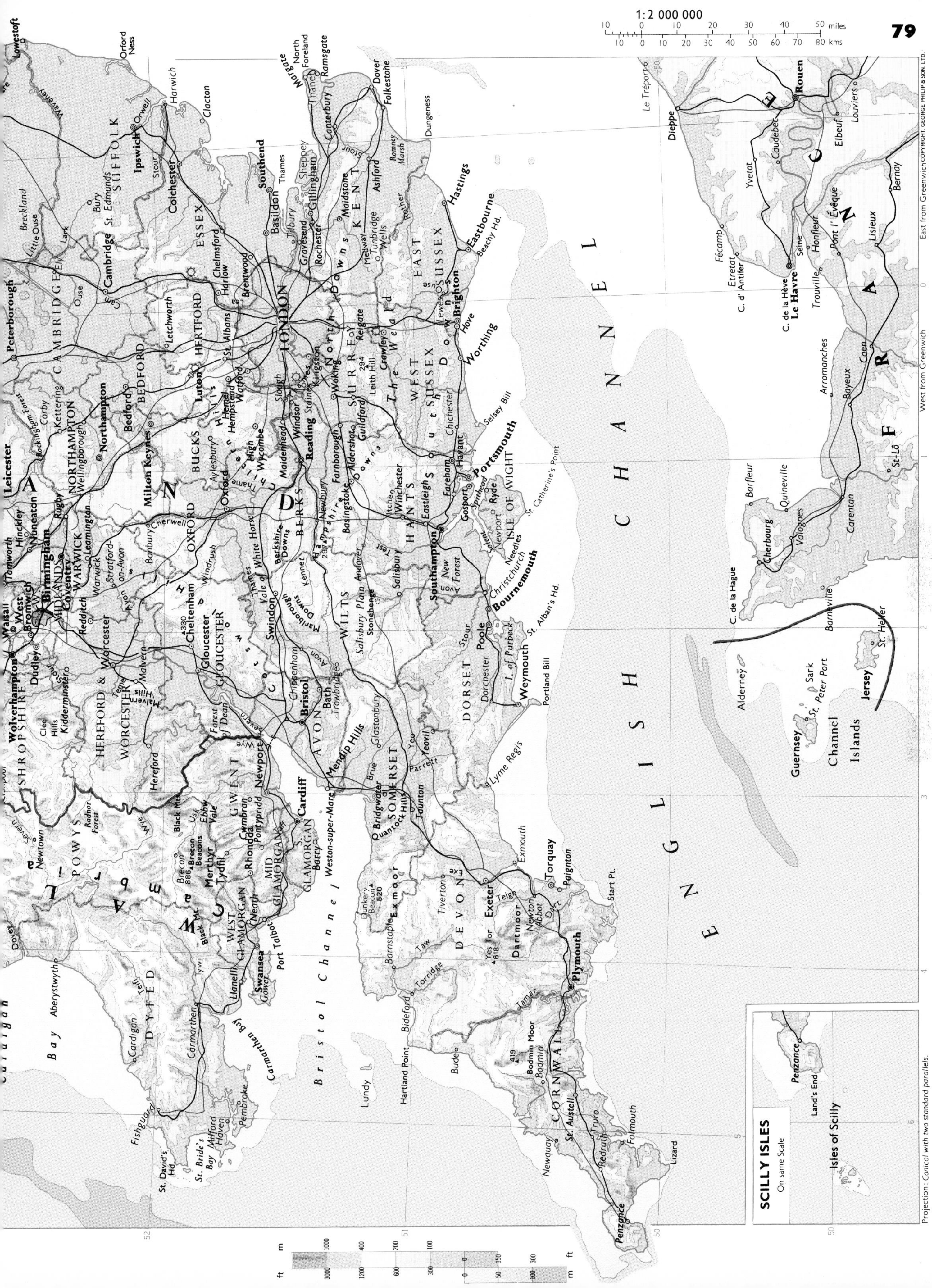
10 0 10 20 30 40 50 miles
10 0 10 20 30 40 50 60 70 80 kms
ENGLISH CHANNEL
ENGLAND
WALES
FRANCE
LONDON
Lowestoft
Orford Ness
Waveney
Harwich
Ipswich
Orwell
SUFFOLK
Clacton
Colchester
Stour
Bury St. Edmunds
Breckland
Little Ouse
Lark
Cambridge
CAMBRIDGE
Peterborough
Ouse
Cam
ESSEX
Chelmsford
Harlow
Brentwood
Southend
Basildon
Tilbury
Thames
Sheppey
Margate
North Foreland
Ramsgate
Thanet
Canterbury
Dover
Folkestone
Dungeness
Romney Marsh
Ashford
Stour
Maidstone
Gillingham
Rochester
Gravesend
KENT
North Downs
Tunbridge Wells
Medway
Rother
Hastings
Eastbourne
Beachy Hd.
EAST SUSSEX
Brighton
Hove
Lewes
Worthing
WEST SUSSEX
South Downs
Chichester
Selsey Bill
The Weald
Crawley
Reigate
Leith Hill
294
SURREY
Guildford
Woking
Kingston
Staines
Aldershot
Farnborough
Letchworth
HERTFORD
St. Albans
Watford
Hemel Hempstead
Luton
Chiltern Hills
BEDFORD
Bedford
Kettering
Corby
Rockingham Forest
NORTHAMPTON
Northampton
Wellingborough
Milton Keynes
BUCKS
Aylesbury
High Wycombe
Slough
Windsor
Maidenhead
Reading
BERKS
Newbury
Berkshire Downs
Vale of White Horse
Oxford
OXFORD
Thame
Cherwell
Banbury
Windrush
Leicester
Nuneaton
Hinckley
Tamworth
Rugby
Coventry
Leamington
WARWICK
Warwick
Stratford-on-Avon
Birmingham
WEST MIDLANDS
West Bromwich
Walsall
Wolverhampton
Dudley
Redditch
Kidderminster
Stour
Worcester
WORCESTER
HEREFORD & WORCESTER
Malvern
Malvern Hills
Teme
Hereford
Clee Hills
SHROPSHIRE
Cheltenham
330
Gloucester
GLOUCESTER
Cotswolds
Forest of Dean
Severn
Wye
Swindon
Marlborough Downs
Kennet
Chippenham
Avon
Bath
Trowbridge
Bristol
AVON
WILTS
Salisbury Plain
Stonehenge
Salisbury
Andover
Test
Basingstoke
Hampshire Downs
HANTS
Winchester
Itchen
Eastleigh
Southampton
New Forest
Fareham
Havant
Portsmouth
Gosport
Spithead
Ryde
Newport
ISLE OF WIGHT
Solent
Needles
St. Catherine's Point
Christchurch
Bournemouth
Poole
St. Alban's Hd.
I. of Purbeck
Weymouth
Portland Bill
Dorchester
DORSET
Stour
Yeovil
Yeo
Parrett
Lyme Regis
Glastonbury
Mendip Hills
Brue
SOMERSET
Bridgwater
Quantock Hills
Taunton
Weston-super-Mare
Bristol Channel
Exmoor
Dunkery Beacon
520
Tiverton
Exe
Exeter
Exmouth
Teign
Torquay
Paignton
Start Pt.
Newton Abbot
Dart
Dartmoor
Yes Tor
618
DEVON
Barnstaple
Taw
Torridge
Bideford
Hartland Point
Lundy
Plymouth
Tamar
Bude
Bodmin Moor
Bodmin
419
CORNWALL
St. Austell
Truro
Falmouth
Redruth
Newquay
Lizard
Penzance
Newport
GWENT
Cardiff
Pontypridd
Cwmbran
Ebbw Vale
Usk
Black Mts.
Brecon
Brecon Beacons
886
Merthyr Tydfil
Rhondda
MID GLAMORGAN
SOUTH GLAMORGAN
Barry
Taff
Neath
WEST GLAMORGAN
Black Mt.
Port Talbot
Swansea
Gower
Llanelli
Tywi
POWYS
Radnor Forest
Newtown
Severn
Wye
Dovey
Aberystwyth
Cardigan Bay
Teifi
Cardigan
DYFED
Carmarthen
Carmarthen Bay
Pembroke
Milford Haven
St. Bride's Bay
St. David's Hd.
Fishguard
Le Tréport
Dieppe
Rouen
Yvetot
Caudebec
Elbeuf
Louviers
Fécamp
Etretat
C. d' Antifer
C. de la Hève
Le Havre
Seine
Honfleur
Trouville
Pont l' Évêque
Lisieux
Bernay
Caen
Bayeux
Arromanches
St-Lô
Carentan
Quineville
Barfleur
Valognes
Cherbourg
C. de la Hague
Barneville
Alderney
Guernsey
St. Peter Port
Sark
Jersey
St. Helier
Channel Islands
SCILLY ISLES
On same Scale
Isles of Scilly
Land's End
Penzance
West from Greenwich
East from Greenwich
ft 3000 1200 600 300 0 50 150 300
m 1000 400 200 100 0 50 100
Projection: Conical with two standard parallels.
COPYRIGHT, GEORGE PHILIP & SON, LTD.

1 : 4 000 000

Projection: Conical with two standard parallels

COPYRIGHT GEORGE PHILIP & SON LTD

1:2 000 000

NORTH SEA

FRISIAN ISLANDS

WADDEN ZEE

NETHERLANDS

Schiermonnikoog
Ostfriesland
Emden
Wiesmoor
Aurich
Yxel

Ameland
Terschelling
Vlieland
Schelling
Dokkum
Leeuwarden
Franeker
Harlingen
Texel
Den Burg
Sneek
Workum
FRIESLAND
Heerenveen
Drachten
Veendam
Winschoten
Groningen
Hoogezand
Leer
Westerstede
Bad Zwischenahn
Oldenburg
Papenburg
Friesoythe

Den Helder
Den Oever
Enkhuizen
Hoorn
Noordoost Polder
Emmeloord
Urk
Steenwijk
Hoogeveen
Meppel
DRENTHE
Assen
Emmen
Coevorden
Meppen
Löningen
NIEDER
SACHSEN
Cloppenburg
Vechta
Quackenbrück
Damme
73

Alkmaar
Castricum
Beverwijk
IJmuiden
Zandvoort
Haarlem
Heemstede
HOLLAND
Edam
Volendam
Marken
Purmerend
Zaandam
AMSTERDAM
Lelystad
FLEVOLAND
Kampen
Zwolle
OVERISSEL
Almelo
Oldenzaal
Hengelo
Enschede
Gronau
Nordhorn
Rheine
Ibbenbüren
Osnabrück
Bersenbrück
Bramsche

Katwijk-aan-Zee
Leiden
Scheveningen
THE HAGUE
Voorburg
Rijswijk
Delft
Hoek van Holland
Europoort
Vlaardingen
Schiedam
ROTTERDAM
Gouda
Oude
Rijn
Alphen
UTRECHT
Zeist
Amersfoort
Soest
Hilversum
Bussum
Huizen
Harderwijk
Nunspeet
107
Apeldoorn
Deventer
Zutphen
Lochem
GELDERLAND
Arnhem
Dieren
Doetinchem
Winterswijk
Ahaus
Coesfeld
Stadtlohn
Borken
Münster
Warendorf
NORD RHEIN
Dülmen
Oelde
Ahlen
Beckum
331

Goeree
Schouwen
Noord Beveland
Zierikzee
Overflakkee
Dordrecht
Sliedrecht
Waalwijk
Oss
's-Hertogenbosch
Veghel
Boxtel
BRABANT
Venraij
Helmond
Kevelaer
Geldern
Weser
Dorsten
Marl
Lippe
Lünen
Gelsenkirchen
Herne
Hamm
Werl
Soest

Walcheren
Middelburg
Flushing
Goes
Bergen-op-Zoom
Roosendaal
Breda
Oosterhout
Tilburg
Eindhoven
Valkenswaard
Maas
Venlo
Moers
Duisburg
Oberhausen
Mülheim
Essen
Bochum
Witten
Iserlohn
Neheim
DORTMUND
Ruhr
Möhne

Knokke
Zeebrugge
Ostend
Nieuwpoort
Bruges
Maldegem
Eeklo
Brasschaat
Schoten
Merksem
ANTWERPEN
Deurne
Antwerp
Hoboken
St. Niklaas
Lokeren
Turnhout
Geel
Herentals
Moll
Maaseik
Weert
Roermond
München-Gladbach
Viersen
Krefeld
Neuss
DÜSSELDORF
Solingen
Remscheid
Wuppertal
Hagen
Lüdenscheid
Plettenberg

Diksmuide
Ostend
Ypres
Roeselare
Ghent
Wetteren
Aalst
FLANDRE
ORIENTALE
Aarschot
Mechelen
Genk
Sittard
Geleen
Heerlen
Jülich
Leverkusen
Opladen
Bergisch Gladbach
COLOGNE
Gummersbach
Olpe
Sauerland
Siegen
WESTFALEN

Menin
Kortrijk
Mouscron
Tourcoing
Roubaix
Lille
Tournai
Oudenaarde
Ronse
Ninove
Jette
Anderlecht
BRUSSELS
Leuven
Halle
Wavre
Tienen
St. Trond
Hasselt
Demer
Maastricht
Tongeren
Aachen
Eschweiler
Stolberg
Düren
Eupen
Verviers
Waldbröl
Siegburg
Bonn
Königswinter
657
Betzdorf

Lens
Orchies
Soignies
HAINAUT
Nivelles
Mons
La Louvière
Binche
Charleroi
Namur
Huy
Liège
Seraing
Spa
Hohe Venn
694
Schleiden
Malmédy
Ahr
Adenau
746
Andernach
Neuwied
Remagen
Westerwald

Arras
PAS-DE-CALAIS
Cambrai
Denain
Valenciennes
Douai
Maubeuge
Hautmont
Avesnes
313
Philippeville
Dinant
Ciney
Marche
Rochefort
Houffalize
652
Clervaux
Prüm
Ernstberg
700
Gerolstein
Daun
Mayen
Cochem
Koblenz
Bad Ems
Diez
RHEINLAND
PFALZ
Bingen
Wiesbaden
Mainz

St.-Quentin
Guise
Hirson
Vervins
Fourmies
Chimay
Revin
Givet
Lesse
St. Hubert
Bastogne
569
Bitburg
Bernkastel
Wittlich
Bad Kreuznach
Nahe
816
Idar-Oberstein
687

SOMME
Ham
Laon
Bohain
Oise
Guise
Charleville-Mézières
Bouillon
Sedan
Neufchâteau
Semois
LUXEMBOURG
Ettelbrück
Sûre
549
Trier
Konz
Saarburg
Hunsrück

Noyon
Chauny
Crépy-en-Valois
Soissons
PICARDIE
OISE
Compiègne
Vesle
Reims
Plaine de
Marne
283
Champagne
Suippes
Aisne
Rethel
Le Chesne
Vouziers
Côtes de Meuse
ARDENNES
Virton
Arlon
Longwy
Villerupt
Longuyon
Luxembourg
Esch
Differdange
Chiers
MEURTHE
ET
Thionville
Dillingen
Merzig
Völklingen
Saarbrücken
Dillingen
SAAR
Sulzbach
Neunkirchen
Homburg
Kaiserslautern
Pirmasens
Landau
Neustadt
St. Wendel
Zweibrücken

MOSELLE
Metz
Montigny
Sarreguemines
St.-Avold
Forbach
Saarlouis
Ingbert

NORTH SEA

GERMANY

FRANCE

BELGIUM

LUXEMBOURG

ft   m
1200 400
600   200
0   0

Projection: Conical with two standard parallels   East from Greenwich   COPYRIGHT GEORGE PHILIP & SON LTD.

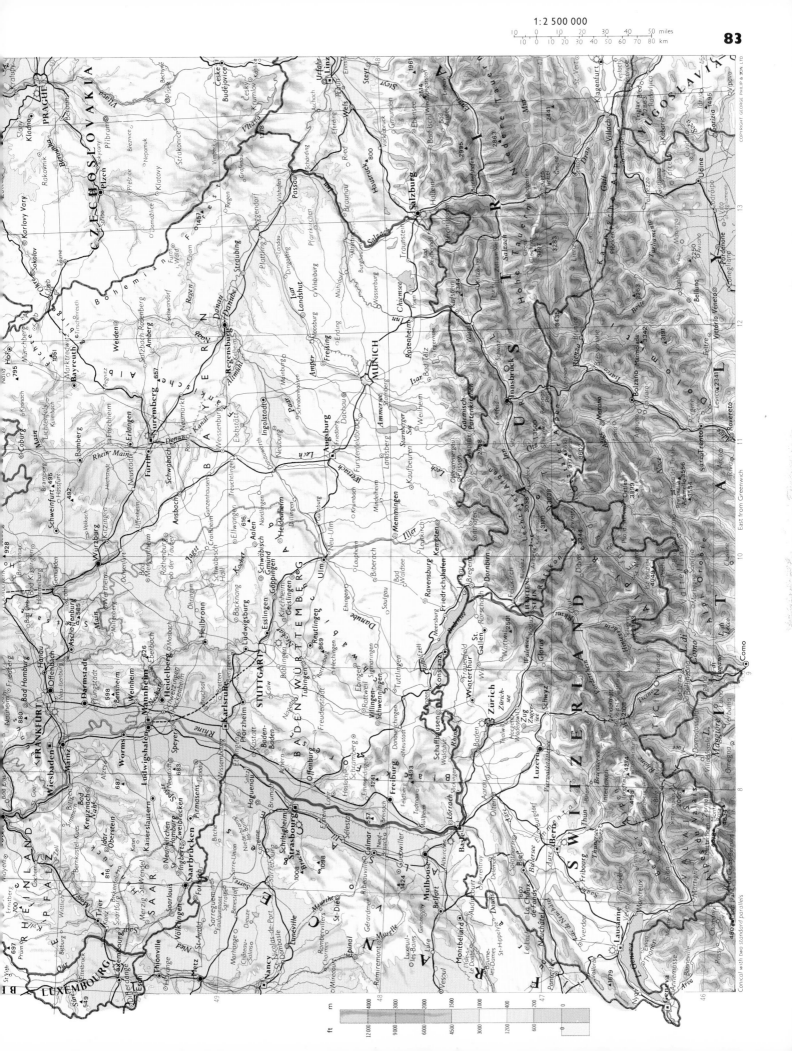

1:5 000 000

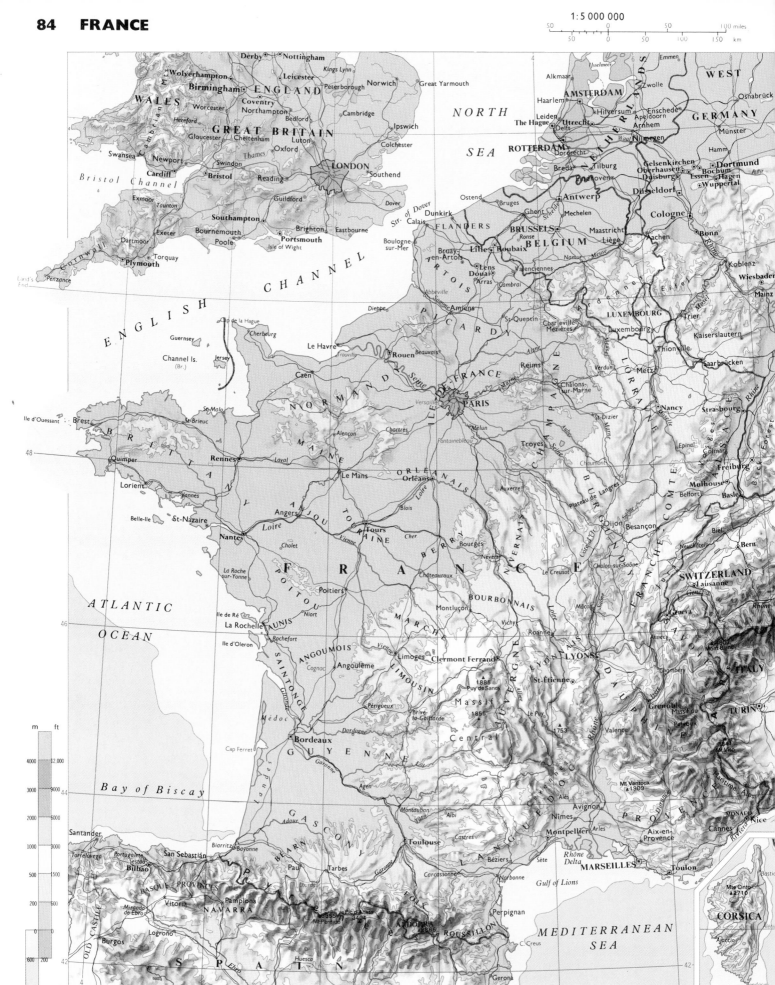

West from Greenwich   East from Greenwich

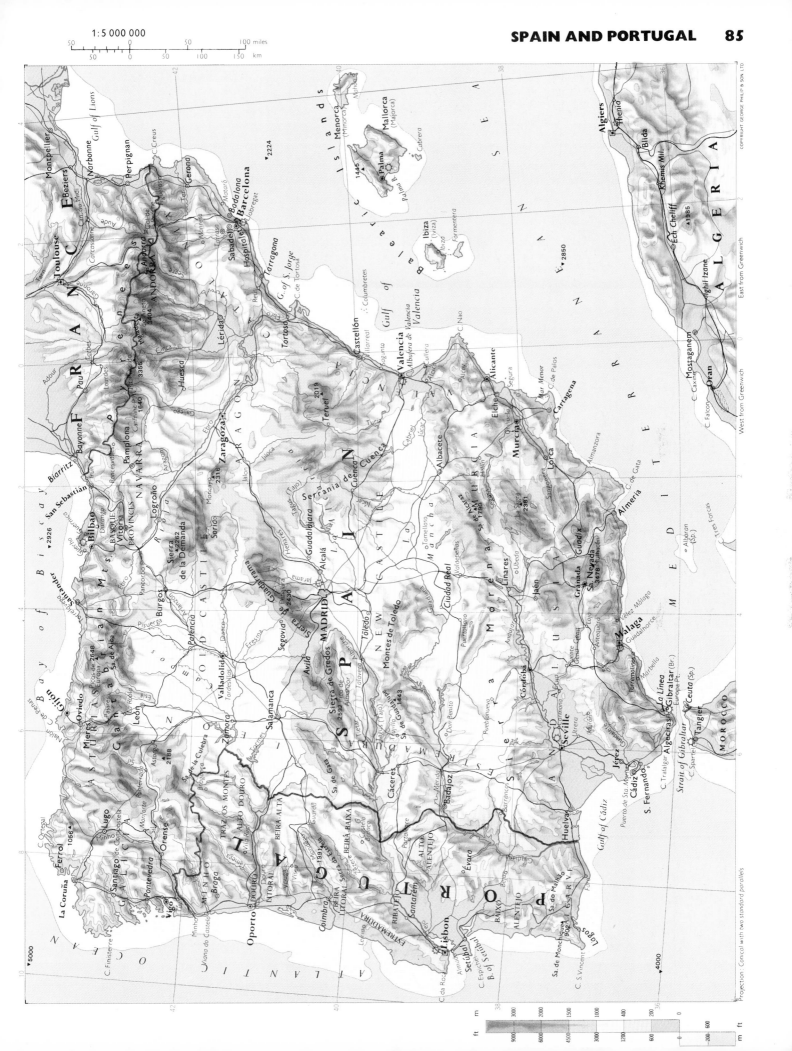

1:5 000 000

COPYRIGHT GEORGE PHILIP & SON, LTD.

East from Greenwich

West from Greenwich

Projection: Conical with two standard parallels

The Hague • Amsterdam
LONDON • Rotterdam • W. • E. BERLIN
Harwich • NETH. • Hanover • Potsdam
Southampton • Ostend • Münster • Brunswick • Magdeburg • Spree
Bristol Chan. • Brighton • Ghent • Antwerp • Essen • Düsseldorf • GERMANY • Halle • Leipzig • Dresde
Exmoor • Bristol • Dover • BELGIUM • Brussels • Aachen • Cologne • Bonn • Wiesbaden • Erfurt • Karl Marx Sta
Dartmoor • Str. of Dover • Lille • Liège • Koblenz • Frankfurt • Erz Geb • Plzen
Land's End • Plymouth • Boulogne • Ardennes • LUX • Mainz • Wurzburg • Nurnberg • Prague
Lizard Pt. • Portsmouth • Amiens • Mannheim • Heidelberg • Bohemian Forest
Scilly Is. • Cherbourg • Somme • St. Quentin • Reims • Metz • Nancy • Karlsruhe • Regensburg
Channel Is. • Dieppe • Nancy • Stuttgart • Augsburg • Linz
Channel Is. • Le Havre • Rouen • Vosges • Strasbourg • Danube • Munich • Salzburg
Ushant • Jersey • Caen • Seine • Troyes • Black Forest • Freiburg • Inn
Pt. de St Mathieu • St. Malo • PARIS • Marne • Freiburg • L. of Constance • Innsbruck • Klagenf
Brest • Versailles • Basle • Zurich
Belle Isle • Rennes • Le Mans • Orleans • Dijon • SWITZERLAND • Bolzano • Udine • Ljubljana
Pt. de Penmarch • Angers • Vienne • Bourges • Bern • Como • Vicenza • Drava
Bay of Biscay • St. Nazaire • Loire • Tours • Chalon • Lausanne • Bergamo • Brescia • Trieste
FRANCE • Poitiers • Geneva • Milan • Verona • Padua • Rijeka
5365 • Limoges • Clermont • Mt. Blanc • Turin • Po • Venice
5098 • La Rochelle • Mt. Dore • Ferrand • St. Étienne • Grenoble • Alessandria • Parma • Modena • Ferrara
C. Ortegal • Bordeaux • Charente • Lyons • Genoa • La Bologna • Forli • Ravenna
La Coruña • Ferrol • Gironde • Dordogne • Cevennes • Riviera • Spezia • Rimini
Santander • Gijón • Oviedo • Picos de Europa 2648 • Lot • Rhône • Ligurian Sea • Florence • San Marino • Ancona
Vigo • Santiago • Bilbao • San Sebastián • Tarn • Nîmes • Avignon • Cannes • Nice • Corse • Elba • Pisa • Leghorn • Arno • Perugia
Orense • León • Vitoria • Pamplona • Toulouse • Montpellier • Marseilles • Toulon • 2710 • Mte. Cinto • ROME
Oporto • Cantabrian Mts • Burgos • Béziers • G. of Lions • Perpignan • Bastia
Braga • Douro • Pyrenees • Pic de Aneto 3404 • Andorra • C. Creus • Corsica • Sabine Mts • Gran Sasso 2914 • Pesca
Sa. da Estrela • Valladolid • Sa. de Gata • Zaragoza • Lérida • Ajaccio • Tiber • Volturno
Coimbra • SPAIN • Sa. de Guadarrama • Barcelona • Caprera • Naples
PORTUGAL • MADRID • Tajo • Tarragona • Str. of Bonifacio • Salerno
Lisbon • Cáceres • Ebro • Castellón • Balearic Is. • Menorca (Minorca) • Sardinia • Mte. del Gennargentu 1834 • 3719 • Capri
Evora • Badajoz • Guadiana • La Mancha • Jucar • Valencia • Palma • Cagliari • Tyrrhenian Sea
Sierra Morena • Albacete • Ibiza • Mallorca (Majorca) • Stromboli
Huelva • Córdoba • Linares • Segura • C. Nao • Cabrera • Lipari Is.
Guadalquivir • Jaén • Murcia • Alicante • Formentera • Palermo
Seville • Granada • Lorca • MEDITERRANEAN • 3340 • Catania • Mess
Tinto • Faro • Genil • Cartagena • Egadi Is. • Sicily
Cádiz • Jerez • Mulhacén 3478 • Almería • Lipari Is.
C. Trafalgar • Málaga • Sa. Nevada • Alboran I. (Sp.) • Palermo • Stromboli
Str. of Gibraltar • Gibraltar (Br.) • C. de Gata • Algiers • Bejaia • Skikda • Annaba • Bizert • C. Bon • Pantelleria (It.)
Tangier • Ceuta (Sp.) • Algeciras • Melilla (Sp.) • Mostaganem • Carthage • Tunis • Gozo • Valletta
Rabat • Oran • Ech Cheliff • Constantine • Kairouan • G. of Hammamet • MALTA
Meknès • Fès • Oujda • Sidi-Bel-Abbès • Sousse • Lampedusa (It.)
Tlemcen • Plateaux • Chott el Hodna • Tébessa • Sfax
MOROCCO • Hauts • Atlas • Djelfa • Biskra • Kerkennah
Great Atlas • Chott ech Chergui • Saharan • Chott Melrhir • Djerba
3737 • W. Djedi • Gabès
ALGERIA • Touggourt • Chott Djerid • Djerba
Béchar • Ghardaïa • Ouargla • Tripoli
Hassi Messaoud • Misratah
Ft. Lallemand • Gebel Nefusa
TUNISIA • Tripolitania

ft • m
12 000 • 4000
6000 • 2000
3000 • 1000
1200 • 400
600 • 200
0 • 0
200 • 600
1000 • 3000
2000 • 6000
3000 • 9000
m • ft

87

------ Division between Greeks and Turks
in Cyprus; Turks to the North.

COPYRIGHT. GEORGE PHILIP & SON. LTD.

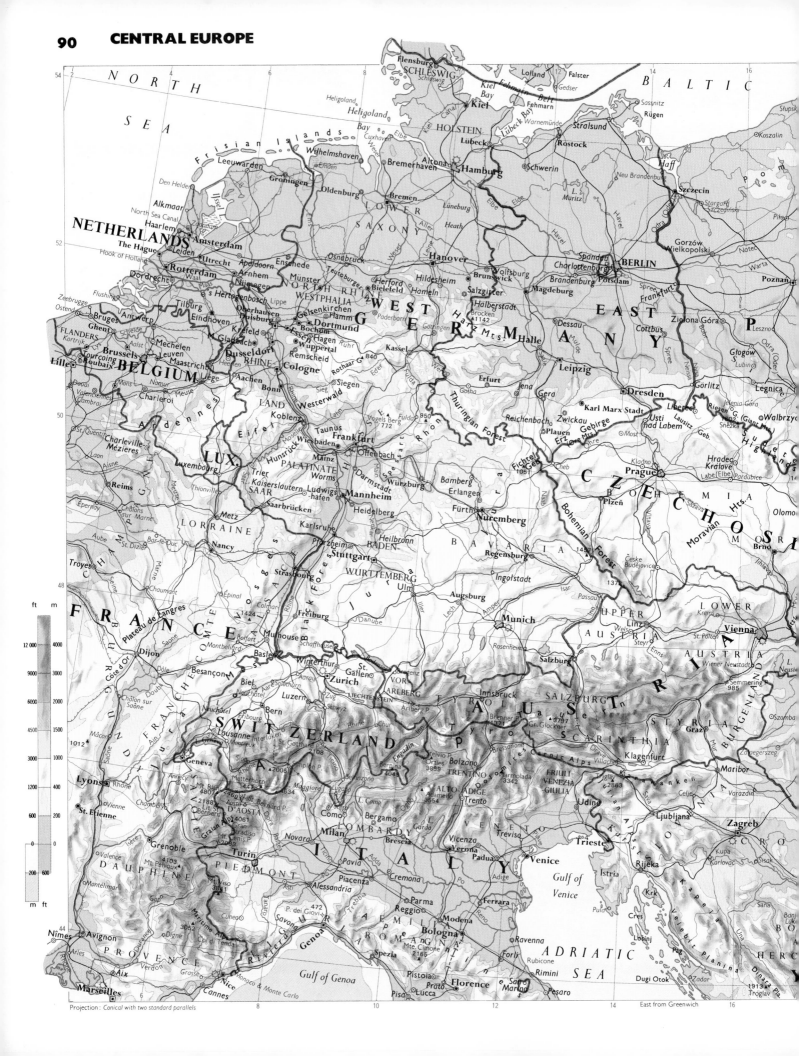

NORTH SEA

BALTIC

Flensburg
SCHLESWIG
Schleswig
Kiel Bay
Kiel
Heligoland
Heligoland Bay
Cuxhaven
HOLSTEIN
Lübeck Bay
Fehmarn
Lolland
Falster
Gedser
Rügen
Sassnitz
Stralsund
Rostock
Warnemünde
Schwerin
Neu Brandenburg
Koszalin
Słupsk
Haff

Den Helder
Frisian Islands
Leeuwarden
Wilhelmshaven
Emden
Bremerhaven
Hamburg
Altona
Lüneburg
Elbe
Lübeck
Heath
Havel
Müritz
Stettin
Szczecin
Stargard
Szczeciński
Piła

NETHERLANDS
Alkmaar
Haarlem
North Sea Canal
Amsterdam
Leiden
The Hague
Hook of Holland
Zeebrugge
Flushing
Ostend
Bruges
Ghent

Groningen
Oldenburg
Bremen
LOWER SAXONY
Aller
Hanover
Brunswick
Wolfsburg
Salzgitter
Magdeburg
Brandenburg
Potsdam
BERLIN
Charlottenburg
Spandau
Frankfurt
Oder
Gorzów
Wielkopolski
Noteć
Warta
Poznań

Utrecht
Apeldoorn
Enschede
Osnabrück
Herford
Bielefeld
Hildesheim
Hameln
Halberstadt
Dessau
Cottbus
Zielona Góra
Legnica

Rotterdam
Dordrecht
Arnhem
Nijmegen
's Hertogenbosch
Münster
NORTH RHINE WESTPHALIA
Lippe
Paderborn
Harz Mts.
Brocken 1142
Halle
Leipzig
Görlitz
Głogów
Lubin

Antwerp
Tilburg
Eindhoven
Oberhausen
Duisburg
Gelsenkirchen
Hamm
Dortmund
Kassel
Göttingen
Erfurt
Jena
Gera
Dresden
EAST GERMANY
Jelenia Góra
Riesen G. (Giant Mts.)
Śnieżka
Sudeten Highlands
Wałbrzych

BELGIUM
Brussels
Leuven
Maastricht
Liège
Aachen
Krefeld
Gladbach
Düsseldorf
Essen
Bochum
Wuppertal
Remscheid
Cologne
Bonn
Siegen
Rothaar G. 840
WEST GERMANY
Thuringian Forest
Gotha
Reichenbach
Zwickau
Plauen
Erz Gebirge
Karl Marx Stadt
Usti nad Labem
Liberec
BOHEMIA

Lille
Tourcoing
Roubaix
FLANDERS
Kortrijk
Mons
Charleroi
Namur
Meuse
Ardennes
Eifel
Westerwald
LAND
RHINE
Koblenz
Lahn
Fulda
Vogels Berg 772
Rhön 950
Cheb
Kladno
Most
Fichtel Geb. 1051
Prague
Hradec Králové
CZECHOSLOVAKIA

St. Quentin
Charleville-Mézières
Laon
Aisne
LUX.
Luxembourg
Trier
Hunsrück
Mosel
Taunus
Wiesbaden
Frankfurt
Offenbach
Mainz
PALATINATE
Worms
Darmstadt
Würzburg
Bamberg
Erlangen
Fürth
Nuremberg
Regensburg
Plzeň
České Budějovice
Moravian
Brno

Reims
Épernay
Châlons sur Marne
Aube
Bar-le-Duc
St. Dizier
Chaumont
Troyes
CHAMPAGNE
Marne
Seine
Metz
LORRAINE
Nancy
Thionville
Saarbrücken
Kaiserslautern
SAAR
Ludwigs-hafen
Mannheim
Heidelberg
Karlsruhe
Heilbronn
BADEN-WÜRTTEMBERG
Stuttgart
Pforzheim
Ulm
Ingolstadt
BAVARIA
Passau
UPPER AUSTRIA
Linz
Krems
LOWER AUSTRIA
Vienna

FRANCE
Plateau de Langres
Dijon
Côte d'Or
FRANCHE-COMTÉ
Belfort
Montbéliard
Mulhouse
Colmar
Freiburg
Black Forest
Strasbourg
Rhine
Danube
Augsburg
Lech
Munich
Rosenheim
Salzburg
Welm
Steyr
Enns
St. Pölten
Wiener Neustadt
Semmering 985
Szombathely

Saône
Mâcon
Chalon sur Saône
Doubs
Besançon
Dôle
JURA
Neuchâtel
Bienne
Solothurn
Aarau
Basle
Schaffhausen
Winterthur
Zürich
St. Gallen
Bregenz
VORARLBERG
Innsbruck
TYROL
Brenner 1371
SALZBURG
STYRIA
Graz
BURGENLAND
Neusi

Lyons
Rhône
St. Vienne
Chambéry
Annecy
Geneva
Lausanne
Montreux
Bern
Fribourg
Luzern
Zug
Schwyz
SWITZERLAND
Chur
Rhine
Arlberg P.
Arlberg
St. Gotthard P. 2108
Splügen P.
Engadin
Bernina 4049
Stelvio P.
Ortles 3899
Bolzano
Bressanone
Dolomites
Gr. Glockner 3797
CARINTHIA
Klagenfurt
Villach
Carnic Alps
Maribor
Varazdin

St. Étienne
Grenoble
Mt. Blanc 4807
Matterhorn 4418
Monte Rosa 4634
Muggiore
Lugano
L. Como
Bellinzona
Como
Bergamo
FRIULI-VENEZIA GIULIA
Udine
Triglav 2863
Ljubljana
Zagreb
CROATIA

DAUPHINÉ
Valence
Mt. Pelvoux 4103
GRAIAN ALPS
Lit. St. Bernard P. 2188
Gr. St. Bernard P. 2473
D'AOSTA 4061
Cenis P. 2083
Novara
Milan
LOMBARDY
Pavia
Brescia
Cremona
VENETO
Vicenza
Verona
Padua
Treviso
Venice
Gulf of Venice
Istria
Rijeka
Kupa
Karlovac
Sisak
Krk
Cres
Lošinj

Montélimar
Gap
Mt. Viso 3841
P. dei Giovi 472
PIEDMONT
Turin
Asti
Alessandria
Piacenza
Parma
Reggio
Modena
Ferrara
Bologna
Ravenna
Rubicone
Forlì
Rimini
Pesaro
ADRIATIC SEA
Pag
Zadar
Troglav 1913 DINARIC

Nîmes
Avignon
Arles
Aix
Digne
Grasse
PROVENCE
RIVIERA
Maritime Alps
Col di Tenda
3052
Cuneo
Savona
Genoa
Gulf of Genoa
Spezia
Mte. Cimone 2165
Pistoia
Prato
Lucca
Pisa
Florence
San Marino
Sana
HERC.

Marseilles
Nice
Monaco & Monte Carlo
Cannes
RIVIERA

ft   m
12 000   4000
9000   3000
6000   2000
4500   1500
3000   1000
1200   400
600   200
0   0
200   600
m   ft

1:5 000 000

50   0   50   100 miles
50   0   50   100   150 km

CENTRAL
EUROPE
POLITICAL
1:25 000 000

DENMARK
Copenhagen
Amsterdam
Hamburg
NETH.
Berlin
WEST   EAST
BELGIUM   GERMANY
LUX.   Bonn
Brussels
Prague
POLAND
Warsaw
U.S.S.R.
Kiev
Lvov
CZECHOSLOVAKIA
FRANCE
Bern   Vienna
SWITZ.   AUSTRIA   Budapest
Liechtenstein   HUNGARY
Monaco   Trieste
ITALY   San Marino
ROMANIA
Bucharest
Belgrade
YUGOSLAVIA
Rome
BULGARIA
Sofia

SEA
Gdańsk Bay
Sopot
Gdynia
Gdańsk ▲329
Elbląg
Tczew
Kaliningrad
Pregel
Chernyakhovsk
LITHUANIA S.S.R.
Vilnius
Lyna
Suwałki
▲309
Neman
Grodno
WHITE
RUSSIA
S.S.R.
Olsztyn
Masurian Lakes Plateau
Grudziądz
Łomża
Ostrołęka
Białystok
Volkovysk
Slonim
Szczara
dgoszcz
Notec
Toruń
Ciechanów
Wkra
Narew
Bug
Inowrocław
Włocławek
Gniezno
Wisła (Vistula)
Płock
Warsaw
Siedlce
Biała Podlaska
Brest
Pripyat
316 ▲
Pripyat Marshes
Uzh
Desna
P   O   L   A   N   D
Kalisz
Łódź
Pabianice
Sieradz
Tomaszów Mazowiecki
Pilica
Radom
Lublin
Chełm
Zamość
Vladimir Volynski
Lutsk
Rovno
Kovel
Styr
Słuch
Korosten
Ostrów elkopolski
Piotrków
cław
Opole
Częstochowa
Kielce ▲612
Ostrowiec Świętokrzyski
Stalowa Wola
Tarnobrzeg
390
San
Rzeszów
Lvov
Zolochev
Ternopol
Shepetovka
Zhitomir
Berdichev
Starokonstantinov
Kazatin
Kiev
Belaya Tserkov
Fastov
Zabrze   Bytom
Gliwice   Sosnowiec
Chorzów
Tychy   Katowice
Kraków
Wisła (Vistula)
Tarnov
Przemyśl
i ▲471
a
Dnestr
Khmelnitskiy
384
Zhmerinka
U   K   R   A   I   N   E
S   S   R
Vinnitsa
Uman
Ostrava
Opava
Frýdek Místek
▲1725
Nowy Sącz
Krosno
Dukla P.
602
Drogobych
Ivano-Frankovsk
Kamenets Podolski
U.   S.   S.   R.
Bug
Pervomalsk
Jablunka Pass
550   West Beskids
High Tatra
▲2655
4780
E   a   s   t   B   e   s   k   i   d   s
Prešov
1881 ▲
931
R   u   t   h   e   n   i   a
Khotin
Chernovtsy
Beltsy
Kotovsk
Gottwaldov
Žilina
Low Tatra
Banská Bystrica
Košice
Uzhgorod
Mukachevo
2061 ▲
of the Tartars
M   o   l   d   a   v   i   a
S.S.R.
lite Mts.
S   L   O   V   A   K   I   A
Slovakian Ore Mts.
Prut
Botoşani
Dnestr
Nitra
Nitra
Hernad
Bodva
M   o   u   n   t   a   i   n   s
429 ▲
Kishinev
Tiraspol
islava
Miskolc
Sajó
Eger
Nyíregyháza
Satu Mare
Baia Mare
Pietrosul
2305 ▲
Suceava
Iaşi
Bendery
Odessa
Györ
Tatabánya
Forest
Hron
Szolnok
Debrecen
Zalău
Someş
2102 ▲
Bistriţa
Pietrosu
Piatra Neamţ
Bacău
Vaslui
Belgorod Dnestrovski
Újpest
BUDAPEST
Cegléd
Oradea
Cluj
Tîrgu Mureş
Miercurea Ciuc
Siret
Odessa
Székesfehérvár
Kecskemét
Körös
Crişu
Black
1848 ▲
Mt. Bihor
T   r   a   n   s   y   l   v   a   n   i   a
Sfântu Gheorghe
Focşani
Galaţi
Izmail
kony   H   U   N   G   A   R   Y
szprém
Balaton
Hódmezővásárhely
White Crişu
Mureş
Alba-Iulia
Deva
Sibiu
Braşov
2535 ▲
Mt. Negoiu
Buzău
Buzău
Braila
467 ▲
Tulcea
Kaposvár
Szekszárd
Szeged
Arad
R   O   M   A   N   I   A
Hunedoara
Transylvanian Alps
Red Tower 350
2607 ▲ Mt. Omul
Ploeşti
Danube
Dobrogea
BLACK
Pécs
Subotica
Senta
Kikinda
Timişoara
B   a   n   a   t
▲ Peleaga
2509
2518 ▲ Păringul Mare
Rimnicu Vîlcea
Tîrgovişte
Slobozia
Ialomiţa
SEA
Drava
Sombor
Novi Sad
Zrenjanin
Resiţa
Porta Orientalis
Tîrgu-Jiu
Jiu
W   a   l   l
Piteşti
Argeş
Bucharest
Dîmboviţa
Călăraşi
Constanţa
Osijek
Sremska Mitrovica
Bela Crkva
Iron Gate
Turnu-Severin
Arges
Ruse
Trajans Wall
44
A
Sava
Belgrade
Smederevo
Craiova
Statina
Vedea
Giurgiu
Danube
Talbukhin
OVINA
Tuzla
▲1346
Sarajevo
Y   U   G   O   S   L   A   V   I   A
Morava
Kragujevac
Timok
Danube
Alexandria
B   U   L   G   A   R   I   A

ICELAND

At the same scale as main map

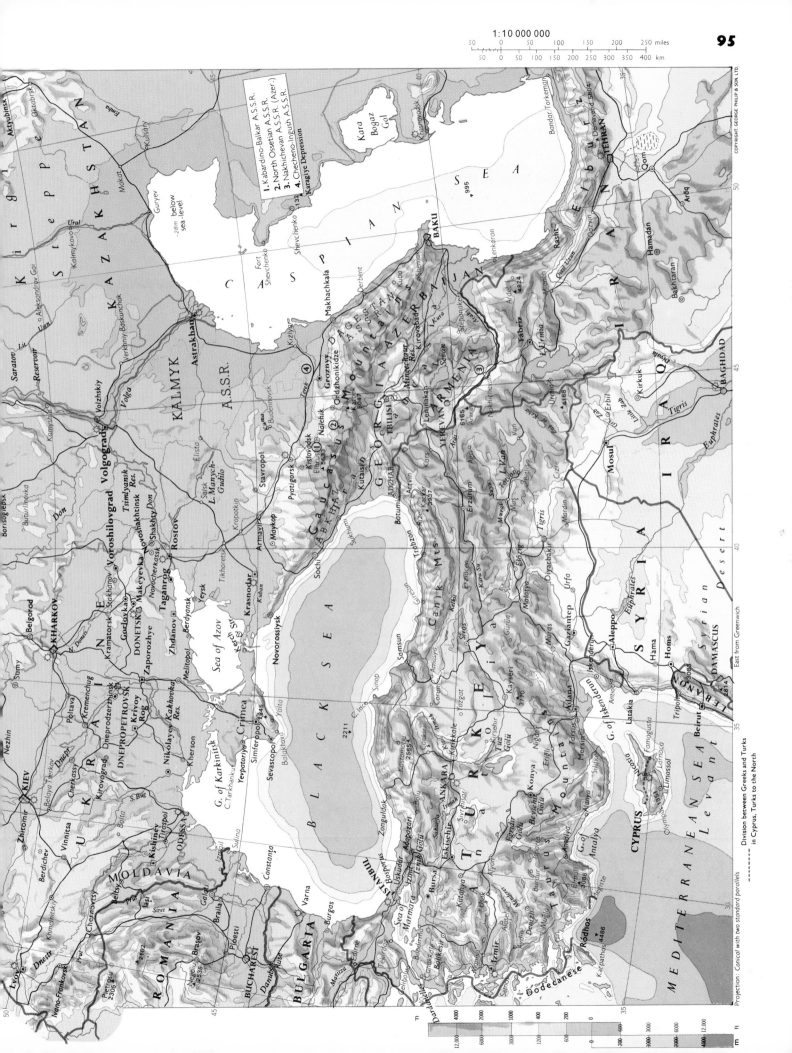

1:10 000 000

50   0   50   100   150   200   250 miles
50   0   50   100   150   200   250   300   350   400 km

1. Kabardino-Balkar A.S.S.R.
2. North Ossetian A.S.S.R.
3. Nakhichevan A.S.S.R. (Azer.)
4. Checheno-Ingush A.S.S.R.
Karagiye Depression

CASPIAN SEA

Kara Bogaz Gol

−28m below sea level

K I R G I Z   S T E P P E

K A Z A K H S T A N

KALMYK A.S.S.R.

Astrakhan

Volgograd

Voroshilovgrad

Rostov

DONETSK

Taganrog

Sea of Azov

Krasnodar

Novorossiysk

B L A C K   S E A

Crimea

Sevastopol

U K R A I N E

KHARKOV

KIEV

MOLDAVIA

ROMANIA

BUCHAREST

BULGARIA

Varna

Burgas

Istanbul

Sea of Marmara

Ankara

T U R K E Y

C Y P R U S

M E D I T E R R A N E A N   S E A

DAGESTAN A.S.S.R.

C a u c a s u s   M o u n t a i n s

Elbrus 5633

G E O R G I A

ABKHAZ

ADZHAR

Sochi

Batumi

Trabzon

Samsun

Canik Mts.

AZERBAIJAN

Baku

Derbent

ARMENIA

YEREVAN

TBILISI

Sevan

L. Van

Erzurum

S Y R I A

Aleppo

LEBANON

DAMASCUS

Beirut

I R A Q

BAGHDAD

Mosul

Kirkuk

Tigris

Euphrates

Syrian Desert

I R A N

TEHRAN

Qom

Tabriz

L. Urmia

Hamadan

Elburz

Demavend 5604

Levant

East from Greenwich

Projection: Conical with two standard parallels

Division between Greeks and Turks
in Cyprus, Turks to the North

COPYRIGHT. GEORGE PHILIP & SON LTD.

m   ft
12,000   12,000
6000   6000
3000   3000
1200   4000
600   2000
400   1000
200   600
0   200
0

R.S.F.S.R.
1. Daghestan A.S.S.R.
2. Kabardino–Balkar A.S.S.R.
3. Mari A.S.S.R.
4. Mordovian A.S.S.R.
5. North Ossetian A.S.S.R.
6. Tatar A.S.S.R.
7. Udmurt A.S.S.R.
8. Chuvash A.S.S.R.
9. Checheno–Ingush A.S.S.R.
AZERBAIJAN
10. Nakhichevan A.S.S.R.
GEORGIA
11. Abkhaz A.S.S.R.
12. Adzhar A.S.S.R.

Projection: Conical Orthomorphic with two standard parallels

East from Greenwich

1:20 000 000

100   0   100   200   300   400   500 miles

100   0   200   400   600   800 km

C. Dezhneva

OCEAN

Komsomolets I.

965 ▲ October Revolution I.

Severnaya
Zemlya

Bolshevik I.

Boris Vilkitski Str.

Chukchi
Sea

St. Lawrence I.
(U.S.A.)

De Long Is.

New Siberian Is.   East Siberian Sea   Wrangel I.

Faddeyev I.   New Siberia

Medvezhi Is.

Gulf of Anadyr

Komandorskiye
Is.

Bering
Sea

3800

Koryak Range   2562

Katelny Is.   Lyakhov Is.   Bolshoi

374   Dimitri Laptev Str.

Laptev
Sea   1853   1752

1146

Byrrang Mts.   Begichev I.

T a i m y r   L. Taimyr

Upper Taimyr Pena.   Nordvik

Pyasina

Volochanka   Kheta   Khatanga   Olenek   Tiksi

Kolyma Ra.   Petchina G.

Gizhiga

Omolon   Gizhiga G.

Shelekhov Gulf

Mt. Klyuchevskaya 4750

Kamchatka Pena.

Petropavlovsk-
Kamchatskiy

Norilsk

Kheta   Anabar   Buluna   Yana   Pobeda 3147   Srednekolymsk

Saskylakh   Olenek

1701   Yessey   Kolyma   Okhotsk

Olenek   Zhigansk   Lena

962   Arctic Circle   Omyakon 2959   Sea of Okhotsk

Cherskiy Range   1780

Vilyuy   Ust-Maya   Aldan Ra.

Verkhoyansk   2389   Dzhugdzhur Ra.

Vilyuysk   Yakutsk   Ayan

Vilyuy   Ust Maya

Lensk (Mukhtuya)   Olekminsk   2246   Shantar Is.   Sakhalin Str.

1104   Bodaibo   2482   Nikolayevsk   1609

Vitim   Stanovoy Ra.   Sikhote Alin Ra.   Sakhalin

Kirensk   2599   Komsomolsk

Ust-Kut   Skovorodino   Khabarovsk   7290

Bratsk   Chita   Blagoveshchensk   Birobidzhan

Krasnoyarsk   2078

Eastern Sayan   1620   2840   Sretensk   Hokkaido   Sapporo

Zima   Nerchinsk   Manchuria   Sikhote   Hakodate

Cheremkhovo   Ulan Ude   Borzya   Vladivostok   3669

Irkutsk   Manzhouli   Qiqihar   Ussuriysk   JAPAN

Munku Sardyk 3491   Kyakhta   Hulun Nur   Harbin   Sea of JAPAN

Kyzyl   Petrovsk   Khilok   Mudanjiang   Honshū

Hentiyn Nuruu   Choybalsan   Changchun   Niigata

Ulys Nuur   2800   Inner Mongolia   Manchuria   Kanazawa

Hyargas Nuur   Ulaanbaatar   1949   Fushin   North

4362   Shenyang   Anshan   Wŏnsan

MONGOLIA   Pyongyang   Seoul   South

4925   Gaxan Nur   Baotou   Dalian   Pusan

Hami   Beijing

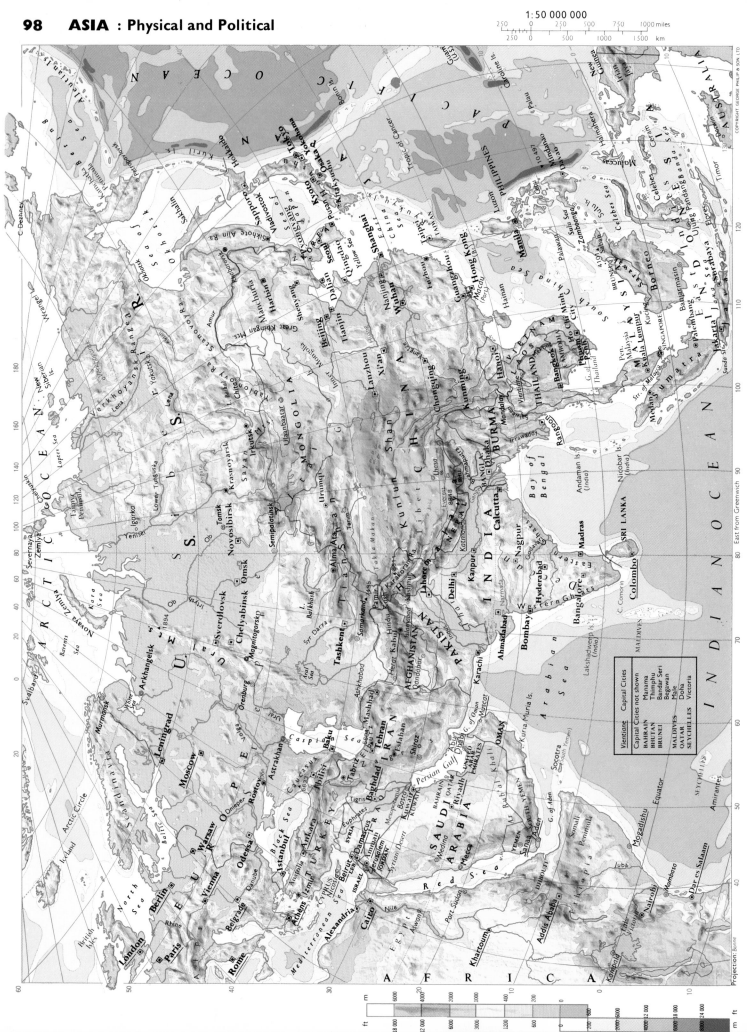

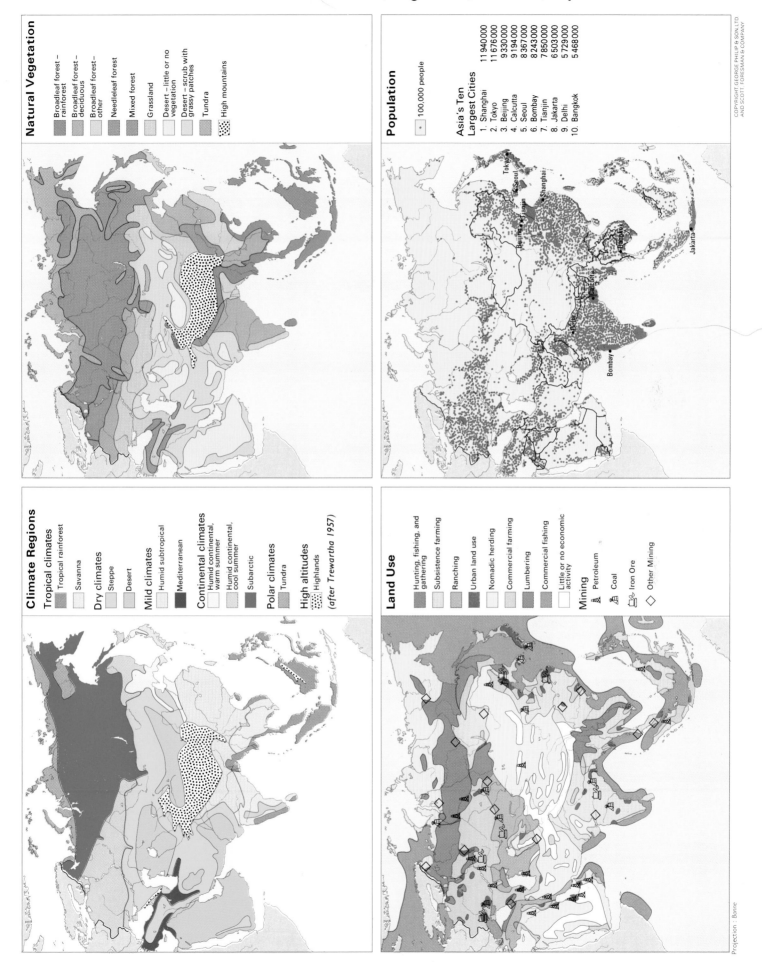

1:110 000 000

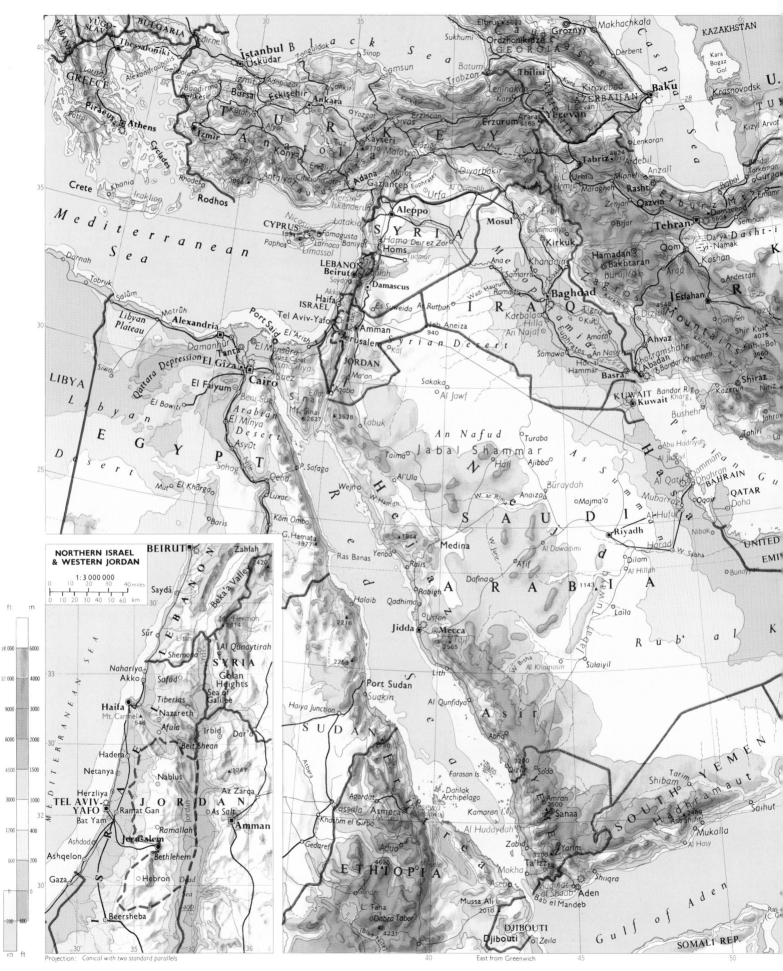

NORTHERN ISRAEL & WESTERN JORDAN

1 : 3 000 000

0 10 20 30 40 miles
0 10 20 30 40 50 60 km

Projection: Conical with two standard parallels

East from Greenwich

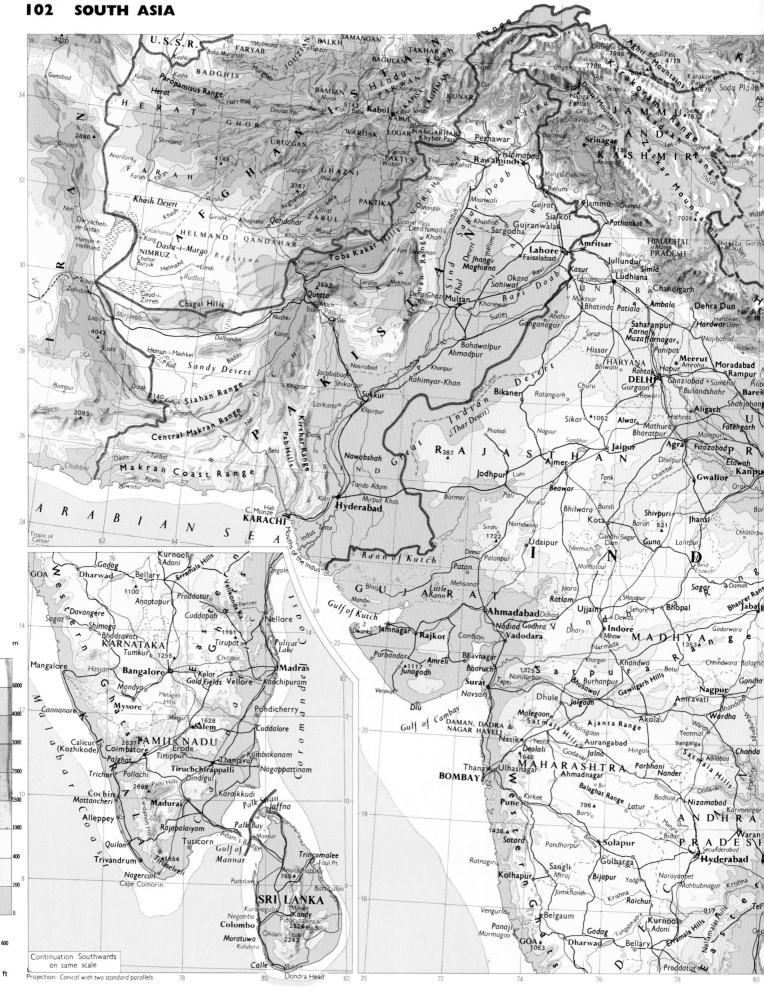

U.S.S.R.

FARYAB • Maimana
BADGHIS
• Kushka
• Konsan
3020 ▲
• Gunabad
• Bala Murghab
SAMANGAN
BALKH
JOUZJAN
• Mazar
• Sabzwar
• Murghab
TAKHAR
Hari Rod
BAGHLAN
HINDU KUSH
Disteghil Sar 7885 ▲
Aghil Mountains 4779
Karakoram Pass
Soda Plains
Rakaposhi 7788 ▲
Gilgit
Skardu
Saser 7672 ▲
Indus

HERAT
• Herat
• Obeh
• Daulat Yar
GHOR
BAMIAN
Koh-i-Baba 5143
PARWAN
Charikar
KAPISA
KUNAR
Chitral
Dir
Dargai
Nanga Parbat
Deosai Mountains
JAMMU
LADAKH
KASHMIR
Leh
Shyok

• Birjand
2886 ▲
URUZGAN
• Uruzgan
4148
AFGHANISTAN
WARDAK
LOGAR
NANGARHAR
Jalalabad
Khyber Pass
Peshawar
Islamabad
Rawalpindi
Srinagar 1135
Baramula
Mangla Dam
7026 ▲
HIMACHAL PRADESH
Simla

FARAH
• Farah
GHAZNI
Ghazni
3787
PAKTYA
Gardez
Wazo
Bannu
Kohat
Thal
WEST FRONTIER
Mianwali
Jhelum
Jammu
Chamba
Pathankot
Shipki-La

Khash Desert
4148
ZABUL
Qalat
PAKTIKA
Manzai
Fort Sandeman
Dera Ismail Khan
Khushab
Sargodha
Gujrat
Sialkot
Gujranwala
Amritsar
Lahore
Jullundur
Ludhiana
Chandigarh
Ambala
Dehra Dun

NIMRUZ
Chahar Burjak
Dasht-i-Margo
Registan
Khugiani
Qandahar
QANDAHAR
HELMAND
Khojak Pass
Loralai
Dera Ghazi Khan
Multan
Khanewal
Sahiwal
Ferozepore
Kasur
Faisalabad
Jhang Maghiana
Okara
Muktsar
Bhatinda
Patiala
Karnal
Saharanpur
Hardwar
Hardwar Dam
Nanda C. 78

2093 ▲
Central Makran Range
Siahan Range
Quetta
3593
Bolan Pass
Sibi
Kalat
Nushki
Khuzdar
Jacobabad
Nasirabad
Shikarpur
Sukkur
Khairpur
Larkana
Rahimyar-Khan
Khanpur
Bahawalpur
Ahmadpur
Sutlej
Abohar
Ganganagar
Sirsa
Hissar
Bikaner
Ratangarh
Churu
HARYANA
Bhiwani
Rohtak
Hapur
Amroha
Moradabad
Rampur

Makran Coast Range
Pasni
Gwadar
Pab Hills
Kirthar Range
Dadu
Bela
Nawabshah
SIND
Tando Adam
Mirpur Khas
Barmer
Nagaur
Sikar 1052
Alwar
Jaipur
Mathura
Bharatpur
Agra
Firozabad
Etawah
Kanpur

ARABIAN SEA
C. Monze
KARACHI
Hab
Kotri
Hyderabad
Mouths of the Indus
Rann of Kutch
Deesa
Palanpur
R 387
Udaipur
Jodhpur
Luni
Pali
Ajmer
Beawar
Bhilwara
Bundi
Kota
RAJASTHAN
Sirohi 1722
Nathdwara
Gandhi Sagar Dam
Guna
Shivpuri
Baran 521
Jhansi
Lalitpur
Chhatarpur

Tropic of Cancer
Totta
Indus
Bhuj
Little Rann
Mandvi
Patan
Mehsana
GUJARAT
Great Indian Desert (Thar Desert)
Phalodi
Ratlam
Jaora
Shajapur
Dewas
Ujjain
Sagar
Damoh
Bina
Etawah
Bhanrer Range

Gulf of Kutch
Dwarka
Jamnagar
Rajkot
Nadiad
Godhra
Dohad
Dhar
Indore
Mhow
Bhopal
MADHYA
Gadarwara

Porbandar
Amreli
Bhavnagar
Bharuch
Cambay
Vadodara
1117
Junagadh
1325
Khargon
Khandwa
Narmada
1353
Betul
Chhindwara
Balaghat
Gondia

Veraval
Diu
Surat
Navsari
Tapti
Nandurbar
Bhusawal
Burhanpur
Gawilgarh Hills
Nagpur
Amravati
Wardha

Gulf of Cambay
DAMAN, DADRA & NAGAR HAVELI
Dhule
Jalgaon
Malegaon
Satmala Hills
Ajanta Range
Akola
Yeotmal
Penganga
Chanda

BOMBAY
Thana
Ulhasnagar
Nasik
Deolali 1646
Aurangabad
Jalna
Hingoli
Parbhani
Nander
Satmala Hills
Adilabad

Kirkee
Pune
Ahmadnagar
Balaghat Range
Latur
Bodhan
Nizamabad
Karimnagar

796 ▲
Barsi
1438
Satara
Bhima
Solapur
Pandharpur
Bidar
MAHARASHTRA
Gulbarga
Secunderabad
Waran
HYDERABAD
ANDHRA PRADESH

Ratnagiri
Sangli
Miraj
Bijapur
Yadgir
Narayanpet
Mahbubnagar
Krishna

Vengurla
Panaji
Marmagoa
GOA 1053
Kolhapur
Jamkhandi
Belgaum
Raichur
917
Kurnool
Adoni
Gadag
Dharwar
Bellary
Tungabhadra
Eramala Hills
Nallamalai Hills

Lower-left inset map:

GOA
Gadag
Kurnool
Adoni
Dharwad
Bellary
Eramala Hills
Ongole
1100
Anantapur
Proddatur
Penner
Nellore
Davangere
Shimoga
Bhadravati
Cuddapah
Pulicat Lake
Mangalore
Hassan
KARNATAKA
Tumkur 1255
Tirupat 1151
Chittoor
Bangalore
Kolar Gold Fields
Vellore
Kanchipuram
MADRAS
Mandya
Melagiri Hills
Mysore
Pondicherry

Cannanore
Salem 1628
Cuddalore
Calicut (Kozhikode)
TAMIL NADU
Coimbatore 2637
Erode
Tiruppur
Mettur
Thanjavur
Kumbakonam
Nagappattinam
Palghat
Tiruchchirappalli
Dindigul
Trichur
Pollachi
Palni Hills 2698
Karaikkudi
Cochin
Mattancheri
Madurai
KERALA
Alleppey
Cardamom Hills
Rajapalaiyam
Jaffna
Palk Strait
Quilon
Tirunelveli 1654
Tuticorin
Palk Bay
Mannar
Adam's Bridge
Gulf of Mannar
Trincomalee
Foul Pt.
Trivandrum
Nagercoil
Cape Comorin
Anuradhapura 766 ▲
Puttalam
Batticaloa

SRI LANKA
Kurunegala
Negombo
Kandy
Pidurutalagala 2524
Colombo
Moratuwa
Badulla
Adam's Peak 2243
Kalutara
Galle
Matara
Dondra Head

Continuation Southwards on same scale

Projection: Conical with two standard parallels

ft   m
18 000   6000
12 000   4000
9000   3000
6000   2000
4500   1500
3000   1000
1200   400
600   200
0   0
200   600
m   ft

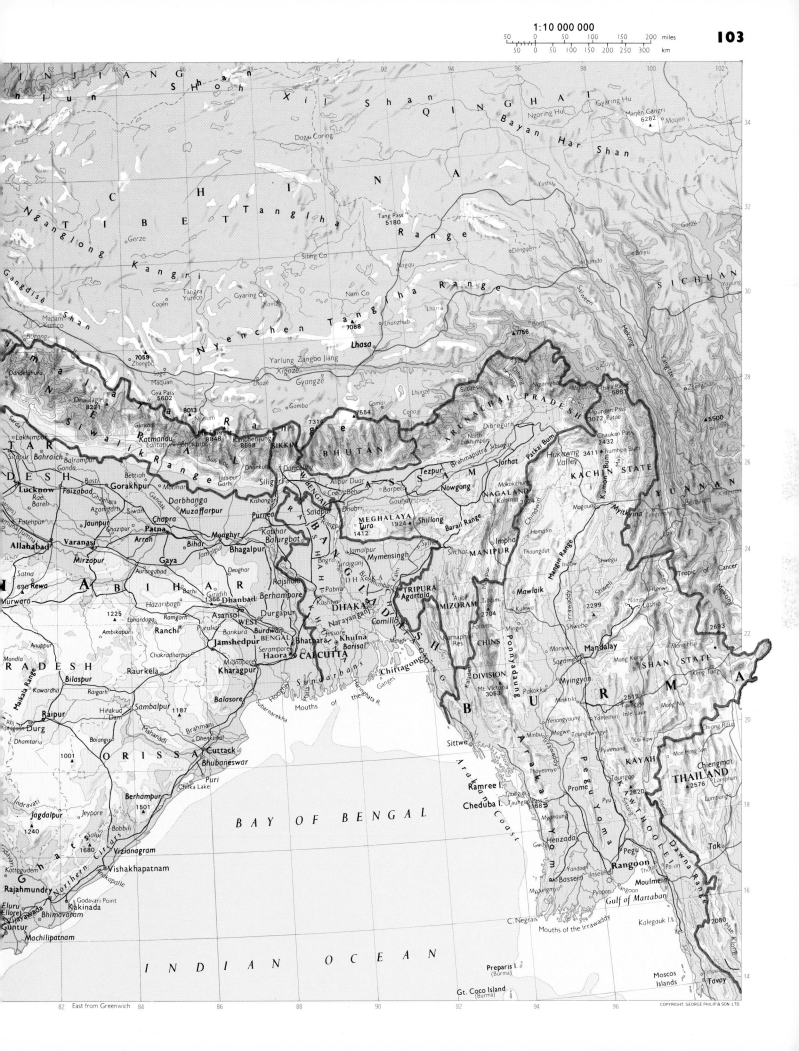

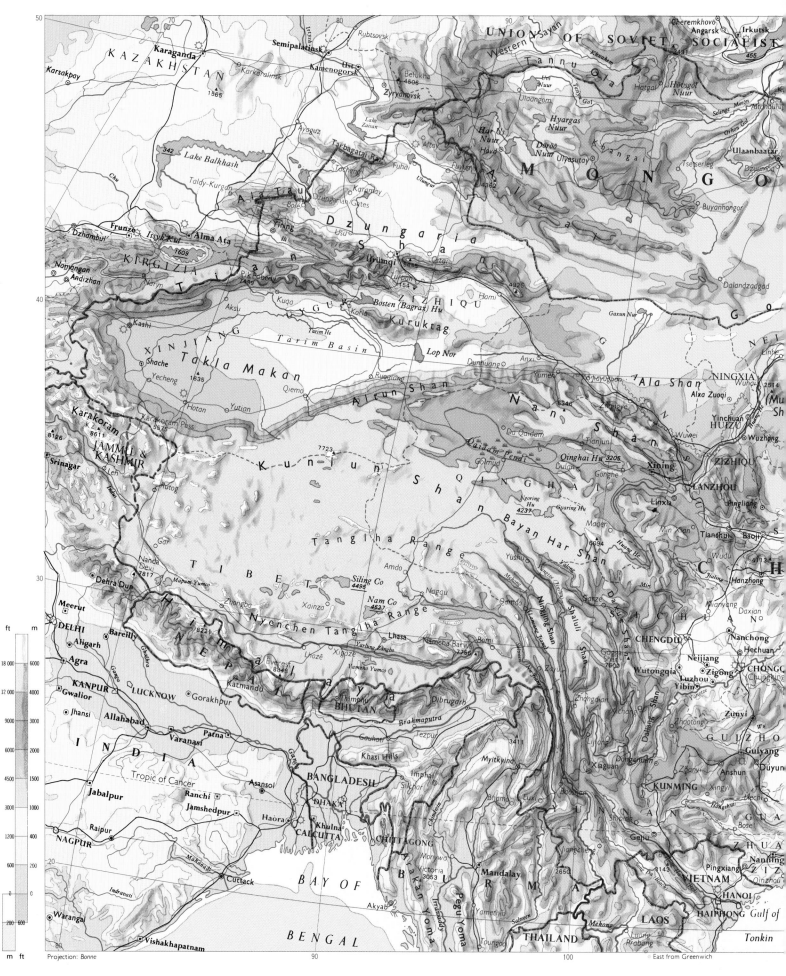

1:15 000 000

100   0   100   200   300   400 miles
100   0   100   200   300   400   500   600 km

REPUBLICS ⊙Chita
Ulan Ude
Lake Baykal
Yablonovyy Range
Nerchinsk
Borzya
Manzhouli
Hulun Nur
Choybalsan
Kerulen
Buir Nur
Saynshand
Dzamin Uud
Erenhot
Abagnar Qi
1949
INNER MONGOLIA
Hohhot
Baotou
Datong
Ordos (Js mo)
GREAT WALL
Jining
Zhangjiakou
Xuanhua
TAIYUAN
Yangquan
Yuci
Fenyang
Tongchuan
Sanmenxia
anyang
XI'AN
Changzhi
Pingdingshan
Nanyang
HUBE
Wanxian Yichang
Shashi
Changde
Yiyang
HUNAN
Xiangtan
Shaoyang
Hengyang
Guilin
GXI
Wuzhou
GZU
thai
Maoming
Zhanjiang
zhou
Hainan
Haikou

C. Terpeniya
Sakhalin
Komsomolsk
Poronaysk
Svobodny
Blagoveshchensk
Aihui
Yuzhno-Sakhalinsk
HEILONGJIANG
Orogen/Zizhiqi
Little Khingan Mts
Birobidzhan
Khabarovsk
Great Khingan Mts
Butha Qi
Nenjiang
Bei'an
Yichun
Hegang
Bikin
Qiqihar
Anda
Suihua
Jiamusi
Shuangyashan
La Perouse Str.
Wakkanai
Horqin Youyi Qianqi
HARBIN
Mudanjiang
Jixi
Mishan
Lake Khanka
Asahigawa
Hokkaido
SAPPORO
Kushiro
Tao'an
Manchuria
Ussuriysk
Otaru
C. Erimo
Hakodate
JILIN
CHANGCHUN
Jilin
Vladivostok
Nakhodka
Tsugaru Strait
Aomori
Hachinohe
Morioka
Shuangliao
Tongliao
Liaoyuan
Yanji
Chongjin
SEA OF
Akita
Siping
Songhua Lake
Chifeng
Fuxin
FUSHUN
Tonghua
NORTH
Hungnam
JAPAN
Sado
Sendai
Chaoyang
Liaoyang
SHENYANG
Benxi
Yalu
Wŏnsan
Niigata
Kōriyama
Jinzhou
ANSHAN
KOREA
Chengde
Jinzhou
Yingkou
Dandong
PYONGYANG
Kaesong
SEOUL
Kanazawa
Toyama
Utsunomiya
TOKYO
Qinhuangdao
G. of Liaodong
Liaodong
Korea Bay
Haeju
INCHON
SOUTH
KAWASAKI
YOKOHAMA
BEIJING (Peking)
Tangshan
DALIAN (Lüda)
NAGOYA
Fuji 3776
Yokosuka
Baoding
TIANJIN (Tientsin)
G. of Chihli (Bo Hai)
Yantai
Weihai
Taejon
TAEGU
OKYO
Shizuoka
Hamamatsu
Cangzhou
HEBE
Shijiazhuang
Ye Xian
Weifang
YELLOW
KOBE
OSAKA
Sakai
Wakayama
Handan
Dezhou
JINAN
Zibo
SEA
Taejon
PUSAN
Okayama
Hiroshima
Kochi
Matsuyama
Xinxiang
Tai'an
Jining
QINGDAO
Kwangju
Masan
1915
Shimonoseki
Shikoku
Luoyang
Kaifeng
HANDONG
Lianyungang
Cheju Do
KITAKYUSHU
FUKUOKA
Sasebo
Kumamoto
ZHENGZHOU
HENAN
Shangqiu
Xuzhou
Qingjiang
1950
Nagasaki
Kyushu
JAPAN
Shangshui
ANGSU
NANJING (Nanking)
Bengbu
Huainan
Kagoshima
Zhenjiang
Changzhou
Wuxi
Suzhou
Tanega
Hefei
ANHUI
Wuhu
SHANGHAI
WUHAN
Tongling
Huangshi
Hangzhou
Hangzhou Wan
Ningbo
EAST CHINA
Amami-ō-Shima
ZHEJIANG
Shaoxing
Jingdezhen
Jinhua
SEA
Nanchang
Shangrao
Wenzhou
JIANGXI
Wuyi Shan 2120
Ryukyu Islands
Changsha
Zhuzhou
Jian
Nanping
Okinawa
Fuzhou
Naha
FUJIAN
Sanming
PACIFIC
Ganzhou
Shaoguan
Zhangzhou
Xiamen (Amoy)
Quanzhou
Chilung
Sakishima Gunto
Tropic of Cancer
GUANGDONG
Mei Xian
Chao'an
Chiai
Yu Shan 3997
TAIPEI
Taichung
OCEAN
GUANGZHOU (Canton)
Shantou
Tainan
TAIWAN
Foshan
KAOHSIUNG
Jiangmen
HONG KONG (Br.)
Macau (Port.)
Batan Is.
SOUTH CHINA
SEA
Hainan Str.
Babuyan Is.

COPYRIGHT GEORGE PHILIP & SON LTD

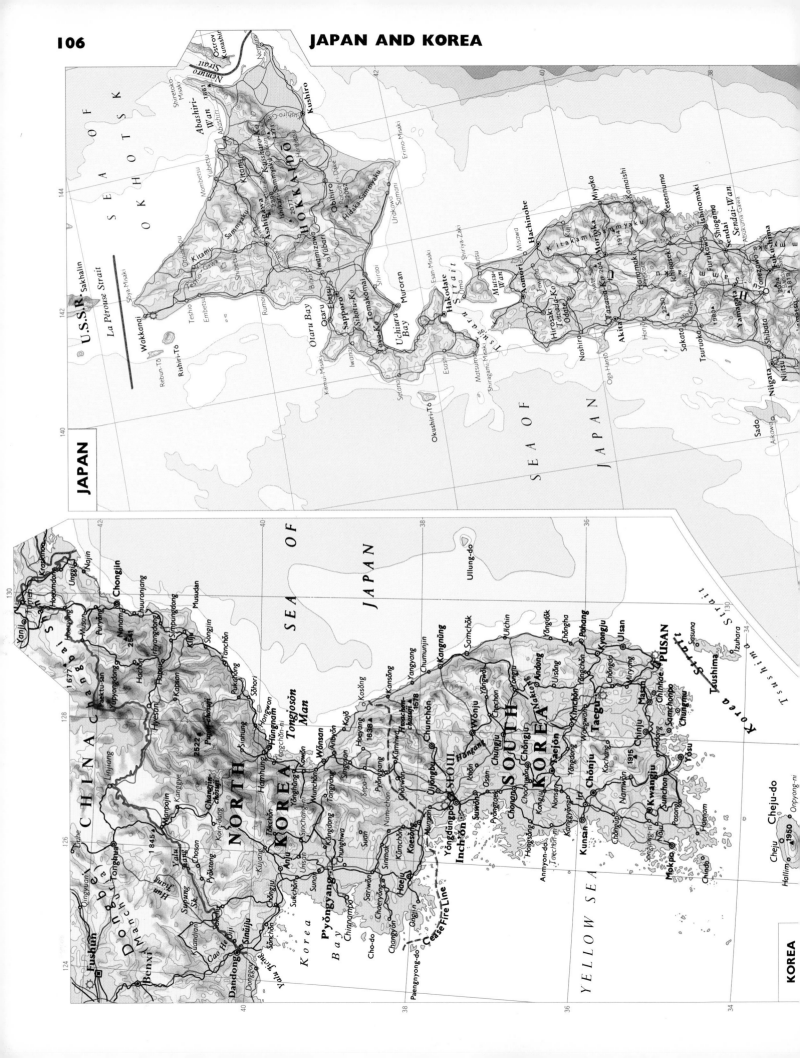

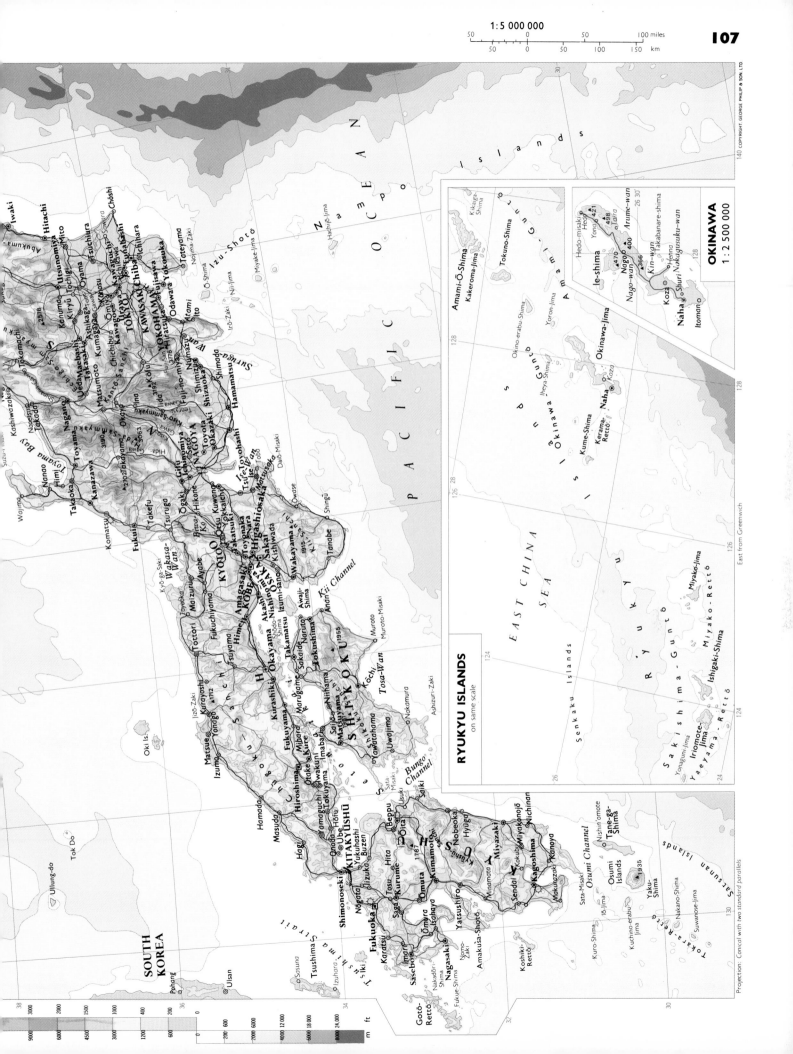

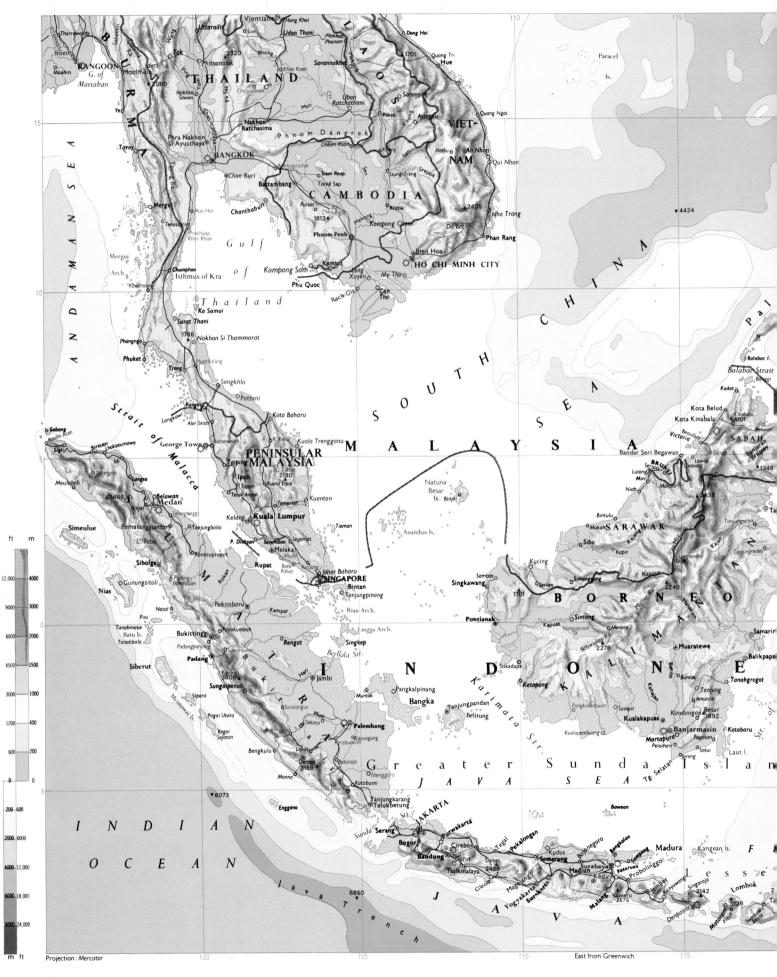

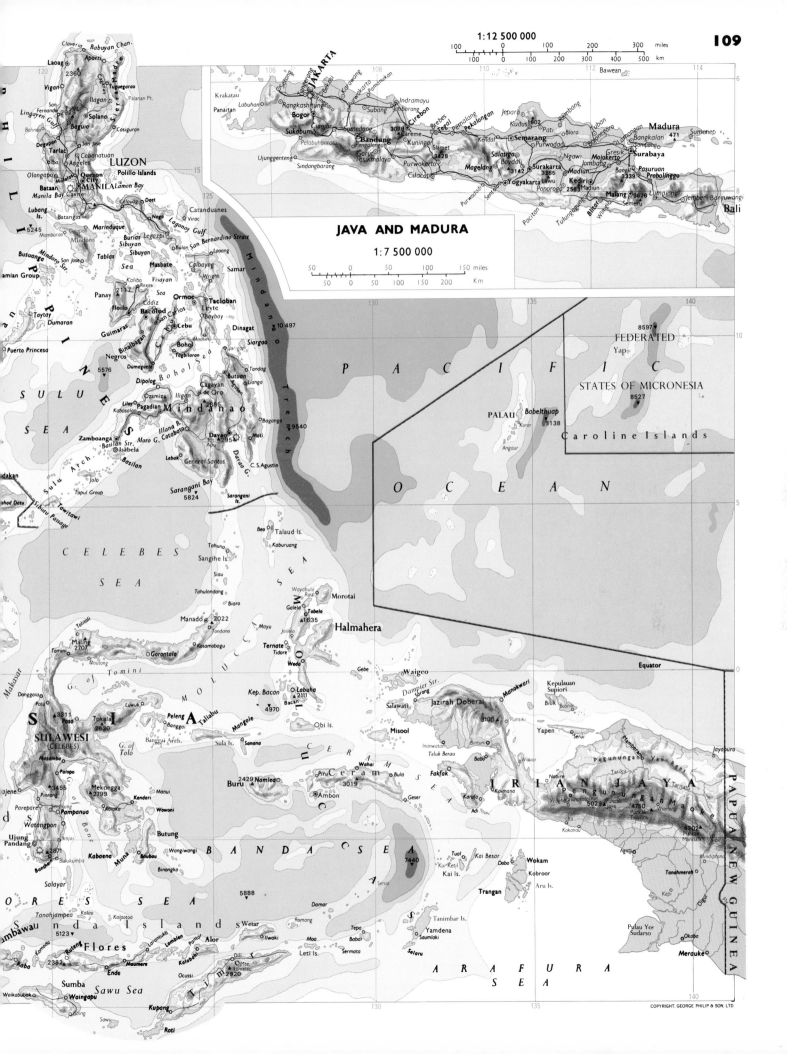

JAVA AND MADURA

1 : 7 500 000

1:12 500 000

1 : 4 000 000

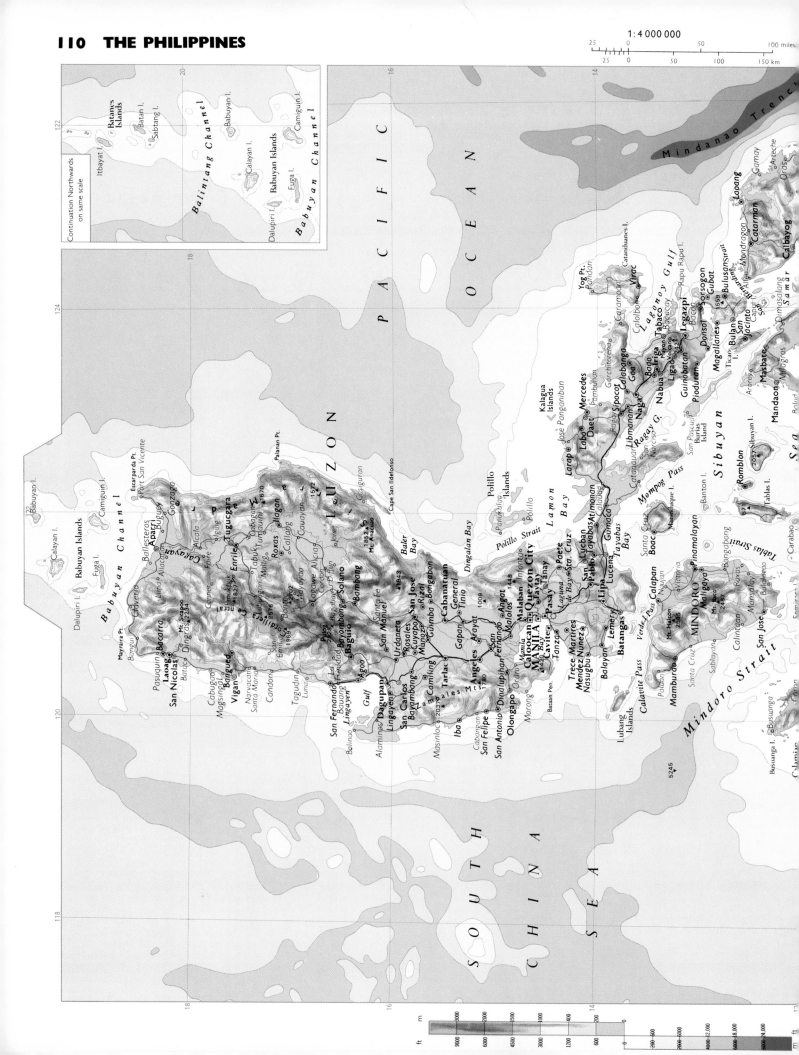

Continuation Northwards
on same scale

Batanes Islands
Itbayat I.
Batan I.
Sabtang I.
Balintang Channel
Babuyan I.
Calayan I.
Babuyan Islands
Dalupiri I.
Fuga I.
Camiguin I.
Babuyan Channel

P A C I F I C   O C E A N

Mindanao Trench

Babuyan I.
Camiguin I.
Babuyan Channel
Babuyan Islands
Calayan I.
Fuga I.
Dalupiri I.
Mayraira Pt.

Escarpada Pt.
Port San Vicente
Gonzaga
Aparri
Buguey
Ballesteros
Cagayan
Claveria
Bangui
Bacarra
Laoag
San Nicolas
Batac
Mt. Sicapoo
Dingras 2334
Bonoan
Vigan
Bongued
Magsingal
Cabugao
Narvacan
Santa Maria
Candon
Togudin
Luna
San Fernando
Bauang
Agoo
Lingayen
Dagupan
Gulf
San Carlos
Bayambong
Lingayen
Iba
San Felipe
Masinloc 2037
Cabangan
San Antonio
Olongapo
Morong
Bolinao Pt.
Alaminos
Bataan Pen.

Pasuquin

Alilem
Abra
Bangued
Tuao
Tabuk
Solana
Tuguegarao
Ilagan
Cabagan
Roxas
Callang
Cauayan
Jones
Bambang
Solano
Bayombong
San Jose
San Manuel
Urdaneta
Rosales
Cuyapo
Munoz
San Carlos
Tarlac
Camiling
Zambales Mts.
Gapan
San Fernando
Angeles
Cabanatuan
General Tinio
Gumba
Bongabon
Arayat
Malolos
Malaban
Caloocan
Cavite
MANILA
Quezon City
Pasay
Tanza
Trece Martires
Mendez Nunez
Nasugbu
Balayan
Batangas
Lemery
Calaca

Baler Bay

Dingalan Bay

Baguio
Trinidad
La Trinidad
Pulog 2929
Cordillera Central
Bontoc
Lubuagan
Banaue
Cervantes
Cervantes 2576
Mt. Data

1572
Mt. Anacuao
1852
1670

Cagayan
Cape San Ildefonso
Casiguran
Palanan Pt.

L U Z O N

Polillo
Polillo Islands
Panukulan
Polillo Strait

Infanta
Paete
Tanay
Laguna de Bay
San Pablo
Sta. Cruz
Lipa
Lucena
Tayabas
Tayabas Bay
Lucban
Gumaca
Atimonan
Guinayangan

Lamon Bay

Calauag
Mompog Pass
Catanauan
Santa Cruz
Boac
Marinduque I.
Calapan
Nauyan
Pinamalayan
Victoria
Pola
MINDORO
Mt. Halcon 2585
Calintaan
Roxas
Bulalacao
Mamburao
Sablayan
Mansalay
San Jose

Verde Pass
Calavite Pass
Lubang Islands

Mindoro Strait

San Jose
Mindoro Strait

Yog Pt.
Pondon
Daet
Mercedes
Labo
Larap
Jose Panganiban
Kalagua Islands

Pambuhan
Colasi
Garchitorena
Cajamoan
Calolbok
Libmanan
Sipocot
Naga
Goa
Nabua
Iriga
Bato
Ligao
Guinobatan
Legazpi
Donsol
Daraga
Mayon Volcano 2421
Tabaco
Bacacay
Bulan
Gubat
Sorsogon
Magallanes
Bulusanstrait
Matnog
San Jacinto
Ticao I.
Burias Island
San Pascual
Masbate
Mandaon
Aroroy
Balud
Mobo
Cataingan

Ragay Gulf
Ragay
Caramoan

S I B U Y A N   S e a

Catanduanes I.
Virac

Lagonoy Gulf

Rapu Rapu
San Miguel

Pio Duran

Romblon
2057 Sibuyan I.
Banton I.
Tablas I.
Carabao
Tablas Strait

Looc
Bongabong
Pinamalayan

Laoang
Catarman
Mondragon
Allen
Calbayog
Catbalogan
S a m a r
Dimasalang
Gamay
Oras
Arteche
Dolores

Busuanga I.
Coron

S I B U Y A N   S e a

S O U T H   C H I N A   S E A

25   0   50   100 miles
25   0   50   100   150 km

m
ft
9000 6000 4500 3000 1500 1000 600 400 200 0
200-600 600-2000 2000-6000 6000-12,000 12,000-18,000 18,000-24,000

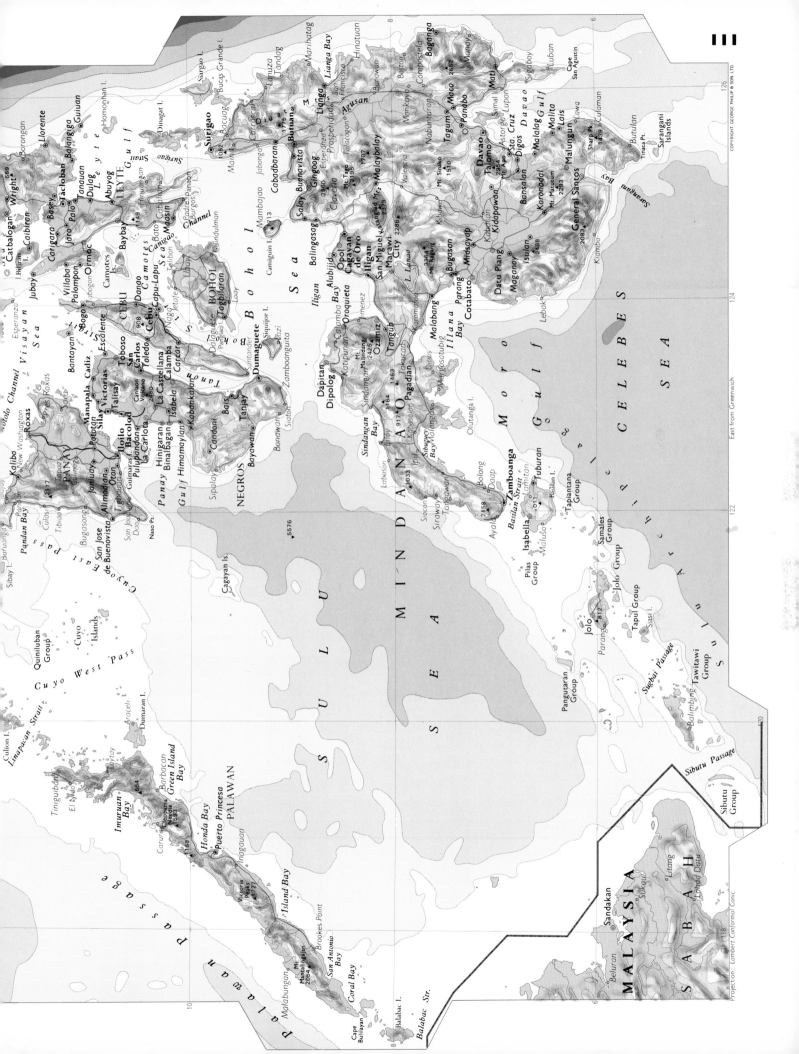

Map labels (Philippines — Mindanao region):

Llorente
Borongan
Catbalogan
Wright
Basey
J. Biliran
Caibiran
Carigara
Tacloban
Tanauan
Dulag
Abuyog
LEYTE
Baybay
Sea
Juban
Villaba
Palompon
Ormoc
Camotes Is.
Danao
Capu-Lapu
CEBU
Cebu
Toledo
Calamba
Cortdor
BOHOL
Tagbilaran
Siquijor I.
Dumaguete
NEGROS
Bacolod
La Carlota
Iloilo
Roxas
PANAY
Kalibo
New Washington

Surigao
Bucas Grande I.
Dinagat I.
Homonhon I.
Sargao I.
Lanuza
Tandag
Marihatag
Lianga Bay
Lianga
Bislig
Hinatuan
Lingig
Cape
San Agustin
Mati
Manay
Baganga
Caraga
Compostela
Monkayo
Davao Gulf
Davao
Digos
Sta. Cruz
Malita
Lais
Malungon
General Santos
Sarangani Islands
Sarangani Bay

Butuan
Cabadbaran
Buenavista
Gingoog
Balingasag
Cagayan de Oro
Opol
Iligan
San Miguel
Marawi City
L. Lanao
Malaybalay
Bugasan
Kidapawan
Midsayap
Cotabato
Datu Piang
Maganoy
Pagadian
Tangub
Ozamiz
Dipolog
Dapitan

MINDANAO

Zamboanga
Basilan
Isabela
Malúso
Jolo
Tapul Group
Siasi
Siasi I.
Balimbing
Tawitawi Group
Bongao
Sibutu Passage
Sibutu Group

SULU SEA

Cuyo West Pass
Cuyo Islands
Quiniluban Group
Cagayan Is.

PALAWAN
Puerto Princesa
Honda Bay
Brookes Point
San Antonio
Coral Bay
Balabac I.
Balabac Str.
Cape Buliluyan

Palawan Passage

CELEBES SEA

Sandakan
MALAYSIA
SABAH
Lahad Datu

COPYRIGHT GEORGE PHILIP & SON LTD

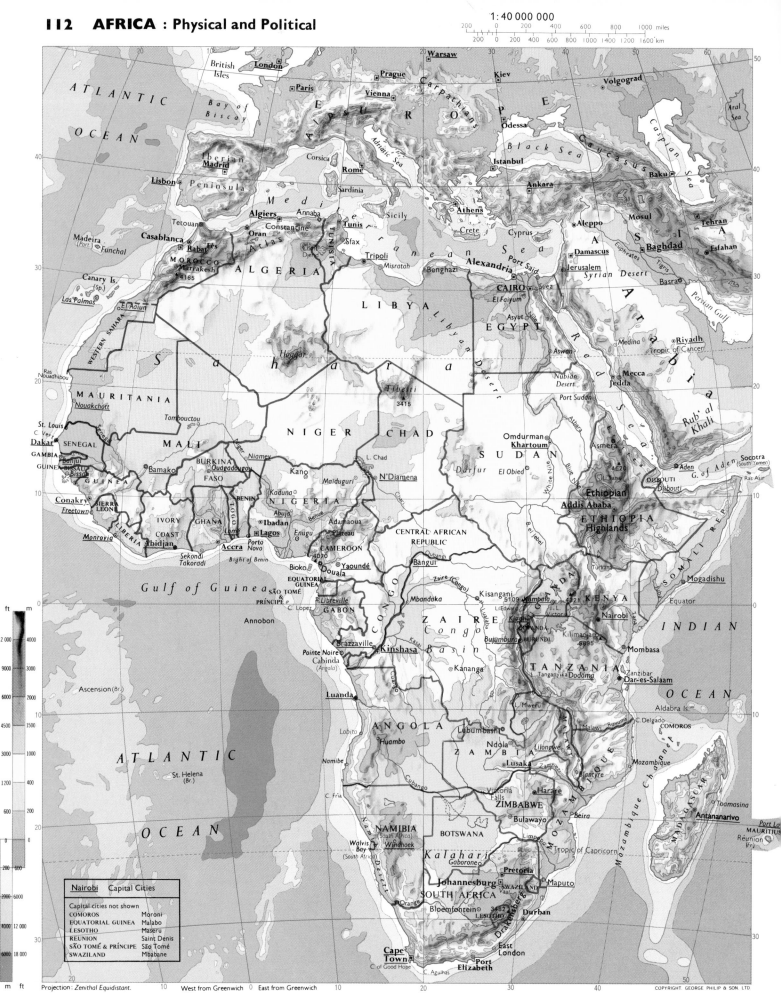

1 : 40 000 000

ATLANTIC OCEAN

British Isles
London
Paris
Warsaw
Prague
Vienna
Kiev
Volgograd
Aral Sea

Bay of Biscay
Madeira (Port.) Funchal
Iberian Peninsula
Madrid
Lisbon
Corsica
Rome
Sardinia
Adriatic Sea
Athens
Crete
Cyprus
Black Sea
Caucasus
Baku
Caspian Sea
Istanbul
Ankara
Aleppo
Mosul
Tehran
Esfahan
ASIA

Tetouan
Algiers
Annaba
Constantine
Tunis
Sfax
Tripoli
Misratah
Benghazi
Alexandria
Port Said
Damascus
Baghdad
Basra
Persian Gulf

Casablanca
Rabat
Fès
Oran
Atlas
Chott
Djelfa
Jerusalem
Syrian Desert
Euphrates
Tigris

MOROCCO
Marrakesh
4165
ALGERIA
LIBYA
Libyan Desert
EGYPT
CAIRO
Suez
El Faiyum
Asyut
Medina
Riyadh
Tropic of Cancer

Canary Is. (Sp.)
Las Palmas
El Aaiún
WESTERN SAHARA
Sahara
Hoggar
Tibesti 3415
Aswan
Nubian Desert
Port Sudan
Mecca
Jedda
Rub' al Khali
Arabia

Ras Nouadhibou
MAURITANIA
Nouakchott
Tombouctou
NIGER
CHAD
Omdurman
Khartoum
Asmera 4620
Socotra (South Yemen)

St. Louis
C. Vert
Dakar
SENEGAL
GAMBIA
Banjul
GUINEA-BISSAU
Bissau
MALI
Bamako
BURKINA FASO
Ouagadougou
Niamey
Kano
L. Chad
N'Djamena
SUDAN
Darfur
El Obeid
Blue Nile
L. Tana
DJIBOUTI
Djibouti
Aden
G. of Aden
Ras Asir

Conakry
Freetown
SIERRA LEONE
GUINEA
IVORY COAST
GHANA
BENIN
TOGO
NIGERIA
Kaduna
Abuja
Ibadan
Enugu
Benue
Adamaoua Plateau
CENTRAL AFRICAN REPUBLIC
Bangui
White Nile
Ethiopian Highlands
Addis Ababa
ETHIOPIA
Shabelle

LIBERIA
Monrovia
Abidjan
Sekondi Takoradi
Accra
Lomé
Porto Novo
Lagos
Bight of Benin
CAMEROON 4070
Yaoundé
Douala
Bioko
EQUATORIAL GUINEA
Oubangui
Uele
Bangui
Zaire (Congo)
SOMALI REP.
Mogadishu

Gulf of Guinea
São Tomé & Príncipe
C. Lopez
Libreville
GABON
CONGO
Kisangani 5109
UGANDA
Kampala
L. Edward
4321
KENYA
Nairobi
Equator

Annobon
Mbandaka
ZAIRE
Congo Basin
L. Victoria
Kigali
RWANDA
BURUNDI
Bujumbura
Kilimanjaro 5895
Mombasa

Brazzaville
Kinshasa
Kasai
Kananga
L. Tanganyika
TANZANIA
Dodoma
Zanzibar
Dar-es-Salaam

Pointe Noire
Cabinda (Angola)
INDIAN OCEAN

Ascension (Br.)
Luanda
L. Mweru
Mweru
Malawi
Ruvuma
C. Delgado
COMOROS
Aldabra Is.

ANGOLA
Lobito
Huambo
Namibe
Lubumbashi
Ndola
ZAMBIA
Lilongwe
Mozambique

ATLANTIC OCEAN
St. Helena (Br.)
Lusaka
Zambezi
Blantyre
MOZAMBIQUE

C. Fria
Victoria Falls
ZIMBABWE
Harare
Beira
Toamasina
Antananarivo
MADAGASCAR
Port Lo
MAURITIUS
Réunion (Fr.)

Cubango
Bulawayo
Limpopo
Tropic of Capricorn

NAMIBIA (South Africa)
Windhoek
BOTSWANA
Maputo
Mozambique Channel

Walvis Bay (South Africa)
Kalahari Desert
Gaborone
Pretoria
SWAZILAND
Maputo

ATLANTIC OCEAN
Orange
Johannesburg
Vaal
SOUTH AFRICA
Bloemfontein 3482
LESOTHO
Drakensberg
Durban
East London

Cape Town
C. of Good Hope
C. Agulhas
Port Elizabeth

Legend:
Nairobi Capital Cities
Capital cities not shown
COMOROS — Moroni
EQUATORIAL GUINEA — Malabo
LESOTHO — Maseru
RÉUNION — Saint Denis
SÃO TOMÉ & PRÍNCIPE — São Tomé
SWAZILAND — Mbabane

ft m
12 000 4000
9000 3000
6000 2000
4500 1500
3000 1000
1200 400
600 200
0 0
200 600
2000 6000
4000 12 000
6000 18 000
m ft

Projection: Zenithal Equidistant.
West from Greenwich
East from Greenwich
COPYRIGHT GEORGE PHILIP & SON LTD

1:100 000 000

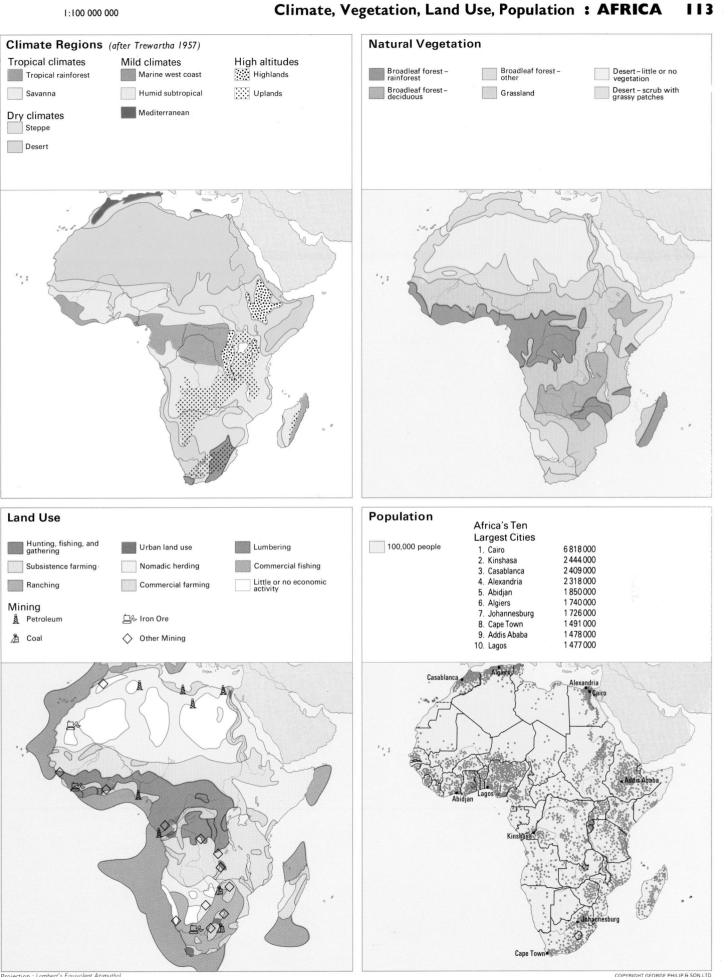

Climate Regions *(after Trewartha 1957)*

Tropical climates
- Tropical rainforest
- Savanna

Dry climates
- Steppe
- Desert

Mild climates
- Marine west coast
- Humid subtropical
- Mediterranean

High altitudes
- Highlands
- Uplands

Natural Vegetation

- Broadleaf forest – rainforest
- Broadleaf forest – deciduous
- Broadleaf forest – other
- Grassland
- Desert – little or no vegetation
- Desert – scrub with grassy patches

Land Use

- Hunting, fishing, and gathering
- Subsistence farming
- Ranching
- Urban land use
- Nomadic herding
- Commercial farming
- Lumbering
- Commercial fishing
- Little or no economic activity

Mining
- Petroleum
- Coal
- Iron Ore
- Other Mining

Projection : *Lambert's Equivalent Azimuthal*

Population

- 100,000 people

Africa's Ten Largest Cities
1. Cairo — 6 818 000
2. Kinshasa — 2 444 000
3. Casablanca — 2 409 000
4. Alexandria — 2 318 000
5. Abidjan — 1 850 000
6. Algiers — 1 740 000
7. Johannesburg — 1 726 000
8. Cape Town — 1 491 000
9. Addis Ababa — 1 478 000
10. Lagos — 1 477 000

Casablanca · Algiers · Alexandria · Cairo · Addis Ababa · Lagos · Abidjan · Kinshasa · Johannesburg · Cape Town

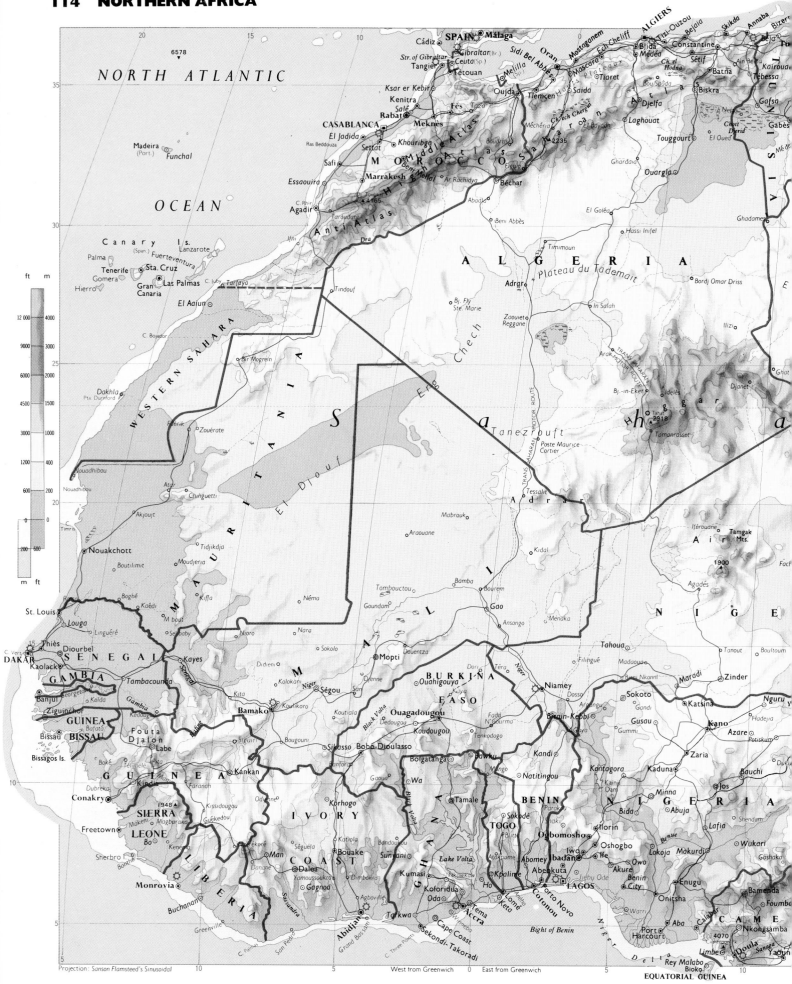

NORTH ATLANTIC

OCEAN

SPAIN

Str. of Gibraltar
Tangier
Ceuta(Sp.)
Tétouan
Melilla(Sp.)
ALGIERS
Tizi-Ouzou
Béjaïa
Skikda
Annaba
Bizer
Deja
Tu

Málaga
Cádiz
Gibraltar(Br.)
Sidi Bel Abbès
Oran
Mostaganem
Ech Cheliff
Blida
Médéa
Constantine
Sétif
Batna
Kairoua

Ksar er Kebir
Kenitra
Salé
Rabat
Fès
Meknès
Oujda
Tlemcen
Saïda
Tiaret
Bou Saâda
Ch. el Hodna
Ain Beïda
Tébessa
Gafsa

CASABLANCA
El Jadida
Khouribga
Settat
Ras Beddouza
MOROCCO
Middle Atlas
Béchar
Djelfa
Laghouat
Touggourt
El Oued
Gabès
Chott Djerid
Mé

Safi
Essaouira
Marrakesh
Beni Mellal
Ar Rachidya
Figuig
Méchéria
El Bayadh
Ghardaïa
Ouargla

Agadir
High Atlas
4165
Taroudant
Abadla
El Goléa
Hassi Inifel
Ghadames

NORTH ATLANTIC
6578

Madeira
(Port.)
Funchal

C. Rhir
Anti Atlas
Dra
Beni Abbès
Timimoun
ALGERIA
Plateau du Tademaït
Bordj Omar Driss
Ghat

Canary Is.
(Span.)
Lanzarote
Fuerteventura
Tarfaya
Ifni
Tindouf
Adrar
In Salah
Ilizi

Palma
Tenerife
Gomera
Hierro
Sta. Cruz
Gran Canaria
Las Palmas
C. Juby
El Aaiun
Bj. Fly
Ste. Marie
Zaouïet Reggane
Djanet

WESTERN SAHARA
C. Bojador
Bir Mogreïn
Chech
Bj.-in-Eker
Idelès
Tahat
2918
a
h
g
g
a
Djanet

Dakhla
Pta. Durnford
Fdérik
Zouérate
MAURITANIA
Sahara
El
Tanezrouft
Poste Maurice Cortier
TRANS-SAHARAN MOTOR ROUTE
ARAK MOTOR ROUTE
Tamanrasset
a

Nouadhibou
Atar
Chinguetti
El Djouf
Adrar
Tessalit
Iférouane
Tamgak Mts.
Air

Timris
Akjoujt
Mabrouk
1900
Agadès

Nouakchott
Tidjikdja
Araouane
Kidal
NIGER

Boutilimit
Moudjéria
Kiffa
Néma
Tombouctou
Goundam
Bamba
Bourem
Menaka
Tahoua
Tanout
Boultum

St. Louis
Louga
Kaédi
M'bout
Selibaby
Nioro
Nara
Sokolo
MALI
Gao
Ansongo
Filingué
Madaoua
Birni Nkonni
Maradi
Zinder
Nguru

DAKAR
Thiès
Diourbel
SENEGAL
Kayes
Didiéni
Kolokani
Mopti
Douentza
Dori
Niamey
Dosso
Gaya
Sokoto
Gusau
Katsina
Hadejia

Kaolack
GAMBIA
Banjul
Tambacounda
Kita
Ségou
San
Djenné
BURKINA
FASO
Téra
Birnin-Kebbi
Gandi
Kano
Azare
Potiskum

Ziguinchor
GUINEA
BISSAU
Bissau
Kolda
Kédougou
Koulikoro
Bamako
Koutiala
Sikasso
Ouahigouya
Ouagadougou
Dédougou
Fada N'Gourma
Tenkodogo
Kaya
Bida
Minna
Zaria
Kaduna
Bauchi

Bissagos Is.
Boké
Fouta
Djalon
Labé
Siguiri
Bougouni
Bobo-Dioulasso
Banfora
Gaoua
Bolgatanga
Dawku
Kandi
Kontagora
Abuja
Jos
Lafia
Shendam

Conakry
Kindia
Faranah
Kankan
Odienné
Korhogo
Wa
Mango
Natitingou
BENIN
Minna
NIGERIA

SIERRA
LEONE
Freetown
Makeni
Magburaka
Bo
1948
Kissidougou
Guéckédou
Séguéla
Katiola
Bouaké
Sunyani
Tamale
Sokodé
TOGO
Parakou
Ilorin
Oshogbo
Ife
Owo
Wukari
Gashaka

LIBERIA
Monrovia
Buchanan
Man
Danané
IVORY
COAST
Daloa
Gagnoa
Yamoussoukro
Dimbokro
Bouaké
Bondoukou
GHANA
Kumasi
Koforidua
Oda
Ho
Kpalime
Lome
Abomey
Ibadan
Iwo
Abeokuta
Ijebu Ode
Benin
City
Enugu
Onitsha
Bamenda
Foumb

Greenville
San Pedro
C. Palmas
Sassandra
Tabou
Torkwa
Sekondi-Takoradi
Cape Coast
Accra
Tema
Keta
Cotonou
Porto Novo
LAGOS
Warri
Port Harcourt
Aba
Calabar
CAME
Limbe
Douala
Rey Malabo
Bioko

Bight of Benin
Niger Delta
EQUATORIAL GUINEA
4070
Sanaga
Yaou

West from Greenwich   East from Greenwich

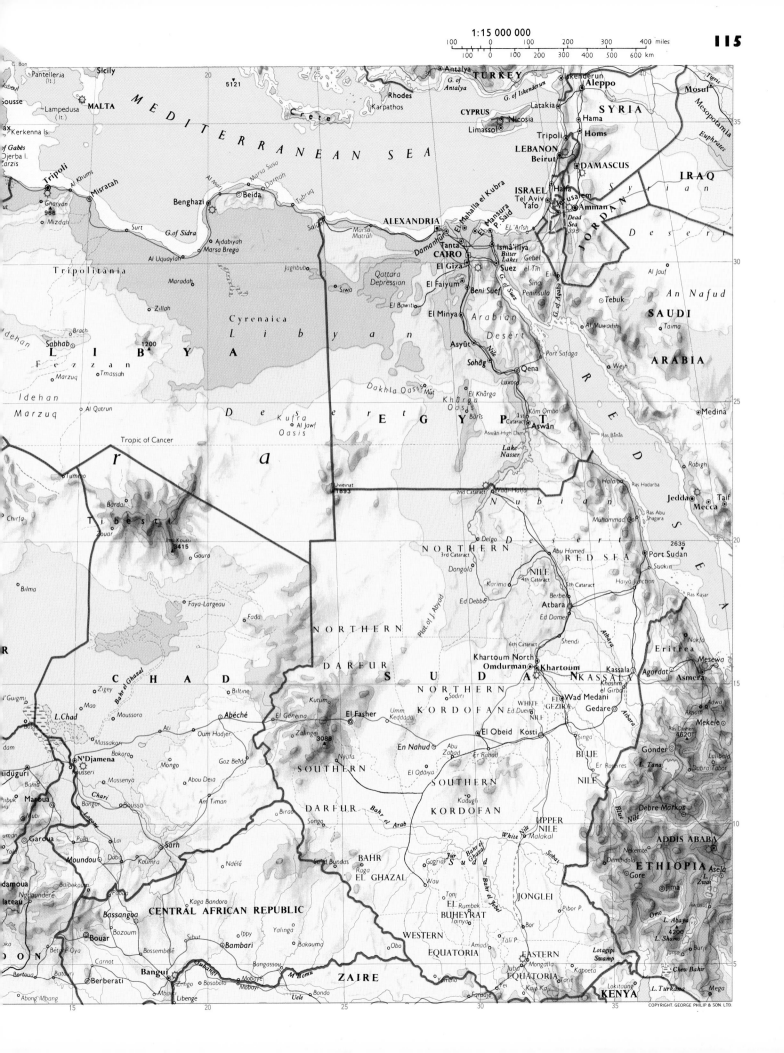

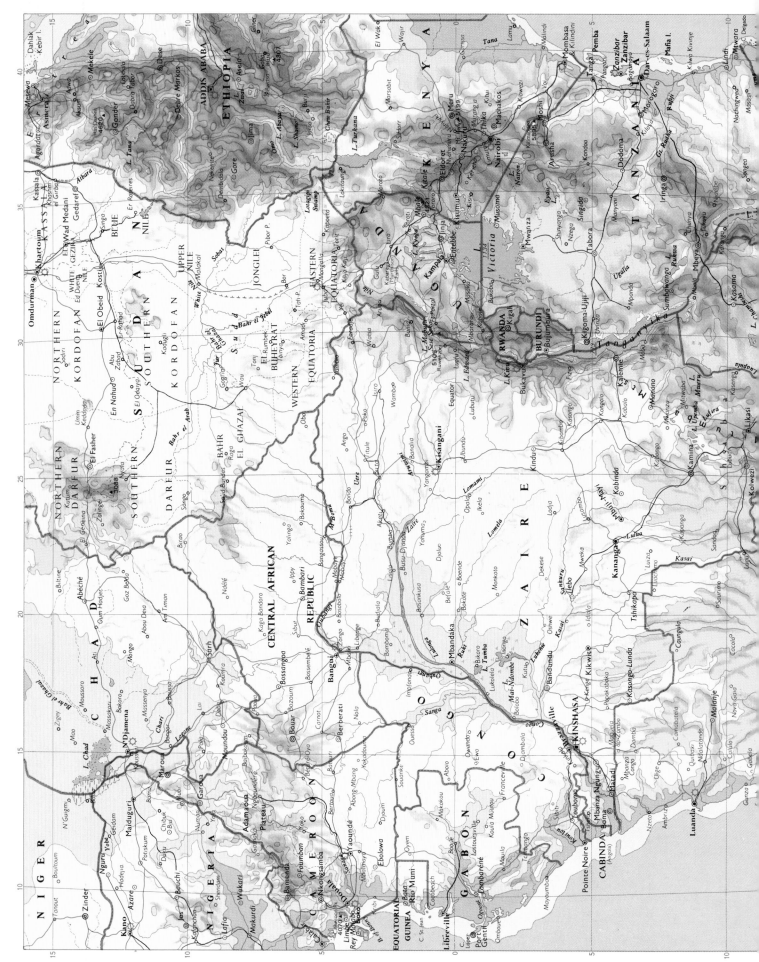

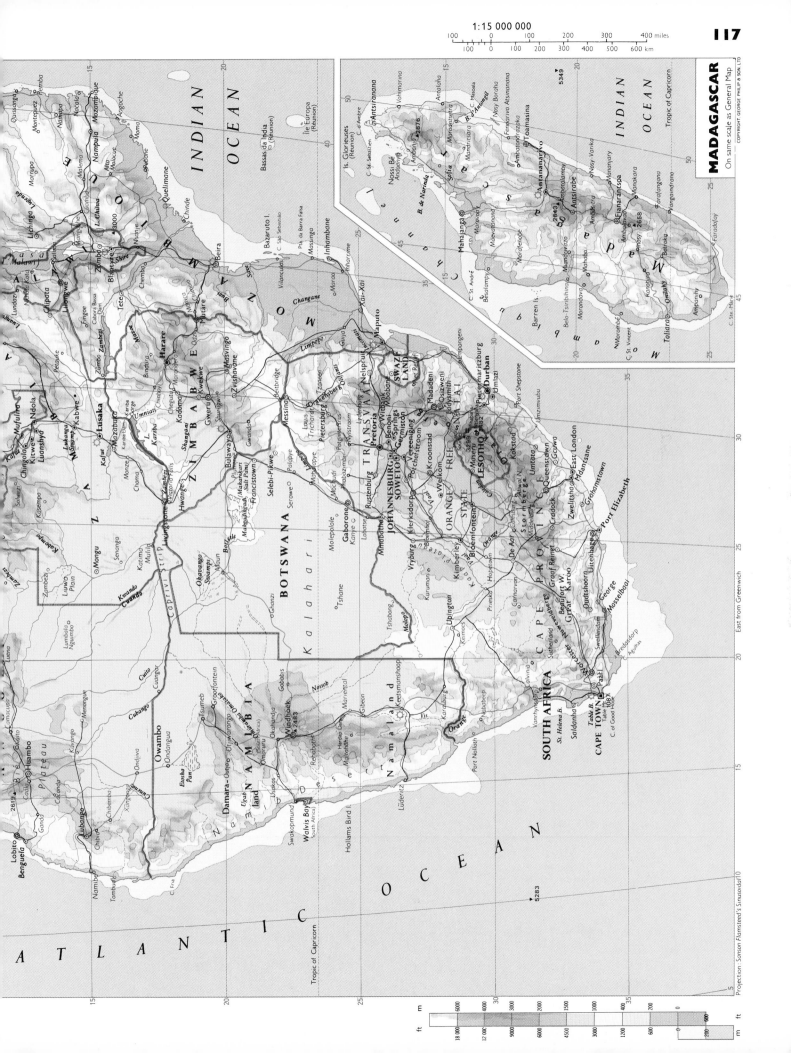

1:15 000 000

100   0   100   200   300   400 miles
100   0   100   200   300   400   500   600 km

MADAGASCAR
On same scale as General Map

INDIAN

OCEAN

INDIAN

OCEAN

Tropic of Capricorn

ATLANTIC   OCEAN

Projection : Sanson Flamsteed's Sinusoidal 10

m
ft   6000   4000   3000   2000   1500   1000   400   200   0
ft   18 000   12 000   9000   6000   4500   3000   1200   600   0   m

Equatorial Scale 1:50 000 000

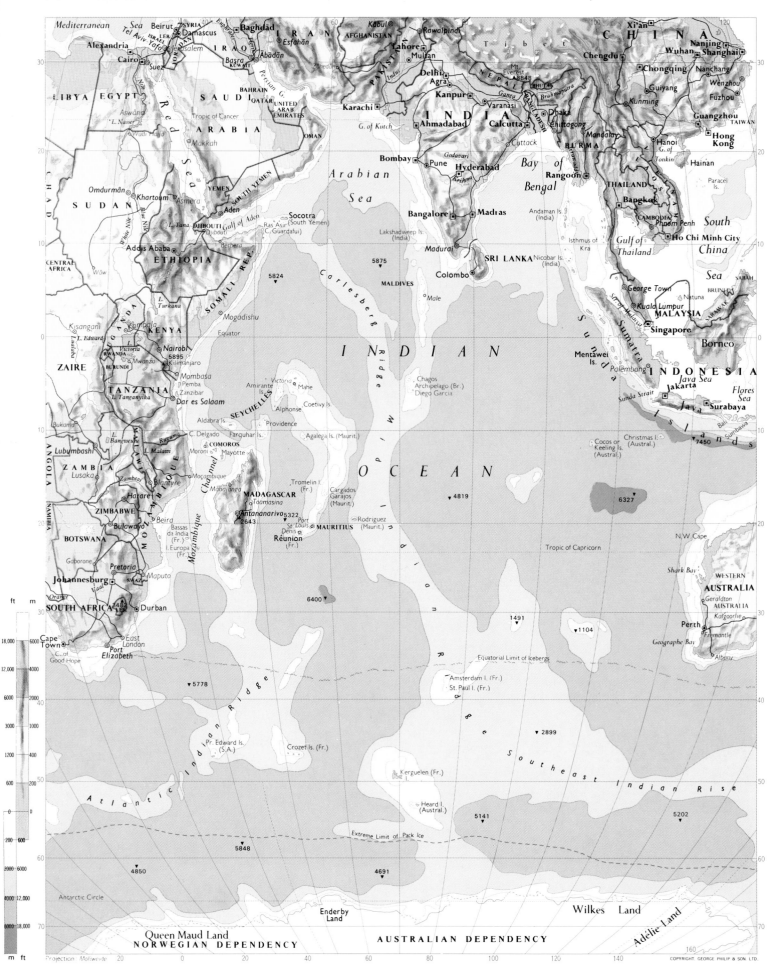

Mediterranean Sea Beirut SYRIA
Tel Aviv Yafo ISRAEL Damascus
Alexandria JERUSALEM JORDAN
Cairo Suez IRAQ Baghdad Esfahān IRAN
LIBYA EGYPT Basra KUWAIT Ābādān
SAUDI BAHRAIN QATAR
Aswān L. Nasser ARABIA UNITED ARAB EMIRATES
Tropic of Cancer
Wadi Halfa Makkah OMAN
CHAD SUDAN
Omdurmān Khartoum Asmera YEMEN SOUTH YEMEN
L. Tana DJIBOUTI Aden Gulf of Aden Socotra (South Yemen)
Djibouti Ras Asir (C. Guardafui)
Addis Ababa Berbera
CENTRAL AFRICA ETHIOPIA
SOMALI REP.
Wāw Mogadishu
UGANDA L. Turkana Equator
Kisangani Kampala KENYA
L. Edward L. Victoria Nairobi 5895
RWANDA Mwanza Kilimanjaro
ZAIRE BURUNDI Mombasa Pemba
Lualaba Zanzibar
Bukama TANZANIA Dar es Salaam
L. Tanganyika
L. Bangweulu Ruvuma C. Delgado
Lubumbashi L. Malawi COMOROS Moroni Mayotte
ZAMBIA Zambezi Moçambique
Lusaka Blantyre Mohoanga
ANGOLA Harare MADAGASCAR Toamasina
ZIMBABWE Beira Antananarivo 2643
Bulawayo MOZAMBIQUE Bassas da India (Fr.) St Louis Port
BOTSWANA I. Europa (Fr.) Réunion (Fr.)
Gaborone Maputo
NAMIBIA Pretoria SWAZI
Johannesburg

Red Sea
Persian G.
Zāhedān
AFGHANISTAN Kabul Rawalpindi
PAKISTAN Lahore Multan
Indus Delhi Agra NEPAL Mt Everest 8848 BHUTAN
Karachi Kanpur Ganga Brahmaputra
G. of Kutch Ahmadabad INDIA Varanasi Dhaka BANGLADESH Chittagong
Bombay Pune Godavari Calcutta Cuttack BURMA Mandalay
Hyderabad Krishna
Bangalore Madras Bay of Bengal Rangoon
Lakshadweep Is. (India) Andaman Is. (India)
Madurai SRI LANKA Nicobar Is. (India)
Colombo
MALDIVES Male

Tibet CHINA Xi'an
Chengdu Chongqing Nanjing Shanghai
Wuhan Nanchang
Guiyang Kunming Wenzhou
Guangzhou Fūzhou
Hanoi G. of Tonkin Hong Kong TAIWAN Hainan
THAILAND Paracel Is.
Bangkok South China Sea
CAMBODIA Phnom Penh
Gulf of Thailand Ho Chi Minh City
Isthmus of Kra
George Town Natuna BRUNEI
Kuala Lumpur SARAWAK SABAH
MALAYSIA Singapore Borneo
Mentawei Is. Sumatra INDONESIA
Palembang Java Sea Jakarta
Sunda Strait Surabaya Flores Sea
Java Islands Bali Sumbawa
Cocos or Keeling Is. (Austral.) Christmas I. (Austral.)

Arabian Sea
▼5875
5824▼
Carlesberg Ridge
INDIAN OCEAN
Chagos Archipelago (Br.) Diego Garcia
Amirante Is. Victoria Mahe
SEYCHELLES Coetivy Is. Alphonse
Aldabra Is. Providence
Farquhar Is. Agalega Is. (Maurit.)
▼4819
Tromelin I. (Fr.)
Cargados Garajos (Maurit.)
5322 Rodriguez (Maurit.)
MAURITIUS
Denis
Tropic of Capricorn
6327
6400▼
N.W. Cape
Shark Bay WESTERN AUSTRALIA
AUSTRALIA Geraldton
1491▼ ▼1104 Geographe Bay Perth Fremantle Kalgoorlie
Equatorial Limit of Icebergs Albany
5778▼ Amsterdam I. (Fr.) St. Paul I. (Fr.)
Atlantic Indian Ridge
Pr. Edward Is. (S.A.) Crozet Is. (Fr.)
▼2899 Southeast Indian Rise
Kerguelen (Fr.)
Heard I. (Austral.) 5141 5202
5848
4850 4691
Antarctic Circle
Enderby Land Wilkes Land Adélie Land
Queen Maud Land Projection: Mollweide NORWEGIAN DEPENDENCY AUSTRALIAN DEPENDENCY

ft m
18,000 6000
12,000 4000
6000 2000
3000 1000
1200 400
600 200
0 0
200 600
2000 6000
4000 12,000
6000 18,000
m ft

COPYRIGHT GEORGE PHILIP & SON LTD.

Climate Regions

Tropical climates
- Tropical rainforest
- Savanna

Mild climates
- Marine west coast
- Humid subtropical
- Mediterranean

Dry climates
- Steppe
- Desert

High altitudes
- Highlands

(after Trewartha 1957)

Natural Vegetation

- Broadleaf forest – rainforest
- Broadleaf forest – deciduous
- Broadleaf forest – other
- Mixed forest
- Grassland
- Desert – little or no vegetation
- Desert – scrub with grassy patches

Land Use

- Hunting, fishing, and gathering
- Subsistence farming
- Ranching
- Urban land use
- Commercial farming
- Lumbering
- Commercial fishing
- Little or no economic activity

Mining

- Petroleum
- Coal
- Iron Ore
- Other Minerals

Population

- 100,000 people

Oceania's Ten Largest Cities
1. Sydney   3 335 000
2. Melbourne   2 865 000
3. Brisbane   1 138 000
4. Adelaide   969 000
5. Perth   969 000
6. Auckland   864 000
7. Newcastle   414 000
8. Wellington   343 000
9. Christchurch   322 000
10. Canberra   256 000

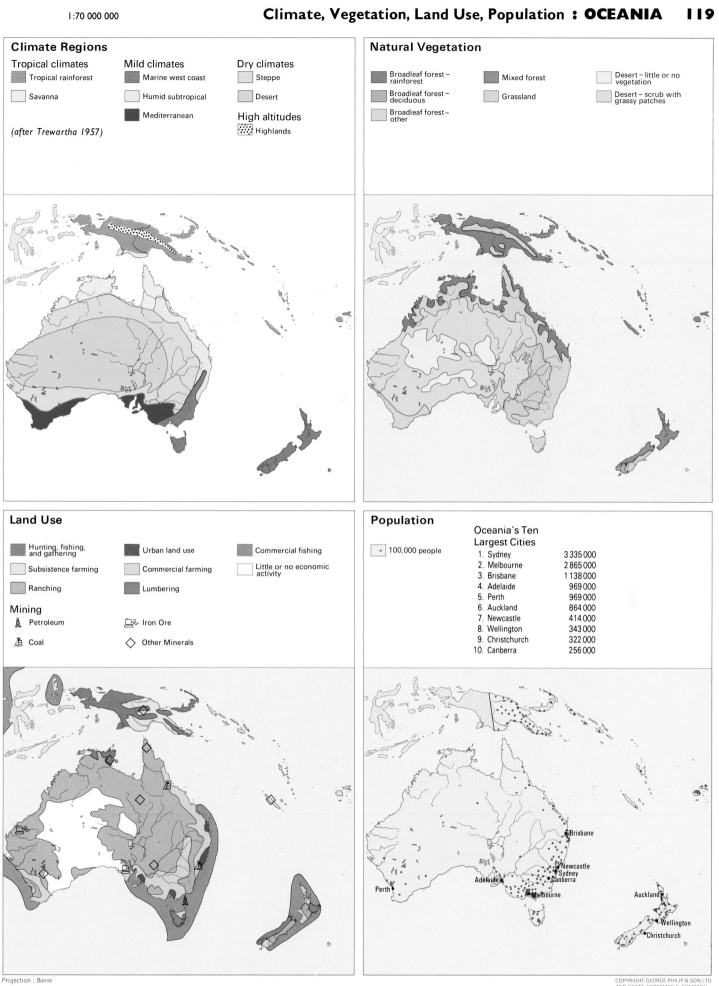

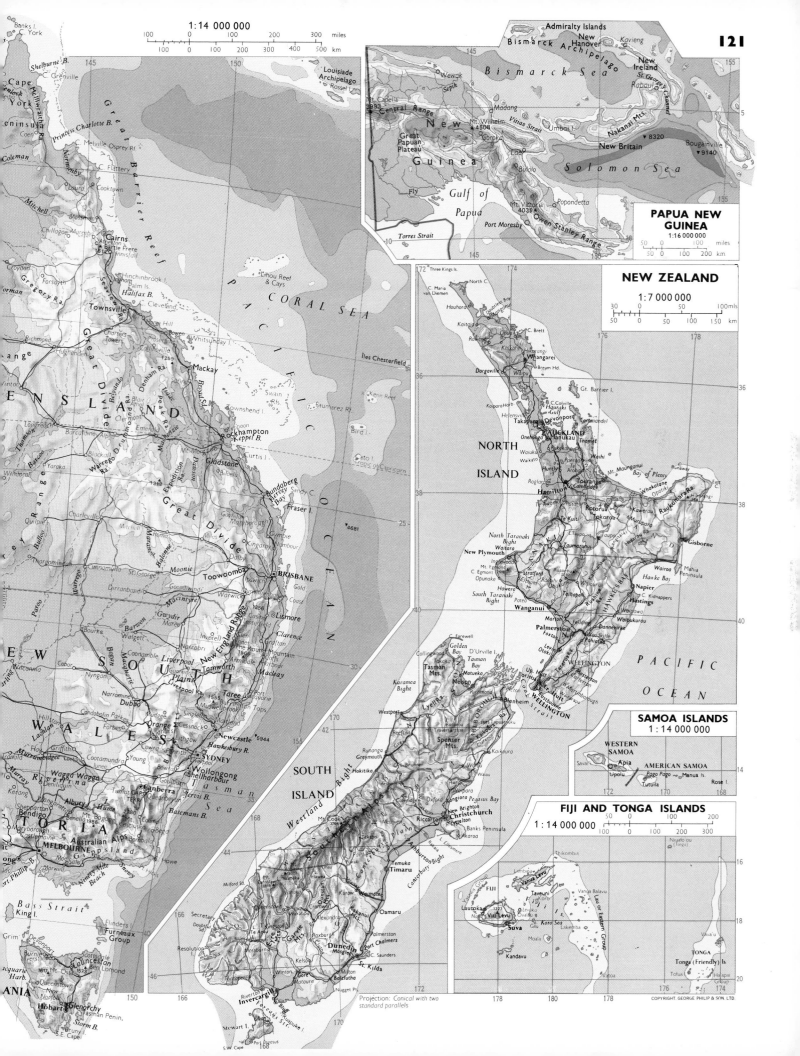

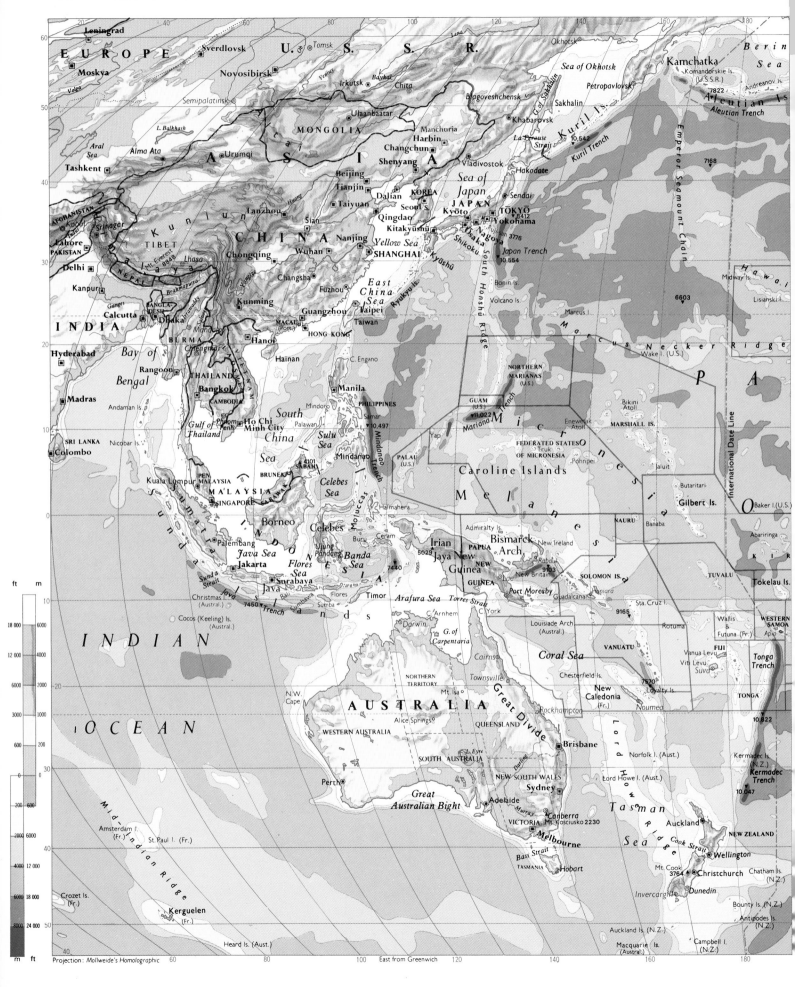

ALASKA
(U.S.)
▼6050
Bristol Bay
Gulf of Alaska
Juneau
Prince of Wales I.
Queen Charlotte Is.
Kitimat
Prince Rupert

Hudson Bay
GREENLAND
C. Farewell
Labrador
Newfoundland
Pr. Edward I.

CANADA

NORTH AMERICA

NORTH

Edmonton
L. Winnipeg
Regina
Winnipeg
Calgary
Vancouver I.
Vancouver
Victoria
Seattle
Portland
Boise
Salt Lake City
▼6741

Montréal
Québec
Saint John
C. Sable
Ottawa
Toronto
L. Ontario
Boston
L. Superior
L. Huron
Michigan
Minneapolis
Erie
Buffalo
Pittsburgh
NEW YORK
Philadelphia
Baltimore
Washington
CHICAGO
Detroit
Cincinnati
L. Winnipeg
Missouri

ATLANTIC

Rocky Mountains

Denver
Kansas City
St. Louis
Memphis
Atlanta
C. Hatteras
UNITED STATES
Oklahoma
Dallas
Mississippi
Jacksonville
Bermuda (U.K.)
▼4418
C. Mendocino
San Francisco
Los Angeles
San Diego
▼6225
Ciudad Juárez

OCEAN

Sierra Madre
Gulf of California
Houston
San Antonio
New Orleans
Gulf of Mexico
Monterrey
Miami
Florida Strait
BAHAMAS
Havana
CUBA
West Indies
Hispaniola
9200
DOM. REP.
HAITI
PUERTO RICO (U.S.)
Leeward Is.
Tropic of Cancer

Hawaiian Is.
(U.S.)
Honolulu
Oahu
Hawaii

Revilla Gigedo Is.
(Mexico)
México
Guadalajara
Puebla ▼5700
Acapulco
BELIZE
Mérida
Yucatan Channel
JAMAICA
▼7680
Kingston
Caribbean Sea
BARBADOS
Windward Is.
TRINIDAD & TOBAGO

PACIFIC

Christmas Island Ridge
Palmyra Is. (U.S.)
Teraina
Tabuaeran
Kiritimati
Jarvis I. (U.S.)
Johnston I. (U.S.)

GUATEMALA
Guatemala ▼4220
Salvador
EL SALVADOR
HONDURAS
NICARAGUA
Managua
San José
CENTRAL AMERICA
COSTA RICA
Colón
PANAMA
Panama Canal
Clipperton I. (Fr.)
Cocos I.
Barranquilla
Caracas
Maracaibo
VENEZUELA
Orinoco
Medellín
Bogotá
Cali
COLOMBIA
Galápagos
(Ecuador)
Quito
ECUADOR
Guayaquil
Iquitos
Manaus
Amazon
BRAZIL
SOUTH
C. Pariñas

OCEAN

Phoenix Is.
Canterbury I.
Phoenix Is.
Malden I.
Starbuck I.
Tongareva
Penrhyn Is.
Manihiki
Suwarrow Is.
Pukapuka
AMER. SAMOA (U.S.)
Cook Islands
(N.Z.)
Niue (N.Z.)
Rarotonga
Manuae
Society Is.
Windward Is.
Tahiti
Leeward Is.
Vostok I.
Flint I.
Caroline I.
Marquesas Is.
Tuamotu Archipelago
FRENCH POLYNESIA
Austral
Tubuai Is.
(Austral Is.)
Rapa Iti

Trujillo
6369 ▼
PERU
Lima
Cuzco
SOUTH
AMERICA
Arequipa
L. Titicaca
Illampu & Ancohuma 6550
La Paz
▼6866
BOLIVIA
Peru-
Iquique
Chile
Antofagasta Trench
▼8050
Tropic of Capricorn
San Félix (Chile)
San Ambrosio (Chile)
Sala-y-Gomez (Chile)
Easter Is. (Chile)
Tucumán
PARAGUAY
Asunción

East Pacific Ridge

Pitcairn I. (U.K.)
Ducie I. (U.K.)

Pacific-Antarctic Ridge

Equator

Seamount Chain

Arch. de Juan Fernández (Chile)
▼6960
Córdoba
Rosario
Valparaíso
Santiago
Buenos Aires
Concepción
URUGUAY
Montevideo
Río de la Plata
Pto. Alegre

Chile Rise

ARGENTINA

SOUTH

Chonos Arch.
Andes
Patagonia
G. of Penas
▼6212
Falkland Is. (U.K.)
Punta Arenas
Str. of Magellan
Tierra del Fuego
C. Horn
South Georgia

ATLANTIC

OCEAN

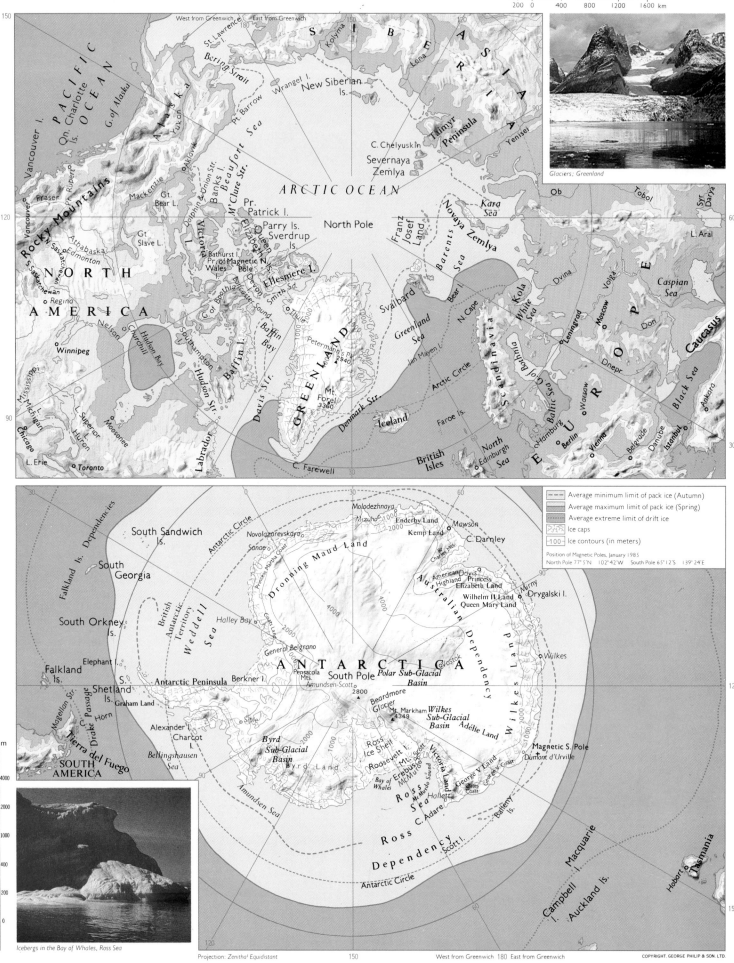

1 : 50 000 000

Glaciers; Greenland

Icebergs in the Bay of Whales, Ross Sea

Projection: Zenithal Equidistant

COPYRIGHT. GEORGE PHILIP & SON. LTD.

Flag	Country or Dependency	Capital	Area	Population	Major or Official Languages	Important Products
	Afghanistan	Kabul	250,000 (mi²) 647,497 (km²)	19,000,000	Pushtu, Dari Persian	carpets, natural gas, fruit, salt, coal, wheat
	Albania	Tirana	11,099 28,748	3,000,000	Albanian	minerals, metals, olives, cereals, tobacco, lumber
	Algeria	Algiers	919,591 2,381,741	23,000,000	Arabic, French	wheat, barley, petroleum, wine, fruit, iron ore
	Andorra	Andorra la Vella	175 453	47,000	French, Spanish	livestock, tobacco, cereals, potatoes, iron ore
	Angola	Luanda	481,351 1,246,700	8,000,000	Bantu languages, Portuguese	coffee, diamonds, cotton, oil, fish, iron ore
	Anguilla (UK)	The Valley	35 91	8,000	English	fruit, vegetables, lobsters, fish, salt
	Antigua and Barbuda	St. Johns	171 442	83,000	English	cotton, clothing, rum, molasses, sugar, bananas
	Argentina	Buenos Aires	1,068,297 2,766,889	31,000,000	Spanish	meat, wool, hides, wheat, corn, fruit, vegetables
	Australia	Canberra	2,967,895 7,686,848	16,000,000	English	wheat, wool, livestock, metal ores, coal, bauxite
	Austria	Vienna	32,374 83,849	8,000,000	German	lumber, metal products, paper, textiles, food
	Azores (PO)	Ponta Delgada	902 2,335	280,000	Portuguese	farm products, fish, fruit, grains
	Bahamas	Nassau	5,380 13,935	232,000	English	pharmaceuticals, salt, fish, lobsters, rum
	Bahrain	Manama	254 659	400,000	Arabic, English, French	petroleum products, fish, aluminum processing
	Bangladesh	Dhaka	55,598 143,998	104,000,000	Bengali, English	jute goods, tea, fish, leather, seafood, hides
	Barbados	Bridgetown	166 431	280,000	English	clothing, molasses, rum, sugar, fish, lime
	Belgium	Brussels	11,781 30,513	10,000,000	Dutch, French	precious stones, iron and steel products
	Belize	Belmopan	8,867 22,965	161,000	English, Spanish	molasses, rice, lumber, livestock, fish, fruit
	Benin	Porto-Novo	43,483 112,622	4,000,000	French, others	palm oil, cotton, cocoa beans, fish, iron ore
	Bermuda (UK)	Hamilton	20 53	60,000	English	perfumes, petroleum products, pharmaceuticals
	Bhutan	Thimphu	18,147 47,000	1,000,000	Dzongkha, Nepali	lumber, fruit, coal, vegetables, cement
	Bolivia	La Paz, Sucre	424,163 1,098,581	7,000,000	Spanish, Quechua, Aymara	petroleum, tin, gold, lead, zinc, coffee
	Botswana	Gaborone	231,804 600,372	1,000,000	English, Setswana	livestock, diamonds, copper, nickel, salt
	Brazil	Brasília	3,286,473 8,511,965	140,000,000	Portuguese	iron ore, steel, motor vehicles, coffee, sugar
	Brunei	Bandar Seri Begawan	2,226 5,765	221,000	Malay, English, Chinese	petroleum, rubber, lumber, rice, pepper, bananas

(UK) United Kingdom   (PO) Portugal

Flag	Country or Dependency	Capital	Area	Population	Major or Official Languages	Important Products
	Bulgaria	Sofia	42,823 (mi²) 110,912 (km²)	9,000,000	Bulgarian	farm products, minerals, machinery, equipment
	Burkina Faso	Ouaga-dougou	105,869 274,200	8,000,000	French, others	livestock, cotton, peanuts, sesame, grains
	Burma	Rangoon	261,216 676,552	37,000,000	Burmese	teak, rice, sugar, precious stones, rubber
	Burundi	Bujumbura	10,747 27,834	5,000,000	Kirundi, French	cotton, hides, tea, coffee, bananas, grain
	Cambodia	Phnom Penh	69,898 181,035	6,000,000	Khmer	fish, rubber, paper, timber, rice, sugar
	Cameroon	Yaoundé	183,568 475,442	10,000,000	English, French, others	cotton, coffee, cocoa beans, tea, rubber
	Canada	Ottawa	3,851,791 9,976,139	27,000,000	English, French	motor vehicles, machinery, lumber, metal ores
	Canary Islands (SP)	Las Palmas	2,808 7,273	1,000,000	Spanish	fish, fruit, grains, wine, vegetables, sugar
	Cape Verde	Praia	1,557 4,033	356,000	Portuguese	fish, shellfish, salt, bananas, coffee, sugar
	Cayman Islands (UK)	Georgetown	100 259	20,000	English	turtle products, fish, lobsters
	Central African Republic	Bangui	240,534 622,984	3,000,000	French, Sango	coffee, diamonds, cocoa beans, lumber, cotton
	Chad	N'Djamena	495,752 1,284,000	5,000,000	French, Arabic, others	livestock, cotton, rice, animal products, fish
	Chile	Santiago	292,256 756,945	12,000,000	Spanish	paper, lumber, copper, iron, nitrates, fish
	China	Beijing	3,705,390 9,596,961	1,000,000,000	Mandarin Chinese, others	farm products, petroleum, minerals, metals
	Colombia	Bogotá	439,735 1,138,914	30,000,000	Spanish	petroleum, coffee, sugar, cotton, textiles
	Comoros	Moroni	719 1,862	469,000	Arabic, French	vanilla, copra, cloves, perfume essences, sugar
	Congo	Brazzaville	132,046 342,000	2,000,000	French, Lingala, Kokongo	lumber, petroleum, cocoa beans, palm oil, sugar
	Cook Islands (NZ)	Avarua	93 241	21,000	English	citrus, clothing, canned fruit, vegetables
	Costa Rica	San José	19,575 50,700	3,000,000	Spanish	livestock, sugar, cocoa beans, coffee, palm oil
	Cuba	Havana	44,218 114,524	10,000,000	Spanish	sugar, rice, citrus, tobacco, nickel, fish
	Cyprus	Nicosia	3,572 9,251	700,000	Greek, Turkish	cereals, citrus, grapes, potatoes, copper, cement
	Czechoslovakia	Prague	49,370 127,869	16,000,000	Czech, Slovak, Hungarian	iron and steel, machinery, beer, wheat, potatoes
	Denmark	Copenhagen	16,629 43,069	5,000,000	Danish	machinery, textiles, dairy products, clothing
	Djibouti	Djibouti	8,494 22,000	481,000	Arabic, French, Afar, Somali	salt, livestock, hides
	Dominica	Roseau	290 751	88,000	English, French patois	cocoa beans, lime juice, bananas, pumice, fruit

(SP) Spain   (NZ) New Zealand

Flag	Country or Dependency	Capital	Area	Population	Major or Official Languages	Important Products
	Dominican Republic	Santo Domingo	18,816 (mi²) 48,734 (km²)	7,000,000	Spanish	coffee, tobacco, bauxite, nickel, sugar, cocoa
	Ecuador	Quito	109,483 283,561	10,000,000	Spanish, Quechua	bananas, coffee, cocoa beans, fish, petroleum
	Egypt	Cairo	386,659 1,001,449	48,000,000	Arabic	cotton, textiles, chemicals, rice, petrochemicals
	El Salvador	San Salvador	8,124 21,041	6,000,000	Spanish	cotton, coffee, sugar, livestock, lumber, rice
	Equatorial Guinea	Malabo	10,830 28,051	282,000	Spanish, Fang, Bubi	lumber, coffee, cocoa beans, bananas, fish
	Ethiopia	Addis Ababa	471,776 1,221,900	36,000,000	Amharic, others	hides, coffee, oilseeds, fruits, vegetables, metals
	Falkland Islands (UK)	Stanley	4,700 12,173	3,000	English	wool, hides, whales
	Fiji	Suva	7,056 18,274	700,000	Fijian, Hindi, English	copra, sugar, gold, lumber, bananas, ginger
	Finland	Helsinki	130,128 337,032	5,000,000	Finnish, Swedish	lumber, paper, manufactured goods, glassware
	France	Paris	211,207 547,026	55,000,000	French	machinery, clothing, farm products, textiles
	French Guiana (FR)	Cayenne	35,135 91,000	82,000	French, Creole	shrimp, rice, lumber, gold, bauxite, sugar
	French Polynesia (FR)	Papeete	1,544 4,014	166,000	French, Polynesian languages	coconuts, citrus, bananas, sugar, vanilla, pearls
	Gabon	Libreville	103,346 267,667	1,000,000	French, Bantu languages	coffee, petroleum, lumber, manganese, iron ore, gold
	Gambia	Banjul	4,361 11,295	751,000	English, others	fish, peanuts, cotton, grains, livestock
	Germany, East	East Berlin	41,767 108,178	17,000,000	German	machinery, precision instruments, textiles
	Germany, West	Bonn	95,976 248,577	60,000,000	German	manufactured goods, chemicals, motor vehicles
	Ghana	Accra	92,099 238,537	14,000,000	English, others	lumber, petroleum, gold, manganese, cocoa beans
	Greece	Athens	50,944 131,944	10,000,000	Greek	textiles, minerals, fish, fruit, cotton, tobacco
	Greenland (DE)	Godthab	840,000 2,175,600	54,000	Danish, Greenlande	metallic ore, fish, fish products, seals
	Grenada	St. George's	133 344	116,000	English	cocoa beans, citrus, fish, nutmeg, bananas, sugar
	Guadeloupe (FR)	Basse-Terre	687 1,779	335,000	French, Creole	fruits, vegetables, sugar, vanilla, cocoa beans, fish
	Guam (US)	Agana	212 549	115,000	Chamorro, English	palm oil, fish, copra, citrus, bananas, sugar
	Guatemala	Guatemala	42,042 108,889	9,000,000	Spanish, Indian languages	cotton, sugar, livestock, bananas, coffee, lumber
	Guinea	Conakry	94,925 245,857	6,000,000	French, Fulani, others	bauxite, fruit, coffee, iron ore, rice, bananas
	Guinea-Bissau	Bissau	13,948 36,125	640,000	Portuguese	peanuts, palm oil, fish, shrimp, lumber, coconuts
	Guyana	Georgetown	83,000 214,969	1,000,000	English, Hindi, Urdu	bauxite, aluminum, sugar, rice, shrimp, coffee

(FR) France   (DE) Denmark   (US) United States

Flag	Country or Dependency	Capital	Area	Population	Major or Official Languages	Important Products
	Haiti	Port-au-Prince	10,714 (mi²) 27,750 (km²)	7,000,000	French, Creole	coffee, sugar, rice, textiles, bauxite
	Honduras	Tegucigalpa	43,277 112,088	5,000,000	Spanish, Indian languages	bananas, coffee, sugar, lumber, livestock
	Hong Kong (UK)	Victoria	403 1,045	6,000,000	Chinese, English	textiles, clothing, electronic goods, cameras, shoes
	Hungary	Budapest	35,919 93,030	11,000,000	Hungarian	consumer goods, tools, machinery, wheat, fruit
	Iceland	Reykjavik	39,768 103,000	245,000	Icelandic	fish, livestock, dairy products, chemicals
	India	New Delhi	1,269,339 3,287,590	767,000,000	Hindi, others	clothing, textiles, jute, machinery, cars, steel
	Indonesia	Jakarta	788,421 2,042,012	164,000,000	Bahasa Indonesia, others	petroleum, tin, lumber, rubber, tea, rice
	Iran	Tehran	636,293 1,648,000	45,000,000	Persian, Kurdish, Azerbaijani	wheat, petroleum, livestock, textiles, cement
	Iraq	Baghdad	167,925 434,924	16,000,000	Arabic, Kurdish	petroleum, cement, livestock, cotton, textiles
	Ireland	Dublin	27,136 70,283	4,000,000	Irish, English	chemicals, dairy products, textiles, machinery
	Israel	Jerusalem	8,019 20,770	4,000,000	Hebrew, Arabic	citrus, chemicals, clothing, machinery, food products
	Italy	Rome	116,303 301,225	58,000,000	Italian	clothing, shoes, textiles, machinery, foods, cars
	Ivory Coast	Abidjan	124,503 322,463	10,000,000	French, others	lumber, coffee, cocoa beans, sugar, cotton
	Jamaica	Kingston	4,244 10,991	2,000,000	English	bauxite, bananas, sugar, citrus, rum, cocoa beans
	Japan	Tokyo	143,750 372,313	121,000,000	Japanese	cars, metal products, textiles, electronics
	Jordan	Amman	37,737 97,740	4,000,000	Arabic	phosphates, fruits, olives, copper, sulfur
	Kenya	Nairobi	244,960 582,646	20,000,000	Swahili, Bantu languages, English	livestock, coffee, tea, hides, cement, sugar
	Kiribati	Bairiki	281 728	68,000	English, Gilbertese	copra, fish, mother-of-pearl, phosphates
	Korea, North	Pyongyang	46,540 120,538	21,000,000	Korean	chemicals, minerals, rice, wheat, cement
	Korea, South	Seoul	38,025 98,484	42,000,000	Korean	machinery, steel, clothing, footwear
	Kuwait	Kuwait	6,880 17,818	2,000,000	Arabic, English	petroleum, shrimp, fertilizer
	Laos	Vientiane	91,429 236,800	4,000,000	Lao	lumber, tin, coffee, textiles, fruits, rice
	Lebanon	Beirut	4,015 10,400	3,000,000	Arabic, French	textiles, fruits, lumber, jewelry, cotton, tobacco
	Lesotho	Maseru	11,720 30,355	2,000,000	English, Sesotho	livestock, diamonds, hides, wool, wheat
	Liberia	Monrovia	43,000 111,800	2,000,000	English, others	lumber, iron ore, gold, cocoa beans, coffee, fish
	Libya	Tripoli	679,359 1,759,540	4,000,000	Arabic	petroleum, olives, dates, barley, citrus fruit

Flag	Country or Dependency	Capital	Area	Population	Major or Official Languages	Important Products
	Liechtenstein	Vaduz	61 (mi²) 157 (km²)	27,000	German	chemicals, metal products machinery, optical lenses
	Luxembourg	Luxembourg	998 2,586	367,000	Luxembourgish, German, French	chemicals, steel, oats, barley, potatoes, wheat
	Macao (PO)	Macao	6 16	320,000	Chinese, Portuguese	manufactured goods, fish, electronic goods, clothing
	Madagascar	Antananarivo	226,657 587,041	10,000,000	Malagasy, French	chromium, graphite, cloves, cotton, coffee
	Malawi	Lilongwe	45,747 118,484	8,000,000	English, Chichewa	fish, tobacco, peanuts, fertilizer, textiles
	Malaysia	Kuala Lumpur	127,316 329,749	16,000,000	Malay, Chinese, Tamil, English	petroleum, lumber, tin, rubber, palm oil, textiles
	Maldives	Male	115 298	177,000	Divehi	coconuts, fish, millet, breadfruit, vegetables
	Mali	Bamako	478,764 1,240,000	8,000,000	French, others	fish, livestock, cotton, peanuts, textiles, rice
	Malta	Valletta	122 316	360,000	Maltese, English	manufactured goods, ships, textiles, fruits
	Marshall Islands (US)	Majuro	70 183	31,000	English, others	copra, tortoise shell, mother-of-pearl, fish
	Martinique (FR)	Fort-de-France	425 1,102	329,000	French, Creole	bananas, rum, sugar, pineapples, vegetables
	Mauritania	Nouakchott	397,953 1,030,700	2,000,000	Arabic, French	copper, iron ore, dates, cereals, vegetables
	Mauritius	Port Louis	790 2,045	1,000,000	English, others	molasses, sugar, tea, iron ore, rice, fish
	Mexico	Mexico City	761,601 1,972,547	80,000,000	Spanish, Indian languages	cotton, petroleum, corn, livestock, coffee, minerals
	Micronesia (US)	Kolonia	280 726	80,000	English, others	copra, fish, handicrafts
	Monaco	Monaco-Ville	.73 1.90	26,000	French, Monégasque	industrial products, chemicals, perfume
	Mongolia	Ulaanbaatar	604,247 1,565,000	2,000,000	Mongolian	livestock, wheat, oats, footwear, minerals
	Montserrat (UK)	Plymouth	40 104	14,000	English	cotton, mangoes, citrus, livestock, potatoes
	Morocco	Rabat	172,413 446,550	25,000,000	Arabic, Berber, French, Spanish	phosphates, citrus, carpets, chemicals
	Mozambique	Maputo	309,494 801,590	14,000,000	Portuguese, Bantu languages	cotton, cashew nuts, sugar, copra, tea
	Namibia (SA)	Windhoek	318,259 824,292	1,000,000	Afrikaans, English, others	sheepskins, diamonds, uranium, copper, lead
	Nauru	Yaren	8 21	8,000	Nauruan, English	phosphates
	Nepal	Katmandu	54,362 140,797	17,000,000	Nepali, Newari	rice, lumber, grain, sugar, jute, cotton
	Netherlands	Amsterdam, The Hague	16,041 41,548	14,000,000	Dutch	manufactured goods, foods, flower bulbs
	Netherlands Antilles (NE)	Willemstad	383 993	152,000	Dutch	oil refining, phosphates, livestock

(SA) South Africa   (NE) Netherlands

Flag	Country or Dependency	Capital	Area	Population	Major or Official Languages	Important Products
	New Caledonia (FR)	Nouméa	7,358 (mi²) 19,058 (km²)	148,000	French, Melanesian languages	nickel, coffee, copra, chrome, iron, cobalt
	New Zealand	Wellington	103,736 268,676	3,000,000	English, Maori	lumber, dairy products, wool, manufactured goods
	Nicaragua	Managua	50,193 130,000	3,000,000	Spanish, Indian languages	coffee, cotton, sugar, chemicals, livestock
	Niger	Niamey	489,189 1,267,000	6,000,000	French, Hausa, others	coal, iron, uranium, peanuts, livestock
	Nigeria	Lagos	356,667 923,768	91,000,000	English, others	petroleum, lumber, tin, cotton, palm oil
	Northern Marianas (US)	Saipan	185 480	18,000	Chamorro, English	copra, livestock, fish, fruits, vegetables
	Norway	Oslo	125,182 324,219	4,000,000	Norwegian, Lapp	petroleum, lumber, fish, ships, chemicals
	Oman	Muscat	105,000 271,950	1,000,000	Arabic	petroleum, fish, asbestos, dates
	Pakistan	Islamabad	310,402 809,943	103,000,000	Urdu, English, others	cotton, rice, fish, sugar, leather
	Palau (US)	Koror	191 494	16,000	English, others	bauxite, yams, copra, fruits, fish, handicrafts
	Panama	Panama City	29,761 77,082	2,000,000	Spanish, English	bananas, sugar, rice, coffee, lumber, corn
	Papua New Guinea	Port Moresby	178,259 461,691	4,000,000	Melanesian languages, English	cocoa beans, copra, lumber, copper, rubber
	Paraguay	Asunción	157,047 406,752	4,000,000	Spanish, Guarani	livestock, tobacco, cotton, oilseeds, lumber
	Peru	Lima	496,222 1,285,216	21,000,000	Spanish, Quechua, Aymara	coffee, cotton, sugar, fish, copper, silver
	Philippines	Manila	115,830 300,000	57,000,000	Pilipino, English, others	lumber, sugar, textiles, coconuts, tobacco
	Poland	Warsaw	120,725 312,677	38,000,000	Polish	machinery, textiles, coal, iron, steel
	Portugal	Lisbon	35,552 92,082	10,000,000	Portuguese	cork, fish, wine, olives, textiles
	Puerto Rico (US)	San Juan	3,435 8,897	3,000,000	Spanish, English	chemicals, clothing, fish, electronic goods, sugar
	Qatar	Doha	4,247 11,000	300,000	Arabic	petroleum, fish, steel
	Réunion (FR)	Saint-Denis	969 2,510	571,000	French, Creole	sugar, beans, vanilla, molasses, rum, bananas
	Romania	Bucharest	91,699 237,500	23,000,000	Romanian, Hungarian, others	lumber, petroleum, coal, machinery, minerals
	Rwanda	Kigali	10,169 26,338	6,000,000	Kinyarwandu, French	coffee, tea, beans, potatoes, livestock
	St. Christopher and Nevis	Basseterre	100 258	50,000	English	molasses, sugar, cotton, salt, fish, spices
	St. Helena (UK)	Jamestown	47 122	5,000	English	fruits, vegetables, handicrafts
	St. Lucia	Castries	238 619	130,000	English, French patois	bananas, coconuts, fish, cocoa beans, spices
	St. Vincent and the Grenadines	Kingstown	150 390	138,000	English	bananas, arrowroot, copra, nutmeg, sugar

Flag	Country or Dependency	Capital	Area	Population	Major or Official Languages	Important Products
	Samoa, American (US)	Pago Pago	76 (mi²) 198 (km²)	34,000	Samoan, English	tuna, pet food, fish meal, handicrafts
	Samoa, Western	Apia	1,093 2,831	163,000	Samoan, English	copra, cocoa beans, lumber, bananas
	San Marino	San Marino	23 61	21,000	Italian	lime, building stone, wheat, textiles, wine
	São Tomé and Príncipe	São Tomé	372 964	106,000	Portuguese	copra, palm oil, cocoa beans, lumber, bananas
	Saudi Arabia	Riyadh	829,996 2,149,690	11,000,000	Arabic	petroleum, cement, dates, chemicals, livestock
	Senegal	Dakar	75,750 196,192	7,000,000	French, Wolof, others	phosphates, fertilizer, peanut oil, cotton, fish
	Seychelles	Victoria	108 280	69,000	English, French	copra, vanilla, fish, livestock, cinnamon
	Sierra Leone	Freetown	27,699 71,740	4,000,000	English, Mende, others	coffee, cocoa beans, fish, ginger, peanuts, sugar
	Singapore	Singapore	224 581	3,000,000	English, Chinese, Malay, Tamil	manufactured goods, fish, electronic goods, textiles
	Solomon Islands	Honiara	10,983 28,446	273,000	Melanesian languages, English	lumber, fish, copra, rice, palm oil, spices
	Somalia	Mogadishu	246,199 637,657	6,000,000	Somali	spices, iron ore, livestock, bananas, peanuts
	South Africa	Capetown, Pretoria	471,443 1,221,037	33,000,000	Afrikaans, English, Bantu languages	gold, diamonds, uranium, wool, fruits, chrome
	Spain	Madrid	194,896 504,782	39,000,000	Spanish, Catalan, Galician, Basque	footwear, fruit, vegetables, cars, clothing
	Sri Lanka	Colombo	25,332 65,610	17,000,000	Sinhala, Tamil, English	rubber, tea, graphite, petroleum, spices, fish
	Sudan	Khartoum	967,495 2,505,813	22,000,000	Arabic, others	livestock, peanuts, copper, cotton, sesame seeds
	Suriname	Paramaribo	63,251 163,820	460,000	Dutch, Surinamese, English	aluminum, bauxite, citrus, lumber, shrimp, sugar
	Swaziland	Mbabane	6,704 17,363	671,000	English, Siswati	coal, iron ore, citrus, cotton, livestock, sugar
	Sweden	Stockholm	173,731 449,964	8,000,000	Swedish	lumber, motor vehicles, machinery, iron and steel
	Switzerland	Bern	15,941 41,288	6,000,000	German, French, Italian	precision instruments, dairy products, chemicals
	Syria	Damascus	71,498 185,180	11,000,000	Arabic	clothing, fruits, vegetables, cotton, petroleum
	Taiwan	Taipei	13,885 35,961	20,000,000	Mandarin Chinese	electrical machinery, footwear, textiles, citrus
	Tanzania	Dar es Salaam	364,898 945,087	22,000,000	Swahili, Bantu languages, English	diamonds, cashews, sisal, cloves, coffee, tea
	Thailand	Bangkok	198,456 514,000	54,000,000	Thai, Chinese	rubber, tapioca, tin, rice, textiles, lumber
	Togo	Lomé	21,925 56,785	3,000,000	Ewe, Mina, others	coffee, cocoa beans, rice, phosphates, cotton, iron
	Tonga	Nuku'alofa	290 751	107,000	Tongan, English	coconuts, bananas, vanilla, pineapples, papayas, fish

FACTS ABOUT THE NORTHEASTERN STATES

State	Population per Square Mile	Percent Urban	Largest City
Connecticut	647	79	Bridgeport
Maine	37	48	Portland
Massachusetts	741	84	Boston
New Hampshire	109	52	Manchester
New Jersey	1,006	89	Newark
New York	374	85	New York City
Pennsylvania	265	69	Philadelphia
Rhode Island	912	87	Providence
Vermont	57	34	Burlington

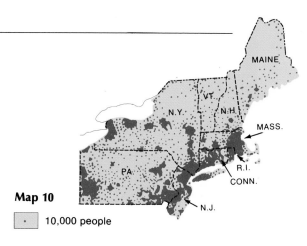

Map 10

· = 10,000 people

State Flag	State	Origin of State Name	State Nickname	State Capital	Year Admitted to Union	Population	Number of Representatives in Congress
	Connecticut	Algonquin, "beside the long river"	Nutmeg State	Hartford	1788	3,189,000	6
	Maine	after former French province of Mayne	Pine Tree State	Augusta	1820	1,173,000	2
	Massachusetts	Algonquin, "large mountain place"	Bay State	Boston	1788	5,832,000	11
	New Hampshire	after English county of Hampshire	Granite State	Concord	1788	1,027,000	2
	New Jersey	after island of Jersey in English Channel	Garden State	Trenton	1787	7,619,000	14
	New York	honors English Duke of York	Empire State	Albany	1788	17,772,000	34
	Pennsylvania	honors Admiral William Penn, father of founder of colony	Keystone State	Harrisburg	1787	11,888,000	23
	Rhode Island	after Greek island of Rhodes	Ocean State	Providence	1790	975,000	2
	Vermont	French, "green mountain"	Green Mountain State	Montpelier	1791	541,000	1

FACTS ABOUT THE SOUTHERN STATES
(including District of Columbia)

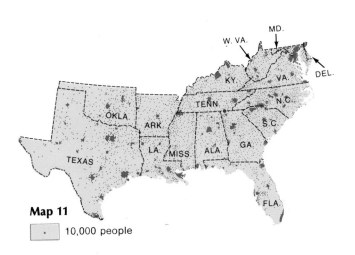

Map 11

| . | 10,000 people |

State	Population per Square Mile	Percent Urban	Largest City
Alabama	79	60	Birmingham
Arkansas	45	52	Little Rock
Delaware	317	71	Wilmington
District of Columbia	9,886	100	Washington
Florida	203	84	Jacksonville
Georgia	101	62	Atlanta
Kentucky	94	51	Louisville
Louisiana	100	69	New Orleans
Maryland	442	80	Baltimore
Mississippi	55	47	Jackson
North Carolina	126	48	Charlotte
Oklahoma	48	67	Oklahoma City
South Carolina	109	54	Columbia
Tennessee	115	60	Memphis
Texas	61	80	Houston
Virginia	142	66	Norfolk
West Virginia	81	36	Charleston

State Flag	State	Origin of State Name	State Nickname	State Capital	Year Admitted to Union	Population	Number of Representatives in Congress
	Alabama	tribe of the Creek confederacy	Yellowhammer State	Montgomery	1819	4,052,000	7
	Arkansas	French version of "Kansas," a Sioux word meaning "south wind people"	Land of Opportunity	Little Rock	1836	2,372,000	4
	Delaware	honors Lord De La Warr, early governor of Virginia	Diamond State	Dover	1787	633,000	1
	District of Columbia	honors Columbus	—	—	—	—	—
	Florida	Spanish, "feast of flowers"	Sunshine State	Tallahassee	1845	11,675,000	19
	Georgia	honors King George II	Peach State	Atlanta	1788	6,104,000	10
	Kentucky	Iroquois, "meadowland"	Bluegrass State	Frankfort	1792	3,729,000	7

(continued on next page)

FACTS ABOUT THE SOUTHERN STATES
(including District of Columbia)

(continued from previous page)

State Flag	State	Origin of State Name	State Nickname	State Capital	Year Admitted to Union	Population	Number of Representatives in Congress
	Louisiana	honors Louis XIV of France	Pelican State	Baton Rouge	1812	4,501,000	8
	Maryland	honors Queen Henrietta Marie	Free State	Annapolis	1788	4,463,000	8
	Mississippi	Chippewa, "great river"	Magnolia State	Jackson	1817	2,625,000	5
	North Carolina	honors King Charles I	Tar Heel State	Raleigh	1789	6,333,000	11
	Oklahoma	Choctaw, "red people"	Sooner State	Oklahoma City	1907	3,305,000	6
	South Carolina	honors King Charles I	Palmetto State	Columbia	1788	3,377,000	6
	Tennessee	name of Cherokee villages on the Little Tennessee River	Volunteer State	Nashville	1796	4,803,000	9
	Texas	Caddo, "friendly tribe"	Lone Star State	Austin	1845	16,685,000	27
	Virginia	honors "Virgin Queen" Elizabeth I	The Old Dominion	Richmond	1788	5,787,000	10
	West Virginia	honors "Virgin Queen" Elizabeth I	Mountain State	Charleston	1863	1,918,000	4

FACTS ABOUT THE MIDWESTERN STATES

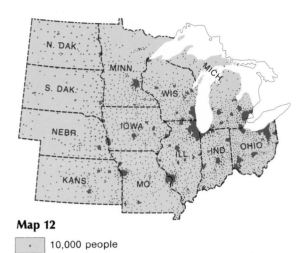

Map 12

▫ 10,000 people

State	Population per Square Mile	Percent Urban	Largest City
Illinois	207	83	Chicago
Indiana	153	64	Indianapolis
Iowa	52	59	Des Moines
Kansas	30	67	Wichita
Michigan	159	71	Detroit
Minnesota	52	67	Minneapolis
Missouri	73	68	St. Louis
Nebraska	21	63	Omaha
North Dakota	10	49	Fargo
Ohio	262	73	Cleveland
South Dakota	9	46	Sioux Falls
Wisconsin	88	64	Milwaukee

State Flag	State	Origin of State Name	State Nickname	State Capital	Year Admitted to Union	Population	Number of Representatives in Congress
	Illinois	Algonquin, "men" or "warriors"	Prairie State	Springfield	1818	11,552,000	22
	Indiana	land of the Indians	Hoosier State	Indianapolis	1816	5,504,000	10
	Iowa	Sioux, "beautiful land"	Hawkeye State	Des Moines	1846	2,851,000	6
	Kansas	Sioux, "south wind people"	Sunflower State	Topeka	1861	2,460,000	5
	Michigan	Chippewa, "great water"	Wolverine State	Lansing	1837	9,145,000	18
	Minnesota	Sioux, "sky-tinted water"	North Star State	St. Paul	1858	4,214,000	8
	Missouri	tribe named after Missouri River, or "muddy water"	Show Me State	Jefferson City	1821	5,066,000	9

(continued on next page)

FACTS ABOUT THE MIDWESTERN STATES

(continued from previous page)

State Flag	State	Origin of State Name	State Nickname	State Capital	Year Admitted to Union	Population	Number of Representatives in Congress
	Nebraska	Omaha name for Platte River, "broad river"	Cornhusker State	Lincoln	1867	1,598,000	3
	North Dakota	Sioux, "friend" or "ally"	Sioux State	Bismarck	1889	679,000	1
	Ohio	Iroquois, "beautiful river"	Buckeye State	Columbus	1803	10,752,000	21
	South Dakota	Sioux, "friend" or "ally"	Sunshine State	Pierre	1889	708,000	1
	Wisconsin	Chippewa, "grassy place"	Badger State	Madison	1848	4,785,000	9

FACTS ABOUT THE WESTERN STATES

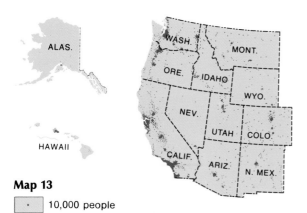

Map 13

▫ · 10,000 people

State	Population per Square Mile	Percent Urban	Largest City
Alaska	1	65	Anchorage
Arizona	27	84	Phoenix
California	164	91	Los Angeles
Colorado	31	81	Denver
Hawaii	162	87	Honolulu
Idaho	12	54	Boise
Montana	6	53	Billings
Nevada	8	85	Las Vegas
New Mexico	12	72	Albuquerque
Oregon	28	68	Portland
Utah	20	84	Salt Lake City
Washington	65	38	Seattle
Wyoming	5	63	Casper

State Flag	State	Origin of State Name	State Nickname	State Capital	Year Admitted to Union	Population	Number of Representatives in Congress
	Alaska	Russian version of Aleut word meaning "great land"	The Last Frontier	Juneau	1959	534,000	1
	Arizona	Spanish version of Pima word meaning "little spring place"	Grand Canyon State	Phoenix	1912	3,319,000	5
	California	mythical island paradise in Spanish literature	Golden State	Sacramento	1850	26,981,000	45
	Colorado	Spanish, "red"	Centennial State	Denver	1876	3,267,000	6
	Hawaii	Polynesian word for "homeland"	Aloha State	Honolulu	1959	1,062,000	2
	Idaho	Shoshone, "salmon tribe" or "light on the mountains"	Gem State	Boise	1890	1,002,000	2
	Montana	Spanish, "mountainous"	Treasure State	Helena	1889	819,000	2

(continued on next page)

The following is a list of the principal abbreviations used in the index.

PAGE	PLACE NAME	LATITUDE	LONGITUDE
54	Andreanof Is., *Pac. Oc.*	52 0N	178 0W
88	Ándria, *Italy*	41 13N	16 17 E
94	Andropov, *U.S.S.R.*	58 5N	38 50 E
68	Andros I., *Bahamas*	24 30N	78 0W
97	Angara —►, *U.S.S.R.*	58 30N	97 0 E
97	Angarsk, *U.S.S.R.*	52 30N	104 0 E
110	Angeles, *Phil.*	15 9N	120 33 E
84	Angers, *France*	47 30N	0 35W
78	Anglesey, *U.K.*	53 17N	4 20W
117	Angola ■, *Africa*	12 0S	18 0 E
84	Angoulême, *France*	45 39N	0 10 E
67	Anguilla, *W. Indies*	18 14N	63 5W
105	Anhui □, *China*	32 0N	117 0 E
84	Anjou, *France*	47 20N	0 15W
95	Ankara, *Turkey*	40 0N	32 54 E
56	Ann Arbor, *U.S.A.*	42 17N	83 45W
114	Annaba, *Algeria*	36 50N	7 46 E
56	Annapolis, *U.S.A.*	39 0N	76 30W
84	Annecy, *France*	45 55N	6 8 E
57	Anniston, *U.S.A.*	33 45N	85 50W
105	Anshan, *China*	41 5N	122 58 E
104	Anshun, *China*	26 18N	105 57 E
95	Antalya, *Turkey*	36 52N	30 45 E
117	Antananarivo, *Madag.*	18 55S	47 31 E
124	Antarctic Pen., *Antarct.*	67 0S	60 0W
124	Antarctica	90 0S	0 0 E
51	Anticosti, I. d', *Canada*	49 30N	63 0W
68	Antigua, *W. Indies*	17 0N	61 50W
67	Antigua & Barbuda ■, *W. Indies*	17 20N	61 48W
74	Antofagasta, *Chile*	23 50S	70 30W
80	Antrim, Mts. of, *U.K.*	54 57N	6 8W
117	Antsiranana, *Madag.*	12 25S	49 20 E
81	Antwerp, *Belgium*	51 13N	4 25 E
105	Anyang, *China*	36 5N	114 21 E
96	Anzhero-Sudzhensk, *U.S.S.R.*	56 10N	86 0 E
106	Aomori, *Japan*	40 45N	140 45 E
57	Apalachicola —►, *U.S.A.*	29 40N	85 0W
110	Aparri, *Phil.*	18 22N	121 38 E
81	Apeldoorn, *Neth.*	52 13N	5 57 E
88	Apennines, *Italy*	44 20N	10 20 E
121	Apia, *W. Samoa*	13 50S	171 50W
57	Appalachian Mts., *U.S.A.*	38 0N	80 0W
58	Appleton, *U.S.A.*	44 17N	88 25W
115	Arabian Desert, *Egypt*	26 0N	33 30 E
101	Arabian Sea, *Ind. Oc.*	16 0N	65 0 E
73	Aracaju, *Brazil*	10 55S	37 4W
73	Araçatuba, *Brazil*	21 10S	50 30W
91	Arad, *Romania*	46 10N	21 20 E
122	Arafura Sea, *E. Indies*	9 0S	135 0 E
85	Aragón □, *Spain*	41 25N	1 0W
73	Araguaia —►, *Brazil*	5 21S	48 41W
103	Arakan Yoma, *Burma*	20 0N	94 40 E
96	Aral Sea, *U.S.S.R.*	44 30N	60 0 E
96	Aralsk, *U.S.S.R.*	46 50N	61 20 E
73	Arapiraca, *Brazil*	9 45S	36 39W
120	Ararat, *Australia*	37 16S	143 0 E
124	Arctic Ocean, *Arctic*	78 0N	160 0W
50	Arctic Red River, *Canada*	67 15N	134 0W
100	Ardebil, *Iran*	38 15N	48 18 E
81	Ardennes, *Belgium*	50 0N	5 10 E
59	Ardmore, *U.S.A.*	34 10N	97 5W
69	Arecibo, *Puerto Rico*	18 29N	66 42W
93	Arendal, *Norway*	58 28N	8 46 E
72	Arequipa, *Peru*	16 20S	71 30W
74	Argentina ■, *S. Amer.*	35 0S	66 0W
120	Argyle, L., *Australia*	16 20S	128 40 E
72	Arica, *Chile*	18 32S	70 20W
67	Arima, *Trin. & Tob.*	10 38N	61 17W
61	Arizona □, *U.S.A.*	34 20N	111 30W
59	Arkansas □, *U.S.A.*	35 0N	92 30W
59	Arkansas —►, *U.S.A.*	33 48N	91 4W
59	Arkansas City, *U.S.A.*	37 4N	97 3W
94	Arkhangelsk, *U.S.S.R.*	64 40N	41 0 E
84	Arles, *France*	43 41N	4 40 E
56	Arlington, *Va., U.S.A.*	38 52N	77 5W
60	Arlington, *Wash., U.S.A.*	48 11N	122 4W
81	Arlon, *Belgium*	49 42N	5 49 E
80	Armagh, *U.K.*	54 22N	6 40W
72	Armenia, *Colombia*	4 35N	75 45W
95	Armenia □, *U.S.S.R.*	40 0N	41 0 E
81	Arnhem, *Neth.*	51 58N	5 55 E
120	Arnhem Land, *Australia*	13 10S	134 30 E
78	Arran, *U.K.*	55 34N	5 12W
84	Arras, *France*	50 17N	2 46 E
103	Arunachal Pradesh □, *India*	28 0N	95 0 E
116	Arusha, *Tanzania*	3 20S	36 40 E
100	As Salt, *Jordan*	32 2N	35 43 E
100	As Summān, *Si. Arabia*	25 0N	47 0 E
106	Asahigawa, *Japan*	43 46N	142 22 E
103	Asansol, *India*	23 40N	87 1 E
75	Ascension I., *Atl. Oc.*	8 0S	14 15W
120	Ashburton —►, *Australia*	21 40S	114 56 E
57	Asheville, *U.S.A.*	35 39N	82 30W
96	Ashkhabad, *U.S.S.R.*	38 0N	57 50 E
100	Ashqelon, *Israel*	31 42N	34 35 E
56	Ashtabula, *U.S.A.*	41 52N	80 50W
98	Asia	45 0N	75 0 E
100	Asīr □, *Si. Arabia*	18 40N	42 30 E
115	Asmera, *Ethiopia*	15 19N	38 55 E
103	Assam □, *India*	26 0N	93 0 E
81	Assen, *Neth.*	53 0N	6 35 E
88	Asti, *Italy*	44 54N	8 11 E
60	Astoria, *U.S.A.*	46 16N	123 50W
95	Astrakhan, *U.S.S.R.*	46 25N	48 5 E
74	Asunción, *Paraguay*	25 10S	57 30W
115	Aswân, *Egypt*	24 4N	32 57 E
74	Atacama Desert, *Chile*	24 0S	69 20W
115	Atbara, *Sudan*	17 42N	33 59 E
50	Athabasca, L., *Canada*	59 15N	109 15W
89	Athens, *Greece*	37 58N	23 46 E
57	Athens, *Ala., U.S.A.*	34 49N	86 58W
57	Athens, *Ga., U.S.A.*	33 56N	83 24W
80	Athlone, *Ireland*	53 26N	7 57W
57	Atlanta, *U.S.A.*	33 50N	84 24W
56	Atlantic City, *U.S.A.*	39 25N	74 25W
75	Atlantic Ocean	0 0	20 0W
57	Auburn, *U.S.A.*	32 37N	85 30W
121	Auckland, *N.Z.*	36 52S	174 46 E
83	Augsburg, *W. Germany*	48 22N	10 54 E
57	Augusta, *Ga., U.S.A.*	33 29N	81 59W
57	Augusta, *Maine, U.S.A.*	44 20N	69 46W
102	Aurangabad, *India*	19 50N	75 23 E
58	Aurora, *Colo., U.S.A.*	39 44N	104 55W
58	Aurora, *Ill., U.S.A.*	41 42N	88 12W
58	Austin, *Minn., U.S.A.*	43 37N	92 59W
59	Austin, *Tex., U.S.A.*	30 20N	97 45W
120	Australia ■, *Oceania*	23 0S	135 0 E
121	Australian Alps, *Australia*	36 30S	148 30 E
121	Australian Capital Territory □, *Australia*	35 30S	149 0 E
90	Austria ■, *Europe*	47 0N	14 0 E
84	Auxerre, *France*	47 48N	3 32 E
88	Avellino, *Italy*	40 54N	14 46 E
84	Avignon, *France*	43 57N	4 50 E
85	Ávila, *Spain*	40 39N	4 43W
120	Ayers Rock, *Australia*	25 23S	131 5 E
78	Ayr, *U.K.*	55 28N	4 37W
100	Az Zarqā, *Jordan*	32 5N	36 4 E
96	Azerbaijan □, *U.S.S.R.*	40 20N	48 0 E
75	Azores, *Atl. Oc.*	38 44N	29 0W
95	Azov, Sea of, *U.S.S.R.*	46 0N	36 30 E
66	Azuero, Pen. de, *Panama*	7 30N	80 30W

B

PAGE	PLACE NAME	LATITUDE	LONGITUDE
101	Bābol, *Iran*	36 40N	52 50 E
110	Babuyan Is., *Phil.*	19 15N	121 40 E
73	Bacabal, *Brazil*	4 15S	44 45W
91	Bacău, *Romania*	46 35N	26 55 E
111	Bacolod, *Phil.*	10 40N	122 57 E
58	Bad Lands, *U.S.A.*	43 40N	102 10W
85	Badajoz, *Spain*	38 50N	6 59W
85	Badalona, *Spain*	41 26N	2 15 E
51	Baffin B., *Canada*	72 0N	64 0W
51	Baffin I., *Canada*	68 0N	75 0W
111	Baganga, *Phil.*	7 34N	126 33 E
100	Baghdād, *Iraq*	33 20N	44 30 E
110	Baguio, *Phil.*	16 26N	120 34 E
68	Bahamas ■, *Atl. Oc.*	24 0N	75 0W
102	Bahawalpur, *Pakistan*	29 24N	71 40 E
74	Bahía Blanca, *Argentina*	38 35S	62 13W
101	Bahrain ■, *Asia*	26 0N	50 35 E
91	Baia Mare, *Romania*	47 40N	23 35 E
64	Baja California □, *Mexico*	31 10N	115 12W
60	Baker, Mt., *U.S.A.*	48 50N	121 49W
61	Bakersfield, *U.S.A.*	35 25N	119 0W
100	Bākhtarān, *Iran*	34 23N	47 0 E
95	Baku, *U.S.S.R.*	40 25N	49 45 E
91	Balaton, *Hungary*	46 50N	17 40 E
110	Balayan, *Phil.*	13 57N	120 44 E
69	Balboa, *Panama*	9 0N	79 30W
85	Balearic Is., *Spain*	39 30N	3 0 E
108	Bali, *Indonesia*	8 20S	115 0 E
95	Balikesir, *Turkey*	39 35N	27 58 E
108	Balikpapan, *Indonesia*	1 10S	116 55 E
89	Balkan Mts., *Bulgaria*	43 15N	23 0 E
96	Balkhash, L., *U.S.S.R.*	46 0N	74 50 E
121	Ballarat, *Australia*	37 33S	143 50 E
64	Balsas —►, *Mexico*	17 55N	102 10W
93	Baltic Sea, *Europe*	56 0N	20 0 E
56	Baltimore, *U.S.A.*	39 18N	76 37W
102	Baluchistan □, *Pakistan*	27 30N	65 0 E
103	Balurghat, *India*	25 15N	88 44 E
114	Bamako, *Mali*	12 34N	7 55W
83	Bamberg, *W. Germany*	49 54N	10 53 E
116	Bamenda, *Cameroon*	5 57N	10 11 E
108	Banda Aceh, *Indonesia*	5 35N	95 20 E
109	Banda Sea, *Indonesia*	6 0S	130 0 E
101	Bandār 'Abbās, *Iran*	27 15N	56 15 E
108	Bandar Seri Begawan, *Brunei*	4 52N	115 0 E
116	Bandundu, *Zaire*	3 15S	17 22 E
109	Bandung, *Indonesia*	6 54S	107 36 E
102	Bangalore, *India*	12 59N	77 40 E
108	Bangka, *Indonesia*	2 30S	105 30 E
108	Bangkok, *Thailand*	13 45N	100 35 E
103	Bangladesh ■, *Asia*	24 0N	90 0 E
57	Bangor, *U.S.A.*	44 48N	68 42W
116	Bangui, *C.A.R.*	4 23N	18 35 E
108	Banjarmasin, *Indonesia*	3 20S	114 35 E
114	Banjul, *Gambia*	13 28N	16 40W
50	Banks I., *Canada*	73 15N	121 30W
111	Bantayan, *Phil.*	11 10N	123 43 E
105	Baoding, *China*	38 50N	115 28 E
104	Baoji, *China*	34 20N	107 5 E
105	Baotou, *China*	40 32N	110 2 E
67	Barahona, *Dom. Rep.*	18 13N	71 7W
67	Barbados ■, *W. Indies*	13 0N	59 30W
85	Barcelona, *Spain*	41 21N	2 10 E
102	Bareilly, *India*	28 22N	79 27 E
96	Barents Sea, *Arctic*	73 0N	39 0 E
88	Bari, *Italy*	41 6N	16 52 E
102	Bari Doab, *Pakistan*	30 20N	73 0 E
103	Barisal, *Bangla.*	22 45N	90 20 E
120	Barkly Tableland, *Australia*	17 50S	136 40 E
88	Barletta, *Italy*	41 20N	16 17 E
96	Barnaul, *U.S.S.R.*	53 20N	83 40 E
72	Barquísimeto, *Venezuela*	10 4N	69 19W
72	Barrancabermeja, *Colombia*	7 0N	73 50W
72	Barranquilla, *Colombia*	11 0N	74 50W
78	Barrow-in-Furness, *U.K.*	54 8N	3 15W
61	Barstow, *U.S.A.*	34 58N	117 2W
59	Bartlesville, *U.S.A.*	36 50N	95 58W
83	Basle, *Switz.*	47 35N	7 35 E
85	Basque Provinces, *Spain*	42 50N	2 45W
101	Basra, *Iraq*	30 30N	47 50 E
120	Bass Str., *Australia*	39 15S	146 30 E
67	Basse-Terre, *Guadeloupe*	16 0N	61 40W
103	Bassein, *Burma*	16 45N	94 30 E
67	Basseterre, *St. Christopher-Nevis*	17 17N	62 43W
84	Bastia, *France*	42 40N	9 30 E
116	Bata, *Eq. Guin.*	1 57N	9 50 E
110	Batangas, *Phil.*	13 35N	121 10 E
79	Bath, *U.K.*	51 22N	2 22W
120	Bathurst, *Australia*	33 25S	149 31 E
51	Bathurst, *Canada*	47 37N	65 43W
54	Bathurst, C., *Canada*	70 34N	128 0W
114	Batna, *Algeria*	35 34N	6 15 E
59	Baton Rouge, *U.S.A.*	30 30N	91 5W
56	Battle Creek, *U.S.A.*	42 20N	85 6W
95	Batumi, *U.S.S.R.*	41 30N	41 30 E
73	Bauru, *Brazil*	22 10S	49 0W
83	Bavaria □, *W. Germany*	49 7N	11 30 E
56	Bay City, *U.S.A.*	43 35N	83 51W
66	Bayamo, *Cuba*	20 20N	76 40W
69	Bayamón, *Puerto Rico*	18 24N	66 10W
104	Bayan Har Shan, *China*	34 0N	98 0 E
84	Bayeux, *France*	49 17N	0 42W
97	Baykal, L., *U.S.S.R.*	53 0N	108 0 E
84	Bayonne, *France*	43 30N	1 28W
59	Baytown, *U.S.A.*	29 42N	94 57W
74	Beagle Channel, *S. Amer.*	55 0S	68 30W
124	Beardmore Glacier, *Antarct.*	84 30S	170 0 E
124	Beaufort Sea, *Arctic*	72 0N	140 0W
59	Beaumont, *U.S.A.*	30 5N	94 8W
84	Beauvais, *France*	49 25N	2 8 E
114	Béchar, *Algeria*	31 38N	2 18W
100	Beersheba, *Israel*	31 15N	34 48 E
105	Bei'an, *China*	48 10N	126 20 E
105	Beijing, *China*	39 55N	116 20 E
117	Beira, *Mozam.*	19 50S	34 52 E
85	Beira-Baixa, *Portugal*	40 2N	7 30W
100	Beirut, *Lebanon*	33 53N	35 31 E
114	Bejaïa, *Algeria*	36 42N	5 13 E
51	Belcher Is., *Canada*	56 15N	78 45W
73	Belém, *Brazil*	1 20S	48 30W
80	Belfast, *U.K.*	54 35N	5 56W
84	Belfort, *France*	47 38N	6 50 E
81	Belgium ■, *Europe*	50 30N	5 0 E
95	Belgorod, *U.S.S.R.*	50 35N	36 35 E
89	Belgrade, *Yugoslavia*	44 50N	20 37 E
108	Beliton Is., *Indonesia*	3 10S	107 50 E
66	Belize ■, *Cent. Amer.*	17 0N	88 30W
66	Belize City, *Belize*	17 25N	88 0W
102	Bellary, *India*	15 10N	76 56 E
84	Belle-Ile, *France*	47 20N	3 10W

PAGE	PLACE NAME	LATITUDE	LONGITUDE
51	Belle Isle, Str. of, *Canada*	51 30N	56 30W
58	Belleville, *U.S.A.*	38 30N	90 0W
60	Bellingham, *U.S.A.*	48 45N	122 27W
66	Belmopan, *Belize*	17 18N	88 30W
73	Belo Horizonte, *Brazil*	19 55S	43 56W
58	Beloit, *U.S.A.*	42 35N	89 0W
94	Beloye More, *U.S.S.R.*	66 30N	38 0E
58	Bemidji, *U.S.A.*	47 30N	94 50W
80	Ben Nevis, *U.K.*	56 48N	5 0W
60	Bend, *U.S.A.*	44 2N	121 15W
88	Benevento, *Italy*	41 7N	14 45E
103	Bengal, Bay of, *Ind. Oc.*	18 0N	90 0E
105	Bengbu, *China*	32 58N	117 20E
115	Benghazi, *Libya*	32 11N	20 3E
115	Beni Suef, *Egypt*	29 5N	31 6E
114	Benin ■, *Africa*	10 0N	2 0E
114	Benin, Bight of, *W. Afr.*	5 0N	3 0E
114	Benin City, *Nigeria*	6 20N	5 31E
117	Benoni, *S. Africa*	26 11S	28 18E
120	Bentinck I., *Australia*	17 3S	139 35E
56	Benton Harbor, *U.S.A.*	42 10N	86 28W
114	Benue →, *Nigeria*	7 48N	6 46E
105	Benxi, *China*	41 20N	123 48E
116	Berbérati, *C.A.R.*	4 15N	15 40E
94	Berezniki, *U.S.S.R.*	59 24N	56 46E
88	Bérgamo, *Italy*	45 42N	9 40E
93	Bergen, *Norway*	60 23N	5 20E
81	Bergen-op-Zoom, *Neth.*	51 30N	4 18E
84	Bergerac, *France*	44 51N	0 30E
81	Bergisch-Gladbach, *W. Germany*	50 59N	7 9E
103	Berhampore, *India*	24 2N	88 27E
103	Berhampur, *India*	19 15N	84 54E
54	Bering Sea, *Pac. Oc.*	58 0N	167 0E
124	Bering Str., *N. Amer.*	66 0N	170 0W
60	Berkeley, *U.S.A.*	37 52N	122 20W
82	Berlin, *Germany*	52 32N	13 24E
68	Bermuda ■, *Atl. Oc.*	32 45N	65 0W
83	Bern, *Switz.*	46 57N	7 28E
78	Berwick-upon-Tweed, *U.K.*	55 47N	2 0W
84	Besançon, *France*	47 15N	6 0E
57	Bessemer, *U.S.A.*	33 25N	86 57W
54	Bethel, *U.S.A.*	60 50N	161 50W
100	Bethlehem, *Jordan*	31 43N	35 12E
56	Bethlehem, *U.S.A.*	40 39N	75 24W
84	Béthune, *France*	50 30N	2 38E
61	Beverly Hills, *U.S.A.*	34 4N	118 29W
81	Beverwijk, *Neth.*	52 28N	4 38E
84	Béziers, *France*	43 20N	3 12E
103	Bhagalpur, *India*	25 10N	87 0E
102	Bhatinda, *India*	30 15N	74 57E
103	Bhatpara, *India*	22 50N	88 25E
102	Bhavnagar, *India*	21 45N	72 10E
103	Bhimavaram, *India*	16 30N	81 30E
102	Bhopal, *India*	23 20N	77 30E
103	Bhubaneshwar, *India*	20 15N	85 50E
103	Bhutan ■, *Asia*	27 25N	90 30E
91	Białystok, *Poland*	53 10N	23 10E
84	Biarritz, *France*	43 29N	1 33W
57	Biddeford, *U.S.A.*	43 30N	70 28W
117	Bié Plateau, *Angola*	12 0S	16 0E
83	Biel, *Switz.*	47 8N	7 14E
82	Bielefeld, *W. Germany*	52 2N	8 31E
59	Big Spring, *U.S.A.*	32 10N	101 25W
60	Bighorn →, *U.S.A.*	46 9N	107 28W
60	Bighorn Mts., *U.S.A.*	44 30N	107 30W
103	Bihar □, *India*	25 0N	86 0E
102	Bikaner, *India*	28 2N	73 18E
55	Bikini Atoll, *Pac. Oc.*	12 0N	167 30E
85	Bilbao, *Spain*	43 16N	2 56W
60	Billings, *U.S.A.*	45 43N	108 29W
59	Biloxi, *U.S.A.*	30 24N	88 53W
111	Binalbagan, *Phil.*	10 12N	122 50E
60	Bingham Canyon, *U.S.A.*	40 31N	112 10W
56	Binghamton, *U.S.A.*	42 9N	75 54W
116	Bioko, *Eq. Guin.*	3 30N	8 40E
120	Birdum, *Australia*	15 39S	133 13E
79	Birmingham, *U.K.*	52 30N	1 55W
57	Birmingham, *U.S.A.*	33 31N	86 50W
84	Biscay, B. of, *Atl. Oc.*	45 0N	2 0W
114	Biskra, *Algeria*	34 50N	5 44E
58	Bismarck, *U.S.A.*	46 49N	100 49W
121	Bismarck Arch., *Papua N. G.*	2 30S	150 0E
121	Bismarck Sea, *Papua N. G.*	4 10S	146 50E
114	Bissau, *Guin.-Biss.*	11 45N	15 45W
89	Bitola, *Yugoslavia*	41 5N	21 10E
60	Bitterroot Range, *U.S.A.*	46 0N	114 20W
107	Biwa-Ko, *Japan*	35 15N	136 10E
96	Biysk, *U.S.S.R.*	52 40N	85 0E
83	Black Forest, *W. Germany*	48 0N	8 0E
58	Black Hills, *U.S.A.*	44 0N	103 50W
95	Black Sea, *Europe*	43 30N	35 0E

PAGE	PLACE NAME	LATITUDE	LONGITUDE
114	Black Volta →, *Africa*	8 41N	1 33W
78	Blackburn, *U.K.*	53 44N	2 30W
78	Blackpool, *U.K.*	53 48N	3 3W
97	Blagoveshchensk, *U.S.S.R.*	50 20N	127 30E
84	Blanc, Mont, *Europe*	45 48N	6 50E
61	Blanca Peak, *U.S.A.*	37 35N	105 29W
117	Blantyre, *Malawi*	15 45S	35 0E
121	Blenheim, *N.Z.*	41 38S	173 57E
117	Bloemfontein, *S. Africa*	29 6S	26 14E
84	Blois, *France*	47 35N	1 20E
58	Bloomington, *Ill., U.S.A.*	40 27N	89 0W
56	Bloomington, *Ind., U.S.A.*	39 10N	86 30W
60	Blue Mts., *Oreg., U.S.A.*	45 15N	119 0W
56	Blue Mts., *Pa., U.S.A.*	40 30N	76 30W
115	Blue Nile →, *Sudan*	12 30N	34 30E
57	Blue Ridge Mts., *U.S.A.*	36 30N	80 15W
74	Blumenau, *Brazil*	27 0S	49 0W
114	Bobo-Dioulasso, *Burkina Faso*	11 8N	4 13W
57	Boca Raton, *U.S.A.*	26 21N	80 5W
81	Bocholt, *W. Germany*	51 50N	6 35E
81	Bochum, *W. Germany*	51 28N	7 12E
83	Bodensee, *W. Germany*	47 35N	9 25E
92	Bodø, *Norway*	67 17N	14 24E
59	Bogalusa, *U.S.A.*	30 50N	89 55W
111	Bogo, *Phil.*	11 3N	124 0E
109	Bogor, *Indonesia*	6 36S	106 48E
72	Bogota, *Colombia*	4 34N	74 0W
90	Bohemian Forest, *Czech.*	49 20N	13 0E
111	Bohol, *Phil.*	9 50N	124 10E
60	Boise, *U.S.A.*	43 43N	116 9W
59	Boise City, *U.S.A.*	36 45N	102 30W
114	Bolgatanga, *Ghana*	10 44N	0 53W
72	Bolivia ■, *S. Amer.*	17 6S	64 0W
88	Bologna, *Italy*	44 30N	11 20E
97	Bolshevik I., *U.S.S.R.*	78 30N	102 0E
94	Bolshezemelskaya Tundra, *U.S.S.R.*	67 0N	56 0E
78	Bolton, *U.K.*	53 35N	2 26W
92	Bolungavík, *Iceland*	66 9N	23 15W
88	Bolzano, *Italy*	46 30N	11 20E
116	Boma, *Zaire*	5 50S	13 4E
102	Bombay, *India*	18 55N	72 50E
88	Bonifacio, Str. of, *France*	41 12N	9 15E
81	Bonn, *W. Germany*	50 43N	7 6E
51	Boothia, Gulf of, *Canada*	71 0N	90 0W
50	Boothia Pen., *Canada*	71 0N	94 0W
93	Borås, *Sweden*	57 43N	12 56E
84	Bordeaux, *France*	44 50N	0 36W
92	Borgarnes, *Iceland*	64 32N	21 55W
59	Borger, *U.S.A.*	35 40N	101 20W
108	Borneo, *E. Indies*	1 0N	115 0E
93	Bornholm, *Denmark*	55 10N	15 0E
95	Bosporus, *Turkey*	41 10N	29 10E
56	Boston, *U.S.A.*	42 20N	71 0W
92	Bothnia, G. of, *Europe*	63 0N	20 0E
117	Botswana ■, *Africa*	22 0S	24 0E
81	Bottrop, *W. Germany*	51 34N	6 59E
114	Bouaké, *Ivory C.*	7 40N	5 2W
116	Bouar, *C.A.R.*	6 0N	15 40E
121	Bougainville I., *Solomon Is.*	6 0S	155 0E
58	Boulder, *U.S.A.*	40 3N	105 10W
84	Boulogne-sur-Mer, *France*	50 42N	1 36E
84	Bourges, *France*	47 9N	2 25E
79	Bournemouth, *U.K.*	50 43N	1 53W
75	Bouvet I., *Antarct.*	54 26S	3 24E
60	Bozeman, *U.S.A.*	45 40N	111 0W
57	Bradenton, *U.S.A.*	27 25N	82 35W
78	Bradford, *U.K.*	53 47N	1 45W
85	Braga, *Portugal*	41 35N	8 25W
103	Brahmaputra →, *India*	24 2N	90 59E
91	Brăila, *Romania*	45 19N	27 59E
72	Branco →, *Brazil*	1 20S	61 50W
50	Brandon, *Canada*	49 50N	99 57W
73	Brasília, *Brazil*	15 47S	47 55E
91	Braşov, *Romania*	45 38N	25 35E
91	Bratislava, *Czech.*	48 10N	17 7E
97	Bratsk, *U.S.S.R.*	56 10N	101 30E
61	Brawley, *U.S.A.*	32 58N	115 30W
73	Brazil ■, *S. Amer.*	10 0S	50 0W
73	Brazilian Highlands, *Brazil*	18 0S	46 30W
59	Brazos →, *U.S.A.*	28 53N	95 23W
116	Brazzaville, *Congo*	4 9S	15 12E
81	Breda, *Neth.*	51 35N	4 45E
92	Breiðafjörður, *Iceland*	65 15N	23 15W
82	Bremen, *W. Germany*	53 4N	8 47E
88	Bremerhaven, *W. Germany*	53 34N	8 35E
60	Bremerton, *U.S.A.*	47 30N	122 38W
83	Brenner Pass, *Alps*	47 0N	11 30E
88	Bréscia, *Italy*	45 33N	10 13E
84	Brest, *France*	48 24N	4 31W
94	Brest, *U.S.S.R.*	52 10N	23 40E
94	Brezhnev, *U.S.S.R.*	55 42N	52 19E

PAGE	PLACE NAME	LATITUDE	LONGITUDE
56	Bridgeport, *U.S.A.*	41 12N	73 12W
67	Bridgetown, *Barbados*	13 0N	59 30W
60	Brigham City, *U.S.A.*	41 30N	112 1W
79	Brighton, *U.K.*	50 50N	0 9W
89	Bríndisi, *Italy*	40 39N	17 55E
121	Brisbane, *Australia*	27 25S	153 2E
79	Bristol, *U.K.*	51 26N	2 35W
57	Bristol, *U.S.A.*	36 36N	82 11W
79	Bristol Channel, *U.K.*	51 18N	4 30W
50	British Columbia □, *Canada*	55 0N	125 15W
80	British Isles, *Europe*	55 0N	4 0W
84	Brittany, *France*	48 0N	3 0W
90	Brno, *Czech.*	49 10N	16 35E
120	Broken Hill, *Australia*	31 58S	141 29E
50	Brooks, *Canada*	50 35N	111 55W
54	Brooks Ra., *U.S.A.*	68 40N	147 0W
120	Broome, *Australia*	18 0S	122 15E
59	Brownsville, *U.S.A.*	25 56N	97 25W
59	Brownwood, *U.S.A.*	31 45N	99 0W
84	Bruay-en-Artois, *France*	50 29N	2 33E
81	Bruges, *Belgium*	51 13N	3 13E
108	Brunei ■, *E. Indies*	4 50N	115 0E
57	Brunswick, *U.S.A.*	31 10N	81 30W
82	Brunswick, *W. Germany*	52 17N	10 28E
81	Brussels, *Belgium*	50 51N	4 21E
59	Bryan, *U.S.A.*	30 40N	96 27W
94	Bryansk, *U.S.S.R.*	53 13N	34 25E
72	Bucaramanga, *Colombia*	7 0N	73 0W
91	Bucharest, *Romania*	44 27N	26 10E
91	Budapest, *Hungary*	47 29N	19 5E
72	Buenaventura, *Colombia*	3 53N	77 4W
74	Buenos Aires, *Argentina*	34 30S	58 20W
56	Buffalo, *U.S.A.*	42 55N	78 50W
91	Bug →, *Poland*	52 31N	21 5E
95	Bug →, *U.S.S.R.*	46 59N	31 58E
116	Bujumbura, *Burundi*	3 16S	29 18E
116	Bukavu, *Zaire*	2 20S	28 52E
96	Bukhara, *U.S.S.R.*	39 48N	64 25E
110	Bulan, *Phil.*	12 40N	123 52E
117	Bulawayo, *Zimbabwe*	20 7S	28 32E
89	Bulgaria ■, *Europe*	42 35N	25 30E
121	Bundaberg, *Australia*	24 54S	152 22E
100	Buraydah, *Si. Arabia*	26 20N	44 8E
103	Burdwan, *India*	23 14N	87 39E
89	Burgas, *Bulgaria*	42 33N	27 29E
85	Burgos, *Spain*	42 21N	3 41W
84	Burgundy, *France*	47 0N	4 50E
114	Burkina Faso ■, *Africa*	12 0N	1 0W
58	Burlington, *Iowa, U.S.A.*	40 50N	91 5W
57	Burlington, *N.C., U.S.A.*	36 7N	79 27W
56	Burlington, *Vt., U.S.A.*	44 27N	73 14W
103	Burma ■, *Asia*	21 0N	96 30E
95	Bursa, *Turkey*	40 15N	29 5E
101	Burujird, *Iran*	33 55N	48 50E
116	Burundi ■, *Africa*	3 15S	30 0E
97	Buryat A.S.S.R. □, *U.S.S.R.*	53 0N	110 0E
101	Būshehr, *Iran*	28 20N	51 45E
60	Butte, *U.S.A.*	46 0N	112 31W
111	Butuan, *Phil.*	8 57N	125 33E
91	Buzău, *Romania*	45 10N	26 50E
91	Bydgoszcz, *Poland*	53 10N	18 0E
124	Byrd Land, *Antarct.*	79 30S	125 0W
97	Byrrang Mts., *U.S.S.R.*	75 0N	100 0E
91	Bytom, *Poland*	50 25N	18 54E

C

PAGE	PLACE NAME	LATITUDE	LONGITUDE
110	Cabanatuan, *Phil.*	15 30N	120 58E
72	Cabimas, *Venezuela*	10 23N	71 25W
116	Cabinda □, *Angola*	5 0S	12 30E
60	Cabinet Mts., *U.S.A.*	48 0N	115 30W
89	Čačak, *Yugoslavia*	43 54N	20 20E
85	Cáceres, *Spain*	39 26N	6 23W
74	Cachoeira do Sul, *Brazil*	30 3S	52 53W
111	Cadiz, *Phil.*	10 57N	123 15E
85	Cádiz, *Spain*	36 30N	6 20W
84	Caen, *France*	49 10N	0 22W
111	Cagayan de Oro, *Phil.*	8 30N	124 40E
88	Cágliari, *Italy*	39 15N	9 6E
69	Caguas, *Puerto Rico*	18 14N	66 4W
67	Caicos Is., *W. Indies*	21 40N	71 40W
121	Cairns, *Australia*	16 57S	145 45E
115	Cairo, *Egypt*	30 1N	31 14E
59	Cairo, *U.S.A.*	37 0N	89 10W
72	Cajamarca, *Peru*	7 5S	78 28W
114	Calabar, *Nigeria*	4 57N	8 20E
88	Calábria □, *Italy*	39 24N	16 30E
84	Calais, *France*	50 57N	1 50E
111	Calamba, *Phil.*	10 11N	123 17E
110	Calbayog, *Phil.*	12 4N	124 38E
103	Calcutta, *India*	22 36N	88 24E
60	Caldwell, *U.S.A.*	43 45N	116 42W
50	Calgary, *Canada*	51 0N	114 10W

PAGE	PLACE NAME	LATITUDE	LONGITUDE
74	Córdoba, *Argentina*	31 20 S	64 10 W
65	Córdoba, *Mexico*	18 50 N	97 0 W
85	Córdoba, *Spain*	37 50 N	4 50 W
54	Cordova, *U.S.A.*	60 36 N	145 45 W
89	Corinth, G. of, *Greece*	38 16 N	22 30 E
80	Cork, *Ireland*	51 54 N	8 30 W
51	Corner Brook, *Canada*	48 57 N	57 58 W
72	Coro, *Venezuela*	11 25 N	69 41 W
102	Coromandel Coast, *India*	12 30 N	81 0 E
50	Coronation Gulf, *Canada*	68 25 N	110 0 W
59	Corpus Christi, *U.S.A.*	27 50 N	97 28 W
74	Corrientes, *Argentina*	27 30 S	58 45 W
64	Corrientes, C., *Mexico*	20 25 N	105 42 W
84	Corsica, *Medit. S.*	42 0 N	9 0 E
59	Corsicana, *U.S.A.*	32 5 N	96 30 W
72	Corumbá, *Brazil*	19 0 S	57 30 W
60	Corvallis, *U.S.A.*	44 36 N	123 15 W
88	Cosenza, *Italy*	39 17 N	16 14 E
66	Costa Rica ■, *Cent. Amer.*	10 0 N	84 0 W
111	Cotabato, *Phil.*	7 14 N	124 15 E
84	Côte d'Or, *France*	47 10 N	4 50 E
114	Cotonou, *Benin*	6 20 N	2 25 E
72	Cotopaxi, *Ecuador*	0 40 S	78 30 W
79	Cotswold Hills, *U.K.*	51 42 N	2 10 W
82	Cottbus, *E. Germany*	51 44 N	14 20 E
58	Council Bluffs, *U.S.A.*	41 20 N	95 50 W
79	Coventry, *U.K.*	52 25 N	1 31 W
56	Covington, *U.S.A.*	39 5 N	84 30 W
91	Craiova, *Romania*	44 21 N	23 48 E
50	Cranbrook, *Canada*	49 30 N	115 46 W
60	Crazy Mts., *U.S.A.*	46 14 N	110 30 W
88	Cremona, *Italy*	45 8 N	10 2 E
89	Crete, *Greece*	35 15 N	25 0 E
78	Crewe, *U.K.*	53 6 N	2 28 W
95	Crimea, *U.S.S.R.*	45 0 N	34 0 E
68	Crooked I., *Bahamas*	22 50 N	74 10 W
118	Crozet Is., *Ind. Oc.*	46 27 S	52 0 E
72	Cruzeiro do Sul, *Brazil*	7 35 S	72 35 W
66	Cuba ■, *W. Indies*	22 0 N	79 0 W
72	Cúcuta, *Colombia*	7 54 N	72 31 W
72	Cuenca, *Ecuador*	2 50 S	79 9 W
85	Cuenca, *Spain*	40 5 N	2 10 W
65	Cuernavaca, *Mexico*	18 55 N	99 15 W
73	Cuiabá, *Brazil*	15 30 S	56 0 W
64	Culiacán, *Mexico*	24 50 N	107 23 W
72	Cumaná, *Venezuela*	10 30 N	64 5 W
56	Cumberland, *U.S.A.*	39 40 N	78 43 W
78	Cumbrian Mts., *U.K.*	54 30 N	3 0 W
88	Cúneo, *Italy*	44 23 N	7 31 E
74	Curitiba, *Brazil*	25 20 S	49 10 W
103	Cuttack, *India*	20 25 N	85 57 E
72	Cuzco, *Peru*	13 32 S	72 0 W
95	Cyprus ■, *Medit. S.*	35 0 N	33 0 E
90	Czechoslovakia ■, *Europe*	49 0 N	17 0 E
91	Częstochowa, *Poland*	50 49 N	19 7 E

D

PAGE	PLACE NAME	LATITUDE	LONGITUDE
108	Da Lat, *Vietnam*	11 56 N	108 25 E
108	Da Nang, *Vietnam*	16 4 N	108 13 E
110	Daet, *Phil.*	14 2 N	122 55 E
110	Dagupan, *Phil.*	16 3 N	120 20 E
114	Dakar, *Senegal*	14 34 N	17 29 W
114	Dakhla, *W. Sahara*	23 50 N	15 53 W
121	Dalby, *Australia*	27 10 S	151 17 E
105	Dalian, *China*	38 50 N	121 40 E
59	Dallas, *U.S.A.*	32 50 N	96 50 W
89	Dalmatia, *Yugoslavia*	43 20 N	17 0 E
114	Daloa, *Ivory C.*	7 0 N	6 30 W
57	Dalton, *U.S.A.*	34 47 N	84 58 W
100	Damascus, *Syria*	33 30 N	36 18 E
101	Dammām, *Si. Arabia*	26 20 N	50 5 E
120	Dampier, *Australia*	20 41 S	116 42 E
120	Dampier Arch., *Australia*	20 38 S	116 32 E
56	Danbury, *U.S.A.*	41 23 N	73 29 W
105	Dandong, *China*	40 10 N	124 20 E
91	Danube →, *Europe*	45 20 N	29 40 E
57	Danville, *U.S.A.*	36 40 N	79 20 W
111	Dapitan, *Phil.*	8 39 N	123 25 E
116	Dar-es-Salaam, *Tanzania*	6 50 S	39 12 E
100	Dar'ā, *Syria*	32 36 N	36 7 E
95	Dardanelles, *Turkey*	40 0 N	26 0 E
66	Darién, G. of, *Colombia*	9 0 N	77 0 W
120	Darling →, *Australia*	34 4 S	141 54 E
120	Darling Ra., *Australia*	32 30 S	116 0 E
83	Darmstadt, *W. Germany*	49 51 N	8 40 E
79	Dartmoor, *U.K.*	50 36 N	4 0 W
51	Dartmouth, *Canada*	44 40 N	63 30 W
120	Darwin, *Australia*	12 25 S	130 51 E
101	Dasht-e Kavīr, *Iran*	34 30 N	55 0 E
101	Dasht-e Lūt, *Iran*	31 30 N	58 0 E
105	Datong, *China*	40 6 N	113 18 E
111	Datu Piang, *Phil.*	7 2 N	124 30 E
50	Dauphin, *Canada*	51 9 N	100 5 W
84	Dauphiné, *France*	45 15 N	5 25 E
111	Davao, *Phil.*	7 0 N	125 40 E
111	Davao, G. of, *Phil.*	6 30 N	125 48 E
58	Davenport, *U.S.A.*	41 30 N	90 40 W
66	David, *Panama*	8 30 N	82 30 W
51	Davis Str., *N. Amer.*	65 0 N	58 0 W
50	Dawson, *Canada*	64 10 N	139 30 W
50	Dawson Creek, *Canada*	55 45 N	120 15 W
56	Dayton, *U.S.A.*	39 45 N	84 10 W
57	Daytona Beach, *U.S.A.*	29 14 N	81 0 W
117	De Aar, *S. Africa*	30 39 S	24 0 E
100	Dead Sea, *Asia*	31 30 N	35 30 E
50	Dease Lake, *Canada*	58 25 N	130 6 W
61	Death Valley, *U.S.A.*	36 19 N	116 52 W
91	Debrecen, *Hungary*	47 33 N	21 42 E
57	Decatur, *Ala., U.S.A.*	34 35 N	87 0 W
58	Decatur, *Ill., U.S.A.*	39 50 N	89 0 W
102	Deccan, *India*	18 0 N	79 0 E
102	Dehra Dun, *India*	30 20 N	78 4 E
61	Delano, *U.S.A.*	35 48 N	119 13 W
56	Delaware □, *U.S.A.*	39 0 N	75 40 W
56	Delaware →, *U.S.A.*	39 20 N	75 25 W
81	Delft, *Neth.*	52 1 N	4 22 E
102	Delhi, *India*	28 38 N	77 17 E
101	Demavend, *Iran*	35 56 N	52 10 E
81	Den Helder, *Neth.*	52 57 N	4 45 E
95	Denizli, *Turkey*	37 42 N	29 2 E
93	Denmark ■, *Europe*	55 30 N	9 0 E
75	Denmark Str., *Atl. Oc.*	66 0 N	30 0 W
59	Denton, *U.S.A.*	33 12 N	97 10 W
58	Denver, *U.S.A.*	39 45 N	105 0 W
78	Derby, *U.K.*	52 55 N	1 28 W
80	Derryveagh Mts., *Ireland*	55 0 N	8 40 W
58	Des Moines, *U.S.A.*	41 35 N	93 37 W
58	Des Moines →, *U.S.A.*	40 23 N	91 25 W
82	Dessau, *E. Germany*	51 49 N	12 15 E
56	Detroit, *U.S.A.*	42 23 N	83 5 W
81	Deurne, *Belgium*	51 12 N	4 24 E
81	Deventer, *Neth.*	52 15 N	6 10 E
101	Dhahran, *Si. Arabia*	26 10 N	50 7 E
103	Dhaka, *Bangla.*	23 43 N	90 26 E
103	Dhanbad, *India*	23 50 N	86 30 E
102	Dharwad, *India*	15 22 N	75 15 E
102	Dhule, *India*	20 58 N	74 50 E
118	Diego Garcia, *Ind. Oc.*	7 50 S	72 50 E
84	Dieppe, *France*	49 54 N	1 4 E
84	Dijon, *France*	47 20 N	5 0 E
54	Dillingham, *U.S.A.*	59 5 N	158 30 W
111	Dinagat, *Phil.*	10 10 N	125 40 E
88	Dinaric Alps, *Yugoslavia*	44 0 N	16 30 E
60	Dinosaur National Monument, *U.S.A.*	40 30 N	108 58 W
111	Dipolog, *Phil.*	8 36 N	123 20 E
120	Dirk Hartog I., *Australia*	25 50 S	113 5 E
120	Disappointment L., *Australia*	23 20 S	122 40 E
95	Diyarbakir, *Turkey*	37 55 N	40 18 E
101	Dizful, *Iran*	32 20 N	48 30 E
100	Djibouti ■, *Africa*	12 0 N	43 0 E
94	Dnepr →, *U.S.S.R.*	46 30 N	32 18 E
95	Dneprodzerzhinsk, *U.S.S.R.*	48 32 N	34 37 E
95	Dnepropetrovsk, *U.S.S.R.*	48 30 N	35 0 E
95	Dnestr →, *U.S.S.R.*	46 18 N	30 17 E
89	Dodecanese, *Greece*	36 35 N	27 0 E
59	Dodge City, *U.S.A.*	37 42 N	100 0 W
116	Dodoma, *Tanzania*	6 8 S	35 45 E
101	Doha, *Qatar*	25 15 N	51 35 E
88	Dolomites, *Italy*	46 30 N	11 40 E
67	Dominica ■, *W. Indies*	15 20 N	61 20 W
67	Dominican Rep. ■, *W. Indies*	19 0 N	70 30 W
95	Don →, *U.S.S.R.*	47 4 N	39 18 E
102	Dondra Head, *Sri Lanka*	5 55 N	80 40 E
80	Donegal, *Ireland*	54 39 N	8 8 W
80	Donegal B., *Ireland*	54 30 N	8 35 W
95	Donetsk, *U.S.S.R.*	48 0 N	37 45 E
105	Dongting Hu, *China*	29 18 N	112 45 E
81	Dordrecht, *Neth.*	51 48 N	4 39 E
81	Dortmund, *W. Germany*	51 32 N	7 28 E
57	Dothan, *U.S.A.*	31 10 N	85 25 W
84	Douai, *France*	50 21 N	3 4 E
116	Douala, *Cameroon*	4 0 N	9 45 E
78	Douglas, *U.K.*	54 9 N	4 29 W
61	Douglas, *U.S.A.*	31 21 N	109 30 W
85	Douro →, *Portugal*	41 8 N	8 40 W
79	Dover, *U.K.*	51 7 N	1 19 E
84	Dover, Str. of, *Europe*	51 0 N	1 30 E
124	Drake Passage, *S. Ocean*	58 0 S	68 0 W
117	Drakensberg, *S. Africa*	31 0 S	28 0 E
93	Drammen, *Norway*	59 42 N	10 12 E
91	Drava →, *Yugoslavia*	45 33 N	18 55 E
81	Drenthe □, *Neth.*	52 52 N	6 40 E
82	Dresden, *E. Germany*	51 2 N	13 45 E
89	Drina →, *Yugoslavia*	44 53 N	19 21 E
80	Drogheda, *Ireland*	53 45 N	6 20 W
124	Dronning Maud Land, *Antarct.*	72 30 S	12 0 E
50	Drumheller, *Canada*	51 25 N	112 40 W
101	Dubai, *United Arab Emirates*	25 18 N	55 20 E
121	Dubbo, *Australia*	32 11 S	148 35 E
80	Dublin, *Ireland*	53 20 N	6 18 W
57	Dublin, *U.S.A.*	32 30 N	82 34 W
89	Dubrovnik, *Yugoslavia*	42 39 N	18 6 E
85	Duero →, *Spain*	41 8 N	8 40 W
81	Duisburg, *W. Germany*	51 27 N	6 42 E
101	Dukhān, *Qatar*	25 25 N	50 50 E
58	Duluth, *U.S.A.*	46 48 N	92 10 W
111	Dumaguete, *Phil.*	9 17 N	123 15 E
78	Dumfries, *U.K.*	55 4 N	3 37 W
80	Dun Laoghaire, *Ireland*	53 17 N	6 9 W
59	Duncan, *U.S.A.*	34 25 N	98 0 W
80	Dundalk, *Ireland*	54 1 N	6 25 W
80	Dundee, *U.K.*	56 29 N	3 0 W
121	Dunedin, *N.Z.*	45 50 S	170 33 E
84	Dunkirk, *France*	51 2 N	2 20 E
64	Durango, *Mexico*	24 3 N	104 39 W
117	Durban, *S. Africa*	29 49 S	31 1 E
81	Düren, *W. Germany*	50 48 N	6 30 E
103	Durg, *India*	21 15 N	81 22 E
103	Durgapur, *India*	23 30 N	87 20 E
57	Durham, *U.S.A.*	36 0 N	78 55 W
89	Durrësi, *Albania*	41 19 N	19 28 E
96	Dushanbe, *U.S.S.R.*	38 33 N	68 48 E
81	Düsseldorf, *W. Germany*	51 15 N	6 46 E
54	Dutch Harbor, *U.S.A.*	53 54 N	166 35 W
104	Duyun, *China*	26 18 N	107 29 E
59	Dyersburg, *U.S.A.*	36 2 N	89 20 W
94	Dzerzhinsk, *U.S.S.R.*	56 14 N	43 30 E
96	Dzhambul, *U.S.S.R.*	42 54 N	71 22 E
104	Dzungaria, *China*	44 10 N	88 0 E

E

PAGE	PLACE NAME	LATITUDE	LONGITUDE
105	East China Sea, *Asia*	30 5 N	126 0 E
82	East Germany ■, *Europe*	52 0 N	12 0 E
98	East Indies, *Asia*	0 0	120 0 E
117	East London, *S. Africa*	33 0 S	27 55 E
56	East Orange, *U.S.A.*	40 46 N	74 13 W
58	East St. Louis, *U.S.A.*	38 37 N	90 4 W
97	East Siberian Sea, *U.S.S.R.*	73 0 N	160 0 E
123	Easter Islands, *Pac. Oc.*	27 0 S	109 0 W
102	Eastern Ghats, *India*	14 0 N	78 50 E
58	Eau Claire, *U.S.A.*	44 46 N	91 30 W
85	Ebro →, *Spain*	40 43 N	0 54 E
114	Ech Cheliff, *Algeria*	36 10 N	1 20 E
50	Echo Bay, *Canada*	66 5 N	117 55 W
72	Ecuador ■, *S. Amer.*	2 0 S	78 0 W
81	Edam, *Neth.*	52 31 N	5 3 E
81	Ede, *Neth.*	52 4 N	5 40 E
59	Edinburg, *U.S.A.*	26 22 N	98 10 W
78	Edinburgh, *U.K.*	55 57 N	3 12 W
50	Edmonton, *Canada*	53 30 N	113 30 W
51	Edmundston, *Canada*	47 23 N	68 20 W
116	Edward, L., *Africa*	0 25 S	29 40 E
59	Edwards Plateau, *U.S.A.*	30 30 N	101 5 W
93	Egersund, *Norway*	58 26 N	6 1 E
121	Egmont, Mt., *N.Z.*	39 17 S	174 5 E
115	Egypt ■, *Africa*	28 0 N	31 0 E
81	Eifel, *W. Germany*	50 10 N	6 45 E
120	Eighty Mile Beach, *Australia*	19 30 S	120 40 E
81	Eindhoven, *Neth.*	51 26 N	5 30 E
114	El Aaiún, *W. Sahara*	27 9 N	13 12 W
61	El Centro, *U.S.A.*	32 50 N	115 40 W
59	El Dorado, *Ark., U.S.A.*	33 10 N	92 40 W
59	El Dorado, *Kans., U.S.A.*	37 55 N	96 56 W
115	El Faiyûm, *Egypt*	29 19 N	30 50 E
115	El Fâsher, *Sudan*	13 33 N	25 26 E
115	El Gîza, *Egypt*	30 0 N	31 10 E
114	El Jadida, *Morocco*	33 11 N	8 17 W
115	El Mahalla el Kubra, *Egypt*	31 0 N	31 0 E
115	El Mansûra, *Egypt*	31 0 N	31 19 E
115	El Minyâ, *Egypt*	28 7 N	30 33 E
115	El Obeid, *Sudan*	13 8 N	30 10 E
61	El Paso, *U.S.A.*	31 50 N	106 30 W
59	El Reno, *U.S.A.*	35 30 N	98 0 W
66	El Salvador ■, *Cent. Amer.*	13 50 N	89 0 W
88	Elba, *Italy*	42 48 N	10 15 E
89	Elbasani, *Albania*	41 9 N	20 9 E
82	Elbe →, *W. Germany*	53 50 N	9 0 E
61	Elbert, Mt., *U.S.A.*	39 5 N	106 27 W
91	Elbląg, *Poland*	54 10 N	19 25 E
95	Elbrus, *U.S.S.R.*	43 21 N	42 30 E
101	Elburz Mts., *Iran*	36 0 N	52 0 E
85	Elche, *Spain*	38 15 N	0 42 W
116	Eldoret, *Kenya*	0 30 N	35 17 E
68	Eleuthera, *Bahamas*	25 0 N	76 20 W
58	Elgin, *U.S.A.*	42 0 N	88 20 W

PAGE	PLACE NAME	LATITUDE	LONGITUDE
56	Elizabeth, *U.S.A.*	40 37N	74 12W
57	Elizabeth City, *U.S.A.*	36 18N	76 16W
57	Elizabethton, *U.S.A.*	36 20N	82 13W
56	Elkhart, *U.S.A.*	41 42N	85 55W
60	Elko, *U.S.A.*	40 50N	115 50W
124	Ellesmere I., *Canada*	79 30N	80 0W
103	Eluru, *India*	16 48N	81 8 E
79	Ely, *U.K.*	52 24N	0 16 E
101	Emāmrūd, *Iran*	36 30N	55 0 E
81	Emden, *W. Germany*	53 22N	7 12 E
121	Emerald, *Australia*	23 32 S	148 10 E
81	Emmeloord, *Neth.*	52 44N	5 46 E
81	Emmen, *Neth.*	52 48N	6 57 E
81	Ems →, *W. Germany*	52 37N	9 26 E
122	Enderbury I., *Pac. Oc.*	3 8 S	171 5W
124	Enderby Land, *Antarct.*	66 0 S	53 0 E
78	England □, *U.K.*	53 0N	2 0W
58	Englewood, *U.S.A.*	39 40N	105 0W
79	English Channel, *Europe*	50 0N	2 0W
59	Enid, *U.S.A.*	36 26N	97 52W
80	Enniskillen, *U.K.*	54 20N	7 40W
81	Enschede, *Neth.*	52 13N	6 53 E
64	Ensenada, *Mexico*	31 50N	116 50W
116	Entebbe, *Uganda*	0 4N	32 28 E
114	Enugu, *Nigeria*	6 20N	7 30 E
116	Equatorial Guinea ■, *Africa*	2 0 S	8 0 E
124	Erebus, Mt., *Antarct.*	77 35 S	167 0 E
82	Erfurt, *E. Germany*	50 58N	11 2 E
56	Erie, *U.S.A.*	42 10N	80 7W
56	Erie, L., *N. Amer.*	42 15N	81 0W
115	Eritrea □, *Ethiopia*	14 0N	41 0 E
83	Erlangen, *W. Germany*	49 35N	11 0 E
102	Erode, *India*	11 24N	77 45 E
95	Erzurum, *Turkey*	39 57N	41 15 E
93	Esbjerg, *Denmark*	55 29N	8 29 E
81	Esch, *Neth.*	51 37N	5 17 E
81	Eschweiler, *W. Germany*	50 49N	6 14 E
101	Eşfahān, *Iran*	33 0N	53 0 E
92	Eskifjörður, *Iceland*	65 3N	13 55W
93	Eskilstuna, *Sweden*	59 22N	16 32 E
50	Eskimo Pt., *Canada*	61 10N	94 15W
95	Eskişehir, *Turkey*	39 50N	30 35 E
72	Esmeraldas, *Ecuador*	1 0N	79 40W
120	Esperance, *Australia*	33 45 S	121 55 E
73	Espinhaço, Serra do, *Brazil*	17 30 S	43 30W
81	Essen, *W. Germany*	51 28N	6 59 E
94	Estonia □, *U.S.S.R.*	58 30N	25 30 E
114	Ethiopia ■, *Africa*	8 0N	40 0 E
88	Etna, *Italy*	37 45N	15 0 E
57	Eufaula, *U.S.A.*	31 55N	85 11W
60	Eugene, *U.S.A.*	44 0N	123 8W
100	Euphrates →, *Asia*	31 0N	47 25 E
60	Eureka, *U.S.A.*	40 50N	124 0W
76	Europe	50 0N	20 0 E
58	Evanston, *U.S.A.*	42 0N	87 40W
56	Evansville, *U.S.A.*	38 0N	87 35W
104	Everest, Mt., *Nepal*	28 5N	86 58 E
60	Everett, *U.S.A.*	48 0N	122 10W
57	Everglades Nat. Park, *U.S.A.*	25 27N	80 53W
85	Évora, *Portugal*	38 33N	7 57W
84	Évreux, *France*	49 0N	1 8 E
89	Évvoia, *Greece*	38 30N	24 0 E
79	Exeter, *U.K.*	50 43N	3 31W
79	Exmoor, *U.K.*	51 10N	3 59W
120	Eyre, L., *Australia*	29 30 S	137 26 E
120	Eyre Pen., *Australia*	33 30 S	137 17 E

F

PAGE	PLACE NAME	LATITUDE	LONGITUDE
55	Fagatogo, *Amer. Samoa*	14 17 S	170 41W
54	Fairbanks, *U.S.A.*	64 50N	147 50W
57	Fairfield, *Ala., U.S.A.*	33 30N	87 0W
60	Fairfield, *Calif., U.S.A.*	38 14N	122 1W
102	Faisalabad, *Pakistan*	31 30N	73 5 E
103	Faizabad, *India*	26 45N	82 10 E
69	Fajardo, *Puerto Rico*	18 20N	65 39W
93	Falkenberg, *Sweden*	56 54N	12 30 E
74	Falkland Is., *Atl. Oc.*	51 30 S	59 0W
56	Fall River, *U.S.A.*	41 45N	71 5W
93	Falun, *Sweden*	60 37N	15 37 E
95	Famagusta, *Cyprus*	35 8N	33 55 E
58	Fargo, *U.S.A.*	46 52N	96 40W
75	Faroe Is., *Atl. Oc.*	62 0N	7 0W
118	Farquhar Is., *Ind. Oc.*	11 0 S	52 0 E
115	Faya-Largeau, *Chad*	17 58N	19 6 E
59	Fayetteville, *Ark., U.S.A.*	36 0N	94 5W
57	Fayetteville, *N.C., U.S.A.*	35 0N	78 58W
114	Fdérik, *Mauritania*	22 40N	12 45W
60	Feather →, *U.S.A.*	38 47N	121 36W
73	Feira de Santana, *Brazil*	12 15 S	38 57W
78	Fens, *U.K.*	52 45N	0 2 E
96	Fergana, *U.S.S.R.*	40 23N	71 19 E
88	Ferrara, *Italy*	44 50N	11 36 E
114	Fès, *Morocco*	34 0N	5 0W
117	Fianarantsoa, *Madag.*	21 26 S	47 5 E
121	Fiji ■, *Pac. Oc.*	17 20 S	179 0 E
85	Finisterre, C., *Spain*	42 50N	9 19W
92	Finland ■, *Europe*	63 0N	27 0 E
93	Finland, G. of, *Europe*	60 0N	26 0 E
92	Finnmark □, *Norway*	69 30N	25 0 E
102	Firozabad, *India*	27 10N	78 25 E
120	Fitzroy Crossing, *Australia*	18 9 S	125 38 E
61	Flagstaff, *U.S.A.*	35 10N	111 40W
60	Flaming Gorge Res., *U.S.A.*	41 15N	109 30W
84	Flanders, *Belgium*	51 10N	3 15 E
92	Flatey, *Iceland*	65 22N	22 56W
60	Flathead L., *U.S.A.*	47 50N	114 0W
82	Flensburg, *W. Germany*	54 46N	9 28 E
120	Flinders →, *Australia*	17 36 S	140 36 E
120	Flinders B., *Australia*	34 19 S	115 19 E
120	Flinders I., *Australia*	40 0 S	148 0 E
120	Flinders Ranges, *Australia*	31 30 S	138 30 E
56	Flint, *U.S.A.*	43 5N	83 40W
88	Florence, *Italy*	43 47N	11 15 E
57	Florence, *Ala., U.S.A.*	34 50N	87 40W
57	Florence, *S.C., U.S.A.*	34 12N	79 44W
109	Flores, *Indonesia*	8 35 S	121 0 E
109	Flores Sea, *Indonesia*	6 30 S	124 0 E
74	Florianópolis, *Brazil*	27 30 S	48 30W
57	Florida □, *U.S.A.*	28 30N	82 0W
66	Florida Str., *U.S.A.*	25 0N	80 0W
121	Fly →, *Papua N. G.*	8 25 S	143 0 E
88	Fóggia, *Italy*	41 28N	15 31 E
79	Folkestone, *U.K.*	51 5N	1 11 E
58	Fond du Lac, *U.S.A.*	43 46N	88 26W
84	Fontainebleau, *France*	48 24N	2 40 E
84	Forbach, *France*	49 10N	6 52 E
105	Formosa = Taiwan ■, *Asia*	23 30N	121 0 E
105	Formosa Strait, *Asia*	24 40N	120 0 E
58	Fort Collins, *U.S.A.*	40 30N	105 4W
67	Fort-de-France, *Martinique*	14 36N	61 2W
58	Fort Dodge, *U.S.A.*	42 29N	94 10W
51	Fort George, *Canada*	53 50N	79 0W
57	Fort Lauderdale, *U.S.A.*	26 10N	80 5W
50	Fort McMurray, *Canada*	56 44N	111 7W
57	Fort Myers, *U.S.A.*	26 39N	81 51W
60	Fort Peck L., *U.S.A.*	47 40N	107 0W
57	Fort Pierce, *U.S.A.*	27 29N	80 19W
59	Fort Scott, *U.S.A.*	37 50N	94 40W
59	Fort Smith, *U.S.A.*	35 25N	94 25W
57	Fort Walton Beach, *U.S.A.*	30 25N	86 40W
56	Fort Wayne, *U.S.A.*	41 5N	85 10W
59	Fort Worth, *U.S.A.*	32 45N	97 25W
73	Fortaleza, *Brazil*	3 45 S	38 35W
78	Forth, Firth of, *U.K.*	56 5N	2 55W
105	Foshan, *China*	23 4N	113 5 E
51	Foxe Chan., *Canada*	65 0N	80 0W
84	France ■, *Europe*	47 0N	3 0 E
83	Frankfurt am Main, *W. Germany*	50 7N	8 40 E
96	Franz Josef Land, *U.S.S.R.*	82 0N	55 0 E
50	Fraser →, *Canada*	49 7N	123 11W
121	Fraser I., *Australia*	25 15 S	153 10 E
56	Fredericksburg, *U.S.A.*	38 16N	77 29W
51	Fredericton, *Canada*	45 57N	66 40W
93	Frederikshavn, *Denmark*	57 28N	10 31 E
93	Fredrikstad, *Norway*	59 13N	10 57 E
58	Freeport, *U.S.A.*	42 18N	89 40W
114	Freetown, *S. Leone*	8 30N	13 17W
83	Freiburg, *W. Germany*	48 0N	7 52 E
61	Fremont, *U.S.A.*	37 32N	122 1W
73	French Guiana ■, *S. Amer.*	4 0N	53 0W
123	French Polynesia □, *Pac. Oc.*	20 0 S	145 0 E
64	Fresnillo, *Mexico*	23 10N	103 0W
61	Fresno, *U.S.A.*	36 47N	119 50W
81	Friesland □, *Neth.*	53 5N	5 50 E
81	Frisian Is., *Europe*	53 30N	6 0 E
51	Frobisher B., *Canada*	62 30N	66 0W
60	Front Range, *U.S.A.*	40 0N	105 40W
96	Frunze, *U.S.S.R.*	42 54N	74 46 E
107	Fuji-San, *Japan*	35 22N	138 44 E
105	Fujian □, *China*	26 0N	118 0 E
107	Fukui, *Japan*	36 0N	136 10 E
107	Fukuoka, *Japan*	33 39N	130 21 E
106	Fukushima, *Japan*	37 44N	140 28 E
107	Fukuyama, *Japan*	34 35N	133 20 E
61	Fullerton, *U.S.A.*	33 52N	117 58W
51	Fundy, B. of, *Canada*	45 0N	66 0W
120	Furneaux Group, *Australia*	40 10 S	147 50 E
83	Fürth, *W. Germany*	49 29N	11 0 E
51	Fury and Hecla Str., *Canada*	69 56N	84 0W
105	Fushun, *China*	41 50N	123 56 E
105	Fuxin, *China*	42 5N	121 48 E
105	Fuzhou, *China*	26 5N	119 16 E
93	Fyn, *Denmark*	55 20N	10 30 E

G

PAGE	PLACE NAME	LATITUDE	LONGITUDE
114	Gabès, *Tunisia*	33 53N	10 2 E
116	Gabon ■, *Africa*	0 10 S	10 0 E
117	Gaborone, *Botswana*	24 45 S	25 57 E
89	Gabrovo, *Bulgaria*	42 52N	25 19 E
57	Gadsden, *U.S.A.*	34 1N	86 0W
57	Gainesville, *Fla., U.S.A.*	29 38N	82 20W
57	Gainesville, *Ga., U.S.A.*	34 17N	83 47W
59	Gainesville, *Tex., U.S.A.*	33 40N	97 10W
123	Galápagos, *Pac. Oc.*	0 0	89 0W
91	Galaţi, *Romania*	45 27N	28 2 E
58	Galesburg, *U.S.A.*	40 57N	90 23W
100	Galilee, Sea of = Kinneret, Yam, *Israel*	32 45N	35 35 E
102	Galle, *Sri Lanka*	6 5N	80 10 E
92	Gällivare, *Sweden*	67 9N	20 40 E
59	Galveston, *U.S.A.*	29 15N	94 48W
80	Galway B., *Ireland*	53 10N	9 20W
114	Gambia ■, *W. Afr.*	13 25N	16 0W
69	Gamboa, *Panama*	9 8N	79 42W
105	Gan Jiang →, *China*	29 15N	116 0 E
102	Ganganagar, *India*	29 56N	73 56 E
103	Ganges →, *India*	23 20N	90 30 E
104	Gansu □, *China*	36 0N	104 0 E
114	Gao, *Mali*	16 15N	0 5W
84	Gap, *France*	44 33N	6 5 E
55	Garapan, *Pac. Oc.*	15 12N	145 53 E
88	Garda, L., *Italy*	45 40N	10 40 E
59	Garden City, *U.S.A.*	38 0N	100 45W
61	Garden Grove, *U.S.A.*	33 47N	117 55W
60	Garland, *U.S.A.*	41 47N	112 10W
84	Garonne →, *France*	45 2N	0 36W
116	Garoua, *Cameroon*	9 19N	13 21 E
56	Gary, *U.S.A.*	41 35N	87 20W
104	Garzê, *China*	31 39N	99 58 E
84	Gascony, *France*	43 45N	0 20 E
51	Gaspé Pen., *Canada*	48 45N	65 40W
57	Gastonia, *U.S.A.*	35 17N	81 10W
78	Gateshead, *U.K.*	54 57N	1 37W
69	Gatun, *Panama*	9 16N	79 55W
69	Gatun, L., *Panama*	9 7N	79 56W
93	Gävle, *Sweden*	60 40N	17 9 E
103	Gaya, *India*	24 47N	85 4 E
100	Gaza, *Egypt*	31 30N	34 28 E
95	Gaziantep, *Turkey*	37 6N	37 23 E
91	Gdańsk, *Poland*	54 22N	18 40 E
91	Gdańsk Bay, *Poland*	54 30N	19 20 E
91	Gdynia, *Poland*	54 35N	18 33 E
121	Geelong, *Australia*	38 10 S	144 22 E
104	Gejiu, *China*	23 20N	103 10 E
81	Gelderland □, *Neth.*	52 5N	6 10 E
81	Gelsenkirchen, *W. Germany*	51 30N	7 5 E
111	General Santos, *Phil.*	6 5N	125 14 E
83	Geneva, *Switz.*	46 12N	6 9 E
83	Geneva, L., *Switz.*	46 26N	6 30 E
81	Genk, *Belgium*	50 58N	5 32 E
88	Gennargentu, Mt., *Italy*	40 0N	9 10 E
88	Genoa, *Italy*	44 24N	8 56 E
117	George, *S. Africa*	33 58 S	22 29 E
108	George Town, *Malaysia*	5 25N	100 15 E
72	Georgetown, *Guyana*	6 50N	58 12W
57	Georgia □, *U.S.A.*	32 0N	82 0W
95	Georgia □, *U.S.S.R.*	42 0N	43 0 E
51	Georgian B., *Canada*	45 15N	81 0W
82	Gera, *E. Germany*	50 53N	12 11 E
117	Germiston, *S. Africa*	26 15 S	28 10 E
85	Gerona, *Spain*	41 58N	2 46 E
56	Gettysburg, *U.S.A.*	39 47N	77 18W
103	Ghaghara →, *India*	25 45N	84 40 E
114	Ghana ■, *W. Afr.*	6 0N	1 0W
102	Ghaziabad, *India*	28 42N	77 26 E
81	Ghent, *Belgium*	51 2N	3 42 E
85	Gibraltar, *Europe*	36 7N	5 22W
85	Gibraltar, Str. of, *Medit. S.*	35 55N	5 40W
120	Gibson Desert, *Australia*	24 0 S	126 0 E
107	Gifu, *Japan*	35 30N	136 45 E
85	Gijón, *Spain*	43 32N	5 42W
61	Gila →, *U.S.A.*	32 43N	114 33W
123	Gilbert Is., *Pac. Oc.*	1 0N	176 0 E
121	Gippsland, *Australia*	37 45 S	147 15 E
84	Gironde →, *France*	45 32N	1 7W
121	Gisborne, *N.Z.*	38 39 S	178 5 E
97	Gizhiga, *U.S.S.R.*	62 3N	160 30 E
97	Gizhiga, G., *U.S.S.R.*	61 0N	158 0 E
120	Gladstone, *Australia*	33 15 S	138 22 E
78	Glasgow, *U.K.*	55 52N	4 14W
61	Glen Canyon Nat. Recreation Area, *U.S.A.*	37 30N	111 0W
56	Glen Falls, *U.S.A.*	43 20N	73 40W
61	Glendale, *U.S.A.*	34 7N	118 18W
91	Gliwice, *Poland*	50 22N	18 41 E

PAGE	PLACE NAME	LATITUDE	LONGITUDE

PAGE	PLACE NAME	LATITUDE	LONGITUDE
50	Lethbridge, *Canada*	49 45N	112 45W
81	Leverkusen, *W. Germany*	51 2N	6 59 E
80	Lewis, *U.K.*	58 10N	6 40W
60	Lewis Ra., *U.S.A.*	48 15N	114 0W
60	Lewiston, *Idaho, U.S.A.*	46 25N	117 0W
57	Lewiston, *Maine, U.S.A.*	44 3N	70 10W
56	Lexington, *Ky., U.S.A.*	38 6N	84 30W
57	Lexington, *N.C., U.S.A.*	35 50N	80 13W
111	Leyte, *Phil.*	11 0N	125 0 E
111	Leyte Gulf, *Phil.*	10 50N	125 25 E
104	Lhasa, *China*	29 50N	91 3 E
111	Lianga, *Phil.*	8 38N	126 6 E
105	Liaodong, Gulf of, *China*	40 20N	121 10 E
105	Liaoning □, *China*	41 40N	122 30 E
105	Liaoyang, *China*	41 15N	123 10 E
105	Liaoyüan, *China*	42 55N	125 10 E
59	Liberal, *U.S.A.*	37 4N	101 0W
114	Liberia ■, *W. Afr.*	6 30N	9 30W
116	Libreville, *Gabon*	0 25N	9 26 E
115	Libya ■, *N. Afr.*	27 0N	17 0 E
115	Libyan Desert, *Africa*	25 0N	25 0 E
117	Lichinga, *Mozam.*	13 13S	35 11 E
83	Liechtenstein ■, *Europe*	47 8N	9 35 E
81	Liège, *Belgium*	50 38N	5 35 E
94	Liepaja, *U.S.S.R.*	56 30N	21 0 E
88	Ligurian Sea, *Italy*	43 20N	9 0 E
116	Likasi, *Zaire*	10 55S	26 48 E
84	Lille, *France*	50 38N	3 3 E
93	Lille Bælt, *Denmark*	55 20N	9 45 E
93	Lillehammer, *Norway*	61 8N	10 30 E
117	Lilongwe, *Malawi*	14 0S	33 48 E
72	Lima, *Peru*	12 0S	77 0W
56	Lima, *U.S.A.*	40 42N	84 5W
95	Limassol, *Cyprus*	34 42N	33 1 E
81	Limburg □, *Neth.*	51 20N	5 55 E
80	Limerick, *Ireland*	52 40N	8 38W
89	Límnos, *Greece*	39 50N	25 5 E
84	Limoges, *France*	45 50N	1 15 E
117	Limpopo →, *Mozam.*	25 15S	33 30 E
85	Linares, *Spain*	38 10N	3 40W
58	Lincoln, *U.S.A.*	40 50N	96 42W
93	Linköping, *Sweden*	58 28N	15 36 E
104	Linxia, *China*	35 36N	103 10 E
83	Linz, *Austria*	48 18N	14 18 E
84	Lions, G. of, *France*	43 0N	4 0 E
110	Lipa, *Phil.*	13 57N	121 10 E
88	Lípari Is., *Italy*	38 30N	14 50 E
94	Lipetsk, *U.S.S.R.*	52 37N	39 35 E
85	Lisbon, *Portugal*	38 42N	9 10W
94	Lithuania □, *U.S.S.R.*	55 30N	24 0 E
58	Little Missouri →, *U.S.A.*	47 30N	102 25W
59	Little Rock, *U.S.A.*	34 41N	92 10W
105	Liuzhou, *China*	24 22N	109 22 E
78	Liverpool, *U.K.*	53 25N	3 0W
121	Liverpool Plains, *Australia*	31 15S	150 15 E
117	Livingstone, *Zambia*	17 46S	25 52 E
88	Ljubljana, *Yugoslavia*	46 4N	14 33 E
59	Llano Estacado, *U.S.A.*	34 0N	103 0W
72	Llanos, *S. Amer.*	5 0N	71 35W
117	Lobito, *Angola*	12 18S	13 35 E
100	Lod, *Israel*	31 57N	34 54 E
60	Lodi, *U.S.A.*	38 12N	121 16W
91	Łódź, *Poland*	51 45N	19 27 E
92	Lofoten, *Norway*	68 30N	15 0 E
60	Logan, *U.S.A.*	41 45N	111 50W
50	Logan, Mt., *Canada*	60 31N	140 22W
85	Logroño, *Spain*	42 28N	2 27W
84	Loire →, *France*	47 16N	2 10W
93	Lolland, *Denmark*	54 45N	11 30 E
88	Lombardy □, *Italy*	45 35N	9 45 E
114	Lomé, *Togo*	6 9N	1 20 E
78	Lomond, L., *U.K.*	56 8N	4 38W
91	Łomza, *Poland*	53 10N	22 2 E
51	London, *Canada*	42 59N	81 15W
79	London, *U.K.*	51 30N	0 5W
80	Londonderry, *U.K.*	55 0N	7 20W
120	Londonderry, C., *Australia*	13 45S	126 55 E
74	Londrina, *Brazil*	23 18S	51 10W
61	Long Beach, *U.S.A.*	33 46N	118 12W
68	Long I., *Bahamas*	23 20N	75 10W
56	Long I., *U.S.A.*	40 50N	73 20W
59	Longview, *Tex., U.S.A.*	32 30N	94 45W
60	Longview, *Wash., U.S.A.*	46 9N	122 58W
81	Löningen, *W. Germany*	52 43N	7 44 E
104	Lop Nor, *China*	40 20N	90 10 E
110	Lopez, *Phil.*	13 53N	122 15 E
56	Lorain, *U.S.A.*	41 28N	82 55W
85	Lorca, *Spain*	37 41N	1 42W
84	Lorient, *France*	47 45N	3 23W
61	Los Alamos, *U.S.A.*	35 57N	106 17W
74	Los Angeles, *Chile*	37 28S	72 23W
61	Los Angeles, *U.S.A.*	34 0N	118 10W
64	Los Mochis, *Mexico*	25 45N	108 57W
121	Louisiade Arch., *Papua N. G.*	11 10S	153 0 E
59	Louisiana □, *U.S.A.*	30 50N	92 0W
56	Louisville, *U.S.A.*	38 15N	85 45W
84	Lourdes, *France*	43 6N	0 3W
56	Lowell, *U.S.A.*	42 38N	71 19W
121	Lower Hutt, *N.Z.*	41 10S	174 55 E
97	Lower Tunguska →, *U.S.S.R.*	64 20N	93 0 E
116	Luanda, *Angola*	8 50S	13 15 E
117	Luanshya, *Zambia*	13 3S	28 28 E
59	Lubbock, *U.S.A.*	33 40N	101 53W
82	Lübeck, *W. Germany*	53 52N	10 41 E
91	Lublin, *Poland*	51 12N	22 38 E
117	Lubumbashi, *Zaire*	11 40S	27 28 E
103	Lucknow, *India*	26 50N	81 0 E
102	Ludhiana, *India*	30 57N	75 56 E
83	Ludwigshafen, *W. Germany*	49 27N	8 27 E
59	Lufkin, *U.S.A.*	31 25N	94 40W
83	Lugano, *Switz.*	46 0N	8 57 E
85	Lugo, *Spain*	43 2N	7 35W
92	Luleå, *Sweden*	65 35N	22 10 E
55	Luma, *Amer. Samoa*	14 15S	169 32W
79	Lundy, *U.K.*	51 10N	4 41W
81	Lünen, *W. Germany*	51 36N	7 31 E
105	Luoyang, *China*	34 40N	112 26 E
117	Lusaka, *Zambia*	15 28S	28 16 E
79	Luton, *U.K.*	51 53N	0 24W
81	Luxembourg, *Lux.*	49 37N	6 9 E
81	Luxembourg ■, *Europe*	50 0N	6 0 E
83	Luzern, *Switz.*	47 3N	8 18 E
104	Luzhou, *China*	28 52N	105 20 E
110	Luzon, *Phil.*	16 0N	121 0 E
95	Lvov, *U.S.S.R.*	49 50N	24 0 E
97	Lyakhov Is., *U.S.S.R.*	73 40N	141 0 E
56	Lynchburg, *U.S.A.*	37 23N	79 10W
50	Lynn Lake, *Canada*	56 51N	101 3W
84	Lyons, *France*	45 46N	4 50 E

M

PAGE	PLACE NAME	LATITUDE	LONGITUDE
100	Ma'ān, *Jordan*	30 12N	35 44 E
93	Maarianhamina, *Finland*	60 5N	19 55 E
81	Maastricht, *Neth.*	50 50N	5 40 E
59	McAllen, *U.S.A.*	26 12N	98 15W
73	Macapá, *Brazil*	0 5N	51 4W
105	Macau ■, *Asia*	22 16N	113 35 E
124	McClure Str., *Canada*	75 0N	119 0W
59	McComb, *U.S.A.*	31 13N	90 30W
118	McDonald Is., *Ind. Oc.*	53 0S	73 0 E
120	Macdonnell Ranges, *Australia*	23 40S	133 0 E
89	Macedonia □, *Greece*	40 39N	22 0 E
89	Macedonia □, *Yugoslavia*	41 53N	21 40 E
73	Maceió, *Brazil*	9 40S	35 41W
80	Macgillycuddy's Reeks, *Ireland*	52 2N	9 45W
116	Machakos, *Kenya*	1 30S	37 15 E
72	Machala, *Ecuador*	3 20S	79 57W
120	Mackay, L., *Australia*	22 30S	129 0 E
50	Mackenzie →, *Canada*	69 10N	134 20W
50	Mackenzie Mts., *Canada*	64 0N	130 0W
54	McKinley, Mt., *U.S.A.*	63 2N	151 0W
59	McKinney, *U.S.A.*	33 10N	96 40W
120	McLeod L., *Australia*	24 9S	113 47 E
50	M'Clintock Chan., *Canada*	72 0N	102 0W
57	Macon, *U.S.A.*	32 50N	83 37W
122	Macquarie Is., *S. Ocean*	54 36S	158 55 E
117	Madadeni, *S. Africa*	27 43S	30 3 E
117	Madagascar ■, *Africa*	20 0S	47 0 E
114	Madeira, *Atl. Oc.*	32 50N	17 0W
72	Madeira →, *Brazil*	3 22S	58 45W
103	Madhya Pradesh □, *India*	21 50N	81 0 E
100	Madīnat al Shaab, *S. Yemen*	12 50N	45 0 E
58	Madison, *U.S.A.*	43 5N	89 25W
109	Madiun, *Indonesia*	7 38S	111 32 E
102	Madras, *India*	13 8N	80 19 E
59	Madre, L., *U.S.A.*	26 0N	97 40W
65	Madre, Sierra, *Mexico*	16 0N	93 0W
85	Madrid, *Spain*	40 25N	3 45W
102	Madurai, *India*	9 55N	78 10 E
97	Magadan, *U.S.S.R.*	59 38N	150 50 E
72	Magdalena →, *Colombia*	11 6N	74 51W
82	Magdeburg, *E. Germany*	52 8N	11 36 E
109	Magelang, *Indonesia*	7 29S	110 13 E
74	Magellan's Str., *Chile*	52 30S	75 0W
88	Maggiore, L., *Italy*	46 0N	8 35 E
94	Magnitogorsk, *U.S.S.R.*	53 27N	59 4 E
117	Mahajanga, *Madag.*	17 0S	47 0 E
118	Mahé, *Ind. Oc.*	5 0S	55 30 E
115	Maiduguri, *Nigeria*	12 0N	13 20 E
57	Maine □, *U.S.A.*	45 20N	69 0W
81	Mainz, *W. Germany*	50 0N	8 17 E
109	Makasar, Str. of, *Indonesia*	1 0S	118 20 E
95	Makeyevka, *U.S.S.R.*	48 0N	38 0 E
95	Makhachkala, *U.S.S.R.*	43 0N	47 30 E
102	Makran Coast Range, *Pakistan*	25 40N	64 0 E
111	Malabang, *Phil.*	7 36N	124 3 E
102	Malabar Coast, *India*	11 0N	75 0 E
108	Malacca, Str. of, *Indonesia*	3 0N	101 0 E
85	Málaga, *Spain*	36 43N	4 23W
109	Malang, *Indonesia*	7 59S	112 45 E
116	Malanje, *Angola*	9 36S	16 17 E
93	Mälaren, *Sweden*	59 30N	17 10 E
95	Malatya, *Turkey*	38 25N	38 20 E
117	Malawi = Nyasa, L., *Africa*	12 30S	34 30 E
117	Malawi ■, *Africa*	13 0S	34 0 E
111	Malaybalay, *Phil.*	8 5N	125 7 E
108	Malaysia ■, *Asia*	5 0N	110 0 E
118	Maldives ■, *Ind. Oc.*	5 0N	73 0 E
114	Mali ■, *Africa*	15 0N	2 0W
85	Mallorca, *Spain*	39 30N	3 0 E
81	Malmédy, *Belgium*	50 25N	6 2 E
93	Malmö, *Sweden*	55 36N	12 59 E
88	Malta ■, *Europe*	35 50N	14 30 E
78	Man, I. of, *U.K.*	54 15N	4 30W
102	Manaar, Gulf of, *Asia*	8 30N	79 0 E
109	Manado, *Indonesia*	1 29N	124 51 E
66	Managua, *Nic.*	12 6N	86 20W
101	Manama, *Bahrain*	26 10N	50 30 E
72	Manaus, *Brazil*	3 0S	60 0W
78	Manchester, *U.K.*	53 30N	2 15W
56	Manchester, *U.S.A.*	42 58N	71 29W
105	Manchuria, *China*	42 0N	125 0 E
103	Mandalay, *Burma*	22 0N	96 4 E
110	Mandaon, *Phil.*	12 13N	123 17 E
102	Mangalore, *India*	12 55N	74 47 E
110	Manila, *Phil.*	14 40N	121 3 E
50	Manitoba □, *Canada*	55 30N	97 0W
58	Manitowoc, *U.S.A.*	44 8N	87 40W
72	Manizales, *Colombia*	5 5N	75 32W
83	Mannheim, *W. Germany*	49 28N	8 29 E
56	Mansfield, *U.S.A.*	40 45N	82 30W
84	Mantes-la-Jolie, *France*	49 0N	1 41 E
88	Mantua, *Italy*	45 20N	10 42 E
55	Manua Is., *Amer. Samoa*	14 13S	169 35W
121	Manukau, *N.Z.*	37 1S	174 55 E
105	Manzhouli, *China*	49 35N	117 25 E
105	Maoming, *China*	21 50N	110 54 E
117	Maputo, *Mozam.*	25 58S	32 32 E
74	Mar del Plata, *Argentina*	38 0S	57 30W
72	Maracaibo, *Venezuela*	10 40N	71 37W
72	Maracaibo, L., *Venezuela*	9 40N	71 30W
72	Maracay, *Venezuela*	10 15N	67 28W
73	Marajó, I. de, *Brazil*	1 0S	49 30W
72	Marañón →, *Peru*	4 30S	73 35W
111	Marawi City, *Phil.*	8 0N	124 21 E
72	Margarita I., *Venezuela*	11 0N	64 0W
55	Mariana Trench, *Pac. Oc.*	13 0N	145 0 E
88	Maribor, *Yugoslavia*	46 36N	15 40 E
51	Maricourt, *Canada*	56 34N	70 49W
73	Marília, *Brazil*	22 13S	50 0W
110	Marinduque, *Phil.*	13 25N	122 0 E
74	Maringá, *Brazil*	23 26S	52 2W
59	Marion, *U.S.A.*	37 45N	88 55W
95	Marmara, Sea of, *Turkey*	40 45N	28 15 E
84	Marne →, *France*	48 48N	2 24 E
116	Maroua, *Cameroon*	10 40N	14 20 E
123	Marquesas Is., *Pac. Oc.*	9 30S	140 0W
58	Marquette, *U.S.A.*	46 30N	87 21W
114	Marrakesh, *Morocco*	31 9N	8 0W
84	Marseilles, *France*	43 18N	5 23 E
59	Marshall, *U.S.A.*	32 29N	94 20W
55	Marshall Is. ■, *Pac. Oc.*	9 0N	171 0 E
58	Marshalltown, *U.S.A.*	42 5N	92 56W
103	Martaban, G. of, *Burma*	16 5N	96 30 E
67	Martinique □, *W. Indies*	14 40N	61 0W
57	Martinsville, *U.S.A.*	36 41N	79 52W
121	Maryborough, *Australia*	37 0S	143 44 E
56	Maryland □, *U.S.A.*	39 10N	76 40W
106	Masan, *S. Korea*	35 11N	128 32 E
110	Masbate, *Phil.*	12 21N	123 36 E
117	Maseru, *Lesotho*	29 18S	27 30 E
101	Mashhad, *Iran*	36 20N	59 35 E
58	Mason City, *U.S.A.*	43 9N	93 12W
56	Massachusetts □, *U.S.A.*	42 25N	72 0W
56	Massena, *U.S.A.*	44 52N	74 55W
84	Massif Central, *France*	45 30N	3 0 E
117	Masvingo, *Zimbabwe*	20 8S	30 49 E
116	Matadi, *Zaire*	5 52S	13 31 E
64	Matamoros, *Mexico*	25 33N	103 15W
88	Matera, *Italy*	40 40N	16 37 E
73	Mato Grosso □, *Brazil*	14 0S	55 0W
107	Matsue, *Japan*	35 25N	133 10 E
107	Matsuyama, *Japan*	33 45N	132 45 E
83	Matterhorn, *Switz.*	45 58N	7 39 E

PAGE	PLACE NAME	LATITUDE	LONGITUDE
72	Maturín, *Venezuela*	9 45N	63 11W
84	Maubeuge, *France*	50 17N	3 57 E
54	Maui, *U.S.A.*	20 45N	156 20 E
54	Mauna Kea, *U.S.A.*	19 50N	155 28W
54	Mauna Loa, *U.S.A.*	21 8N	157 10W
114	Mauritania ■, *Africa*	20 50N	10 0W
118	Mauritius ■, *Ind. Oc.*	20 0S	57 0 E
103	Mawlaik, *Burma*	23 40N	94 26 E
66	May Pen, *Jamaica*	17 58N	77 15W
68	Mayaguana, *Bahamas*	22 30N	72 44W
69	Mayagüez, *Puerto Rico*	18 12N	67 9W
101	Mazar-e Sharīf, *Afghan.*	36 41N	67 0 E
64	Mazatlán, *Mexico*	23 13N	106 25W
117	Mbabane, *Swaziland*	26 18S	31 6 E
116	Mbandaka, *Zaire*	0 1N	18 18 E
116	Mbanza Ngungu, *Zaire*	5 12S	14 53 E
116	Mbeya, *Tanzania*	8 54S	33 29 E
116	Mbuji-Mayi, *Zaire*	6 9S	23 40 E
117	Mdantsane, *S. Africa*	32 56S	27 46 E
61	Mead, L., *U.S.A.*	36 1N	114 44W
100	Mecca, *Si. Arabia*	21 30N	39 54 E
81	Mechelen, *Belgium*	50 58N	5 41 E
108	Medan, *Indonesia*	3 40N	98 38 E
72	Medellín, *Colombia*	6 15N	75 35W
60	Medford, *U.S.A.*	42 20N	122 52W
60	Medicine Bow Ra., *U.S.A.*	41 10N	106 25W
50	Medicine Hat, *Canada*	50 0N	110 45W
100	Medina, *Si. Arabia*	24 35N	39 52 E
86	Mediterranean Sea, *Europe*	35 0N	15 0 E
50	Medley, *Canada*	54 25N	110 16W
120	Meekatharra, *Australia*	26 32S	118 29 E
102	Meerut, *India*	29 1N	77 42 E
105	Mei Xian, *China*	24 16N	116 6 E
114	Meknès, *Morocco*	33 57N	5 33W
108	Mekong →, *Asia*	9 30N	106 15 E
122	Melanesia, *Pac. Oc.*	4 0S	155 0 E
121	Melbourne, *Australia*	37 50S	145 0 E
57	Melbourne, *U.S.A.*	28 4N	80 35W
95	Melitopol, *U.S.S.R.*	46 50N	35 22 E
120	Melville I., *Australia*	11 30S	131 0 E
51	Melville Pen., *Canada*	68 0N	84 0W
59	Memphis, *U.S.A.*	35 7N	90 0W
60	Mendocino, C., *U.S.A.*	40 26N	124 25W
74	Mendoza, *Argentina*	32 50S	68 52W
58	Menominee, *U.S.A.*	45 9N	87 39W
85	Menorca, *Spain*	40 0N	4 0 E
61	Merced, *U.S.A.*	37 18N	120 30W
65	Mérida, *Mexico*	20 58N	89 37W
72	Mérida, *Venezuela*	8 24N	71 8W
59	Meridian, *U.S.A.*	32 20N	88 42W
95	Mersin, *Turkey*	36 51N	34 36 E
116	Meru, *Tanzania*	3 15S	36 46 E
61	Mesa, *U.S.A.*	33 20N	111 56W
100	Mesopotamia, *Asia*	33 30N	44 0 E
88	Messina, *Italy*	38 10N	15 32 E
88	Messina, Str. of, *Italy*	38 5N	15 35 E
59	Metairie, *U.S.A.*	29 59N	90 9W
84	Metz, *France*	49 8N	6 10 E
84	Meuse →, *Europe*	50 45N	5 41 E
64	Mexicali, *Mexico*	32 40N	115 29W
65	México, *Mexico*	19 20N	99 10W
65	Mexico ■, *Cent. Amer.*	20 0N	100 0W
65	Mexico, G. of, *Cent. Amer.*	25 0N	90 0W
57	Miami, *U.S.A.*	25 45N	80 15W
57	Miami Beach, *U.S.A.*	25 49N	80 6W
56	Michigan □, *U.S.A.*	44 40N	85 40W
56	Michigan, L., *U.S.A.*	44 0N	87 0W
64	Michoacan □, *Mexico*	19 0N	102 0W
55	Micronesia, Federated States of ■, *Pac. Oc.*	11 0N	160 0 E
78	Middlesbrough, *U.K.*	54 35N	1 14W
59	Midland, *U.S.A.*	32 0N	102 3W
111	Midsayap, *Phil.*	7 12N	124 32 E
122	Midway Is., *Pac. Oc.*	28 13N	177 22W
85	Mieres, *Spain*	43 18N	5 48W
92	Mikkeli, *Finland*	61 43N	27 15 E
88	Milan, *Italy*	45 28N	9 10 E
79	Milford Haven, *U.K.*	51 43N	5 2W
57	Millinocket, *U.S.A.*	45 45N	68 45W
58	Milwaukee, *U.S.A.*	43 9N	87 58W
73	Minas Gerais □, *Brazil*	18 50S	46 0W
65	Minatitlán, *Mexico*	17 59N	94 31W
111	Mindanao, *Phil.*	8 0N	125 0 E
110	Mindoro, *Phil.*	13 0N	121 0 E
110	Mindoro Strait, *Phil.*	12 30N	120 30 E
58	Minneapolis, *U.S.A.*	44 58N	93 20W
58	Minnesota □, *U.S.A.*	46 40N	94 0W
58	Minot, *U.S.A.*	48 10N	101 15W
94	Minsk, *U.S.S.R.*	53 52N	27 30 E
103	Mirzapur, *India*	25 10N	82 34 E
91	Miskolc, *Hungary*	48 7N	20 50 E
115	Misrātah, *Libya*	32 24N	15 3 E
59	Mississippi □, *U.S.A.*	33 0N	90 0W
59	Mississippi →, *U.S.A.*	29 0N	89 15W
59	Mississippi, Delta of the, *U.S.A.*	29 15N	90 30W
60	Missoula, *U.S.A.*	46 52N	114 0W
58	Missouri □, *U.S.A.*	38 25N	92 30W
58	Missouri →, *U.S.A.*	38 50N	90 8W
58	Mitchell, *U.S.A.*	43 40N	98 0W
116	Mitumba Mts., *Zaire*	6 0S	29 0 E
107	Miyazaki, *Japan*	31 56N	131 30 E
103	Mizoram □, *India*	23 30N	92 40 E
117	Mmabatho, *S. Africa*	25 49S	25 30 E
92	Mo i Rana, *Norway*	66 15N	14 7 E
57	Mobile, *U.S.A.*	30 41N	88 3W
116	Mobutu Sese Seko, L., *Africa*	1 30N	31 0 E
88	Módena, *Italy*	44 39N	10 55 E
61	Modesto, *U.S.A.*	37 43N	121 0W
112	Mogadishu, *Somalia*	2 2N	45 25 E
94	Mogilev, *U.S.S.R.*	53 55N	30 18 E
61	Mojave Desert, *U.S.A.*	35 0N	116 30W
95	Moldavia □, *U.S.S.R.*	47 0N	28 0 E
58	Moline, *U.S.A.*	41 30N	90 30W
72	Mollendo, *Peru*	17 0S	72 0W
93	Mölndal, *Sweden*	57 40N	12 3 E
54	Molokai, *U.S.A.*	21 8N	157 0W
109	Moluccas, *Indonesia*	1 0S	127 0 E
116	Mombasa, *Kenya*	4 2S	39 43 E
67	Mona Passage, *W. Indies*	18 0N	67 40W
84	Monaco ■, *Europe*	43 46N	7 23 E
80	Monaghan, *Ireland*	54 15N	6 58W
59	Monahans, *U.S.A.*	31 35N	102 50W
81	Mönchen-Gladbach, *W. Germany*	51 12N	6 23 E
64	Monclova, *Mexico*	26 50N	101 30W
51	Moncton, *Canada*	46 7N	64 51W
103	Monghyr, *India*	25 23N	86 30 E
104	Mongolia ■, *Asia*	47 0N	103 0 E
117	Mongu, *Zambia*	15 16S	23 12 E
59	Monroe, La., *U.S.A.*	32 32N	92 4W
57	Monroe, N.C., *U.S.A.*	35 2N	80 37W
114	Monrovia, *Liberia*	6 18N	10 47W
81	Mons, *Belgium*	50 27N	3 58 E
60	Montana □, *U.S.A.*	47 0N	110 0W
84	Montbéliard, *France*	47 31N	6 48 E
84	Montceau-les-Mines, *France*	46 40N	4 23 E
66	Montego Bay, *Jamaica*	18 30N	78 0W
61	Monterey, *U.S.A.*	36 35N	121 57W
72	Montería, *Colombia*	8 46N	75 53W
64	Monterrey, *Mexico*	25 40N	100 30W
73	Montes Claros, *Brazil*	16 30S	43 50W
74	Montevideo, *Uruguay*	34 50S	56 11W
57	Montgomery, *U.S.A.*	32 20N	86 20W
84	Montluçon, *France*	46 22N	2 36 E
84	Montpellier, *France*	43 37N	3 52 E
51	Montréal, *Canada*	45 31N	73 34W
61	Montrose, *U.S.A.*	38 30N	107 52W
67	Montserrat, *W. Indies*	16 40N	62 10W
50	Moose Jaw, *Canada*	50 24N	105 30W
114	Mopti, *Mali*	14 30N	4 0W
102	Moradabad, *India*	28 50N	78 50 E
80	Moray Firth, *U.K.*	57 50N	3 30W
78	Morecambe B., *U.K.*	54 7N	3 0W
64	Morelia, *Mexico*	19 42N	101 7W
65	Morelos □, *Mexico*	18 40N	99 10W
85	Morena, Sierra, *Spain*	38 20N	4 0W
59	Morgan City, *U.S.A.*	29 40N	91 15W
120	Mornington I., *Australia*	16 30S	139 30 E
114	Morocco ■, *N. Afr.*	32 0N	5 50W
116	Morogoro, *Tanzania*	6 50S	37 40 E
57	Morristown, *U.S.A.*	36 18N	83 20W
60	Moscow, *U.S.A.*	46 45N	116 59W
94	Moscow, *U.S.S.R.*	55 45N	37 35 E
84	Moselle →, *Europe*	50 22N	7 36 E
116	Moshi, *Tanzania*	3 22S	37 18 E
73	Mossoró, *Brazil*	5 10S	37 15W
114	Mostaganem, *Algeria*	35 54N	0 5 E
89	Mostar, *Yugoslavia*	43 22N	17 50 E
100	Mosul, *Iraq*	36 15N	43 5 E
78	Motherwell, *U.K.*	55 48N	4 0W
103	Moulmein, *Burma*	16 30N	97 40 E
120	Mount Enid, *Australia*	21 42S	116 26 E
120	Mount Gambier, *Australia*	37 50S	140 46 E
120	Mount Magnet, *Australia*	28 2S	117 47 E
121	Mount Morgan, *Australia*	23 40S	150 25 E
56	Mount Vernon, *U.S.A.*	40 57N	73 49W
61	Mountain View, *U.S.A.*	37 26N	122 5W
81	Mouscron, *Belgium*	50 45N	3 12 E
117	Mozambique ■, *Africa*	19 0S	35 0 E
117	Mozambique Chan., *Africa*	20 0S	39 0 E
100	Mubarraz, *Si. Arabia*	25 29N	49 40 E
105	Mudanjiang, *China*	44 38N	129 30 E
117	Mufulira, *Zambia*	12 32S	28 15 E
81	Mülheim, *W. Germany*	51 26N	6 53 E
84	Mulhouse, *France*	47 40N	7 20 E
80	Mull, *U.K.*	56 27N	6 0W
102	Multan, *Pakistan*	30 15N	71 36 E
56	Muncie, *U.S.A.*	40 10N	85 20W
83	Munich, *W. Germany*	48 8N	11 33 E
81	Münster, *W. Germany*	51 58N	7 37 E
85	Murcia, *Spain*	38 20N	1 10W
91	Mureş →, *Romania*	46 15N	20 13 E
57	Murfreesboro, *U.S.A.*	35 50N	86 21W
94	Murmansk, *U.S.S.R.*	68 57N	33 10 E
120	Murray →, *Australia*	35 20S	139 22 E
121	Murrumbidgee →, *Australia*	34 43S	143 12 E
101	Muscat, *Oman*	23 40N	58 38 E
58	Muscatine, *U.S.A.*	41 25N	91 5W
120	Musgrave Ranges, *Australia*	26 0S	132 0 E
59	Muskogee, *U.S.A.*	35 50N	95 25W
117	Mutare, *Zimbabwe*	18 58S	32 38 E
103	Muzaffarpur, *India*	26 7N	85 23 E
116	Mwanza, *Tanzania*	2 30S	32 58 E
103	Myitkyina, *Burma*	25 24N	97 26 E
103	Mymensingh, *Bangla.*	24 45N	90 24 E
102	Mysore, *India*	12 17N	76 41 E

N

PAGE	PLACE NAME	LATITUDE	LONGITUDE
100	Nāblus, *Jordan*	32 14N	35 15 E
110	Nabua, *Phil.*	13 24N	123 22 E
59	Nacogdoches, *U.S.A.*	31 33N	94 39W
110	Naga, *Phil.*	13 38N	123 15 E
103	Nagaland □, *India*	26 0N	94 30 E
107	Nagano, *Japan*	36 40N	138 10 E
107	Nagaoka, *Japan*	37 27N	138 51 E
107	Nagasaki, *Japan*	32 47N	129 50 E
107	Nago, *Japan*	26 36N	128 0 E
107	Nagoya, *Japan*	35 10N	136 50 E
102	Nagpur, *India*	21 8N	79 10 E
107	Naha, *Japan*	26 13N	127 42 E
116	Nairobi, *Kenya*	1 17S	36 48 E
116	Nakuru, *Kenya*	0 15S	36 4 E
95	Nalchik, *U.S.S.R.*	43 30N	43 33 E
104	Nam Co, *China*	30 30N	90 45 E
96	Namangan, *U.S.S.R.*	41 0N	71 40 E
117	Namib Desert, *Namibia*	22 30S	15 0 E
117	Namibe, *Angola*	15 7S	12 11 E
117	Namibia ■, *Africa*	22 0S	18 9 E
60	Nampa, *U.S.A.*	43 34N	116 34W
117	Nampula, *Mozam.*	15 6N	39 15 E
81	Namur, *Belgium*	50 27N	4 52 E
104	Nan Shan, *China*	38 30N	99 0 E
50	Nanaimo, *Canada*	49 10N	124 0W
105	Nanchang, *China*	28 42N	115 55 E
104	Nanchong, *China*	30 43N	106 2 E
84	Nancy, *France*	48 42N	6 12 E
102	Nanda Devi, *India*	30 23N	79 59 E
105	Nanking = Nanjing, *China*	32 2N	118 47 E
104	Nanning, *China*	22 48N	108 20 E
105	Nanping, *China*	26 38N	118 10 E
84	Nantes, *France*	47 12N	1 33W
105	Nantong, *China*	32 1N	120 52 E
60	Napa, *U.S.A.*	38 18N	122 17W
121	Napier, *N.Z.*	39 30S	176 56 E
88	Naples, *Italy*	40 50N	14 17 E
57	Naples, *U.S.A.*	26 10N	81 45W
107	Nara, *Japan*	34 40N	135 49 E
103	Narayanganj, *Bangla.*	23 40N	90 33 E
102	Narmada →, *India*	21 38N	72 36 E
120	Narrogin, *Australia*	32 58S	117 14 E
92	Narvik, *Norway*	68 28N	17 26 E
57	Nashville, *U.S.A.*	36 12N	86 46W
102	Nasik, *India*	19 58N	73 50 E
68	Nassau, *Bahamas*	25 0N	77 20W
115	Nasser, L., *Egypt*	23 0N	32 30 E
93	Nässjö, *Sweden*	57 39N	14 42 E
117	Natal, *Brazil*	5 47S	35 13W
73	Natal □, *S. Africa*	28 30S	30 30 E
59	Natchez, *U.S.A.*	31 35N	91 25W
120	Naturaliste C., *Australia*	40 50S	148 15 E
122	Nauru ■, *Pac. Oc.*	1 0S	166 0 E
89	Náxos, *Greece*	37 8N	25 25 E
64	Nayarit □, *Mexico*	22 0N	105 0W
100	Nazareth, *Israel*	32 42N	35 17 E
115	N'Djamena, *Chad*	12 10N	14 59 E
117	Ndola, *Zambia*	13 0S	28 34 E
80	Neagh, Lough, *U.K.*	54 35N	6 25W
54	Near Is., *U.S.A.*	53 0N	172 0 E
58	Nebraska □, *U.S.A.*	41 30N	100 0W
79	Needles, *U.K.*	50 39N	1 35W
74	Negro →, *Argentina*	41 2S	62 47W
72	Negro →, *Brazil*	3 0S	60 0W
111	Negros, *Phil.*	9 30N	122 40 E
104	Neijiang, *China*	29 35N	104 55 E
72	Neiva, *Colombia*	2 56N	75 18W

PAGE	PLACE NAME	LATITUDE	LONGITUDE
102	Nellore, *India*	14 27N	79 59 E
121	Nelson, *N.Z.*	41 18S	173 16 E
50	Nelson →, *Canada*	54 33N	98 2W
117	Nelspruit, *S. Africa*	25 29S	30 59 E
103	Nepal ■, *Asia*	28 0N	84 30 E
80	Ness, Loch, *U.K.*	57 15N	4 30W
100	Netanya, *Israel*	32 20N	34 51 E
81	Netherlands ■, *Europe*	52 0N	5 30 E
67	Netherlands Antilles ■, *S. Amer.*	12 15N	69 0W
65	Netzahualcoyotl, Presa, *Mexico*	17 10N	93 30W
83	Neuchâtel, *Switz.*	47 0N	6 55 E
81	Neukirchen, *W. Germany*	54 52N	8 44 E
81	Neuss, *W. Germany*	51 12N	6 39 E
81	Neustadt, *W. Germany*	49 21N	8 10 E
81	Neuwied, *W. Germany*	50 26N	7 29 E
60	Nevada □, *U.S.A.*	39 20N	117 0W
85	Nevada, Sierra, *Spain*	37 3N	3 15W
60	Nevada, Sierra, *U.S.A.*	39 0N	120 30W
84	Nevers, *France*	47 0N	3 9 E
73	New Amsterdam, *Guyana*	6 15N	57 36W
56	New Bedford, *U.S.A.*	41 40N	70 52W
57	New Bern, *U.S.A.*	35 8N	77 3W
121	New Britain, *Papua N. G.*	5 50S	150 20 E
56	New Britain, *U.S.A.*	41 41N	72 47W
51	New Brunswick □, *Canada*	46 50N	66 30W
122	New Caledonia, *Pac. Oc.*	21 0S	165 0 E
85	New Castile, *Spain*	39 45N	3 20W
121	New England Ra., *Australia*	30 20S	151 45 E
122	New Guinea, *Pac. Oc.*	4 0S	136 0 E
56	New Hampshire □, *U.S.A.*	43 40N	71 40W
56	New Haven, *U.S.A.*	41 20N	72 54W
121	New Ireland, *Papua N. G.*	3 20S	151 50 E
56	New Jersey □, *U.S.A.*	40 30N	74 10W
56	New London, *U.S.A.*	41 23N	72 8W
61	New Mexico □, *U.S.A.*	34 30N	106 0W
59	New Orleans, *U.S.A.*	30 0N	90 5W
121	New Plymouth, *N.Z.*	39 4S	174 5 E
97	New Siberian Is., *U.S.S.R.*	75 0N	142 0 E
121	New South Wales □, *Australia*	33 0S	146 0 E
56	New York □, *U.S.A.*	42 40N	76 0W
56	New York City, *U.S.A.*	40 45N	74 0W
121	New Zealand ■, *Oceania*	40 0S	176 0 E
56	Newark, *U.S.A.*	40 41N	74 12W
56	Newburgh, *U.S.A.*	41 30N	74 1W
121	Newcastle, *Australia*	33 0S	151 46 E
78	Newcastle-upon-Tyne, *U.K.*	54 59N	1 37W
51	Newfoundland □, *Canada*	53 0N	58 0W
79	Newport, *U.K.*	51 35N	3 0W
56	Newport, *U.S.A.*	41 13N	71 19W
56	Newport News, *U.S.A.*	37 2N	76 30W
80	Newry, *U.K.*	54 10N	6 20W
108	Nha Trang, *Vietnam*	12 16N	109 10 E
51	Niagara Falls, *N. Amer.*	43 7N	79 5W
114	Niamey, *Niger*	13 27N	2 6 E
66	Nicaragua ■, *Cent. Amer.*	11 40N	85 30W
66	Nicaragua, L., *Nic.*	12 0N	85 30W
84	Nice, *France*	43 42N	7 14 E
118	Nicobar Is., *Ind. Oc.*	9 0N	93 0 E
95	Nicosia, *Cyprus*	35 10N	33 25 E
66	Nicoya, Pen. de, *C. Rica*	9 45N	85 40W
114	Niger ■, *W. Afr.*	13 30N	10 0 E
114	Niger →, *W. Afr.*	5 33N	6 33 E
114	Nigeria ■, *W. Afr.*	8 30N	8 0 E
106	Niigata, *Japan*	37 58N	139 0 E
54	Niihau, *U.S.A.*	21 55N	160 10W
81	Nijmegen, *Neth.*	51 50N	5 52 E
95	Nikolayev, *U.S.S.R.*	46 58N	32 0 E
97	Nikolayevsk, *U.S.S.R.*	50 0N	45 35 E
115	Nile →, *Africa*	30 10N	31 6 E
84	Nîmes, *France*	43 50N	4 23 E
121	Ninety Mile Beach, *Australia*	38 15S	147 24 E
105	Ningbo, *China*	29 51N	121 28 E
104	Ningxia Huizu Zizhiqu □, *China*	38 0N	106 0 E
58	Niobrara →, *U.S.A.*	42 45N	98 0W
84	Niort, *France*	46 19N	0 29W
51	Nipigon, L., *Canada*	49 50N	88 30W
89	Niš, *Yugoslavia*	43 19N	21 58 E
107	Nishinomiya, *Japan*	34 45N	135 20 E
73	Niterói, *Brazil*	22 52S	43 0W
94	Nizhniy Tagil, *U.S.S.R.*	57 55N	59 57 E
116	Nkongsamba, *Cameroon*	4 55N	9 55 E
107	Nobeoka, *Japan*	32 36N	131 41 E
64	Nogales, *Mexico*	31 20N	110 56W
61	Nogales, *U.S.A.*	31 33N	110 56W
54	Nome, *U.S.A.*	64 30N	165 24W
81	Nordhorn, *W. Germany*	52 27N	7 4 E
97	Nordvik, *U.S.S.R.*	74 2N	111 32 E
56	Norfolk, *U.S.A.*	36 40N	76 15W
122	Norfolk I., *Pac. Oc.*	28 58S	168 3 E
97	Norilsk, *U.S.S.R.*	69 20N	88 6 E
59	Norman, *U.S.A.*	35 12N	97 30W
84	Normandy, *France*	48 45N	0 10 E
120	Normanton, *Australia*	17 40S	141 10 E
92	Norrbotten □, *Sweden*	66 30N	22 30 E
93	Norrköping, *Sweden*	58 37N	16 11 E
92	Norrland, *Sweden*	66 50N	18 0 E
48	North America	40 0N	100 0W
75	North Atlantic Ocean, *Atl. Oc.*	30 0N	50 0W
50	North Battleford, *Canada*	52 50N	108 17W
51	North Bay, *Canada*	46 20N	79 30W
60	North Bend, *U.S.A.*	43 28N	124 14W
92	North Cape, *Norway*	71 15N	25 40 E
57	North Carolina □, *U.S.A.*	35 30N	80 0W
78	North Channel, *British Is.*	55 0N	5 30W
58	North Dakota □, *U.S.A.*	47 30N	100 0W
121	North I., *N.Z.*	38 0S	175 0 E
106	North Korea ■, *Asia*	40 0N	127 0 E
80	North Minch, *U.K.*	58 5N	5 55W
58	North Platte, *U.S.A.*	41 10N	100 50W
58	North Platte →, *U.S.A.*	41 15N	100 45W
124	North Pole, *Arctic*	90 0N	0 0 E
90	North Rhine Westphalia □, *W. Germany*	51 55N	7 0 E
76	North Sea, *Europe*	56 0N	4 0 E
80	North West Highlands, *U.K.*	57 35N	5 2W
50	North West Territories □, *Canada*	67 0N	110 0W
78	North York Moors, *U.K.*	54 25N	0 50W
79	Northampton, *U.K.*	52 14N	0 54W
80	Northern Ireland □, *U.K.*	54 45N	7 0W
55	Northern Marianas □, *Pac. Oc.*	17 0N	145 0 E
120	Northern Territory □, *Australia*	16 0S	133 0 E
51	Northumberland Str., *Canada*	46 20N	64 0W
92	Norway ■, *Europe*	63 0N	11 0 E
92	Norwegian Sea, *Atl. Oc.*	66 0N	1 0 E
79	Norwich, *U.K.*	52 38N	1 17 E
78	Nottingham, *U.K.*	52 57N	1 10W
114	Nouâdhibou, *Mauritania*	20 54N	17 0W
114	Nouakchott, *Mauritania*	18 9N	15 58W
122	Nouméa, *N. Cal.*	22 17S	166 30 E
51	Nova Scotia □, *Canada*	45 10N	63 0W
88	Novara, *Italy*	45 27N	8 36 E
96	Novaya Zemlya, *U.S.S.R.*	75 0N	56 0 E
89	Novi Sad, *Yugoslavia*	45 18N	19 52 E
95	Novocherkassk, *U.S.S.R.*	47 27N	40 5 E
96	Novokuznetsk, *U.S.S.R.*	53 45N	87 10 E
94	Novomoskovsk, *U.S.S.R.*	54 5N	38 15 E
95	Novorossiysk, *U.S.S.R.*	44 43N	37 46 E
95	Novoshakhtinsk, *U.S.S.R.*	47 46N	39 58 E
96	Novosibirsk, *U.S.S.R.*	55 0N	83 5 E
115	Nubian Desert, *Sudan*	21 30N	33 30 E
65	Nuevo Laredo, *Mexico*	27 30N	99 30W
120	Nullarbor, *Australia*	31 28S	130 55 E
54	Nunivak I., *U.S.A.*	60 0N	166 0W
83	Nuremburg, *W. Germany*	49 26N	11 5 E
117	Nyasa, L., *Africa*	12 30S	34 30 E
91	Nyíregyháza, *Hungary*	47 58N	21 47 E
93	Nykøbing, *Denmark*	56 48N	8 51 E

O

PAGE	PLACE NAME	LATITUDE	LONGITUDE
58	Oahe, L., *U.S.A.*	45 30N	100 25W
54	Oahu, *U.S.A.*	21 30N	158 0W
58	Oak Park, *U.S.A.*	41 55N	87 45W
57	Oak Ridge, *U.S.A.*	36 1N	84 12W
61	Oakland, *U.S.A.*	37 50N	122 18W
121	Oamaru, *N.Z.*	45 5S	170 59 E
65	Oaxaca, *Mexico*	17 2N	96 40W
65	Oaxaca □, *Mexico*	17 0N	97 0W
96	Ob →, *U.S.S.R.*	66 45N	69 30 E
96	Ob, G. of, *U.S.S.R.*	70 0N	73 0 E
81	Oberhausen, *W. Germany*	51 28N	6 50 E
57	Ocala, *U.S.A.*	29 11N	82 5W
61	Oceanside, *U.S.A.*	33 13N	117 26W
97	October Revolution I., *U.S.S.R.*	79 30N	97 0 E
93	Odense, *Denmark*	55 22N	10 23 E
59	Odessa, *U.S.A.*	31 51N	102 23W
95	Odessa, *U.S.S.R.*	46 30N	30 45 E
90	Odra →, *Poland*	53 33N	14 38 E
83	Offenbach, *W. Germany*	50 6N	8 46 E
55	Ofu, *Amer. Samoa*	14 11S	169 41W
114	Ogbomosho, *Nigeria*	8 1N	4 11 E
60	Ogden, *U.S.A.*	41 13N	112 1W
56	Ogdensburg, *U.S.A.*	44 40N	75 27W
56	Ohio □, *U.S.A.*	40 20N	84 10W
56	Ohio →, *U.S.A.*	38 0N	86 0W
107	Ōita, *Japan*	33 14N	131 36 E
60	Okanogan →, *U.S.A.*	48 6N	119 43W
117	Okavango Swamps, *Botswana*	18 45S	22 45 E
107	Okayama, *Japan*	34 40N	133 54 E
107	Okazaki, *Japan*	34 57N	137 10 E
57	Okeechobee, L., *U.S.A.*	27 0N	80 50W
57	Okefenokee Swamp, *U.S.A.*	30 50N	82 15W
97	Okhotsk, *U.S.S.R.*	59 20N	143 10 E
97	Okhotsk, Sea of, *Asia*	55 0N	145 0 E
59	Oklahoma □, *U.S.A.*	35 20N	97 30W
59	Oklahoma City, *U.S.A.*	35 25N	97 30W
59	Okmulgee, *U.S.A.*	35 38N	96 0W
92	Ólafsfjörður, *Iceland*	66 4N	18 39W
93	Öland, *Sweden*	56 45N	16 38 E
85	Old Castile, *Spain*	41 55N	4 0W
81	Oldenburg, *W. Germany*	53 10N	8 10 E
97	Olekminsk, *U.S.S.R.*	60 25N	120 30 E
73	Olinda, *Brazil*	8 1S	34 51W
90	Olomouc, *Czech.*	49 38N	17 12 E
55	Olosega, *Amer. Samoa*	14 11S	169 38W
91	Olsztyn, *Poland*	53 48N	20 29 E
89	Olympia, *Greece*	37 39N	21 39 E
60	Olympia, *U.S.A.*	47 0N	122 58W
60	Olympic Mts., *U.S.A.*	47 50N	123 45W
89	Olympus, Mt., *Greece*	40 6N	22 23 E
80	Omagh, *U.K.*	54 36N	7 20W
58	Omaha, *U.S.A.*	41 15N	96 0W
101	Oman ■, *Si. Arabia*	23 0N	58 0 E
101	Oman, G. of, *Asia*	24 30N	58 30 E
115	Omdurmân, *Sudan*	15 40N	32 28 E
107	Ōmiya, *Japan*	35 54N	139 38 E
96	Omsk, *U.S.S.R.*	55 0N	73 12 E
107	Ōmuta, *Japan*	33 0N	130 26 E
94	Onega →, *U.S.S.R.*	63 58N	37 55 E
94	Onega, G. of, *U.S.S.R.*	64 30N	37 0 E
94	Onega, L., *U.S.S.R.*	62 0N	35 30 E
114	Onitsha, *Nigeria*	6 6N	6 42 E
51	Ontario □, *Canada*	52 0N	88 10W
56	Ontario, L., *N. Amer.*	43 40N	78 0W
91	Opole, *Poland*	50 42N	17 58 E
85	Oporto, *Portugal*	41 8N	8 40W
91	Oradea, *Romania*	47 2N	21 58 E
114	Oran, *Algeria*	35 45N	0 39W
59	Orange, *U.S.A.*	30 10N	93 50W
117	Orange →, *S. Africa*	28 41S	16 28 E
117	Orange Free State □, *S. Africa*	28 30S	27 0 E
57	Orangeburg, *U.S.A.*	33 35N	80 53W
105	Ordos, *China*	39 0N	109 0 E
95	Ordzhonikidze, *U.S.S.R.*	43 0N	44 35 E
93	Örebro, *Sweden*	59 20N	15 18 E
60	Oregon □, *U.S.A.*	44 0N	121 0W
94	Orekhovo-Zuyevo, *U.S.S.R.*	55 50N	38 55 E
94	Orel, *U.S.S.R.*	52 57N	36 3 E
94	Orenburg, *U.S.S.R.*	51 45N	55 6 E
85	Orense, *Spain*	42 19N	7 55W
72	Orinoco →, *Venezuela*	9 15N	61 30W
103	Orissa □, *India*	20 0N	84 0 E
88	Oristano, *Italy*	39 54N	8 35 E
65	Orizaba, *Mexico*	18 51N	97 6W
80	Orkney Is., *U.K.*	59 0N	3 0W
57	Orlando, *U.S.A.*	28 30N	81 25W
84	Orléans, *France*	47 54N	1 52 E
111	Ormoc, *Phil.*	11 0N	124 37 E
92	Örnsköldsvik, *Sweden*	63 17N	18 40 E
94	Orsk, *U.S.S.R.*	51 12N	58 34 E
72	Oruro, *Bolivia*	18 0S	67 9W
107	Ōsaka, *Japan*	34 40N	135 30 E
96	Osh, *U.S.S.R.*	40 37N	72 49 E
51	Oshawa, *Canada*	43 50N	78 50W
58	Oshkosh, *U.S.A.*	41 27N	102 20W
114	Oshogbo, *Nigeria*	7 48N	4 37 E
89	Osijek, *Yugoslavia*	45 34N	18 41 E
117	Osizweni, *S. Africa*	27 49S	30 7 E
93	Oslo, *Norway*	59 55N	10 45 E
93	Oslo Fjord, *Norway*	58 30N	10 0 E
81	Osnabrück, *W. Germany*	52 16N	8 2 E
74	Osorno, *Chile*	40 25S	73 0W
81	Ostend, *Belgium*	51 15N	2 50 E
92	Östersund, *Sweden*	63 10N	14 38 E
91	Ostrava, *Czech.*	49 51N	18 18 E
107	Osumi, Is., *Japan*	30 30N	130 45 E
56	Oswego, *U.S.A.*	43 29N	76 30W
121	Otago □, *N.Z.*	44 44S	169 10 E
106	Otaru, *Japan*	43 10N	141 0 E
89	Otranto, Str. of, *Italy*	40 15N	18 40 E
107	Ōtsu, *Japan*	35 0N	135 50 E
51	Ottawa, *Canada*	45 27N	75 42W
51	Ottawa →, *Canada*	45 27N	74 8W
58	Ottumwa, *U.S.A.*	41 0N	92 25W
59	Ouachita Mts., *U.S.A.*	34 50N	94 30W
114	Ouagadougou, *Burkina Faso*	12 25N	1 30W
114	Oujda, *Morocco*	34 41N	1 55W
92	Oulu, *Finland*	65 1N	25 29 E
92	Oulu, L., *Finland*	64 25N	27 0 E

PAGE	PLACE NAME	LATITUDE	LONGITUDE
80	Outer Hebrides, *U.K.*	57 30N	7 40W
85	Oviedo, *Spain*	43 25N	5 50W
121	Owen Stanley Range, *Papua N. G.*	8 30S	147 0E
60	Owyhee →, *U.S.A.*	43 46N	117 2W
79	Oxford, *U.K.*	51 45N	1 15W
61	Oxnard, *U.S.A.*	34 10N	119 14W
111	Ozamis, *Phil.*	8 15N	123 50E
59	Ozark Plateau, *U.S.A.*	37 20N	91 40W

P

PAGE	PLACE NAME	LATITUDE	LONGITUDE
117	Paarl, *S. Africa*	33 45S	18 56E
72	Pacaraima, Sierra, *Venezuela*	4 0N	62 30W
65	Pachuca, *Mexico*	20 10N	98 40W
122	Pacific Ocean	10 0N	140 0W
108	Padang, *Indonesia*	1 0S	100 20E
82	Paderborn, *W. Germany*	51 42N	8 44E
88	Padua, *Italy*	45 24N	11 52E
56	Paducah, *U.S.A.*	37 0N	88 40W
111	Pagadian, *Phil.*	7 55N	123 30E
55	Pago Pago, *Amer. Samoa*	14 16S	170 43W
61	Painted Desert, *U.S.A.*	36 0N	111 30W
78	Paisley, *U.K.*	55 51N	4 27W
102	Pakistan ■, *Asia*	30 0N	70 0E
55	Palau □, *Pac. Oc.*	7 30N	134 30E
111	Palawan, *Phil.*	9 30N	118 30E
108	Palembang, *Indonesia*	3 0S	104 50E
85	Palencia, *Spain*	42 1N	4 34W
88	Palermo, *Italy*	38 8N	13 20E
59	Palestine, *U.S.A.*	31 42N	95 35W
102	Palk Strait, *Asia*	10 0N	79 45E
61	Palm Springs, *U.S.A.*	33 51N	116 35W
85	Palma de Mallorca, *Spain*	39 35N	2 39E
121	Palmerston North, *N.Z.*	40 21S	175 39E
72	Palmira, *Colombia*	3 32N	76 16W
96	Pamirs, *U.S.S.R.*	37 40N	73 0E
57	Pamlico Sd., *U.S.A.*	35 20N	76 0W
59	Pampa, *U.S.A.*	35 35N	100 58W
74	Pampas, *Argentina*	35 0S	63 0W
85	Pamplona, *Spain*	42 48N	1 38W
69	Panamá, *Panama*	9 0N	79 25W
66	Panama ■, *Cent. Amer.*	8 48N	79 55W
66	Panamá, G. of, *Panama*	8 4N	79 20W
69	Panama Canal, *Panama*	9 10N	79 37W
57	Panama City, *U.S.A.*	30 10N	85 41W
111	Panay, *Phil.*	11 10N	122 30E
89	Pančevo, *Yugoslavia*	44 52N	20 41E
88	Pantelleria, *Italy*	36 52N	12 0E
121	Papua, Gulf of, *Papua N. G.*	9 0S	144 50E
121	Papua New Guinea ■, *Oceania*	8 0S	145 0E
73	Pará □, *Brazil*	3 20S	52 0W
74	Paraguay ■, *S. Amer.*	23 0S	57 0W
74	Paraguay →, *Paraguay*	27 18S	58 38W
73	Paramaribo, *Suriname*	5 50N	55 10W
74	Paraná, *Argentina*	31 45S	60 30W
74	Paraná →, *Argentina*	33 43S	59 15W
72	Parecis, Serra dos, *Brazil*	13 0S	60 0W
109	Parepare, *Indonesia*	4 0S	119 40E
84	Paris, *France*	48 50N	2 20E
59	Paris, *U.S.A.*	33 40N	95 30W
60	Park Range, *U.S.A.*	40 0N	106 30W
56	Parkersburg, *U.S.A.*	39 18N	81 31W
121	Parkes, *Australia*	33 9S	148 11E
88	Parma, *Italy*	44 50N	10 20E
73	Parnaíba →, *Brazil*	3 0S	41 50W
61	Pasadena, *Calif., U.S.A.*	34 5N	118 9W
59	Pasadena, *Tex., U.S.A.*	29 45N	95 14W
57	Pascagoula, *U.S.A.*	30 21N	88 30W
60	Pasco, *U.S.A.*	46 10N	119 0W
72	Pasto, *Colombia*	1 13N	77 17W
74	Patagonia, *Argentina*	45 0S	69 0W
56	Paterson, *U.S.A.*	40 55N	74 10W
103	Patna, *India*	25 35N	85 12E
89	Pátrai, *Greece*	38 14N	21 47E
84	Pau, *France*	43 19N	0 25W
88	Pavia, *Italy*	45 10N	9 10E
96	Pavlodar, *U.S.S.R.*	52 33N	77 0E
56	Pawtucket, *U.S.A.*	41 51N	71 22W
89	Pazardzhik, *Bulgaria*	42 12N	24 20E
50	Peace →, *Canada*	59 0N	111 25W
94	Pechora →, *U.S.S.R.*	68 13N	54 15E
59	Pecos →, *U.S.A.*	29 42N	102 30W
91	Pécs, *Hungary*	46 5N	18 15E
103	Pegu, *Burma*	17 20N	96 29E
103	Pegu Yoma, *Burma*	19 0N	96 0E
108	Pekanbaru, *Indonesia*	0 30N	101 15E
58	Pekin, *U.S.A.*	40 35N	89 40W
105	Peking = Beijing, *China*	39 55N	116 20E
89	Peloponnese □, *Greece*	37 10N	22 0E
74	Pelotas, *Brazil*	31 42S	52 23W

PAGE	PLACE NAME	LATITUDE	LONGITUDE
84	Pelvoux, Massif de, *France*	44 52N	6 20E
108	Pematangsiantar, *Indonesia*	2 57N	99 5E
116	Pemba, *Tanzania*	5 0S	39 45E
60	Pend Oreille, L., *U.S.A.*	48 0N	116 30W
60	Pendleton, *U.S.A.*	45 35N	118 50W
108	Peninsular Malaysia □, *Malaysia*	4 0N	102 0E
78	Pennines, *U.K.*	54 50N	2 20W
56	Pennsylvania □, *U.S.A.*	40 50N	78 0W
120	Penong, *Australia*	31 59S	133 5E
57	Pensacola, *U.S.A.*	30 30N	87 10W
80	Pentland Firth, *U.K.*	58 43N	3 10W
94	Penza, *U.S.S.R.*	53 15N	45 5E
58	Peoria, *U.S.A.*	40 40N	89 40W
72	Pereira, *Colombia*	4 49N	75 43W
94	Perm, *U.S.S.R.*	58 0N	57 10E
84	Perpignan, *France*	42 42N	2 53E
101	Persian Gulf, *Asia*	27 0N	50 0E
120	Perth, *Australia*	31 57S	115 52E
80	Perth, *U.K.*	56 24N	3 27W
56	Perth Amboy, *U.S.A.*	40 31N	74 16W
72	Peru ■, *S. Amer.*	8 0S	75 0W
88	Perúgia, *Italy*	43 6N	12 24E
88	Pescara, *Italy*	42 28N	14 13E
102	Peshawar, *Pakistan*	34 2N	71 37E
51	Peterborough, *Canada*	44 20N	78 20W
79	Peterborough, *U.K.*	52 35N	0 14W
80	Peterhead, *U.K.*	57 30N	1 49W
56	Petersburg, *U.S.A.*	37 17N	77 26W
96	Petropavlovsk, *U.S.S.R.*	54 53N	69 13E
97	Petropavlovsk-Kamchatskiy, *U.S.S.R.*	53 3N	158 43E
73	Petrópolis, *Brazil*	22 33S	43 9W
94	Petrozavodsk, *U.S.S.R.*	61 41N	34 20E
83	Pforzheim, *W. Germany*	48 53N	8 43E
57	Phenix City, *U.S.A.*	32 30N	85 0W
56	Philadelphia, *U.S.A.*	40 0N	75 10W
110	Philippines ■, *Asia*	12 0N	123 0E
108	Phnom Penh, *Cambodia*	11 33N	104 55E
61	Phoenix, *U.S.A.*	33 30N	112 10W
123	Phoenix Is., *Pac. Oc.*	3 30S	172 0W
88	Piacenza, *Italy*	45 2N	9 42E
91	Piatra Neamţ, *Romania*	46 56N	26 21E
84	Picardie, *France*	49 50N	3 0E
75	Pico, *Azores*	38 28N	28 20W
88	Piedmont □, *Italy*	45 0N	7 30E
64	Piedras Negras, *Mexico*	28 42N	100 31W
117	Pietermaritzburg, *S. Africa*	29 35S	30 25E
74	Pilcomayo →, *Paraguay*	25 21S	57 42W
110	Pinamalayan, *Phil.*	13 2N	121 29E
108	Pinang, *Malaysia*	5 25N	100 15E
89	Pindus Mts., *Greece*	40 0N	21 0E
59	Pine Bluff, *U.S.A.*	34 10N	92 0W
104	Pingxiang, *China*	22 6N	106 46E
91	Piotrków Trybunalski, *Poland*	51 23N	19 43E
74	Piracicaba, *Brazil*	22 45S	47 40W
89	Piraiévs, *Greece*	37 57N	23 42E
81	Pirmasens, *W. Germany*	49 12N	7 30E
88	Pisa, *Italy*	43 43N	10 23E
88	Pistóia, *Italy*	43 57N	10 53E
123	Pitcairn I., *Pac. Oc.*	25 5S	130 5W
91	Piteşti, *Romania*	44 52N	24 54E
59	Pittsburg, *U.S.A.*	37 21N	94 43W
56	Pittsburgh, *U.S.A.*	40 25N	79 55W
72	Piura, *Peru*	5 15S	80 38W
59	Plainview, *U.S.A.*	34 10N	101 40W
74	Plata, Río de la, *S. Amer.*	34 45S	57 30W
58	Platte →, *U.S.A.*	39 16N	94 50W
82	Plauen, *E. Germany*	50 29N	12 9E
121	Plenty, Bay of, *N.Z.*	37 45S	177 0E
89	Pleven, *Bulgaria*	43 26N	24 37E
91	Płock, *Poland*	52 32N	19 40E
91	Ploieşti, *Romania*	44 57N	26 5E
89	Plovdiv, *Bulgaria*	42 8N	24 44E
79	Plymouth, *U.K.*	50 23N	4 9W
90	Plzen, *Czech.*	49 45N	13 22E
88	Po →, *Italy*	44 57N	12 4E
60	Pocatello, *U.S.A.*	42 50N	112 25W
94	Podolsk, *U.S.S.R.*	55 25N	37 30E
55	Pohnpei, *Pac. Oc.*	6 55N	158 10E
67	Pointe-à-Pitre, *Guadeloupe*	16 10N	61 30W
116	Pointe Noire, *Congo*	4 48S	11 53E
84	Poitiers, *France*	46 35N	0 20E
91	Poland ■, *Europe*	52 0N	20 0E
110	Polillo Is., *Phil.*	14 56N	122 0E
95	Poltava, *U.S.S.R.*	49 35N	34 35E
122	Polynesia, *Pac. Oc.*	10 0S	162 0W
59	Ponca City, *U.S.A.*	36 40N	97 5W
69	Ponce, *Puerto Rico*	18 1N	66 37W
102	Pondicherry, *India*	11 59N	79 50E
75	Ponta Delgada, *Azores*	37 44N	25 40W
74	Ponta Grossa, *Brazil*	25 7S	50 10W

PAGE	PLACE NAME	LATITUDE	LONGITUDE
59	Pontchartrain, L., *U.S.A.*	30 12N	90 0W
85	Pontevedra, *Spain*	42 26N	8 40W
56	Pontiac, *U.S.A.*	42 40N	83 20W
108	Pontianak, *Indonesia*	0 3S	109 15E
72	Poopó, L., *Bolivia*	18 30S	67 35W
72	Popayán, *Colombia*	2 27N	76 36W
59	Poplar Bluff, *U.S.A.*	36 45N	90 22W
65	Popocatépetl, *Mexico*	19 2N	98 38W
93	Pori, *Finland*	61 29N	21 48E
92	Porsangen Fjord, *Norway*	70 45N	25 0E
60	Port Angeles, *U.S.A.*	48 7N	123 30W
66	Port Antonio, *Jamaica*	18 10N	76 30W
59	Port Arthur, *U.S.A.*	30 0N	94 0W
67	Port-au-Prince, *Haiti*	18 40N	72 20W
51	Port-Cartier, *Canada*	50 2N	66 50W
117	Port Elizabeth, *S. Africa*	33 58S	25 40E
116	Port-Gentil, *Gabon*	0 40S	8 50E
114	Port Harcourt, *Nigeria*	4 40N	7 10E
120	Port Hedland, *Australia*	20 25S	118 35E
56	Port Huron, *U.S.A.*	43 0N	82 28W
118	Port Louis, *Mauritius*	20 10S	57 30E
121	Port Moresby, *Papua N. G.*	9 24S	147 8E
67	Port of Spain, *Trin. & Tob.*	10 40N	61 31W
121	Port Phillip B., *Australia*	38 10S	144 50E
115	Port Said, *Egypt*	31 16N	32 18E
115	Port Sudan, *Sudan*	19 32N	37 9E
50	Portage La Prairie, *Canada*	49 58N	98 18W
57	Portland, *Maine, U.S.A.*	43 40N	70 15W
60	Portland, *Oreg., U.S.A.*	45 35N	122 40W
74	Pôrto Alegre, *Brazil*	30 5S	51 10W
114	Porto Novo, *Benin*	6 23N	2 42E
72	Pôrto Velho, *Brazil*	8 46S	63 54W
72	Portovíejo, *Ecuador*	1 7S	80 28W
79	Portsmouth, *U.K.*	50 48N	1 6W
56	Portsmouth, *U.S.A.*	36 50N	76 20W
85	Portugal ■, *Europe*	40 0N	7 0W
74	Posadas, *Argentina*	27 30S	55 50W
117	Potchefstroom, *S. Africa*	26 41S	27 7E
88	Potenza, *Italy*	40 40N	15 50E
56	Potomac →, *U.S.A.*	38 0N	76 23W
72	Potosí, *Bolivia*	19 38S	65 50W
82	Potsdam, *E. Germany*	52 23N	13 4E
56	Poughkeepsie, *U.S.A.*	41 40N	73 57W
58	Powder →, *U.S.A.*	46 47N	105 12W
61	Powell, L., *U.S.A.*	37 25N	110 45W
105	Poyang Hu, *China*	29 10N	116 10E
65	Poza Rica, *Mexico*	20 33N	97 27W
90	Poznań, *Poland*	52 25N	16 55E
90	Prague, *Czech.*	50 5N	14 22E
88	Prato, *Italy*	43 53N	11 5E
73	Presidente Prudente, *Brazil*	22 5S	51 25W
57	Presque Isle, *U.S.A.*	46 40N	68 0W
78	Preston, *U.K.*	53 46N	2 42W
117	Pretoria, *S. Africa*	25 44S	28 12E
57	Prichard, *U.S.A.*	30 47N	88 5W
50	Prince Albert, *Canada*	53 15N	105 50W
51	Prince Edward I. □, *Canada*	46 20N	63 20W
50	Prince George, *Canada*	53 55N	122 50W
50	Prince of Wales I., *Canada*	73 0N	99 0W
50	Prince Rupert, *Canada*	54 20N	130 20W
94	Pripyat Marshes, *U.S.S.R.*	52 0N	28 10E
89	Priština, *Yugoslavia*	42 40N	21 13E
89	Prizren, *Yugoslavia*	42 13N	20 45E
96	Prokopyevsk, *U.S.S.R.*	54 0N	86 45E
103	Prome, *Burma*	18 49N	95 13E
84	Provence, *France*	43 40N	5 46E
56	Providence, *U.S.A.*	41 50N	71 28W
60	Provo, *U.S.A.*	40 16N	111 37W
54	Prudhoe Bay, *U.S.A.*	70 20N	148 20W
89	Prut →, *Romania*	46 3N	28 10E
91	Przemyśl, *Poland*	49 50N	22 45E
65	Puebla, *Mexico*	19 3N	98 12W
65	Puebla □, *Mexico*	18 30N	98 0W
58	Pueblo, *U.S.A.*	38 20N	104 40W
72	Puerto La Cruz, *Venezuela*	10 13N	64 38W
74	Puerto Montt, *Chile*	41 28S	73 0W
111	Puerto Princesa, *Phil.*	9 46N	118 45E
69	Puerto Rico ■, *W. Indies*	18 15N	66 45W
60	Puget Sd., *U.S.A.*	47 15N	122 30W
88	Pula, *Italy*	39 0N	9 0E
60	Pullman, *U.S.A.*	46 49N	117 10W
102	Pune, *India*	18 29N	73 57E
102	Punjab □, *India*	31 0N	76 0E
102	Punjab □, *Pakistan*	30 0N	72 0E
74	Punta Arenas, *Chile*	53 10S	71 0W
72	Punto Fijo, *Venezuela*	11 50N	70 13W
103	Purnia, *India*	25 45N	87 31E
72	Purus →, *Brazil*	3 42S	61 28W
106	Pusan, *S. Korea*	35 5N	129 0E
84	Puy-de-Dôme, *France*	45 46N	2 57E
106	Pyŏngyang, *N. Korea*	39 0N	125 30E
84	Pyrenees, *Europe*	42 45N	0 18E

PAGE	PLACE NAME	LATITUDE	LONGITUDE
	Q		
101	Qandahār, *Afghan.*	31 32N	65 30 E
101	Qatar ■, *Asia*	25 30N	51 15 E
115	Qattâra Depression, *Egypt*	29 30N	27 30 E
101	Qazvin, *Iran*	36 15N	50 0 E
115	Qena, *Egypt*	26 10N	32 43 E
105	Qingdao, *China*	36 5N	120 20 E
104	Qinghai □, *China*	36 0N	98 0 E
104	Qinghai Hu, *China*	36 40N	100 10 E
105	Qingjiang, *China*	33 30N	119 2 E
105	Qiqihar, *China*	47 26N	124 0 E
101	Qom, *Iran*	34 40N	51 0 E
51	Québec, *Canada*	46 52N	71 13W
51	Québec □, *Canada*	50 0N	70 0W
50	Queen Charlotte Is., *Canada*	53 20N	132 10W
124	Queen Elizabeth Is., *Canada*	76 0N	95 0W
50	Queen Maud G., *Canada*	68 15N	102 30W
120	Queensland □, *Australia*	22 0S	142 0 E
117	Queenstown, *S. Africa*	31 52S	26 52 E
64	Querétaro, *Mexico*	20 36N	100 23W
102	Quetta, *Pakistan*	30 15N	66 55 E
110	Quezon City, *Phil.*	14 38N	121 0 E
108	Qui Nhon, *Vietnam*	13 40N	109 13 E
84	Quimper, *France*	48 0N	4 9W
58	Quincy, *U.S.A.*	39 55N	91 20W
65	Quintana Roo □, *Mexico*	19 0N	88 0W
72	Quito, *Ecuador*	0 15S	78 35W
	R		
114	Rabat, *Morocco*	34 2N	6 48W
58	Racine, *U.S.A.*	42 41N	87 51W
91	Radom, *Poland*	51 23N	21 12 E
88	Ragusa, *Italy*	36 56N	14 42 E
60	Rainier, Mt., *U.S.A.*	46 50N	121 50W
103	Raipur, *India*	21 17N	81 45 E
103	Rajahmundry, *India*	17 1N	81 48 E
102	Rajasthan □, *India*	26 45N	73 30 E
102	Rajkot, *India*	22 15N	70 56 E
57	Raleigh, *U.S.A.*	35 47N	78 39W
102	Rampur, *India*	28 50N	79 5 E
103	Ramree Kyun, *Burma*	19 0N	94 0 E
74	Rancagua, *Chile*	34 10S	70 50W
103	Ranchi, *India*	23 19N	85 27 E
103	Rangoon, *Burma*	16 45N	96 20 E
58	Rapid City, *U.S.A.*	44 0N	103 0W
101	Rasht, *Iran*	37 20N	49 40 E
103	Raurkela, *India*	22 14N	84 50 E
88	Ravenna, *Italy*	44 28N	12 15 E
102	Rawalpindi, *Pakistan*	33 38N	73 8 E
60	Rawlins, *U.S.A.*	41 50N	107 20W
79	Reading, *U.K.*	51 27N	0 57W
56	Reading, *U.S.A.*	40 20N	75 53W
73	Recife, *Brazil*	8 0S	35 0W
82	Recklinghausen, *W. Germany*	51 36N	7 10 E
104	Red = Hong ⟶, *Vietnam*	20 17N	106 34 E
58	Red ⟶, *N. Amer.*	50 24N	96 48W
59	Red ⟶, *U.S.A.*	31 0N	91 40W
50	Red Deer, *Canada*	52 20N	113 50W
100	Red Sea, *Asia*	25 0N	36 0 E
60	Redding, *U.S.A.*	40 30N	122 25W
61	Redwood City, *U.S.A.*	37 30N	122 15W
83	Regensburg, *W. Germany*	49 1N	12 7 E
88	Réggio di Calábria, *Italy*	38 7N	15 38 E
88	Réggio nell' Emilia, *Italy*	44 42N	10 38 E
50	Regina, *Canada*	50 27N	104 35W
57	Reidsville, *U.S.A.*	36 21N	79 40W
84	Reims, *France*	49 15N	4 1 E
50	Reindeer L., *Canada*	57 15N	102 15W
81	Remscheid, *W. Germany*	51 11N	7 12 E
84	Rennes, *France*	48 7N	1 41W
60	Reno, *U.S.A.*	39 30N	119 50W
58	Republican ⟶, *U.S.A.*	39 3N	96 48W
74	Resistencia, *Argentina*	27 30S	59 0W
89	Réthímnon, *Greece*	35 18N	24 30 E
118	Réunion □, *Ind. Oc.*	21 0S	56 0 E
92	Reykjavík, *Iceland*	64 10N	21 57 E
65	Reynosa, *Mexico*	26 5N	98 18W
81	Rhein = Rhine ⟶, *W. Germany*	51 52N	6 20 E
90	Rhineland-Palatinate □, *W. Germany*	50 0N	7 0 E
56	Rhode Island □, *U.S.A.*	41 38N	71 37W
89	Rhodope Mts., *Bulgaria*	41 40N	24 20 E
79	Rhondda, *U.K.*	51 39N	3 30W
84	Rhône ⟶, *France*	43 28N	4 42 E
73	Ribeirão Prêto, *Brazil*	21 10S	47 50W
60	Richland, *U.S.A.*	46 15N	119 15W
60	Richmond, *Calif., U.S.A.*	37 58N	122 21W
56	Richmond, *Va., U.S.A.*	37 33N	77 27W
94	Riga, *U.S.S.R.*	56 53N	24 8 E
94	Riga, G. of, *U.S.S.R.*	57 40N	23 45 E
88	Rijeka, *Yugoslavia*	45 20N	14 21 E
81	Rijswijk, *Neth.*	52 4N	4 22 E
88	Rímini, *Italy*	44 3N	12 33 E
91	Rîmnicu Vîlcea, *Romania*	45 9N	24 21 E
51	Rimouski, *Canada*	48 27N	68 30W
72	Rio Branco, *Brazil*	9 58S	67 49W
74	Río Cuarto, *Argentina*	33 10S	64 25W
73	Rio de Janeiro, *Brazil*	23 0S	43 12W
74	Río Gallegos, *Argentina*	51 35S	69 15W
74	Rio Grande, *Brazil*	32 0S	52 20W
59	Rio Grande ⟶, *U.S.A.*	25 57N	97 9W
116	Río Muni □, *Eq. Guin.*	1 30N	10 0 E
72	Ríobamba, *Ecuador*	1 50S	78 45W
120	Riverina, *Australia*	29 45S	120 40 E
61	Riverside, *U.S.A.*	34 0N	117 22W
100	Riyadh, *Si. Arabia*	24 41N	46 42 E
84	Roanne, *France*	46 3N	4 4 E
56	Roanoke, *U.S.A.*	37 19N	79 55W
58	Rochester, *Minn., U.S.A.*	44 1N	92 28W
56	Rochester, *N.Y., U.S.A.*	43 10N	77 40W
57	Rock Hill, *U.S.A.*	34 55N	81 2W
58	Rock Island, *U.S.A.*	41 30N	90 35W
60	Rock Springs, *U.S.A.*	41 40N	109 10W
58	Rockford, *U.S.A.*	42 20N	89 0W
121	Rockhampton, *Australia*	23 22S	150 32 E
57	Rocky Mount, *U.S.A.*	35 55N	77 48W
48	Rocky Mts., *N. Amer.*	55 0N	121 0W
89	Ródhos, *Greece*	36 15N	28 10 E
118	Rodriguez, *Ind. Oc.*	19 45S	63 20 E
81	Roeselare, *Belgium*	50 57N	3 7 E
93	Rogaland □, *Norway*	59 12N	6 20 E
91	Romania ■, *Europe*	46 0N	25 0 E
110	Romblon, *Phil.*	12 33N	122 17 E
88	Rome, *Italy*	41 54N	12 30 E
57	Rome, *U.S.A.*	34 20N	85 0W
81	Ronse, *Belgium*	50 45N	3 35 E
81	Roosendaal, *Neth.*	51 32N	4 29 E
73	Roraima, Mt., *Venezuela*	5 10N	60 40W
74	Rosario, *Argentina*	33 0S	60 40W
67	Roseau, *Dominica*	15 20N	61 24W
58	Roseau, *U.S.A.*	48 51N	95 46W
60	Roseburg, *U.S.A.*	43 10N	123 20W
60	Roseville, *U.S.A.*	38 46N	121 17W
93	Roskilde, *Denmark*	55 38N	12 3 E
124	Ross Ice Shelf, *Antarct.*	80 0S	180 0 E
124	Ross Sea, *Antarct.*	74 0S	178 0 E
82	Rostock, *E. Germany*	54 4N	12 9 E
95	Rostov, *U.S.S.R.*	47 15N	39 45 E
59	Roswell, *U.S.A.*	33 26N	104 32W
121	Roto, *Australia*	33 0S	145 30 E
121	Rotorua, *N.Z.*	38 9S	176 16 E
81	Rotterdam, *Neth.*	51 55N	4 30 E
84	Roubaix, *France*	50 40N	3 10 E
84	Rouen, *France*	49 27N	1 4 E
111	Roxas, *Capiz, Phil.*	11 36N	122 49 E
110	Roxas, *Isabela, Phil.*	17 8N	121 36 E
100	Rub' al Khali, *Si. Arabia*	18 0N	48 0 E
89	Ruse, *Bulgaria*	43 48N	25 59 E
94	Russian S.F.S.R. □, *U.S.S.R.*	62 0N	105 0 E
116	Rwanda ■, *Africa*	2 0S	30 0 E
94	Ryazan, *U.S.S.R.*	54 40N	39 40 E
94	Rybinsk Res., *U.S.S.R.*	58 30N	38 0 E
107	Ryūkyū Is., *Japan*	26 0N	128 0 E
91	Rzeszów, *Poland*	50 5N	21 58 E
	S		
81	Saarbrücken, *W. Germany*	49 15N	6 58 E
94	Saaremaa, *U.S.S.R.*	58 30N	22 30 E
81	Saarland □, *W. Germany*	49 15N	7 0 E
67	Saba, *W. Indies*	17 42N	63 26W
85	Sabadell, *Spain*	41 28N	2 7 E
108	Sabah □, *Malaysia*	6 0N	117 0 E
115	Sabhah, *Libya*	27 9N	14 29 E
60	Sacramento, *U.S.A.*	38 33N	121 30W
60	Sacramento ⟶, *U.S.A.*	38 3N	121 56W
61	Sacramento Mts., *U.S.A.*	32 30N	105 30W
114	Safi, *Morocco*	32 18N	9 20W
102	Sagar, *India*	14 14N	75 6 E
56	Saginaw, *U.S.A.*	43 26N	83 55W
114	Sahara, *Africa*	23 0N	5 0 E
114	Saharan Atlas, *Algeria*	34 9N	3 29 E
102	Saharanpur, *India*	29 58N	77 33 E
108	Saigon = Ho Chi Minh City, *Vietnam*	10 58N	106 40 E
80	St. Andrews, *U.K.*	56 20N	2 48W
57	St. Augustine, *U.S.A.*	29 52N	81 20W
50	St. Boniface, *Canada*	49 53N	97 5W
84	St.-Brieuc, *France*	48 30N	2 46W
51	St. Catharines, *Canada*	43 10N	79 15W
67	St. Christopher-Nevis ■, *W. Indies*	17 20N	62 40W
84	St.-Claude, *France*	46 22N	5 52 E
58	St. Cloud, *U.S.A.*	45 30N	94 11W
69	St. Croix, *W. Indies*	17 45N	64 45W
118	St.-Denis, *Réunion*	20 52S	55 27 E
54	St. Elias, Mt., *U.S.A.*	60 14N	140 50W
50	St. Elias Mts., *Canada*	60 33N	139 28W
84	St.-Étienne, *France*	45 27N	4 22 E
83	St. Gallen, *Switz.*	47 25N	9 20 E
67	St. George's, *Grenada*	12 5N	61 43W
80	St. George's Channel, *U.K.*	52 0N	6 0W
75	St. Helena, *Atl. Oc.*	15 55S	5 44W
117	St. Helena B., *S. Africa*	32 40S	18 10 E
78	St. Helens, *U.K.*	53 28N	2 44W
60	St. Helens, Mt., *U.S.A.*	46 12N	122 11W
84	St. Helier, *U.K.*	49 11N	2 6W
51	St-Hyacinthe, *Canada*	45 40N	72 58W
51	St. John, *Canada*	45 20N	66 8W
68	St. John's, *Antigua*	17 6N	61 51W
51	St. John's, *Canada*	47 35N	52 40W
57	St. John's ⟶, *U.S.A.*	30 20N	81 30W
58	St. Joseph, *U.S.A.*	39 46N	94 50W
80	St. Kilda, *U.K.*	57 9N	8 34W
51	St. Lawrence ⟶, *Canada*	49 30N	66 0W
51	St. Lawrence, Gulf of, *Canada*	48 25N	62 0W
54	St. Lawrence I., *U.S.A.*	63 0N	170 0W
84	St.-Lô, *France*	49 7N	1 5W
114	St-Louis, *Senegal*	16 8N	16 27W
58	St. Louis, *U.S.A.*	38 40N	90 12W
67	St. Lucia ■, *W. Indies*	14 0N	60 50W
67	St. Maarten, *W. Indies*	18 0N	63 5W
84	St.-Malo, *France*	48 39N	2 1W
67	St-Martin, *W. Indies*	18 0N	63 0W
84	St.-Nazaire, *France*	47 17N	2 12W
81	St-Niklaas, *Belgium*	51 10N	4 8 E
58	St. Paul, *U.S.A.*	44 54N	93 5W
84	St. Peter Port, *U.K.*	49 27N	2 31W
57	St. Petersburg, *U.S.A.*	27 45N	82 40W
51	St.-Pierre et Miquelon □, *N. Amer.*	46 55N	56 10W
84	St.-Quentin, *France*	49 50N	3 16 E
69	St. Thomas, *W. Indies*	18 21N	64 55W
84	St.-Tropez, *France*	43 17N	6 38 E
67	St. Vincent and the Grenadines ■, *W. Indies*	13 0N	61 10W
55	Saipan, *Pac. Oc.*	15 12N	145 45 E
107	Sakai, *Japan*	34 30N	135 30 E
58	Sakakawea, L., *U.S.A.*	47 30N	102 0W
97	Sakhalin, *U.S.S.R.*	51 0N	143 0 E
74	Salado ⟶, *Argentina*	31 40S	60 41W
85	Salamanca, *Spain*	40 58N	5 39W
102	Salem, *India*	11 40N	78 11 E
60	Salem, *U.S.A.*	45 0N	123 0W
88	Salerno, *Italy*	40 40N	14 44 E
58	Salina, *U.S.A.*	38 50N	97 40W
61	Salinas, *U.S.A.*	36 40N	121 41W
57	Salisbury, *U.S.A.*	35 20N	80 29W
79	Salisbury Plain, *U.K.*	51 13N	1 50W
60	Salmon ⟶, *U.S.A.*	45 51N	116 46W
60	Salmon River Mts., *U.S.A.*	45 0N	114 30W
60	Salt Lake City, *U.S.A.*	40 45N	111 58W
74	Salta, *Argentina*	24 57S	65 25W
64	Saltillo, *Mexico*	25 25N	101 0W
74	Salto, *Uruguay*	31 27S	57 50W
61	Salton Sea, *U.S.A.*	33 20N	115 50W
73	Salvador, *Brazil*	13 0S	38 30W
103	Salween ⟶, *Burma*	16 31N	97 37 E
83	Salzburg, *Austria*	47 48N	13 2 E
82	Salzgitter, *W. Germany*	52 13N	10 22 E
108	Samarinda, *Indonesia*	0 30S	117 9 E
96	Samarkand, *U.S.S.R.*	39 40N	66 55 E
89	Sámos, *Greece*	37 45N	26 50 E
95	Samsun, *Turkey*	41 15N	36 22 E
59	San Angelo, *U.S.A.*	31 30N	100 30W
59	San Antonio, *U.S.A.*	29 30N	98 30W
61	San Bernardino, *U.S.A.*	34 7N	117 18W
110	San Carlos, *Phil.*	15 55N	120 20 E
72	San Cristóbal, *Venezuela*	16 50N	92 40W
61	San Diego, *U.S.A.*	32 43N	117 10W
64	San Fernando, *Mexico*	30 0N	115 10W
110	San Fernando, *Phil.*	16 40N	120 23 E
67	San Fernando, *Trin. & Tob.*	10 20N	61 30W
61	San Fernando, *U.S.A.*	34 15N	118 29W
61	San Francisco, *U.S.A.*	37 47N	122 30W
67	San Francisco de Macorîs, *Dom. Rep.*	19 19N	70 15W
61	San Joaquin ⟶, *U.S.A.*	38 4N	121 51W
74	San Jorge, G., *Argentina*	46 0S	66 0W
66	San José, *C. Rica*	10 0N	84 2W
110	San Jose, *Phil.*	15 45N	120 55 E
61	San Jose, *U.S.A.*	37 20N	121 53W
74	San Juan, *Argentina*	31 30S	68 30W
69	San Juan, *Puerto Rico*	18 28N	66 8W

PAGE	PLACE NAME	LATITUDE	LONGITUDE
58	Springfield, *Ill., U.S.A.*	39 48N	89 40W
56	Springfield, *Mass., U.S.A.*	42 8N	72 37W
59	Springfield, *Mo., U.S.A.*	37 15N	93 20W
56	Springfield, *Ohio, U.S.A.*	39 58N	83 48W
60	Springfield, *Oreg., U.S.A.*	44 2N	123 0W
97	Sredinnyy Ra., *U.S.S.R.*	57 0N	160 0 E
97	Srednekolymsk, *U.S.S.R.*	67 27N	153 40 E
102	Sri Lanka ■, *Asia*	7 30N	80 50 E
102	Srinagar, *India*	34 5N	74 50 E
74	Stanley, *Falkland Is.*	51 40S	59 51W
97	Stanovoy Ra., *U.S.S.R.*	55 0N	130 0 E
89	Stara Zagora, *Bulgaria*	42 26N	25 39 E
56	State College, *U.S.A.*	40 47N	77 1W
57	Statesville, *U.S.A.*	35 48N	80 51W
93	Stavanger, *Norway*	58 57N	5 40 E
95	Stavropol, *U.S.S.R.*	45 5N	42 0 E
98	Steppe, *Asia*	50 0N	50 0 E
94	Sterlitamak, *U.S.S.R.*	53 40N	56 0 E
56	Steubenville, *U.S.A.*	40 21N	80 39W
59	Stillwater, *U.S.A.*	36 5N	97 3W
78	Stirling, *U.K.*	56 7N	3 57W
93	Stockholm, *Sweden*	59 20N	18 3 E
61	Stockton, *U.S.A.*	38 0N	121 20W
78	Stoke-on-Trent, *U.K.*	53 1N	2 11W
82	Stralsund, *E. Germany*	54 17N	13 5 E
84	Strasbourg, *France*	48 35N	7 42 E
83	Stuttgart, *W. Germany*	48 46N	9 10 E
89	Subotica, *Yugoslavia*	46 6N	19 49 E
72	Sucre, *Bolivia*	19 0S	65 15W
114	Sudan ■, *Africa*	15 0N	30 0 E
51	Sudbury, *Canada*	46 30N	81 0W
115	Suez, *Egypt*	29 58N	32 31 E
102	Sukkur, *Pakistan*	27 42N	68 54 E
109	Sulawesi, *Indonesia*	2 0S	120 0 E
111	Sulu Arch., *Phil.*	6 0N	121 0 E
111	Sulu Sea, *E. Indies*	8 0N	120 0 E
108	Sumatra, *Indonesia*	0 40N	100 20 E
109	Sumbawa, *Indonesia*	8 26S	117 30 E
89	Šumen, *Bulgaria*	43 18N	26 55 E
57	Sumter, *U.S.A.*	33 55N	80 22W
95	Sumy, *U.S.S.R.*	50 57N	34 50 E
98	Sunda Is., *Indonesia*	5 0S	105 0 E
108	Sunda Str., *Indonesia*	6 20S	105 30 E
103	Sundarbans, *Asia*	22 0N	89 0 E
78	Sunderland, *U.K.*	54 54N	1 22W
92	Sundsvall, *Sweden*	62 23N	17 17 E
61	Sunnyvale, *U.S.A.*	37 23N	122 2W
58	Superior, *U.S.A.*	46 45N	92 5W
56	Superior, L., *N. Amer.*	47 40N	87 0W
100	Sūr, *Lebanon*	33 19N	35 16 E
109	Surabaya, *Indonesia*	7 17S	112 45 E
109	Surakarta, *Indonesia*	7 35S	110 48 E
102	Surat, *India*	21 12N	72 55 E
96	Surgut, *U.S.S.R.*	61 14N	73 20 E
111	Surigao, *Phil.*	9 47N	125 29 E
73	Suriname ■, *S. Amer.*	4 0N	56 0W
92	Surtsey, *Iceland*	63 20N	20 30W
60	Susanville, *U.S.A.*	40 28N	120 40W
56	Susquehanna →, *U.S.A.*	39 33N	76 5W
102	Sutlej →, *Pakistan*	29 23N	71 3 E
121	Suva, *Fiji*	18 6S	178 30 E
106	Suwŏn, *S. Korea*	37 17N	127 1 E
105	Suzhou, *China*	31 19N	120 38 E
124	Svalbard, *Arctic*	78 0N	17 0 E
93	Svendborg, *Denmark*	55 4N	10 35 E
94	Sverdlovsk, *U.S.S.R.*	56 50N	60 30 E
124	Sverdrup Is., *Canada*	79 0N	97 0W
79	Swansea, *U.K.*	51 37N	3 57W
117	Swaziland ■, *Africa*	26 30S	31 30 E
92	Sweden ■, *Europe*	57 0N	15 0 E
59	Sweetwater, *U.S.A.*	32 30N	100 28W
50	Swift Current, *Canada*	50 20N	107 45W
79	Swindon, *U.K.*	51 33N	1 47W
83	Switzerland ■, *Europe*	46 30N	8 0 E
121	Sydney, *Australia*	33 53S	151 10 E
51	Sydney, *Canada*	46 7N	60 7W
94	Syktyvkar, *U.S.S.R.*	61 45N	50 40 E
56	Syracuse, *U.S.A.*	43 4N	76 11W
96	Syrdarya →, *U.S.S.R.*	46 3N	61 0 E
100	Syria ■, *Asia*	35 0N	38 0 E
100	Syrian Desert, *Asia*	31 0N	40 0 E
94	Syzran, *U.S.S.R.*	53 12N	48 30 E
90	Szczecin, *Poland*	53 27N	14 27 E
91	Szeged, *Hungary*	46 16N	20 10 E
91	Székesfehérvár, *Hungary*	47 15N	18 25 E

T

PAGE	PLACE NAME	LATITUDE	LONGITUDE
110	Tabaco, *Phil.*	13 22N	123 44 E
65	Tabasco □, *Mexico*	17 45N	93 30W
116	Tabora, *Tanzania*	5 2S	32 50 E
100	Tabrīz, *Iran*	38 7N	46 20 E
100	Tabūk, *Si. Arabia*	28 23N	36 36 E
111	Tacloban, *Phil.*	11 15N	124 58 E
72	Tacna, *Peru*	18 0S	70 20W
60	Tacoma, *U.S.A.*	47 15N	122 30W
74	Tacuarembó, *Uruguay*	31 45S	56 0W
96	Tadzhikistan □, *U.S.S.R.*	35 30N	70 0 E
106	Taegu, *S. Korea*	35 50N	128 37 E
106	Taejŏn, *S. Korea*	36 20N	127 28 E
95	Taganrog, *U.S.S.R.*	47 12N	38 50 E
85	Tagus →, *Spain*	38 40N	9 24W
123	Tahiti, *Pac. Oc.*	17 37S	149 27W
60	Tahoe, L., *U.S.A.*	39 0N	120 9W
105	Taichung, *Taiwan*	24 10N	120 35 E
97	Taimyr Pen., *U.S.S.R.*	75 0N	100 0 E
105	Tainan, *Taiwan*	23 17N	120 18 E
105	Taipei, *Taiwan*	25 2N	121 30 E
105	Taiwan ■, *Asia*	23 30N	121 0 E
105	Taiyuan, *China*	37 52N	112 33 E
100	Ta'izz, *Yemen*	13 35N	44 2 E
103	Tak, *Thailand*	16 52N	99 8 E
107	Takamatsu, *Japan*	34 20N	134 5 E
107	Takaoka, *Japan*	36 47N	137 0 E
121	Takapuna, *N.Z.*	36 47S	174 47 E
107	Takasaki, *Japan*	36 20N	139 0 E
104	Takla Makan, *China*	39 0N	83 0 E
74	Talca, *Chile*	35 28S	71 40W
74	Talcahuano, *Chile*	36 40S	73 10W
57	Talladega, *U.S.A.*	33 28N	86 2W
57	Tallahassee, *U.S.A.*	30 25N	84 15W
94	Tallinn, *U.S.S.R.*	59 22N	24 48 E
114	Tamale, *Ghana*	9 22N	0 50W
65	Tamaulipas □, *Mexico*	24 0N	99 0W
94	Tambov, *U.S.S.R.*	52 45N	41 28 E
102	Tamil Nadu □, *India*	11 0N	77 0 E
57	Tampa, *U.S.A.*	27 57N	82 38W
92	Tampere, *Finland*	61 30N	23 50 E
65	Tampico, *Mexico*	22 20N	97 50W
115	Tana, L., *Ethiopia*	13 5N	37 30 E
120	Tanami Desert, *Australia*	18 50S	132 0 E
116	Tanga, *Tanzania*	5 5S	39 2 E
116	Tanganyika, L., *E. Afr.*	6 40S	30 0 E
114	Tangier, *Morocco*	35 50N	5 49W
105	Tangshan, *China*	39 38N	118 10 E
111	Tanjay, *Phil.*	9 30N	123 5 E
116	Tanzania ■, *E. Afr.*	6 40S	34 0 E
73	Tapajós →, *Brazil*	2 24S	54 41W
88	Táranto, *Italy*	40 30N	17 11 E
88	Táranto, G. of, *Italy*	40 0N	17 15 E
84	Tarbes, *France*	43 15N	0 3 E
120	Tarcoola, *Australia*	30 44S	134 36 E
72	Tarija, *Bolivia*	21 30S	64 40W
104	Tarim Basin, *China*	40 0N	84 0 E
110	Tarlac, *Phil.*	15 29N	120 35 E
91	Tarnów, *Poland*	50 3N	21 0 E
85	Tarragona, *Spain*	41 5N	1 17 E
85	Tarrasa, *Spain*	41 34N	2 1 E
96	Tashkent, *U.S.S.R.*	41 20N	69 10 E
120	Tasmania □, *Australia*	42 0S	146 30 E
94	Tatar A.S.S.R. □, *U.S.S.R.*	55 30N	51 30 E
55	Tau, *Samoa*	14 15S	169 30W
121	Taupo, L., *N.Z.*	38 46S	175 55 E
95	Taurus Mts., *Turkey*	37 0N	35 0 E
103	Tavoy, *Burma*	14 2N	98 12 E
95	Tbilisi, *U.S.S.R.*	41 43N	44 50 E
66	Tegucigalpa, *Hond.*	14 5N	87 14W
61	Tehachapi, *U.S.A.*	35 11N	118 29W
101	Tehrān, *Iran*	35 44N	51 30 E
65	Tehuantepec, Gulf of, *Mexico*	15 50N	95 0W
65	Tehuantepec, Isthmus of, *Mexico*	17 0N	94 30W
100	Tel Aviv-Yafo, *Israel*	32 4N	34 48 E
93	Telemark □, *Norway*	59 25N	8 30 E
108	Teluk Betung, *Indonesia*	5 20S	105 10 E
114	Tema, *Ghana*	5 41N	0 0 E
96	Temirtau, *U.S.S.R.*	50 5N	72 56 E
61	Tempe, *U.S.A.*	33 26N	111 59W
59	Temple, *U.S.A.*	31 5N	97 22W
114	Tenerife, *Canary Is.*	28 15N	16 35W
120	Tennant Creek, *Australia*	19 30S	134 15 E
57	Tennessee □, *U.S.A.*	36 0N	86 30W
57	Tennessee →, *U.S.A.*	37 4N	88 34W
73	Teófilo Otoni, *Brazil*	17 50S	41 30W
64	Tepic, *Mexico*	21 30N	104 54W
88	Téramo, *Italy*	42 40N	13 40 E
75	Terceira, *Azores*	38 43N	24 13W
73	Teresina, *Brazil*	5 9S	42 45W
88	Terni, *Italy*	42 34N	12 38 E
56	Terre Haute, *U.S.A.*	39 28N	87 24W
85	Teruel, *Spain*	40 22N	1 8W
54	Tetlin, *U.S.A.*	63 14N	142 50W
114	Tétouan, *Morocco*	35 35N	5 21W
89	Tetovo, *Yugoslavia*	42 1N	21 2 E
59	Texarkana, *U.S.A.*	33 25N	94 3W
59	Texas □, *U.S.A.*	31 40N	98 30W
59	Texas City, *U.S.A.*	29 20N	94 55W
81	Texel, *Neth.*	53 5N	4 50 E
108	Thailand ■, *Asia*	16 0N	102 0 E
108	Thailand, G. of, *Asia*	11 30N	101 0 E
102	Thal Desert, *Pakistan*	31 10N	71 30 E
79	Thames →, *U.K.*	51 30N	0 35 E
102	Thar Desert, *India*	28 0N	72 0 E
81	The Hague, *Neth.*	52 7N	4 17 E
50	The Pas, *Canada*	53 45N	101 15W
89	Thessaloníki, *Greece*	40 38N	22 58 E
89	Thessaloniki, Gulf of, *Greece*	40 15N	22 45 E
89	Thessaly □, *Greece*	39 30N	22 0 E
114	Thies, *Senegal*	14 50N	16 51W
103	Thimphu, *Bhutan*	27 31N	89 45 E
84	Thionville, *France*	49 20N	6 10 E
93	Thisted, *Denmark*	56 58N	8 40 E
57	Thomasville, *Ga., U.S.A.*	30 50N	84 0W
57	Thomasville, *N.C., U.S.A.*	35 55N	80 4W
50	Thompson →, *Canada*	50 15N	121 24W
89	Thrace □, *Greece*	41 9N	25 30 E
124	Thule, *Greenland*	77 40N	69 0W
51	Thunder Bay, *Canada*	48 20N	89 15W
104	Tian Shan, *China*	43 0N	84 0 E
105	Tianjin, *China*	39 10N	117 15 E
104	Tianshui, *China*	34 32N	105 40 E
88	Tiber →, *Italy*	41 44N	12 14 E
100	Tiberias, *Israel*	32 47N	35 32 E
115	Tibesti, *Chad*	21 0N	17 30 E
104	Tibet □, *China*	32 30N	86 0 E
105	Tientsin = Tianjin, *China*	39 10N	117 15 E
74	Tierra del Fuego, *Argentina*	54 0S	67 45W
100	Tigris →, *Iraq*	37 0N	42 30 E
64	Tijuana, *Mexico*	32 30N	117 10W
97	Tiksi, *U.S.S.R.*	71 40N	128 45 E
81	Tilburg, *Neth.*	51 31N	5 6 E
121	Timaru, *N.Z.*	44 23S	171 14 E
114	Timbuktu = Tombouctou, *Mali*	16 50N	3 0W
91	Timişoara, *Romania*	45 43N	21 15 E
51	Timmins, *Canada*	48 28N	81 25W
109	Timor, *Indonesia*	9 0S	125 0 E
55	Tinian, *Pac. Oc.*	15 0N	145 38 E
80	Tipperary, *Ireland*	52 28N	8 10W
89	Tiranë, *Albania*	41 18N	19 49 E
91	Tîrgu Mureş, *Romania*	46 31N	24 38 E
102	Tiruchchirappalli, *India*	10 45N	78 45 E
91	Tisza →, *Hungary*	46 8N	20 2 E
72	Titicaca, L., *Peru*	15 30S	69 30W
89	Titograd, *Yugoslavia*	42 30N	19 19 E
114	Tizi-Ouzou, *Algeria*	36 42N	4 3 E
65	Tlaxcala □, *Mexico*	19 30N	98 20W
117	Toamasina, *Madag.*	18 10S	49 25 E
67	Tobago, *W. Indies*	11 10N	60 30W
96	Tobol →, *U.S.S.R.*	58 10N	68 12 E
73	Tocantins →, *Brazil*	1 45S	49 10W
94	Togliatti, *U.S.S.R.*	53 32N	49 24 E
114	Togo ■, *W. Afr.*	6 15N	1 35 E
122	Tokelau Is., *Pac. Oc.*	9 0S	171 45W
107	Tokushima, *Japan*	34 4N	134 34 E
107	Tōkyō, *Japan*	35 45N	139 45 E
54	Tolageak, *U.S.A.*	70 2N	162 50W
89	Tolbukhin, *Bulgaria*	43 37N	27 49 E
85	Toledo, *Spain*	39 50N	4 2W
56	Toledo, *U.S.A.*	41 37N	83 33W
117	Toliara, *Madag.*	23 21S	43 40 E
65	Toluca, *Mexico*	19 20N	99 40W
114	Tombouctou, *Mali*	16 50N	3 0W
96	Tomsk, *U.S.S.R.*	56 30N	85 5 E
56	Tonawanda, *U.S.A.*	43 0N	78 54W
121	Tonga ■, *Pac. Oc.*	19 50S	174 30W
122	Tonga Trench, *Pac. Oc.*	18 0S	175 0W
58	Tongue →, *U.S.A.*	46 24N	105 52W
104	Tonkin, G. of, *Asia*	20 0N	108 0 E
121	Toowoomba, *Australia*	27 32S	151 56 E
58	Topeka, *U.S.A.*	39 3N	95 40W
92	Torne älv →, *Sweden*	65 50N	24 12 E
51	Toronto, *Canada*	43 39N	79 20W
120	Torrens, L., *Australia*	31 0S	137 50 E
64	Torreón, *Mexico*	25 33N	103 26W
121	Torres Strait, *Australia*	9 50S	142 20 E
69	Tortola, *W. Indies*	18 19N	65 0W
85	Tortosa, *Spain*	40 49N	0 31 E
91	Toruń, *Poland*	53 0N	18 39 E
84	Toulon, *France*	43 10N	5 55 E
84	Toulouse, *France*	43 37N	1 27 E
81	Tournai, *Belgium*	50 35N	3 25 E
84	Tours, *France*	47 22N	0 40 E
121	Townshend, C., *Australia*	22 18S	150 30 E
121	Townsville, *Australia*	19 15S	146 45 E
107	Toyama, *Japan*	36 40N	137 15 E
107	Toyanaka, *Japan*	34 50N	135 28 E
107	Toyohashi, *Japan*	34 45N	137 25 E
107	Toyota, *Japan*	35 3N	137 7 E

PAGE	PLACE NAME	LATITUDE	LONGITUDE
95	Trabzon, *Turkey*	41 0N	39 45 E
50	Trail, *Canada*	49 5N	117 40W
80	Tralee, *Ireland*	52 16N	9 42W
95	Transcaucasia, *U.S.S.R.*	42 0N	44 0 E
117	Transvaal □, *S. Africa*	25 0S	29 0 E
91	Transylvanian Alps, *Romania*	45 30N	25 0 E
88	Trápani, *Italy*	38 1N	12 30 E
88	Trentino-Alto Adige □, *Italy*	46 30N	11 0 E
88	Trento, *Italy*	46 5N	11 8 E
56	Trenton, *U.S.A.*	40 15N	74 41W
81	Trier, *W. Germany*	49 45N	6 37 E
88	Trieste, *Italy*	45 39N	13 45 E
102	Trincomalee, *Sri Lanka*	8 38N	81 15 E
75	Trindade, I., *Atl. Oc.*	20 20S	29 50W
59	Trinidad, *U.S.A.*	37 15N	104 30W
67	Trinidad, *W. Indies*	10 30N	61 15W
67	Trinidad & Tobago ■, *W. Indies*	10 30N	61 20W
59	Trinity →, *U.S.A.*	30 30N	95 0W
60	Trinity Mts., *U.S.A.*	40 20N	118 50W
100	Tripoli, *Lebanon*	34 31N	35 50 E
115	Tripoli, *Libya*	32 49N	13 7 E
75	Tristan da Cunha, *Atl. Oc.*	37 6S	12 20W
102	Trivandrum, *India*	8 41N	77 0 E
51	Trois-Rivières, *Canada*	46 25N	72 34W
93	Trollhättan, *Sweden*	58 17N	12 20 E
92	Troms □, *Norway*	68 56N	19 0 E
92	Tromsø, *Norway*	69 40N	18 56 E
92	Trondheim, *Norway*	63 36N	10 25 E
57	Troy, *Ala., U.S.A.*	31 50N	85 58W
56	Troy, *N.Y., U.S.A.*	42 45N	73 39W
84	Troyes, *France*	48 19N	4 3 E
72	Trujillo, *Peru*	8 6S	79 0W
55	Truk, *Pac. Oc.*	7 25N	151 46 E
96	Tselinograd, *U.S.S.R.*	51 10N	71 30 E
95	Tsimlyansk Res., *U.S.S.R.*	48 0N	43 0 E
107	Tsu, *Japan*	34 45N	136 25 E
106	Tsugaru Str., *Japan*	41 30N	140 30 E
123	Tuamotu Arch., *Pac. Oc.*	17 0S	144 0W
123	Tubuai Is., *Pac. Oc.*	25 0S	150 0W
61	Tucson, *U.S.A.*	32 14N	110 59W
59	Tucumcari, *U.S.A.*	35 12N	103 45W
110	Tuguegarao, *Phil.*	17 35N	121 42 E
94	Tula, *U.S.S.R.*	54 13N	37 38 E
61	Tulare, *U.S.A.*	36 15N	119 26W
72	Tulcán, *Ecuador*	0 48N	77 43W
59	Tulsa, *U.S.A.*	36 10N	96 0W
72	Tulua, *Colombia*	4 6N	76 11W
72	Tumaco, *Colombia*	1 50N	78 45W
114	Tunis, *Tunisia*	36 50N	10 11 E
114	Tunisia ■, *Africa*	33 30N	9 10 E
72	Tunja, *Colombia*	5 33N	73 25W
59	Tupelo, *U.S.A.*	34 15N	88 42W
103	Tura, *India*	25 30N	90 16 E
88	Turin, *Italy*	45 4N	7 40 E
116	Turkana, L., *Kenya*	3 30N	36 5 E
95	Turkey ■, *Eurasia*	39 0N	36 0 E
96	Turkmenistan □, *U.S.S.R.*	39 0N	59 0 E
67	Turks Is., *W. Indies*	21 20N	71 20W
93	Turku, *Finland*	60 30N	22 19 E
91	Turnu-Severin, *Romania*	44 39N	22 41 E
57	Tuscaloosa, *U.S.A.*	33 13N	87 31W
102	Tuticorin, *India*	8 50N	78 12 E
55	Tutuila, *Amer. Samoa*	14 19S	170 50W
122	Tuvalu ■, *Pac. Oc.*	8 0S	178 0 E
65	Tuxtla Gutiérrez, *Mexico*	16 50N	93 10W
95	Tuz Gölü, *Turkey*	38 45N	33 30 E
89	Tuzla, *Yugoslavia*	44 34N	18 41 E
60	Twin Falls, *U.S.A.*	42 30N	114 30W
91	Tychy, *Poland*	50 9N	18 59 E
59	Tyler, *U.S.A.*	32 18N	95 18W
83	Tyrol □, *Austria*	47 3N	10 43 E
88	Tyrrhenian Sea, *Europe*	40 0N	12 30 E
96	Tyumen, *U.S.S.R.*	57 11N	65 29 E

U

PAGE	PLACE NAME	LATITUDE	LONGITUDE
107	Ube, *Japan*	33 56N	131 15 E
73	Uberaba, *Brazil*	19 50S	47 55W
73	Uberlândia, *Brazil*	19 0S	48 20W
72	Ucayali →, *Peru*	4 30S	73 30W
102	Udaipur, *India*	24 36N	73 44 E
93	Uddevalla, *Sweden*	58 21N	11 55 E
88	Údine, *Italy*	46 5N	13 10 E
94	Ufa, *U.S.S.R.*	54 45N	55 55 E
116	Uganda ■, *E. Afr.*	2 0N	32 0 E
60	Uinta Mts., *U.S.A.*	40 45N	110 30W
117	Uitenhage, *S. Africa*	33 40S	25 28 E
109	Ujung Pandang, *Indonesia*	5 10S	119 20 E
95	Ukraine □, *U.S.S.R.*	49 0N	32 0 E
104	Ulaanbaatar, *Mongolia*	47 55N	106 53 E
97	Ulan Ude, *U.S.S.R.*	51 45N	107 40 E
102	Ulhasnagar, *India*	19 15N	73 10 E
83	Ulm, *W. Germany*	48 23N	10 0 E
106	Ulsan, *S. Korea*	35 32N	129 21 E
94	Ulyanovsk, *U.S.S.R.*	54 20N	48 25 E
104	Ulyasutay, *Mongolia*	47 56N	97 28 E
88	Umbria □, *Italy*	42 53N	12 30 E
92	Umeå, *Sweden*	63 45N	20 20 E
117	Umtata, *S. Africa*	31 36S	28 49 E
51	Ungava B., *Canada*	59 30N	67 30W
51	Ungava Pen., *Canada*	60 0N	74 0W
96	Union of Soviet Socialist Republics ■, *Eurasia*	60 0N	100 0 E
101	United Arab Emirates ■, *Asia*	23 50N	54 0 E
76	United Kingdom ■, *Europe*	55 0N	3 0W
52	United States of America ■, *N. Amer.*	37 0N	96 0W
117	Upington, *S. Africa*	28 25S	21 15 E
93	Uppsala, *Sweden*	59 53N	17 38 E
94	Ural Mts., *U.S.S.R.*	60 0N	59 0 E
94	Uralsk, *U.S.S.R.*	51 20N	51 20 E
50	Uranium City, *Canada*	59 34N	108 37W
58	Urbana, *U.S.A.*	40 7N	88 12W
96	Urgench, *U.S.S.R.*	41 40N	60 41 E
100	Urmia, L., *Iran*	37 50N	45 30 E
64	Uruapan, *Mexico*	19 30N	102 0W
74	Uruguay ■, *S. Amer.*	32 30S	56 30W
74	Uruguay →, *S. Amer.*	34 12S	58 18W
104	Ürümqi, *China*	43 45N	87 45 E
95	Üsküdar, *Turkey*	41 0N	29 5 E
96	Ust-Kamenogorsk, *U.S.S.R.*	50 0N	82 36 E
96	Ust Urt Plateau, *U.S.S.R.*	44 0N	55 0 E
94	Ustinov, *U.S.S.R.*	56 51N	53 14 E
60	Utah □, *U.S.A.*	39 30N	111 30W
56	Utica, *U.S.A.*	43 5N	75 18W
81	Utrecht, *Neth.*	52 5N	5 8 E
107	Utsunomiya, *Japan*	36 30N	139 50 E
102	Uttar Pradesh □, *India*	27 0N	80 0 E
96	Uzbekistan □, *U.S.S.R.*	41 30N	65 0 E

V

PAGE	PLACE NAME	LATITUDE	LONGITUDE
92	Vaasa, *Finland*	63 6N	21 38 E
102	Vadodara, *India*	22 20N	73 10 E
92	Vadsø, *Norway*	70 3N	29 50 E
54	Valdez, *U.S.A.*	61 14N	146 17W
74	Valdivia, *Chile*	39 50S	73 14W
57	Valdosta, *U.S.A.*	30 50N	83 20W
84	Valence, *France*	44 57N	4 54 E
85	Valencia, *Spain*	39 27N	0 23W
72	Valencia, *Venezuela*	10 11N	68 0W
84	Valenciennes, *France*	50 20N	3 34 E
85	Valladolid, *Spain*	41 38N	4 43W
72	Valledupar, *Colombia*	10 29N	73 15W
60	Vallejo, *U.S.A.*	38 12N	122 15W
88	Valletta, *Malta*	35 54N	14 30 E
74	Valparaíso, *Chile*	33 2S	71 40W
95	Van, L., *Turkey*	38 30N	43 0 E
120	Van Diemen G., *Australia*	11 45S	132 0 E
50	Vancouver, *Canada*	49 15N	123 10W
60	Vancouver, *U.S.A.*	45 44N	122 41W
50	Vancouver I., *Canada*	49 50N	126 0W
93	Vänern, *Sweden*	58 47N	13 30 E
121	Vanua Levu, *Fiji*	16 33S	179 15 E
122	Vanuatu ■, *Pac. Oc.*	15 0S	168 0 E
103	Varanasi, *India*	25 22N	83 0 E
92	Varangar Fjord, *Norway*	70 3N	29 25 E
89	Vardar →, *Yugoslavia*	40 35N	22 50 E
93	Värmlands □, *Sweden*	60 0N	13 20 E
89	Varna, *Bulgaria*	43 13N	27 56 E
93	Västerås, *Sweden*	59 37N	16 38 E
93	Västmanlands □, *Sweden*	59 45N	16 20 E
92	Vatnajökull, *Iceland*	64 30N	16 48W
93	Vättern, *Sweden*	58 25N	14 30 E
93	Växjö, *Sweden*	56 52N	14 50 E
84	Vendée, *France*	46 50N	1 35W
72	Venezuela ■, *S. Amer.*	8 0N	65 0W
88	Venice, *Italy*	45 27N	12 20 E
81	Venlo, *Neth.*	51 22N	6 11 E
61	Ventura, *U.S.A.*	34 16N	119 18W
65	Veracruz, *Mexico*	19 10N	96 10W
65	Veracruz □, *Mexico*	19 0N	96 15W
88	Vercelli, *Italy*	45 19N	8 25 E
117	Vereeniging, *S. Africa*	26 38S	27 57 E
97	Verkhoyansk, *U.S.S.R.*	67 35N	133 25 E
97	Verkhoyansk Ra., *U.S.S.R.*	66 0N	129 0 E
56	Vermont □, *U.S.A.*	43 40N	72 50W
59	Vernon, *U.S.A.*	34 10N	99 20W
88	Verona, *Italy*	45 27N	11 0 E
84	Versailles, *France*	48 48N	2 8 E
81	Verviers, *Belgium*	50 37N	5 52 E
92	Vestmannaeyjar, *Iceland*	63 27N	20 15W
88	Vesuvius, Mt., *Italy*	40 50N	14 22 E
93	Viborg, *Denmark*	56 27N	9 23 E
59	Vicksburg, *U.S.A.*	32 22N	90 56W
50	Victoria, *Canada*	48 30N	123 25W
59	Victoria, *U.S.A.*	28 50N	97 0W
121	Victoria □, *Australia*	37 0S	144 0 E
116	Victoria, L., *E. Afr.*	1 0S	33 0 E
64	Victoria de Durango, *Mexico*	24 3N	104 39W
117	Victoria Falls, *Zimbabwe*	17 58S	25 52 E
50	Victoria I., *Canada*	71 0N	111 0W
124	Victoria Land., *Antarct.*	75 0S	160 0 E
111	Victorias, *Phil.*	10 54N	123 5 E
90	Vienna, *Austria*	48 12N	16 22 E
108	Vientiane, *Laos*	17 58N	102 36 E
108	Vietnam ■, *Asia*	19 0N	106 0 E
110	Vigan, *Phil.*	17 35N	120 28 E
85	Vigo, *Spain*	42 12N	8 41W
103	Vijayawada, *India*	16 31N	80 39 E
65	Villahermosa, *Mexico*	17 59N	92 55W
84	Villefranche-sur-Saône, *France*	45 59N	4 43 E
94	Vilnius, *U.S.S.R.*	54 38N	25 19 E
97	Vilyuysk, *U.S.S.R.*	63 40N	121 35 E
74	Viña del Mar, *Chile*	33 0S	71 30W
56	Vineland, *U.S.A.*	39 30N	75 0W
95	Vinnitsa, *U.S.S.R.*	49 15N	28 30 E
110	Virac, *Phil.*	13 30N	124 20 E
69	Virgin Gorda, *W. Indies*	18 30N	64 26W
69	Virgin Is., *W. Indies*	18 40N	64 30W
56	Virginia □, *U.S.A.*	37 45N	78 0W
56	Virginia Beach, *U.S.A.*	36 54N	75 58W
59	Visalia, *U.S.A.*	36 25N	119 18W
111	Visayan Sea, *Phil.*	11 30N	123 30 E
50	Viscount Melville Sd., *Canada*	74 10N	108 0W
103	Vishakhapatnam, *India*	17 45N	83 20 E
91	Vistula = Wisła →, *Poland*	54 22N	18 55 E
94	Vitebsk, *U.S.S.R.*	55 10N	30 15 E
88	Viterbo, *Italy*	42 25N	12 8 E
121	Viti Levu, *Fiji*	17 30S	177 30 E
97	Vitim →, *U.S.S.R.*	59 26N	112 34 E
73	Vitória, *Brazil*	20 20S	40 22W
85	Vitoria, *Spain*	42 50N	2 41W
73	Vitória da Conquista, *Brazil*	14 51S	40 51W
81	Vlaardingen, *Neth.*	51 55N	4 21 E
94	Vladimir, *U.S.S.R.*	56 15N	40 30 E
97	Vladivostok, *U.S.S.R.*	43 10N	131 53 E
81	Vlissingen, *Neth.*	51 26N	3 34 E
89	Vlórë, *Albania*	40 32N	19 28 E
94	Volga →, *U.S.S.R.*	48 30N	46 0 E
95	Volgograd, *U.S.S.R.*	48 40N	44 25 E
94	Vologda, *U.S.S.R.*	59 10N	40 0 E
89	Vólos, *Greece*	39 24N	22 59 E
114	Volta, L., *Ghana*	7 30N	0 15 E
73	Volta Redonda, *Brazil*	22 31S	44 5W
95	Volzhskiy, *U.S.S.R.*	48 56N	44 46 E
81	Voorburg, *Neth.*	52 5N	4 24 E
94	Vorkuta, *U.S.S.R.*	67 48N	64 20 E
94	Voronezh, *U.S.S.R.*	51 40N	39 10 E
95	Voroshilovgrad, *U.S.S.R.*	48 38N	39 15 E
84	Vosges, *France*	48 20N	7 10 E
117	Vryburg, *S. Africa*	26 55S	24 45 E

W

PAGE	PLACE NAME	LATITUDE	LONGITUDE
81	Waal →, *Neth.*	51 59N	4 30 E
56	Wabash →, *U.S.A.*	37 46N	88 2W
59	Waco, *U.S.A.*	31 33N	97 5W
115	Wâd Medanî, *Sudan*	14 28N	33 30 E
81	Waddenzee, *Neth.*	53 6N	5 10 E
50	Waddington, Mt., *Canada*	51 23N	125 15W
54	Wahiawa, *U.S.A.*	21 30N	158 2W
107	Wakayama, *Japan*	34 15N	135 15 E
90	Wałbrzych, *Poland*	50 45N	16 18 E
79	Wales □, *U.K.*	52 30N	3 30W
60	Walla Walla, *U.S.A.*	46 3N	118 25W
91	Wallachia, *Romania*	44 35N	25 0 E
122	Wallis & Futuna Is., *Pac. Oc.*	13 18S	176 10W
60	Wallowa Mts., *U.S.A.*	45 20N	117 30W
117	Walvis Bay, *S. Africa*	23 0S	14 28 E
121	Wanganui, *N.Z.*	39 56S	175 3 E
60	Warner Mts., *U.S.A.*	41 30N	120 20W
121	Warrego →, *Australia*	30 24S	145 21 E
57	Warrington, *U.S.A.*	30 22N	87 16W
91	Warsaw, *Poland*	52 13N	21 0 E
91	Warta →, *Poland*	52 35N	14 39 E
60	Wasatch Ra., *U.S.A.*	40 30N	111 15W
78	Wash, The, *U.K.*	52 58N	0 20 E
56	Washington, *U.S.A.*	38 52N	77 0W
60	Washington □, *U.S.A.*	47 45N	120 30W
57	Washington, Mt., *U.S.A.*	44 15N	71 18W
56	Waterbury, *U.S.A.*	41 32N	73 0W
80	Waterford, *Ireland*	52 16N	7 8W
58	Waterloo, *U.S.A.*	42 27N	92 20W
60	Waterton Glacier International Peace Park, *U.S.A.*	48 35N	113 40W
56	Watertown, *U.S.A.*	43 58N	75 57W
57	Waterville, *U.S.A.*	44 35N	69 40W

159

PAGE	PLACE NAME	LATITUDE	LONGITUDE
61	Watsonville, *U.S.A.*	36 55N	121 49W
58	Waukegan, *U.S.A.*	42 22N	87 54W
58	Waukesha, *U.S.A.*	43 0N	88 15W
58	Wausau, *U.S.A.*	44 57N	89 40W
58	Wauwatosa, *U.S.A.*	43 6N	87 59W
59	Waxahachie, *U.S.A.*	32 22N	96 53W
57	Waycross, *U.S.A.*	31 12N	82 25W
79	Weald, The, *U.K.*	51 7N	0 9E
124	Weddell Sea, *Antarct.*	72 30S	40 0W
105	Weifang, *China*	36 47N	119 10E
117	Welkom, *S. Africa*	28 0S	26 50E
120	Wellesley Is., *Australia*	16 42S	139 30E
121	Wellington, *N.Z.*	41 19S	174 46E
90	Wels, *Austria*	48 9N	14 1E
60	Wenatchee, *U.S.A.*	47 30N	120 17W
105	Wenzhou, *China*	28 0N	120 38E
82	Weser →, *W. Germany*	53 33N	8 30E
103	West Bengal □, *India*	23 0N	88 0E
82	West Germany ■, *Europe*	52 0N	9 0E
48	West Indies, *Cent. Amer.*	15 0N	70 0W
57	West Palm Beach, *U.S.A.*	26 44N	80 3W
81	West Schelde →, *Neth.*	51 23N	3 50E
96	West Siberian Plain, *U.S.S.R.*	62 0N	75 0E
56	West Virginia □, *U.S.A.*	39 0N	81 0W
120	Western Australia □, *Australia*	25 0S	118 0E
102	Western Ghats, *India*	14 0N	75 0E
114	Western Sahara ■, *Africa*	25 0N	13 0W
121	Western Samoa ■, *Pac. Oc.*	14 0S	172 0W
121	Westport, *N.Z.*	41 46S	171 37E
121	Whangarei, *N.Z.*	35 43S	174 21E
56	Wheeling, *U.S.A.*	40 2N	80 41W
59	White →, *Ark., U.S.A.*	33 53N	91 3W
56	White →, *Ind., U.S.A.*	38 25N	87 45W
115	White Nile →, *Sudan*	15 38N	32 31E
94	White Russia □, *U.S.S.R.*	53 30N	27 0E
94	White Sea, *U.S.S.R.*	66 30N	38 0E
50	Whitehorse, *Canada*	60 43N	135 3W
61	Whitney, Mt., *U.S.A.*	36 35N	118 14W
120	Whyalla, *Australia*	33 2S	137 30E
59	Wichita, *U.S.A.*	37 40N	97 20W
59	Wichita Falls, *U.S.A.*	33 57N	98 30W
80	Wicklow Mts., *Ireland*	53 0N	6 30W
81	Wiesbaden, *W. Germany*	50 7N	8 17E
79	Wight, I. of, *U.K.*	50 40N	1 20W
120	Wilberforce, C., *Australia*	11 54S	136 35E
124	Wilhelm II Land, *Antarct.*	68 0S	90 0E
82	Wilhelmshaven, *W. Germany*	53 30N	8 9E
56	Wilkes Barre, *U.S.A.*	41 15N	75 52W
124	Wilkes Land, *Antarct.*	69 0S	120 0E
67	Willemstad, *Neths. Antilles*	12 5N	69 0W
56	Williamsburg, *U.S.A.*	37 17N	76 44W
56	Williamsport, *U.S.A.*	41 18N	77 1W
58	Williston, *U.S.A.*	48 10N	103 35W
56	Wilmington, *Del., U.S.A.*	39 45N	75 32W
57	Wilmington, *N.C., U.S.A.*	34 14N	77 54W
57	Wilson, *U.S.A.*	35 44N	77 54W
120	Wimmera, *Australia*	36 30S	142 0E
60	Wind River Range, *U.S.A.*	43 0N	109 30W
117	Windhoek, *Namibia*	22 35S	17 4E
51	Windsor, *Canada*	42 18N	83 0W
79	Windsor, *U.K.*	51 28N	0 36W
67	Windward Is., *Atl. Oc.*	13 0N	63 0W
67	Windward Passage, *W. Indies*	20 0N	74 0W
50	Winnipeg, *Canada*	49 54N	97 9W
50	Winnipeg, L., *Canada*	52 0N	97 0W
58	Winona, *U.S.A.*	44 2N	91 39W
57	Winston-Salem, *U.S.A.*	36 7N	80 15W
83	Winterthur, *Switz.*	47 30N	8 44E
121	Winton, *Australia*	22 24S	143 3E
58	Wisconsin □, *U.S.A.*	44 30N	90 0W
91	Wisła →, *Poland*	54 22N	18 55E
117	Witbank, *S. Africa*	25 51S	29 14E
81	Witten, *W. Germany*	51 26N	7 19E
91	Włocławek, *Poland*	52 40N	19 3E
82	Wolfsburg, *W. Germany*	52 27N	10 49E
121	Wollongong, *Australia*	34 25S	150 54E
79	Wolverhampton, *U.K.*	52 35N	2 6W
106	Wŏnsan, *N. Korea*	39 11N	127 27E
60	Woodland, *U.S.A.*	38 40N	121 50W
50	Woods, L. of the, *Canada*	49 15N	94 45W
117	Worcester, *S. Africa*	33 39S	19 27E
79	Worcester, *U.K.*	52 12N	2 12W
56	Worcester, *U.S.A.*	42 14N	71 49W
83	Worms, *W. Germany*	49 37N	8 21E
97	Wrangel I., *U.S.S.R.*	71 0N	180 0E
91	Wrocław, *Poland*	51 5N	17 5E
105	Wuhan, *China*	30 31N	114 18E
105	Wuhu, *China*	31 22N	118 21E
81	Wuppertal, *W. Germany*	51 15N	7 8E
83	Würzburg, *W. Germany*	49 46N	9 55E
104	Wutongqiao, *China*	29 22N	103 50E
105	Wuxi, *China*	31 30N	120 30E
105	Wuzhou, *China*	23 30N	111 18E
56	Wyandotte, *U.S.A.*	42 14N	83 13W
120	Wyndham, *Australia*	15 33S	128 3E
60	Wyoming □, *U.S.A.*	42 48N	109 0W

X

PAGE	PLACE NAME	LATITUDE	LONGITUDE
104	Xiaguan, *China*	25 32N	100 16E
105	Xiamen, *China*	24 25N	118 4E
105	Xiangfan, *China*	32 2N	112 8E
105	Xiangtan, *China*	27 51N	112 54E
105	Xiangyang, *China*	32 1N	112 8E
73	Xingu →, *Brazil*	1 30S	51 53W
104	Xining, *China*	36 34N	101 40E
104	Xinjiang Uygur Zizhiqu □, *China*	42 0N	86 0E
105	Xuzhou, *China*	34 18N	117 10E

Y

PAGE	PLACE NAME	LATITUDE	LONGITUDE
97	Yablonovy Ra., *U.S.S.R.*	53 0N	114 0E
60	Yakima, *U.S.A.*	46 42N	120 30W
97	Yakut A.S.S.R. □, *U.S.S.R.*	62 0N	130 0E
97	Yakutsk, *U.S.S.R.*	62 5N	129 50E
106	Yamagata, *Japan*	38 15N	140 15E
96	Yamal Peninsula, *U.S.S.R.*	71 0N	70 0E
89	Yambol, *Bulgaria*	42 30N	26 36E
103	Yamuna →, *India*	25 30N	81 53E
97	Yana →, *U.S.S.R.*	71 30N	136 0E
104	Yangtze Kiang →, *China*	31 40N	122 0E
105	Yanji, *China*	42 59N	129 30E
105	Yantai, *China*	37 34N	121 22E
116	Yaoundé, *Cameroon*	3 50N	11 35E
55	Yap Is., *Pac. Oc.*	9 30N	138 10E
94	Yaroslavl, *U.S.S.R.*	57 35N	39 55E
107	Yatsushiro, *Japan*	32 30N	130 40E
101	Yazd, *Iran*	31 55N	54 27E
59	Yazoo →, *U.S.A.*	32 35N	90 50W
105	Yellow Sea, *China*	35 0N	123 0E
50	Yellowknife, *Canada*	62 27N	114 29W
58	Yellowstone →, *U.S.A.*	47 58N	103 59W
60	Yellowstone National Park, *U.S.A.*	44 35N	110 0W
100	Yemen ■, *Asia*	15 0N	44 0E
96	Yenisey →, *U.S.S.R.*	71 50N	82 40E
95	Yerevan, *U.S.S.R.*	40 10N	44 31E
104	Yibin, *China*	28 45N	104 32E
105	Yichang, *China*	30 40N	111 20E
104	Yichuan, *China*	36 2N	110 10E
104	Yining, *China*	43 58N	81 10E
109	Yogyakarta, *Indonesia*	7 49S	110 22E
107	Yokkaichi, *Japan*	35 0N	136 38E
107	Yokohama, *Japan*	35 27N	139 28E
107	Yokosuka, *Japan*	35 20N	139 40E
56	Yonkers, *U.S.A.*	40 57N	73 51W
78	York, *U.K.*	53 58N	1 7W
56	York, *U.S.A.*	39 57N	76 43W
121	York, C., *Australia*	10 42S	142 31E
120	Yorke Pen., *Australia*	34 50S	137 40E
61	Yosemite National Park, *U.S.A.*	38 0N	119 30W
94	Yoshkar Ola, *U.S.S.R.*	56 38N	47 55E
56	Youngstown, *U.S.A.*	41 7N	80 41W
81	Ypres, *Belgium*	50 51N	2 53E
105	Yuan Jiang →, *China*	28 55N	111 50E
60	Yuba City, *U.S.A.*	39 12N	121 37W
65	Yucatan □, *Mexico*	21 30N	86 30W
65	Yucatan Str., *Caribbean*	22 0N	86 30W
89	Yugoslavia ■, *Europe*	44 0N	20 0E
54	Yukon →, *N. Amer.*	65 30N	150 0W
50	Yukon Territory □, *Canada*	63 0N	135 0W
61	Yuma, *U.S.A.*	32 45N	114 37W
104	Yunnan □, *China*	25 0N	102 30E
97	Yuzhno-Sakhalinsk, *U.S.S.R.*	46 58N	142 45E

Z

PAGE	PLACE NAME	LATITUDE	LONGITUDE
81	Zaandam, *Neth.*	52 26N	4 49E
91	Zabrze, *Poland*	50 18N	18 50E
94	Zagorsk, *U.S.S.R.*	56 20N	38 10E
88	Zagreb, *Yugoslavia*	45 50N	16 0E
101	Zagros Mts., *Iran*	33 45N	47 0E
100	Zahlah, *Lebanon*	33 52N	35 50E
116	Zaire ■, *Africa*	3 0S	23 0E
116	Zaire →, *Africa*	6 4S	12 24E
89	Zákinthos, *Greece*	37 47N	20 57E
117	Zambezi →, *Africa*	18 55S	36 4E
117	Zambia ■, *Africa*	15 0S	28 0E
111	Zamboanga, *Phil.*	6 59N	122 3E
85	Zamora, *Spain*	41 30N	5 45W
56	Zanesville, *U.S.A.*	39 56N	82 0W
116	Zanzibar, *Tanzania*	6 12S	39 12E
95	Zaporozhye, *U.S.S.R.*	47 50N	35 10E
85	Zaragoza, *Spain*	41 39N	0 53W
114	Zaria, *Nigeria*	11 0N	7 40E
81	Zeebrugge, *Belgium*	51 19N	3 12E
81	Zeist, *Neth.*	52 5N	5 15E
105	Zhangjiakou, *China*	40 48N	114 55E
105	Zhangzhou, *China*	24 30N	117 35E
105	Zhanjiang, *China*	21 15N	110 20E
95	Zhdanov, *U.S.S.R.*	47 5N	37 31E
105	Zhejiang □, *China*	29 0N	120 0E
105	Zhengzhou, *China*	34 45N	113 34E
95	Zhitomir, *U.S.S.R.*	50 20N	28 40E
105	Zibo, *China*	36 47N	118 3E
90	Zielona Góra, *Poland*	51 57N	15 30E
104	Zigong, *China*	29 15N	104 48E
114	Ziguinchor, *Senegal*	12 35N	16 20W
91	Žilina, *Czech.*	49 12N	18 42E
117	Zimbabwe ■, *Africa*	20 0S	30 0E
61	Zion National Park, *U.S.A.*	37 25N	112 50W
94	Zlatoust, *U.S.S.R.*	55 10N	59 40E
95	Zonguldak, *Turkey*	41 28N	31 50E
89	Zrenjanin, *Yugoslavia*	45 22N	20 23E
83	Zug, *Switz.*	47 10N	8 31E
104	Zunyi, *China*	27 42N	106 53E
83	Zürich, *Switz.*	47 22N	8 32E
82	Zwickau, *E. Germany*	50 43N	12 30E
81	Zwolle, *Neth.*	52 31N	6 6E

Acknowledgment 1988

Photographs:
p.27 Merete Rentsch, Ron Snipe; p.28–29 Gunter Ziesler – Bruce Coleman, Gene Ahrens – Bruce Coleman, South Australian Government, Merete Rentsch, Peter Rentsch; p.30–31 Gerald Cubitt – Bruce Coleman, S.A.S., Alcan Jamaica Ltd., Ron Snipe, Bill Wise –Oxfam, Saskatchewan Government Office, Norman Myers – Bruce Coleman, Merete Rentsch; p.35 Mike Wells – Oxfam, South Australian Government, Norman Myers – Bruce Coleman; p.41 Smithsonian Institution, Washington D.C. – The Bridgeman Art Library; p.124 Merete Rentsch.

Cover: Imtek Imagineering/Masterfile

Title Page: NASA

World Fact Information and Atlas Consultation by Ron Snipe, Ph.D., Geographer, Lawrence, Kansas.

Map projections are the means by which the earth's curved surface can be transferred to or projected upon a flat surface, like the pages of this atlas. They are systematic drawings of lines representing parallels or meridians on a flat surface. They show either the whole earth or some portion of it. No projection can represent the earth's spherical surface without some distortion or areas, shapes, directions, or distances.

Although in practice nearly all projections are derived mathemetically, most are more easily visualized if you think of a light shining through the grid of parallels and meridians on a globe. The shadows these lines would cast on a flat piece of paper would form a projection. The piece of paper could also be rolled into a cylinder or a cone. Thus, there are several kinds of projections. These are azimuthal, cylindrical, and conical.

Azimuthal

Cylindrical

Conical

An Azimuthal projection is constructed by the projection of part of the globe onto a flat surface which touches the globe at only one point. The zenithal gnomonic projection (A) touches the globe at a pole. This projection is good for showing polar air routes, because the shortest distance between any two points is a straight line. Air-route distances from one point (e.g. Capetown) are best shown by the Oblique Zenithal Equidistant projection (B). Azimuthal projections are best for larger scale maps of small areas so that distortion around the edges is not too great.

Cylindrical projections are constructed by projecting a portion of the globe onto a cylinder which touches the globe only along one line, e.g. the equator. This line is the only one true to scale, with distortion of size and shape increasing towards the top and bottom of the cylinder. The Mercator projection (A) is one kind of cylindrical projection. It avoids distortion of shape by making an increase in scale along the parallels. Although there is still size distortion, the Mercator's best use is for navigation since directions can be plotted as straight lines. The Mollweide projection (B) is a cylindrical projection on which the meridians are no longer parallel. This is an equal-area projection, which is useful for mapping distributions. In this case, it is "interrupted" or broken apart in the water areas. Cylindrical projections are best for mapping the whole world.

Conical projections use the projection of the globe onto a cone which caps the globe and touches it along a parallel. The scale is correct along this line and along the meridians. In the simple conic projection (A), the scale is correct along the heavy parallel and the meridians. Bonne's projection (B) is another conical projection. It is an equal-area projection, but there is shape distortion around its edges. Conical projections cannot cover the entire globe. They are best suited for mid-latitude or temperate regions with large longitudinal extent, e.g. Asia.

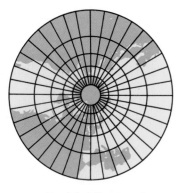

(A) Zenithal Gnomonic

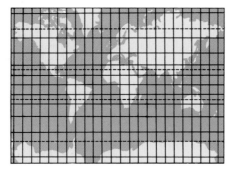

(A) Mercator

(A) Simple Conic

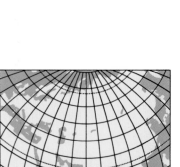

(B) Bonne

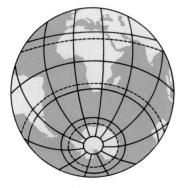

(B) Oblique Zenithal Equidistant

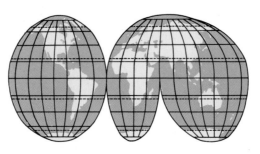

(B) Interrupted Mollweide

In this atlas, many projections are used. They have been carefully chosen for their specific advantages. The names of the projections appear in the lower left-hand margins of the maps. Almost all of the world and continental maps are equal-area projections. Most of the large-scale maps are conical projections, which have correct shapes and true directions.